PUBLIC PLACES – URBAN SPACES

The Dimensions of Urban Design

Matthew Carmona, Tim Heath,
Taner Oc and Steven Tiesdell

Architectural Press

AMSTERDAM   BOSTON   HEIDELBERG   LONDON   NEW YORK   OXFORD
PARIS   SAN DIEGO   SAN FRANCISCO   SINGAPORE   SYDNEY   TOKYO

Architectural Press is an imprint of Elsevier
Linacre House, Jordan Hill, Oxford OX2 8DP, UK
30 Corporate Drive, Suite 400, Burlington, MA 01803, USA

First edition 2003
Reprinted 2003, 2004 (twice), 2005, 2006, 2007, 2008

British Library Cataloguing in Publication Data
Public places – urban spaces: the dimensions of urban design
  1. City planning
  I. Carmona, Matthew II. Heath, Tim
  III. Oc, Tanner IV. Tiesdell, Steven
  711

Library of Congress Cataloging-in-Publication Data
A catalog record for this book is available from the Library of Congress

ISBN: 978-0-7506-3632-2

For information on all Architectural Press publications
visit our website at www.architecturalpress.com

Printed and bound in *Great Britain*

08 09 10   10 9 8

Contents

Acknowledgements

We would like to thank the many people who have helped us in bringing this book to publication. Foremost among them are:

John Henneberry for his valuable comments and positive suggestions on an early draft of what became Chapter 10. Bob Jarvis for his helpful and supportive comments on a draft version of this book. Jim Livingston, Alison Sandison, David Chapman, Elisebete Cidre and Steven Thornton-Jones for their work on the illustrations. Alison Yates, Liz Whiting and Colleagues at the Architectural Press for their patience. Margaret Downing for all her help with editing the final text, and last but not least our students (past and present) at University College London, and the Universities of Nottingham, Aberdeen and Sheffield.

We are grateful to those who have given permission for illustrations to be reproduced. Sources of these are acknowledged in the captions.

All photographic and other non-referenced illustrations supplied by Matthew Carmona and Steven Tiesdell.

Preface

This book provides an exposition of the different, but intimately related, dimensions of urban design. It takes a holistic approach, which neither focuses on a limited checklist of urban design qualities nor – it is hoped – excludes important areas. By this means, it provides a comprehensive overview both for those new to the subject and those requiring a general guide. The structure is easily accessible, with self-contained and well cross-referenced sections and chapters. This enables readers to dip in for specific information, while the incremental layering of concepts aids those reading the book cover to cover.

Urban design is also treated as a design process in which, as in any such process, there are no 'right' or 'wrong' answers – there are only 'better' and 'worse' ones, the quality of which may only be known in time. It is necessary, therefore, to have a continually questioning and inquisitive approach to the subject, rather than a dogmatic view. The book does not, therefore, seek to produce a 'new' theory of urban design in a prescriptive fashion and, hence, no formulaic 'solution' is offered. There is, nevertheless, a broad belief in – and attitude to – urban design as an important part of urban development, renewal, management, planning and conservation processes.

Synthesising and integrating ideas, theories, etc., from a wide range of sources, the book is embedded in a comprehensive reading of existing literature and research. It also draws on the authors' experience in teaching, researching and writing about urban design in schools of planning, architecture and surveying.

The motivation

The genesis of this book came from two distinct sources. First, from a period during the 1990s when the authors worked together at the University of Nottingham on an innovative undergraduate urban planning programme. Its primary motivation was a strong – and, in hindsight, we believe correct – conviction that, by teaching urban design at the core of an interdisciplinary, creative, problem-solving discipline, planning (and other) students would have a superior and more valuable learning experience, which would – in turn – provide a better foundation for their future careers. Although in many schools of planning, urban design is figuratively put into a 'box' and taught by the school's only urban design 'specialist', our contention was that urban design awareness and sensibility should inform all – or, at least, most – parts of the curriculum. The same may be considered to be true of schools of architecture and surveying. Second, there was a need to prepare undergraduate lecture courses presenting ideas, principles, and concepts of the subject to support the programme's design studio teaching. Although many excellent books existed, it soon became apparent that none drew from the full range of urban design thought. The writing of these courses generated the idea for the book, and provided its overall structure.

The structure

The book is in three main parts. It begins with a broad discussion of the context within which urban design takes place. In Chapter 1, the challenge for 'urban design' and for the 'urban designer' – a term used throughout the book in its broadest sense to encompass both 'knowing' and 'unknowing' urban designers – is made explicit. The chapter deliberately adopts a broad understanding, seeing urban design as more than simply the physical or visual appearance of development, and as an integrative (i.e. joined-up) and integrating activity. While urban design's scope may be broad and its boundaries often 'fuzzy', the heart of its concern is about making places for people: this idea forms the kernel of this book. More realistically, it is about

making *better* places than would otherwise be produced. This is – unashamedly and unapologetically – a normative contention about what we believe urban design *should* be about, rather than what at any point in time it *is* about. We thus regard urban design as an ethical activity: first, in an axiological sense (because it is intimately concerned with issues of values); and, second, because it is – or should be – concerned with particular values such as social justice and equity.

In Chapter 2, issues of change in the contemporary urban context are outlined and discussed. Chapter 3 presents a number of overarching

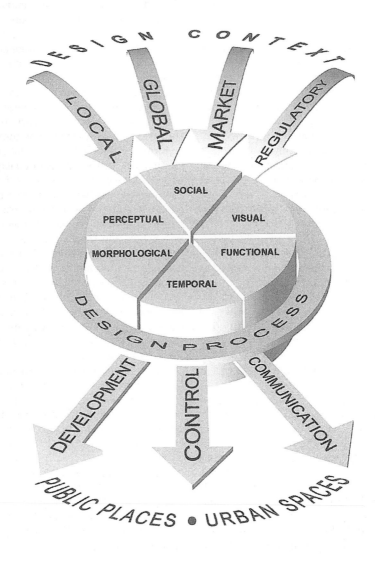

contexts – local, global, market and regulatory – that provide the background for urban design action. These contexts underpin and inform the discussions of the individual dimensions of urban design principles and practice in Part II.

Part II consists of six chapters, each of which reviews a substantive dimension of urban design – 'morphological', 'perceptual', 'social', 'visual', 'functional' and 'temporal'. As urban design is a joined-up activity, this separation is for the purpose of clarity in exposition and analysis only. These six overlapping dimensions are the 'everyday subject matter' of urban design, while the crosscutting contexts outlined in Chapter 3 relate to and inform all the dimensions. The six dimensions and four contexts are also linked and related by the conception of design as a process of problem solving. The chapters are not intended to delimit boundaries around particular areas of urban design. Instead, they emphasise the breadth of the subject area, with the connections between the different broad areas being made explicit. Urban design is only holistic if all the dimensions (the areas of action) are considered simultaneously.

In Part III, implementation and delivery mechanisms are explored – how urban design is procured, controlled, and communicated – stressing the nature of urban design as a process moving from theory to action. The final chapter brings together the various dimensions of the subject to emphasise its holistic nature.

Urban design: an emerging and evolving activity

It is only recently in the UK that urban design has been recognised as an important area of practice by the existing built environment professions, and even more recently that it has been recognised by central and local government, and incorporated more fully into the planning remit. The Urban Design Alliance (UDAL), a multi-profession umbrella organisation, has also been set up by the built environment professional institutes to promote urban design.

In certain states in the US, urban design has often been more fully conceptualised and better integrated into the activities of the established built environment professionals. Examination of the planning history of cities such as San Francisco and Portland clearly demonstrates this. More generally, as in the UK, recent initiatives at both public and professional level have combined to give it a new prominence – in the public sector, through the spread of design review control as a means to promote better design through planning action, and in the professions with the emergence of, for example, the Congress for the New Urbanism. In addition, urban design is the focus of well-developed grass roots activity, with local communities participating in the design, management and reshaping of their own local environments.

Urban design is an expanding discipline. There is unprecedented and increasing demand from the public and private sectors for practitioners – or, more simply, for those with urban design expertise. This demand is being matched by a range of new urban design courses at both graduate and undergraduate levels; by greater recognition in planning, architectural and surveying (real estate) education; and by new demand from private and public practitioners wanting to develop appropriate skills and knowledge.

All urban designers – both knowing and unknowing (see Chapter 1) – need a clear understanding of how their various actions and interventions in the built environment combine to create high quality, people-friendly, vital and viable environments or, conversely, poor quality, alienating or simply monotonous ones. As a field of activity, urban design has been the subject of much recent attention and has secured its place among the other established built environment professions as a key means of addressing interdisciplinary concerns. In this position it is a policy- and practice-based subject which, like architecture and planning, benefits from an extensive and legitimising theoretical underpinning. This book draws on that, now extensive, underpinning, to present many of the key contributions aimed at beneficially influencing the overall quality and liveability of urban environments.

While urban design has developed quickly and continues to evolve, it is hoped that the structure adopted by this book will stand the test of time and, over time, will be able to incorporate advances in our thinking on the practice and process of urban design, as well as any omissions which – through ignorance or lack of appreciation – have not been included from the start. As a contribution to the better understanding of good urban design, it is hoped that it will contribute to the design, development, enhancement and preservation of successful urban spaces and cherished public places.

PART I

THE CONTEXT FOR URBAN DESIGN

1

Urban design today

INTRODUCTION

This book adopts a broad understanding of urban design, which is focused on the making of places for people (Figures 1.1, 1.2). More precisely and realistically, it focuses on urban design as the *process* of making *better* places for people *than would otherwise be produced*. This definition asserts the importance of four themes that occur throughout the book. First, it stresses that urban design is for and about people. Second, it emphasises the value and significance of 'place'. Third, it recognises that urban design operates in the 'real' world, with its field of opportunity constrained and bounded by economic (market) and political (regulatory) forces. Fourth, it asserts the importance of design as a process. The idea that urban design is about making better places is unashamedly and unapologetically a normative contention about what it should be, rather than what it is at any point in time.

Providing an introduction to the concept of urban design, this chapter is in three main parts. The first develops an understanding of the subject. The second discusses the contemporary need for urban design. The third discusses urban design practice.

TOWARDS AN UNDERSTANDING OF URBAN DESIGN

The term 'urban design' was coined in North America in the late 1950s, and replaced the narrower and somewhat outmoded term 'civic design'. Typified by the City Beautiful Movement, civic design focused largely on the siting and design of major civic buildings – city halls, opera houses, museums – and their relationship to open spaces. Urban design denotes a more expansive approach. Evolving from an initial, predominantly aesthetic, concern with the distribution of building masses and the space between buildings, it has become primarily concerned with the quality of the public realm – both physical and sociocultural – and the making of places for people to enjoy and use. Containing two somewhat problematical words, 'urban design' is an inherently ambiguous term. Taken separately, 'urban' and 'design' have clear meanings: 'urban' suggests the characteristics of towns or cities, while 'design' refers to such activities as sketching, planning, arranging, colouring and pattern making. Throughout this book, however, as used generally within the practice of urban design, the term 'urban' has a wide and inclusive meaning, embracing not only the city and town but also the village and hamlet, while 'design', rather than having a narrowly aesthetic interpretation, is as much about effective problem solving and/or the processes of delivering or organising development.

In a wide-ranging review of urban design, Madanipour (1996, pp. 93–117) identified seven areas of ambiguity in its definition:

1. Should urban design be focused at particular scales or levels?
2. Should it focus only on the visual qualities of the urban environment or, more broadly, address the organisation and management of urban space?
3. Should it simply be about transforming spatial arrangements, or about more deeply seated social and cultural relations between spaces and society?

FIGURE 1.1
A place for people –
Harbour Steps, Seattle,
Washington, USA

4. Should the focus of urban design be its product (the urban environment) or the process by which it is produced?
5. Should urban design be the province of architects, planners or landscape architects?
6. Should it be a public or private sector activity?
7. Should it be seen as an objective–rational process (a science) or an expressive–subjective process (an art)?

The first three ambiguities are concerned with the 'product' of urban design, the last three with urban design as a 'process', while the fourth concerns the product–process dilemma. Although Madanipour's ambiguities are deliberately presented as oppositional and mutually exclusive, in most cases, it is a case of 'and/both' rather than 'either/or'. As we 'consciously shape and manage our built environments' (Madanipour, 1996,

FIGURE 1.2
A place for people –
Broadgate, London, UK

p. 117), urban designers are interested in, and engaged with, both process and its product. While, in practice, 'urban design' can be used to refer to all the products and processes of development, it is often useful to use the term in a more restricted sense to mean *adding* of *quality* to them.

Attempting to sum up the remit of urban design, Tibbalds (1988a) notes a definition of it as *'Everything you can see out of the window.'* While this has a basic truth and logic, if 'everything' can be considered to be urban design, then equally perhaps 'nothing' is urban design (Daganhart and Sawicki, 1994). Nevertheless, in acknowledging the potential scope and diversity of urban design, there is little value in putting boundaries around the subject. The real need is for definitions that encapsulate its heart or core rather than prescribe its edge or boundary. That is, for the identification, clarification and debate of central beliefs and activities rather than of boundaries and exclusions.

It is frequently easier to say what urban design is not, than to say precisely what it is. It is not, for example, architecture, civil or highway engineering, landscape architecture, estate management, or town planning. Equally, it is both more and less than any of these long-established activities (University of Reading, 2001). Relational definitions (i.e. those that define something in relation to something else) can, nonetheless, be helpful.

Urban design is typically defined in terms of architecture and town planning – Gosling and Maitland (1984) describe it as the 'common ground' between them, while the UK's Social Science Research Council located urban design at 'the interface between architecture, landscape architecture and town planning, drawing on the design tradition of architecture and landscape architecture, and the environmental management and social science tradition of contemporary planning' (from Bentley and Butina 1991). Urban design is not, however, simply an interface. It encompasses and sometimes subsumes a number of disciplines and activities – prompting Rob Cowan (2001a, p. 9) to ask:

> which profession is best at interpreting policy; assessing the local economy and property market; appraising a site or area in terms of land use, ecology, landscape, ground conditions, social factors, history, archaeology, urban form and transport; managing and facilitating a participative process; drafting and illustrating design principles; and programming the development process?

Cowan contends that while all these skills are likely to be needed in, say, producing an urban design framework or master plan, it is rare for them all to be embodied by a single professional. The best frameworks and master plans are drawn up by a number of people with different skills, working in collaboration. Urban design is inherently collaborative and interdisciplinary, involving an integrated approach, and the skills and expertise of a wide range of professionals and others.

Scale has also been used as a means of defining urban design. Urban design has commonly been considered to function at an intermediate scale between planning (the settlement) and architecture (individual buildings). In 1976 Reyner Banham defined its field of concern as 'urban situations about half a mile square'. This definition is useful only if we see urban design as an activity mediating between architecture and planning. Kevin Lynch (1981, p. 291) defined it more broadly as encompassing a wide range of concerns across different spatial scales, arguing that urban designers may be engaged in preparing a comprehensive regional access study, a new town, a regional park system, and equally, 'may seek to protect neighbourhood streets, revitalise a public square, . . . set regulations for conservation or development, build a participatory process, write an interpretative guide or plan a city celebration'. It is important to appreciate that urban design operates at and across a variety of spatial scales rather than at any particular one.

Although consideration of urban design at a particular scale is a convenient device, it detracts from the fact that urban environments are vertically integrated 'wholes'. Urban designers need to be constantly aware of scales both above and below that at which they are working, and also of the relationship of the parts to the whole, and the whole to the parts. In a necessary reminder to the built environment professions, Francis Tibbalds (1992, p. 9) argued that 'places matter most': 'We seem to be losing the ability to stand back and look at what we are producing as a whole . . . We need to stop worrying quite so much about individual buildings and other physical artefacts and think instead about places in their entirety.' In broad terms, Christopher Alexander's 'pattern language' illustrates the range of scales at which urban design operates, with the patterns being ordered in terms of scale, beginning with patterns for strategic (city-wide) design, and working down to interior design. Alexander et al. (1977, p. xiii), however, stressed that no pattern was an 'isolated entity': 'Each pattern can exist in the world only to the extent that it is supported by other patterns: the larger patterns in which it is embedded, the patterns of the same size that surround it, and the smaller patterns which are embedded in it.'

Traditions of thought in urban design

Two broad traditions of urban design thought stem from different ways of appreciating design and the products of the design process. In his paper 'Urban Environments as Visual Art or Social Settings', Bob Jarvis (1980) discussed this distinction in terms of a 'visual-artistic' tradition emphasising the visual qualities of buildings and space, and a 'social usage' tradition primarily concerned with the social qualities of people, places and activities. In recent years, the two have become synthesised into a third, 'making places' tradition.

(i) The visual-artistic tradition
The visual-artistic tradition was that of an earlier, more 'architectural' and narrower understanding of urban design. Predominantly product-oriented, it focused on the visual qualities and aesthetic experience of urban spaces, rather than on the cultural, social, economic, political and spatial factors and processes contributing to successful urban places. Influenced by Sitte's City Planning According to Artistic Principles (1889) as well as (what appeared to be its aesthetic antithesis) the work of Le Corbusier, the visual-artistic tradition is clearly expressed in Unwin's Town Planning in Practice (1909), and reinforced by the various contributions to MHLG Design in Town and Village (1953). It is typified by Frederick Gibberd's concern for the pictorial composition of front gardens, rather than for considerations of privacy or of opportunities for personalisation (Jarvis, 1980, p. 53). Issues of pictorial composition also predominate in the 'townscape' approach developed by Gordon Cullen and others in the late 1940s and the 1950s. As Punter and Carmona (1997, p. 72) note, while Cullen's Townscape developed his personal and expressive response to urban environments, it largely failed to acknowledge public perceptions of townscapes and places, which – by contrast – Kevin Lynch's contemporaneous The Image of the City highlighted (Lynch, 1960).

(ii) The social usage tradition
The social usage tradition emphasised the way in which people use and colonise space. It encompassed issues of perception and sense of place. Identifying Kevin Lynch (1960) as a key proponent of this approach, Jarvis (1980, p. 58) highlights Lynch's attempt to shift the focus of urban design in two ways:

- *in terms of appreciation of the urban environment*: rejecting the notion that this was an exclusive and elitist concern, Lynch emphasised that pleasure in urban environments was a commonplace experience;
- *in terms of the object of study*: instead of examining the physical and material form of urban environments, Lynch suggested examining people's perceptions and mental images.

Jane Jacobs – whose book *The Death and Life of Great American Cities* attacked many of the fundamental concepts of 'Modernist' urban planning and heralded many aspects of contemporary urban design – was a key proponent of this approach, arguing that the city could never be a work of art because art was made by 'selection from life', while a city was 'life at its most vital, complex and intense' (1961, p. 386). Concentrating on the sociofunctional aspects of streets, sidewalks and parks, Jacobs emphasised their role as containers of human activity and places of social interaction. The same kind of detailed observation informed subsequent work in this tradition, such as Jan Gehl's studies of public space in Scandinavia (1971) and William H. Whyte's (1980) *The Social Life of Small Urban Spaces*.

Christopher Alexander's work also epitomises the social usage tradition. As Jarvis (1980, p. 59) notes in *Notes on the Synthesis of Form* (Alexander, 1964) and *A City is Not a Tree* (Alexander, 1965), Alexander identified both the failings of design philosophies that considered 'form without context' and the dangers of approaching city design in ways that did not allow for a rich diversity of cross connections between activities and places. Alexander's ideas were developed further in *A Pattern Language* (Alexander *et al.*, 1977) and *The Timeless Way of Building* (Alexander *et al.*, 1979), in which he set out a range of 'patterns'. Rather than 'complete designs', each pattern was a 'sketched minimum framework of essentials', a 'few basic instructions' and 'rough freehand sketches' to be shaped and refined (Jarvis, 1980, p. 59). For Alexander, the patterns are intended to provide the designer with a usable – but not predetermined – series of relationships between activities and spaces. Even those patterns closest to the traditional visual or spatial concerns of urban design, in which Alexander frequently cites Camillo Sitte, are grounded in and justified by research and/or observation of people's use of places.

(iii) The making places tradition

Over the past twenty years, the concept of urban design that has become dominant is one of making places for people. This evolution of urban design thought is nicely summed up in the following definitions:

- In 1953, Frederick Gibberd argued that the 'purpose of town design is to see that [the urban] composition not only functions properly, but is pleasing in appearance'.
- In 1961, Jane Jacobs asserted that: '*To approach the city . . . or neighbourhood as if it were a larger architectural problem . . . is to substitute art for life.*'
- In 1988, Peter Buchanan argued that urban design was 'essentially about place making, where places are not just a specific space, but all the activities and events that make it possible'.

Synthesising the earlier traditions, contemporary urban design is simultaneously concerned with the design of urban space as an aesthetic entity and as a behavioural setting. It focuses on the diversity and activity which help to create successful urban places, and, in particular, on how well the physical milieu supports the functions and activities taking place there (Figures 1.3, 1.4). With this concept comes the notion of urban design as the design and management of the 'public realm' – defined as the public face of buildings, the spaces between frontages, the activities taking place in and between these spaces, and the managing of these activities, all of which are affected by the uses of the buildings themselves, i.e. the 'private realm' (Gleave, 1990, p. 64) (see Chapter 6).

In recent years, 'official' definitions have also embraced the concepts of making places, and of the public realm. In England, for example, planning policy guidance states that 'urban design' should be taken to mean:

> the relationship between different buildings; the relationship between buildings and the streets, squares, parks and other spaces which make up the public domain itself; the relationship of one part of a village, town or city with the other parts; and the patterns of movement and activity which are thereby established. In short, the complex relationships between all the elements of built and unbuilt space. (DoE Planning Policy Guidance Note 1, 1997, para. 14)

FIGURE 1.3
A place for people – Darling Harbour, Sydney, Australia

FIGURE 1.4
A place for people – Waterfront Park, Portland, Oregon, USA

The Department of Transport, Environment and the Regions (DTER, previously the DoE) and the Commission for Architecture and the Built Environment (CABE, formerly the Royal Fine Art Commission) subsequently gave a more rounded definition, identifying urban design as the 'art of making places for people':

> It includes the way places work and matters such as community safety, as well as how they look. It concerns the connections between people and places, movement and urban form, nature and the built fabric, and the processes for ensuring successful villages, towns and cities. (DETR/CABE, By Design: Urban Design in the Planning System: Towards Better Practice, 2000a, p. 8)

The guide identified seven objectives of urban design, each relating to the concept of place:

- *Character*: a place with its own identity;
- *Continuity and enclosure*: a place where public and private spaces are clearly distinguished;
- *Quality of the public realm*: a place with attractive and successful outdoor areas;
- *Ease of movement*: a place that is easy to get to and move through;
- *Legibility*: a place that has a clear image and is easy to understand;
- *Adaptability*: a place that can change easily;
- *Diversity*: a place with variety and choice.

Urban design frameworks

As part of the 'making places' tradition, there have been a number of attempts to identify the desirable qualities of successful urban places and/or 'good' urban form. It is useful to note the key content of five such attempts.

Kevin Lynch

Lynch (1981, pp. 118–19) identified five performance dimensions of urban design:

1. *Vitality*, the degree to which the form of places supports the functions, biological requirements and capabilities of human beings.
2. *Sense*, the degree to which places can be clearly perceived and structured in time and space by users.

3. *Fit*, the degree to which the form and capacity of spaces matches the pattern of behaviours that people engage in or want to engage in.
4. *Access*, the ability to reach other persons, activities, resources, services, information, or places, including the quantity and diversity of elements that can be reached.
5. *Control*, the degree to which those who use, work, or reside in places can create and manage access to spaces and activities.

Two meta-criteria underpinned the five dimensions: those of *efficiency*, relating to the costs of creating and maintaining a place for any given level of attainment of the dimensions; and of *justice*, relating to the way in which environmental benefits were distributed. Thus, for Lynch the key questions were: (i) what is the relative cost of achieving a particular degree of vitality, sense, fit, access, or control?; (ii) who is getting how much of it?

Allan Jacobs and Donald Appleyard

In their paper 'Towards an Urban Design Manifesto', Jacobs and Appleyard (1987, pp. 115–16) suggested seven goals that were 'essential for the future of a good urban environment':

1. *Liveability*: A city should be a place where everyone can live in relative comfort.
2. *Identity and control*: People should feel that some part of the environment 'belongs' to them, individually and collectively, whether they own it or not.
3. *Access to opportunities, imagination and joy*: People should find the city a place where they can break from traditional moulds, extend their experience, and have fun.
4. *Authenticity and meaning*: People should be able to understand their (and others') city, its basic layout, public functions and institutions, and the opportunities it offers.
5. *Community and public life*: Cities should encourage participation of their citizens in community and public life.
6. *Urban self-reliance*: Increasingly cities will have to become more self-sustaining in their uses of energy and other scarce resources.
7. *An environment for all*: Good environments should be accessible to all. Every citizen is entitled to a minimal level of environmental liveability, and of identity, control and opportunity.

To achieve these goals, five physical characteristics or 'prerequisites' of a 'sound' urban environment were defined:

1. Liveable streets and neighbourhoods.
2. A minimum density of residential development and intensity of land use.
3. Integrated activities – living, working, shopping – in reasonable proximity to each other.
4. A manmade environment that defines public space, particularly by its buildings (as opposed to buildings that mostly sit in space).
5. Many separate, distinct buildings with complex arrangements and relationships (as opposed to a few, large buildings).

Responsive Environments

During the late 1970s and early 1980s, a team at the then Oxford Polytechnic formulated an approach to urban design, published as *Responsive Environments: A manual for urban designers* (Bentley *et al.*, 1985). The approach stressed the need for more democratic, enriching environments, maximising the degree of choice available to users. The design of a place, it was argued, affected the choices people could make:

• Where they could and could not go.
• The range of uses available.
• How easily they could understand what opportunities its offers.
• The degree to which they could use a given place for different purposes.
• Whether the detailed appearance of the place made them aware of the choice available.
• Their choice of sensory experience.
• The extent to which they could put their own stamp on a place.

The approach respectively focused on seven key issues in making places responsive: those of *permeability, variety, legibility, robustness, visual appropriateness, richness* and *personalisation*. It was later suggested that *resource efficiency, cleanliness* and *biotic support* be added, to include the ecological impact of urban forms and activity patterns (Bentley, 1990). Based on their experience in practice and teaching, McGlynn and Murrain (1994) argued that four qualities appeared to be fundamental – *permeability, variety* (vitality, proximity and concentration), *legibil-*

ity and *robustness* (resilience). Bentley (1999, pp. 215–17) has subsequently proposed a 'responsive city typology' consisting of the deformed grid, the complex use pattern, robust plot development, the positive privacy gradient, the perimeter block, and the native biotic network.

Francis Tibbalds

In 1989, His Royal Highness The Prince of Wales offered a framework for architectural design sparking an important debate. In response, an urban design framework of ten principles was developed by the then-president of the Royal Town Planning Institute and founder of the UK-based Urban Design Group, Francis Tibbalds (1988b, 1992):

1. consider places before buildings;
2. have the humility to learn from the past and respect your context;
3. encourage the mixing of uses in towns and cities;
4. design on a human scale;
5. encourage the freedom to walk about;
6. cater for all sections of the community and consult with them;
7. build legible (recognisable or understandable) environments;
8. build to last and adapt;
9. avoid change on too great a scale at the same time;
10. with all the means available, promote intricacy, joy and visual delight in the built environment.

The Congress for New Urbanism

New Urbanism is a term applied to a set of ideas that appeared in the USA during the second half of the 1980s and early 1990s, including 'neo-traditional neighbourhoods' (NTDs) or 'traditional neighbourhood developments' (TNDs), where the central idea was to design complete neighbourhoods that would be similar to traditional neighbourhoods (e.g. Duany and Plater-Zyberk, 1991), and 'pedestrian pockets' or 'transit-oriented development' (TOD), where the central idea was to design neighbourhoods that were explicitly related to transport connections and of a sufficient density to make public transport viable (e.g. Calthorpe, 1989, 1993). There was some convergence between the ideas, including common preferences for mixed uses; environmental sensitivity; an internally consistent hierarchy of architectural, building and street types; legible edges and centres; walkability; and a reliance on succinct graphic guidelines in lieu of traditional zoning codes (Kelbaugh, 1997). Their origins, however, show a much greater diversity. Coming from an energy and environmental design ethic, pedestrian pockets and TODs were predicated on a regional transit and open space system, while TNDs grew out of a concern to recreate traditional notions of city, town, neighbourhood and architecture.

Formalised through the creation of the *Congress for New Urbanism* (CNU) in 1993 and the publication of a Charter for New Urbanism (www.cnu.org) styled on CIAM's 1933 *Charter of Athens* (see Chapter 2), New Urbanists were 'committed to re-establishing the relationship between the art of building and the making of community, through citizen based participatory planning and design' (CNU, 1999). While explicitly recognising that physical solutions alone cannot solve social and economic problems, the Charter argued that 'neither can economic vitality, community stability, and environmental health be sustained without a coherent and supportive physical framework'. It advocated the restructuring of public policy and development practices to support the following principles:

- Neighbourhoods should be diverse in use and population.
- Communities should be designed for the pedestrian and for transit, as well as for the car.
- Cities and towns should be shaped by physically defined and universally accessible public spaces and community institutions.
- Urban places should be framed by architecture and landscape design that celebrate local history, climate, ecology and building practice.

The Charter also asserted principles to guide public policy, development practice, planning and design, at the scales of region (metropolis, city and town), neighbourhood (district and corridor) and block (street and building).

The frameworks

Each of the above frameworks has a different degree of prescription regarding desirable physical and spatial form. Lynch's framework is least prescriptive and is essentially a series of criteria to guide and evaluate urban design, which leaves others to determine the physical form. Jacobs' and Appleyard's framework is much more prescriptive.

Their criteria suggest the vibrant, lively and well-integrated urban form of cities such as San Francisco and Paris. As is discussed later in this book, urban designers should be wary of being too prescriptive about urban form, since that which is appropriate in one local climate and culture may not be so in another.

While these frameworks are sound in themselves, there is a danger of their treatment as inflexible dogma or their reduction to mechanical formulae. They should be used with the flexibility derived from a deeper understanding and appreciation of their biases, justifications and interrelations. Urban design should not be reduced to a formula. Application of a formula negates the active process of design that relates general principles to specific situations. In any design process there are no wholly 'right' or 'wrong' answers, there are only better and worse ones. Their quality may only be known in time. Furthermore, frameworks may well stress the outcomes or products of urban design rather than the process dimensions, suggesting qualities of 'good' environment or urban design, but not how these can be achieved. The processes through which the urban environment comes about demand cognisance of, and sensitivity to, power dynamics in urban space and its production. Urban designers therefore need to understand the contexts within which they operate (Chapter 3) and the processes by which places and developments come about (Chapters 10 and 11).

As in many spheres, there is often an implementation 'gap' between theory and practice. The experience of New Urbanism provides an illustration of this. Sohmer and Lang (2000, p. 756) argue that New Urbanism can be considered to involve three main components: (i) an architectural style (i.e. neo-traditional, contextualised architecture); (ii) an urban design practice (i.e. prescribed street forms, street profiles, public spaces and densities); and (iii) a set of land use policies (i.e. mixed-use, mixed-income, mixed-tenure, and transit-oriented development). These can be arranged in a pyramid, whereby those at the lower levels are easier to implement and those at the higher levels harder to implement. The pyramid reflects the hierarchy of the use of New Urbanism. The New Urbanist architectural style is often used without the other two components. Housing developments may, for example, feature New Urbanist-inspired neo-traditional homes but on standard suburban lots. While not as readily adopted as the architectural style, the urban design component is more common than New Urbanist land use policies. Sohmer and Lang, therefore, conclude that for 'true' New Urbanism, all three components must be in place. It could, however, be argued that for 'true' New Urbanism, the 'architectural style' component is dispensable (see Chapter 11).

THE NEED FOR URBAN DESIGN

Having clarified the scope of urban design, it is necessary to discuss the contemporary need for urban design. Writing in the mid-1970s, Ian Bentley (1976) saw the emergence of concerns for urban design originating in critiques of: (i) the urban environmental product; (ii) the development process; and (iii) the professional role in controlling its production. Each of these critiques detected various kinds of fragmentation and a lack of concern for the totality and overall quality of the urban environment.

The urban environmental product and the development process

There have been many critiques of the built environment. The poor quality of much of the contemporary urban environment, and the lack of concern for overall quality, are functions of the processes by which the environment is produced, and the forces that act on those processes. Influence and blame is attributed – rightly or wrongly – to the development industry. The authors of the DETR/Housing Corporation's *Urban Design Compendium* (Llewelyn-Davies, 2000) argue that the development process and the actors within it have become 'entangled' in a system that produces 'developments', but not 'places', constrained by the 'predominantly conservative, short-term and supply-driven characteristics of the development industry'. Environmental degradation also results from the cumulative effect of incremental decisions by 'unknowing' urban designers (see below).

In a similar vein, focusing on the product rather than the process of urban design, Loukaitou-Sideris (1996, p. 91) discussed urban quality in terms of 'cracks', seeing the cracks as:

- the gaps in the urban form, where overall continuity is disrupted;
- the residual spaces left undeveloped, underused or deteriorating;

- the physical divides that purposefully or accidentally separate social worlds;
- the spaces that development has passed by or where new development creates fragmentation and interruption.

She gives examples of such cracks in a range of locations. Examples in the urban core include those situations 'where corporate towers assert their dominance over the skies, but turn their back onto the city; where sunken or elevated plazas, skyways and roof gardens disrupt pedestrian activity; and where the asphalt deserts of parking lots fragment the continuity of the street' (p. 91). Elsewhere the cracks include car-oriented commercial strips, with no sidewalks or pedestrian amenities, and walled or gated developments that 'assert their privateness by defying any connection with the surrounding landscape' (pp. 91–2).

Poor quality urban environments also come about in response to various social and economic trends, such as those of homogenisation and standardisation, of a focus on individualism rather than collective issues, of the privatisation of life and culture, and of retreat from and decline of the public realm. Jacobs and Appleyard (1987, p. 113) comment that cities – especially American cities – have become privatised through consumer society's emphasis on the individual and the private sector. Escalated greatly by increasing car use, these trends result in a 'new form of city',

> one of closed, defended islands with blank and windowless façades surrounded by wastelands of parking lots and fast-moving traffic . . . The public environment of many American cities has become an empty desert, leaving public life dependent for its survival solely on planned formal occasions, mostly in protected internal locations.

The role of the built environment professions

The contemporary concern for urban design is also located in critiques of the role of the various built environment professions. As the apparent certainties of Modernism in architecture and planning became increasingly questioned, the period from the 1960s onwards saw a series of crises of confidence in the main environmental professions about what they were doing and how they were doing it. Lang (1994, p. 3) locates the birth of urban design in the recognition that 'the sterile urban environments achieved by applying the ideas of the Modern Movement to both policy-making and to architectural design at the urban scale were a failure in terms of the lives of the people who inhabited them' – people who, in McGlynn's words (1993, p. 3), 'began to challenge the values and assumptions of architects and planners and to distrust their ability to improve upon the spatial and physical forms of pre-modernist urbanism'.

Problems of a lack of quality in contemporary development have also been attributed to well-intentioned but ill-conceived public sector regulation, and to development controls and standards with little holistic awareness. Drawing inspiration from John Ruskin's 'Seven Lamps of Architecture', Jon Rouse (1998) outlined what he described as 'The Seven Clamps of Urban Design', the reasons 'why we are consistently failing to achieve high standards of . . . urban design' (see Box 1.1). Similarly, in discussing planning and development controls in the US, Duany et al. (2000, p. 19) argue that many development codes have a negative effect on the quality of the built environment:

Their size and their result are symptoms of the same problem: they are hollow at the core. They do not emanate from any physical vision. They have no images, no diagrams, no recommended models, only numbers and words. Their authors, it seems, have no clear picture of what they want their communities to be. They are not imagining a place that they admire, or buildings that they hope to emulate. Rather, all they seem to imagine is what they don't want: no mixed uses, no slow-moving cars, no parking shortages, no overcrowding.

Inflexible applications of technical standards frequently frustrate the creation of places. In the US context, Duany et al. (2000, p. xi) observe that: 'one cannot easily build Charleston anymore, because it is against the law. Similarly, Boston's Beacon Hill, Nantucket, Sante Fe, Carmel – all of these well-known places, many of which have become tourist destinations, exist in direct violation of current zoning ordinance.' The problem is particularly pronounced with regard to highway and traffic design standards, the rigid application of which effectively determines the layout of many residential areas. This is partly a consequence of fragmentation: focusing on a part while failing to see the whole, or to recognise design as a process of creating 'wholes'.

BOX 1.1 – THE SEVEN CLAMPS OF URBAN DESIGN

(from Rouse, 1998)

(i) *The Clamp of Strategic Vacuum*
Lack of sufficient national, regional and local policy apparatus to ensure that urban design is placed at the heart of political and administrative decision-making.

(ii) *The Clamp of Reactivity*
Failure of the planning system to adopt a strategic approach to urban design process, and the substitution of reactive and negative regulation for proactive and positive intervention.

(iii) *The Clamp of Over-Regulation*
Regulation in the wrong place and time, that can kill innovation, creativity and risk taking. However, greater flexibility in the processes of development needs to be balanced by stronger control on the quality of design.

(iv) *The Clamp of Meanness*
In an age where we learned the price of everything, but forgot the value of so many things, design in general, and urban design in particular, suffered. Design may cost money, but creates lasting value.

(v) *The Clamp of Illiteracy*
Virtually no one is properly equipped with the skills to demand, create and interpret excellence in urban design – we have become illiterate, and need, collectively, to re-educate ourselves.

(vi) *The Clamp of Small Mindedness*
Contemporary development is characterised by introspection, low ambition, a tendency to revert to the lowest common denominator, and an unhealthy obsession with the successes and failures of the past.

(vii) *The Clamp of Short-Termism*
A systemic, myopic condition means that the shape of new development is dictated not by the projected 100-year life of buildings and the need for aftercare, but by the five-year funding programme, four-year political cycle, three-year public expenditure agreement, and the spectre of annuality.

As is discussed in Chapter 11, rather than controls for the sake of controls, the need is for 'smart' controls that are informed by a holistic awareness.

Bentley (1998, p. 15) argues that one of the most important reasons for urban design arises because of the gaps created by the boundaries set up and institutionalised around the various environmental disciplines and concerns, producing a 'fragmented set of professions', with 'tight boundaries around' and 'gaps between them'. As the gaps between the environmental professions became increasingly hardened and institutionalised, it appeared that what was falling through the gaps was concern for 'the public realm itself – the void between buildings, the streets and spaces which constitute our everyday experiences of urban spaces' (McGlynn, 1993, p. 3). This suggested a need to focus on the integration of professional activity, and a concern for the environment as a whole. From the late 1960s onwards, an increasing number of professionals began to see the hard-edged division of responsibilities as contributing to poor quality urban environments, poor quality development, and poor quality places.

URBAN DESIGN AS JOINING UP

The discussion above gives rise to two related notions of urban design: (i) as a means of joining up a fragmented set of professions and (ii) as a means of restoring or giving qualities of coherence and continuity to individual, often inward-focused urban developments (i.e. to improve overall environmental quality and make better places).

Joining up the professions

Problems of overall urban quality typically have a number of common characteristics, including interconnectivity, complexity, uncertainty, ambiguity and conflict. Such problems are inherently multidimensional, their dimensions interdependent and not forming an easy fit with professions based on functional divisions. Although rigid 'silo-based' specialisation has its place (we need brain surgeons as well as general practitioners), it may also encourage professionals to see things from one narrow disciplinary perspective, fragmenting the pool of skills, and reducing the options for integration and holistic consideration. It is clear that the strands of interest and expertise need to be drawn together. In essence, this becomes an argument for soft-edged rather than hard-edged professionalism, and for collaborative and inclusive working practices.

By the 1970s, some professionals had begun to show concern, and, where possible, to take responsibility, for overall urban quality. They also sought to address aspects of professional practice that were detrimental to quality, arguing for greater consideration of place and the environment in planning, and for greater appreciation and respect for issues of context in architecture (i.e. including consideration of the 'site' as something beyond the immediate ownership boundary).

Recognising the need to join up a fragmented set of professions, certain key individuals – and subsequently organisations – set out to build bridges and to create dialogue and common cause among the established built environment professions. In the UK, the first umbrella organisation, the Urban Design Group (UDG), was founded in 1978. The UDG considered that everyone acting in the environment was an urban designer 'because the decisions they made affected the quality of urban spaces' (Linden and Billingham, 1998, p. 40). The interprofessional nature of urban design was further emphasised in the UK by the launch of the Urban Design Alliance (UDAL) in 1997. Founded by the Civic Trust, the Landscape Institute, the Institution of Civil Engineers, the Royal Institute of British Architects (RIBA), the Royal Institution of Chartered Surveyors (RICS), the Royal Town Planning Institute (RTPI) and the Urban Design Group (UDG), UDAL aims to 'foster greater awareness of urban design and to promote higher standards of urban design'. The campaigning work of these organisations has been partly responsible for a major shift in the UK Government's approach to urban design (see Chapter 11).

Joining up the urban environment

In a complex and sophisticated argument, Sternberg argued that the primary role of urban design is to reassert the 'cohesiveness of the urban experience'. Drawing on the 'organicist' school of thought – which had influenced Patrick Geddes, Lewis Mumford and, more recently, Christopher Alexander, who noted how organicists observed that 'modern society (especially its central dynamic mechanism, the market) atomised community, nature and the city. Inspired by biological metaphors and philosophical concepts of vitalism, the organicists set out to reassert the natural growth and wholeness that a 'mechanical' market society would tend to undermine' (Sternberg, 2000, p. 267). Sternberg suggested that the ideas informing urban design share an intellectual foundation in implicitly acknowledging the 'non-commodifiability' of the human experience across property boundaries (i.e. that it is impossible to separate the parts from the whole). He contended that the leading urban design theorists share 'the view that good design seeks to reintegrate the human experience of urban form in the face of real estate markets that would treat land and buildings as discrete commodities' (p. 265). Here, without conscious concern for urban design as a process of restoring or giving qualities of coherence and continuity to individual, often inward-focused developments, the issue of overall quality will inevitably be neglected.

This is put more directly into an urban design context by Alexander's notion of 'things' and 'relationships'. Alexander (1979) argued that what we perceive to be 'things' in our everyday surroundings – buildings, walls, streets, fences – are better understood as 'patterns' intersecting with other patterns (i.e. as relationships). A window, for example, is a relationship between inside and outside, between public and private. When they cease to be 'relationships' and become 'things' (i.e. they become isolated or removed from their context), patterns lose the quality that Alexander calls 'aliveness'. Thus, just as Alexander *et al.* (1977) argued that no pattern is an isolated entity, but is embedded in the patterns that surround it, so the role of urban design is in large part about joining up the patterns that others (architects, developers, highway engineers, etc.) are primarily concerned with providing.

URBAN DESIGN PRACTICE

Who are the urban designers? An inclusive response is all those who take decisions that shape the urban environment, which includes not just architects, landscape architects, planners, engineers, and surveyors, but also developers, investors, occupiers, civil servants, politicians, events organisers, crime and fire prevention officers, environmental health officials, and many others. Individuals and groups engage in the process of urban design in different capacities and with different objectives. Their influence on design decisions may be direct or indirect, consisting of 'self-conscious urban design' (i.e. what people who see themselves as urban designers create and do) or 'unselfconscious urban design' (resulting from the decisions and actions of those who do not see themselves as urban designers) (Beckley, 1979, from Rowley, 1995, p. 187). In this sense, there is a continuum

from 'knowing' to 'unknowing' urban designers. This is not a distinction in terms of the quality of outcome: the outcomes of both knowing and unknowing can be 'good' and 'bad'. Nevertheless, given the complexity of the contemporary environment, unknowing urban design is not a 'bad thing' *per se*, but – because overall environmental quality is not an explicit consideration – it lessens the likelihood of 'good' places being created. Barnett (1982, p. 9), for example, contends that 'Today's city is not an accident. Its form is usually unintentional, but it is not accidental. It is the product of decisions made for single, separate purposes, whose interrelationships and side effects have not been fully considered.'

'Knowing' urban designers are the professionals employed for their urban design expertise. They may nonetheless have no specific training in the subject, but have learnt from experience following an initial training in architecture, planning or landscape architecture. Further along the continuum are the built environment professionals who, despite having an influence on decisions affecting the quality of the urban environment, do not consider themselves to be urban designers. They nevertheless acknowledge their role in improving environmental quality. This group includes those property developers who recognise the potential of urban design to add value and promote long-term commercial success (University of Reading, 2001).

'Unknowing' urban designers, those who make urban design decisions without appreciating that this is what they are doing (Figures 1.5, 1.6), include the following:

- *Politicians in central/state government*, who set the strategic framework for design within national economic strategy and the policy context for sustainability.
- *Politicians in local or regional government*, who implement central government strategy, interpreting and developing it in the light of local circumstances including the investment of public resources in the public realm.
- *The business community and civil servants*, who make investment decisions, including those relating to the physical infrastructure.
- *Accountants*, who advise the public and private sectors about their investments.
- *Engineers*, who design the roads and public transport infrastructure and integrate it into the public realm.
- *Investors*, who assess investment opportunities,

FIGURE 1.5
The introduction of wheely bins in Greenwich, London, has had an unexpected disruptive impact on the urban scene and represents an example of unknowing urban design

FIGURE 1.6
The location of re-cycling bins can offer a similar example of a disruptive addition to the street scene – in this case an Aberdeen conservation area

and options concerning, for example, developments and developers to back.

- *Urban regeneration agencies*, which invest public money in regeneration projects and balance environmental, social and economic objectives.

- *Providers of infrastructure* (e.g. electricity, gas and telecommunications companies), which invest in the hidden infrastructure and in maintaining the public realm.
- *Community groups*, which support or oppose developments, campaign for improvements, and otherwise involve themselves in the development process.
- *Householders and occupiers*, who maintain and personalise their property.

Without conscious recognition of the qualities and additional value of good urban design, the creation and production of urban environments often occurs by omission rather than commission. The challenge for knowing urban design practitioners is to demonstrate the importance and value of urban design, and to ensure that concern for it is not absent through ignorance or neglect, or omitted for misguided or short-sighted convenience. Part of this role involves educating unknowing urban designers about the important role they play.

TYPES OF URBAN DESIGN PRACTICE

Mainstream practice customarily affords urban designers two basic roles, those of 'planner/urban designer' and 'architect/urban designer'. The former typically guides and co-ordinates the activities of others, but increasingly is called on to establish long-term spatial or physical 'visions' for localities, by means of a master plan or urban design framework. Such control is typically, but not exclusively, exercised by the public sector over private interests, where the public interest is deemed sufficient to justify protection or guidance. The 'architect/urban designer' is directly involved with the design of development, usually in the form of a specific building or series of buildings.

Contemporary urban design practice is, however, much broader than this. Research for DETR (2000) identified four types of contemporary urban design practice: urban development design; design policies, guidance and control; public realm design; and community urban design (see Table 1.1). Lang (1994, pp. 78–89) also outlined four key types of urban design action: the urban designer as total designer; 'all-

TABLE 1.1
Types of urban design practice

	PROFESSIONAL DOMAIN	CHARACTERISTICS	ACTIVITIES
URBAN DEVELOPMENT DESIGN	Traditionally domain of architects supported by landscape architects and other designers	Rooted in the development process. Typically applicable at site and neighbourhood scales	Involves *all-of-a-piece* design situations and some *total* design situations
DESIGN POLICIES, GUIDANCE AND CONTROL	Traditionally domain of planners supported by architects, landscape architects, conservation officers and others	The design dimension of the planning process (e.g. primarily response to anticipated effects of urban change on urban design quality, whereby guidance and control are typically applied from *outside* development process). Range of considerations usually wider than concerns of urban development design. Applicable at all scales of urban design	Includes: (i) area appraisals, design strategy and policy formulation; (ii) preparation of supplementary design guidance and briefs, and (iii) exercise of design or 'aesthetic' control
PUBLIC REALM DESIGN	Engineers, planners, architects, landscape architects and others. But frequently unintentional result of unco-ordinated decisions and actions taken by many different parties	Encompasses design of 'capital web' (e.g. roads and streets, footpaths and pavements, car parks, public transport interchanges, parks and other urban spaces). Relevant over range of scales	Includes: (i) design and implementation of specific projects; (ii) production and application of guidelines for design and improvement of a locality; and (iii) ongoing management and maintenance of places, including programming of activities and events
COMMUNITY URBAN DESIGN	No particular profession	Seeks to work *with* and *in* communities developing proposals from grass-roots level. Particularly applicable to neighbourhood scale	Utilises range of approaches and techniques to engage with those who will use the environment

(Source: adapted from University of Reading, 2001).

of-a-piece' urban designer; the urban designer as infrastructure designer; and the urban designer as guideline designer. Several other important variants of urban designer exist, and ten types are outlined below. These are not mutually exclusive, and within the same project, urban designers may be involved in a number of roles.

- *Total designer*: a single person or team carrying a project from its inception to its completion on site. While an urban designer may be central to the design process for a project, given the multi-disciplinary nature of urban design and the many actors involved in the process, it is unlikely that the total designer will be a single individual.
- *'All-of-a-piece' urban designer*: a single designer or firm prepares a master plan giving detailed guidelines for developers and architects to follow in the design of buildings. Here 'the urban design team acts as the reviewer of each sub-proposal and implicitly, the elements of the whole project are built within a short period of time of each other, if not simultaneously' (Lang, 1994, p. 79).
- *Vision maker (concept provider)*: provides the concept of how to organise the spatial pattern of a city or urban area, communicating it in the form of a framework or set of guidelines for other actors to develop the detailed phases or parts.
- *Infrastructure designer*: closely associated with the civil engineering and, to a lesser degree, the town planning professions. Because much of the character of an urban environment stems from its streets, parks, public spaces and other public facilities, this role is a crucial one which should not be underestimated.
- *Policy maker*: closely involved with politicians and decision-makers in the creation of a positive future for towns and cities. This is a facilitating role, which involves providing guidance and advice to decision-makers regarding the nature of changes to the built environment; establishing goals for development, and guidelines within which others operate; and co-ordinating, monitoring and evaluating work as it is implemented. The policy maker must consider short- and long-term consequences of design decisions, look to the needs of future generations, and have concern for both the community and the environment as a whole.
- *Guideline designer*: establishes detailed design principles in policy form, defining and designing public space, specifying certain uses, encouraging and stimulating development, and conserving existing environments. Used in the public and (increasingly) in the private sector, guidelines link policy with practice.
- *Urban manager*: promotes, develops and undertakes the day-to-day management of urban areas. The role concerns the whole urban environment, and often encompasses many of the activities listed under facilitator of urban events (below), together with the initiation of small-scale initiatives through the assembly of a coalition of interest groups, and management of the servicing and maintenance of the public realm.
- *Facilitator of urban events*: stimulates activity by initiating and/or administering programmes of cultural animation, with social events and spectacles that encourage a diverse range of people to visit, use and linger in urban places. Programmes usually involve a variety of events and activities across a range of times and venues, and require local enthusiasm and, usually, official recognition, partnership and sponsorship. The facilitator must consider why and how events are provided, where they should occur, and who is the target audience.
- *Community motivator or catalyst*: responsible for enabling community participation in the development process, including the urban design, planning and management of the local built environment. A wide range of methods, including meetings, forums and workshops, are typically used to involve all sections of the community, and citizens groups, in planning to suit local circumstances, time scales and resources.
- *Urban conservationist*: influences the decision-making process with regard to the delicate balance between retention and change. This requires a sensitive appreciation of the dynamics and processes of urban change. The scale and level of interest can vary from individual buildings to large areas of townscape, neighbourhoods or quarters of the city, to the whole city. As well as the protection of buildings and areas, the role is concerned with the promotion of change that will positively enhance the existing townscape.

Clients and consumers of urban design

Given their role in the urban environment, urban design practitioners serve a wide range of 'client' interests. The processes and outcomes of urban design involve and affect people and interests in different ways: as individuals; as members of local groups, communities and society as a whole; as occupiers and users; and as members of present and future generations. Lang (1994, pp. 459–62) makes the distinction between 'paying' and 'non-paying' clients of urban design. Paying clients include entrepreneurs and their financial backers. In the public sector, the entrepreneurs are government agencies and politicians and their financial backers are the taxpayers. In the private sector, the entrepreneurs are developers, and their financial backers are the bankers and lending institutions. As Lang notes, these actors often act as surrogates for the people – purchasers, tenants, users – who will ultimately pay for the buildings and environments produced. Lang identifies several types of non-paying client, the main two groups of which are:

- *Occupiers and users*: Non-paying in the sense that they do not hire or interact with the professionals designing for them, thus leaving an administrative and experiential gap between professional and user–client (see Chapters 10 and 11). Users are often represented in the development process by, for example, public agencies or marketing experts, whose professional skills include an understanding of users' needs and how they can be met.
- *The public interest*: While it is easy to assert that urban designers should serve the public interest, ascertaining and defining that interest, in any particular situation, is difficult. Participants in the development process have different, sometimes competing, interests, while built environment professionals' assumptions about the public interest are often based on narrow professional and/or class factors. In practice, defining the public interest often involves bargaining and negotiation among vying parties.

In discussing the clients and consumers for urban design, it is important to note the possibility of a number of 'gaps'. There are, for example, typically gaps between the producers and the users or consumers of the urban environment (see Chapter 10). There are also communication and social gaps between the designer and the user and the professional and the layperson (see Chapter 12). If their desire is to make places for people, urban designers should attempt to narrow rather than exacerbate these gaps.

CONCLUSION

Over the past forty years, urban design has become a recognised field of activity. Although its scope is broad and its boundaries often 'fuzzy' and sometimes contested, this chapter has argued that it should be seen as an integrative 'joined-up' activity, at the heart of which is a concern for making places for people. While it is probably inevitable that different groups, including those with urban design qualifications, will continue to lay claim to it as a discrete profession, urban design is a shared rather than a particular responsibility – not least because the problems posed and challenges presented are often too complex to be handled by a single person or profession, but also because the responsibility for the overall quality of the urban environment often falls between the established built environment professions.

The creation of a good urban environment and an attractive public realm is not just the prerogative of professional specialists and their patrons. As urban design cannot be abstracted from the day-to-day life of urban areas, all those involved in the creation and functioning of such areas have a role to play in ensuring their success. Hence, a multitude of parties are concerned with the creation of urban environments and places – including central and local government, local communities, the business community, property developers and investors, occupiers and users, passers-by and future generations. All of these groups have an interest and a role to play in urban design.

2

Urban change

INTRODUCTION

Urban environments have changed significantly in recent years, as have ideas about how they should be designed, changed and improved. The significance of 'place' (meaning a location whose position relative to other locations is important) has diminished as the means and methods of communication between locations (both physical and electronic) have evolved, and the pace and intensity of globalisation and other processes have accelerated. Traditional, centralised, city form has evolved into a less legible landscape of sprawling polycentric 'cities'. As assumptions of centralised urban form and dominant central business districts become less tenable, and notions of 'city centre', 'suburb', and 'city edge' less meaningful, members of each residential unit 'create their own city from the multitude of destinations that are within suitable driving distance' (Fishman, 1987, p. 185) – although advances in electronic communications increasingly make physical travel unnecessary.

This chapter is in two main sections. The first discusses changing ideas about urban space design. The second discusses the processes of urban change, and their outcomes in terms of industrial, post-industrial and informational age urban form.

URBAN SPACE DESIGN

'Traditional' urban space can be regarded as the evolved state of urban form immediately prior to the onset of large-scale industrialisation and urbanisation. The processes of urban growth in 'traditional' (pre-industrial) cities can be broadly divided into the 'organic' and the 'planned'. Most towns and cities grew by piecemeal *ad hoc* actions, often involving the replacement of buildings on existing plots. Expressly planned settlements, usually in the form of gridded plans including those developed by the Greeks and Romans, are exemplified in the medieval bastide towns in France, and in Edward I's plantation towns in England.

With professional planners/architects assuming the work of building cities and developing theories about how cities ought to be, it was the Renaissance that properly heralded the transition from freely evolved to planned cities which 'became to a greater degree a work of art, conceived, perceived, and executed as a whole' (Gehl, 1996, p. 43). Examples of consciously designed developments include squares and public spaces (e.g. the Place Vendôme and Place des Vosges in Paris); street systems (e.g. Sixtus V's plans for Rome, Haussmann's remodelling of Paris); extensions to existing cities (e.g. Edinburgh New Town, the Cerda plan for Barcelona); and the redevelopment of fortifications (e.g. the Ringstrasse in Vienna). Even planned cities subsequently accrued incremental and organic development, responding to the configuration of land ownership, and to the incremental evolution of road and other infrastructure networks (Kostof, 1991).

Until the Industrial Revolution, urban development was limited in a number of fundamental ways, resulting in urban spaces modestly scaled (by current standards) by:

- Transport methods and speeds limited to those of the pedestrian and the horse and cart.
- Availability of construction materials. Each city was built using locally derived materials, giving it a relatively consistent appearance.

BOX 2.1 – CHARACTERISTICS OF MODERNIST URBAN SPACE DESIGN

Healthier buildings

Early Modernist planning and urban design demonstrated a reaction to the physical conditions of industrial cities. Medical knowledge developed during the nineteenth and early twentieth centuries provided criteria (the need for light, air, sun and ventilation, and access to open spaces) for the design of healthier buildings and environments. It was argued that the best way to achieve this was to detach buildings from each other, orientate them towards the sun (rather than, as previously, towards the street), spread them out to allow light and air to flow freely around them, and build upwards to where light and air were plentiful.

Healthier environments

Modernists strove both to design buildings providing healthier internal conditions, and to create healthier environments. At the larger scale, the generally agreed solution was to provide more light and air by decongestion, lower residential densities, and the segregation or zoning of housing from industry. The concept of functional zoning was fundamental to the *Charter of Athens*, which proposed rigid zoning of city plans, with green belts between areas reserved for different land uses. This was justified not only on environmental grounds, but also because the resulting city would be more efficient and ordered. New modes of transport would tie the separated areas together.

Accommodating the car

The car and the urban highway were potent symbols of the new age. 'The cities will become part of the country: I shall live 30 miles from my office in one direction; my secretary will live thirty miles away from it too, in the other direction, under another pine tree. We shall both own cars. We shall use up tyres, wear out roads surfaces and gears, consume oil and gasoline' (Le Corbusier, 1927). In the *Charter of Athens* it was argued that, because existing cities were ill-equipped to accommodate the car and other forms of mechanised transport, 'great transformations' were necessary, with conflicts resolved by segregation of vehicles and pedestrians, and rejection of 'streets' that slowed cars down.

Architectural design philosophies

To express their function and functional requirements, buildings were designed from the inside-out, responding only to their programme and functional requirements (the importance of light, air, hygiene, aspect, prospect, recreation, movement, and openness). They became sculptures, 'objects in space' following their own internal logic without necessarily responding to the immediate urban context. Designing buildings in this manner also expressed their modernity.

Attitude to the past

Modernism had an enthusiasm for the zeitgeist – the spirit of the age – that was a reaction to nineteenth century historicism, and expressed a sense of a radical break with the past. Differences were emphasised rather than continuities, with the past seen as a hindrance to the future. Although this dismissal of the past was a matter of 'rhetoric rather than reality', it was important in shaping attitudes and values (Middleton, 1983, p. 730).

- Building methods, usually limited to load-bearing masonry and timber construction. These materials – together with the absence of lifts to service high-rise – limited the height that could be built to a maximum of six or seven storeys. Taller buildings were made only occasionally, for special purposes (e.g. cathedrals, watch towers).

Change in the urban fabric was generally gradual, enabling successive generations to derive a sense of continuity and stability from their physical surroundings. With the growth of capitalism and rapid urbanisation, mainly during the nineteenth century, the older scale and pace of city development was overtaken. Limiting factors on construction and scale changed as industrialisation introduced new building materials and construction techniques (e.g. plate glass, steel, concrete, balloon frames). Other influences included technological developments (e.g. railways, the safety elevator, the internal combustion engine) and related social and economic innovations (e.g. social institutions such as hospitals, large offices, hotels, industrial concerns). Architects and engineers sought to create new structures and plans to meet new demands and challenges. These ideas would become known as Modernism.

Modernism emerged in architecture and planning at the end of the nineteenth century and in the first half of the twentieth century. It was driven both by horror at the squalor and slums of nineteenth century industrial cities, and by perception of the start of a new age – the Machine Age – in which society would reap the benefits of, and accompanying, technological development and industrial production. The leading Modernist in the design of cities was the Swiss architect and planner, Le Corbusier. The period's most influential 'urban design' manifesto was *The Charter of Athens*, the report by the 1933 Congress of CIAM, the International Congress of Modern Architecture established in the 1920s by, among others, Le Corbusier.

A number of contemporary problems and opportunities informed Modernists' concepts of urban space design, from which they sought to derive new principles of urban form (Box 2.1). Traditional, relatively low-rise streets, squares and urban blocks were eschewed in favour of a rational, usually orthogonal, distribution of slab and point blocks set in park land and open space. Rather than being enclosed by buildings, urban space would now flow freely around them (Giedion, 1971).

Opportunity and political will to develop Modernist ideas in practice came after 1945 with post-war reconstruction in Europe, and later through slum clearance programmes and as a consequence of road-building schemes in all developed countries. Comprehensive redevelopment, rather than incremental rehabilitation, refurbishment and infill development, ostensibly offered significant physical improvements over earlier urban form and was justified by claims and desires for progress and modernity. The post-war period saw a dramatic acceleration in the pace and physical scale of the cycle of demolition and renewal.

Comprehensive redevelopment offered the prospect of higher quality environments and more efficient transport networks. At the same time, however, urban clearance, together with the design of new developments, destroyed historic street patterns and traditional notions of urban space. The process of redevelopment was highly disruptive to the economic and social infrastructure, while the product was also fatally flawed: large blocks simplified the land-use pattern, removing the 'nooks and crannies' that could house economically marginal but socially desirable uses and activities that gave variety and life to an area. Nevertheless, although often a painful process, for most of the initial post-war period, the destruction of the physical, social and cultural fabric of inner city areas, mixed-use functional neighbourhoods, and poorer, working-class residential areas was accepted without serious question.

There were a number of reactions to, and criticisms of, Modernist ideas of urban space design,

and the prevailing practices and outcomes of urban development (see Box 2.2). Contemporary urban space design has in large part drawn stimulus from these perceived shortcomings. Critiques of Modernism almost inevitably, however, tend towards caricatures, presenting it as more monolithic than it actually was. It is therefore important to recognise the scope for more nuanced and sympathetic discussions of Modernism: as Wells-Thorpe (1998, p. 105) observes, many of the benefits of Modernism are now taken for granted.

In a stimulating article, 'The Contemporary City in Four Movements', Mitchell Schwarzer (2000, pp. 129–36) presents a typology of contemporary urbanisms which neatly encapsulates some of the diversity of contemporary urban development processes and urban design ideas:

1. *Traditional urbanism* looks back 'to an age of grids, public squares, moderately dense housing and pedestrian corridors'. Based on a critique of the placelessness of the modern vehicular city and of urban sprawl, traditional urbanism attempts to recover what it regards as a more 'authentic' urban framework.
2. *Conceptual urbanism* adopts a more radical attitude, attempting to 'shake off assumptions of what the city was, is or should be', and to appreciate the 'fluid instabilities' of cities as well as their 'inertia of material residue'. Instead of denouncing the 'chaos and congestion' of contemporary urban life, conceptual urbanists 'experiment out from disruption and disorder'.
3. *Marketplace urbanism* is characterised by the 'immense financial, technological and political energies' developing at 'those nodes of dynamic intensity coalescing around the intersections of major freeways, atop tens of thousands of acres of farmland or waste land, on the borders of existing cities'. Both the scale of suburban development, and the economic power of edge cities, are seen as 'proof of their harmony with popular values . . . Pragmatism is identified with what sells'.
4. *Social urbanism*: a critique of most aspects of contemporary US cities, in particular the 'uneven consequences' of commodity capitalism. Highlighting areas of the city that 'capital ignores or flees from', such areas are seen as an 'indictment against the ongoing denigration of urban life at the hands of unequal capital concentration, relentless business and real-estate competition and ceaseless social movements'.

BOX 2.2 – CHARACTERISTICS AND CRITIQUES OF MODERNIST URBAN SPACE DESIGN

Participation and involvement

Modernism was perceived to have a lack of dialogue with the end user: Le Corbusier, for example, had suggested that 'people would have to be re-educated to appreciate his visions' (quoted in Knox, 1987, p. 364), while Walter Gropius considered it undesirable to talk to building users because 'they were intellectually undeveloped' (quoted in Knox, 1987, p. 366). Arguments were advanced about the value of consulting with users and local communities in order to understand and perhaps respond to their opinions, preferences and aspirations. Subsequent experience on the ground was generally uneven, with attempts at participation often being top-down, *for* rather than *with* or *by* local people (see Chapter 12).

Conservation

By the late 1960s, the cultural and historic attributes of traditional environments, and the way they seemed better able to accommodate and support urban life and activity, were increasingly recognised in contrast to, and as reaction against, Modernist environments. All over Europe and in the US, during the 1960s and early 1970s, policies that protected historic areas were introduced, and conservation became an integral, rather than peripheral, part of urban planning. With it came concern for context, and (in contrast with the internationalism of Modernism) greater respect for the uniqueness of places and their history, and for the continuity of local patterns and typologies.

Mixed uses

The logic of functional zoning, reinforced by transport developments and by high land values that excluded lower value uses, reduced the complexity and vitality of city centres. The tendency towards sterility was exacerbated by large, generally mono-functional office blocks and shopping malls, which internalised much of the traditional street life and activity.

Urban form

With new awareness of the qualities and scale of the 'traditional' city, some critics advocated a morphological approach to urban design, based on 'tried and tested' spatial precedents and archetypes, and stressing continuity with, rather than a break from, the past. There was a growing influence from theorists unhappy with the achievements of Modernist urban space design: while Modernism's 'best solo performances' may have been 'more virtuoso', they failed to produce 'good' streets or 'good' cities. There was a recognition that 'the typical fabric and its overall orchestration were better in previous eras' (Kelbaugh, 1997, p. 95).

Architecture

Disillusion with Modernist architecture – or, rather, with its debasement through industrialised production and construction techniques – has been well documented in books such as *Form Follows Fiasco* (Blake, 1974) and *From Bauhaus to Our House* (Wolfe, 1981). In his 1966 book *Complexity and Contradiction in Architecture*, Robert Venturi questioned the purist, minimalist and elitist dogma that, in his view, the International Style and architectural Modernism had become. Influenced by this and by Venturi's subsequent book *Learning from Las Vegas*, new ideas about architecture emerged, including stylistic pluralism and recognition of the built environment's decorative and contextual properties.

The centre of many North American cities have become what Kostof terms 'automobile territory', with razed urban blocks given over to car parking next to intensively developed blocks

Cities for people

The ultimate effect of the car on city form is graphically illustrated in the centres of many American cities. Kostof (1992, p. 277) observes how, in Detroit, Houston and Los Angeles especially, there is 'Modernist urbanism', but not of the sort envisaged by Le Corbusier. 'His iconic *ville verte* – a vision of towers in a park – became in America a *ville grise* of towers in a parking lot'. Although European cities were transformed in less dramatic ways, most saw major road building schemes. Roads did not have the social qualities of streets and tended to slice up and fragment urban areas, causing problems of severance (see Chapter 4). As a reaction to the exclusive emphasis on cars, there has been – in part, at least – a new concern for the pedestrian, and a desire to create pedestrian-dominant environments (accessible to cars, but suiting the scale, pace and comfort of pedestrians) and environments that facilitate use by a range of travel modes.

These types constitute two pairs of opposites. Traditional urbanism and conceptual urbanism propose contrasting ideas about what should inform design and the creation of urban form. Market place urbanism is about the forces shaping contemporary urban form, while social urbanism is a critique of the contemporary urban condition. Traditional urbanism is akin to New Urbanism, while conceptual urbanism relates to New Modernism (see Box 2.3). Although primarily based on US precedents and developments, Schwarzer's typology has a more general applicability, although it is not exhaustive. Other approaches are also possible, for example, one that recognises the realities of both market place and social urbanism, respecting the values of traditional urbanism while embracing the opportunities of conceptual urbanism.

TRANSFORMATIONS IN URBAN FORM

Cities and settlements have evolved through three historical eras. In the first, they were primarily market places; in the second, primarily centres of industrial production; and in the third, they are primarily centres of service provision and consumption. The original basis for cities was people's need to come together, for purposes including security and defence; trade and the exchange of goods and services; access to information, other people and place-specific resources; to engage in activities requiring communal effort or organisation; and to use particular equipment, machines, etc. The essential factor was that activities required people to communicate, which, at least initially, meant being in the same place at the same time. The coming together of people in space and time facilitates an important social dimension which has subsequently been taken as the essence of the 'urban' in a cultural sense. Oldenburg (1999, p. xxviii), for example, contends that without public gathering places integral in people's lives, the 'promise of the city' is denied because the urban area 'fails to nourish the kinds of relationships and the diversity of human contact that are the essence of the city' (see Chapter 6).

Since the first settlements, the reasons for people coming together have multiplied massively. So too has the technology and means of effectively being in the same place at the same time. The use of this technology has had significant effects on the form and nature of all settlements. Increased mobility through innovations in transport – canals, railway, automobiles, etc. – has been a key factor in the changing distribution of activities in space, and the changing spatial form of cities and urban areas. These innovations have compressed space–time (the distance that can be travelled in a unit of time), allowing urban areas to spread out. Where fifteen minutes' walking time in a medieval town might cover one mile and take you from one side of the town to the other, fifteen minutes' driving in a city today might cover five or six miles without leaving the city. There have also been innovations in communications technology (e.g. telegraph, telephone, e-mail, video-conferencing), which have provided alternatives to co-presence in communication.

Patterns of urban development can be regarded as the product of successive eras of transport/communication technology. Borchert (1991, from Knox and Pinch, 2000, p. 86), for example, identifies a series of epochs in the development of US cities, each of which produced a distinctive urban form:

- The pre-rail epoch (before 1830).
- The 'iron horse' epoch (1830–1870).
- The streetcar epoch (1870–1920).
- The automobile/cheap oil epoch (1920–1970).
- The jet propulsion/electronic communication epoch (1970 onwards).

In *City of Bits: Space, Place and the Infobahn*, William Mitchell (1994) argues that digital telecommunications networks will transform urban form and function as radically as networks of water supply and sewers, electricity, and mechanised transportation, telegraph and telephone have previously done. By supporting remote and asynchronous interaction, electronic networks will further loosen many of the spatial and temporal linkages that previously bound human activities together.

To illustrate the costs and benefits of local/remote and synchronous/asynchronous communication, Mitchell (1999, p. 136) uses the example of seeking information from a colleague. He puts these modes of communication into a four-stage historical context that *inter alia* helps explain the development of urban form (see Figure 2.1). While face-to-face contact provides the most intense, high quality and potentially enjoyable interaction, it is also the most expensive option, requiring travel, and consuming real estate. By

BOX 2.3 – NEW MODERNISM

Since the mid-1980s, a radical New Modernist approach, closely related to Deconstructivism, has persisted primarily in the ideas – rather than built projects – of an architectural avant-garde aiming to create architecture and urbanism that accurately reflect the contemporary social condition. Jencks (1990, pp. 268–87) identifies elements of the rhetoric of New Modernism that convey its spirit, those of 'hermantic coding', 'disjunctive complexity', 'explosive space', 'frenzied cacophony', 'thematised ornament', 'traces of memory', 'comic destructive' and 'non-place sprawl'. In reflecting – rather than attempting to shape – society, New Modernists have turned away from the social ideals of Modernism. Kelbaugh (1997, p. 70) sees this as 'essentially nihilist', because it 'accepts and even celebrates the fragmentation, dislocation, acuteness, and impermanence of contemporary life'. Similarly, Ellin (1999, p. 14) regards deconstructivism as 'cynical in the extreme' in having no social agenda, 'It says the world is a mess, and that to design honestly, we should express that.'

Many New Modernist projects are recognisable by their use of fractal geometry, a branch of mathematics that has 'discovered' similar shapes occurring in nature at all scales. Exploiting the ability of computers to construct convoluted shapes and structures, New Modernists have sought to 'slice and break their building forms into slivers and shards; others twist and contort them into warped and dishevelled buildings' (Kelbaugh, 1997, p. 71).

New Modernists tend to see urban design as 'big architecture', rather than in the wider sense intended in this book. The theoretical influence has so far outweighed the actual impact on the urban development process. Its main theorists have produced a limited number of buildings and urban projects but, as yet, no larger-scale schemes. Some of those built – Frank Gehry's Guggenheim Museum in Bilbao, Daniel Libeskind's Jewish Museum in Berlin – constitute significant urban events, extreme examples of contextual dissonance and juxtaposition, and rich visual and aesthetic experiences (see Chapter 8). Nevertheless, while New Modernism might produce exciting buildings,

environments and spaces, it arguably produces them for looking at or visiting occasionally rather than for living or working in. Kelbaugh considers Deconstructivism and Modernism to be 'equally solipsistic and distrustful of context', noting that both have produced 'self-centred' buildings: the former of 'pure, Euclidean geometry'; the latter of 'shattered, fractal geometry'. He concludes that by 'celebrating decentered and fragmented contemporary reality, Deconstruction has given up hope of urban clarity, coherence and civility – even of the possibility of urbanism itself' (Kelbaugh, 1997, p. 71).

Guggenheim Museum, Bilbao, designed by Frank Gehry

contrast, despite separating participants in both space and time, remote asynchronous communication can be far more convenient and often much less costly. In general, therefore, increased mobility – both physical and electronic – has reduced the

need for the spatial concentration of activities, and has allowed activities to spread out.

Electronic communication is perhaps the most powerful decentralising and dis-urbanising force ever experienced. Many experts see the information superhighway further dispersing people and their jobs from cities. As Peter Hall (1998, p. 957) observes: 'After all, that was the effect of previous technological breakthroughs, like the telephone and the car; the information superhighway will simply take the trend to its logical conclusion'. For Mitchell (1995, p. 94), the new technology has dissolved the 'glue' that held the old agglomerations together – the need for face-to-face contact with co-workers, for close proximity to expensive information-processing equipment, for access to information held at a central location. As well as transport and communication technologies, forms of social and economic organisation, together with other types of technology (e.g. construction techniques), change over time. Potential changes can be illustrated by comparing a traditional local bookshop with an e-tail bookseller such as Amazon (see Table 2.1).

Nevertheless, due to communication technology, while cities and urban areas are spatially diffuse and fluid, they are also more connected and integrated – albeit electronically rather than physically – than ever before.

Recognition of the importance of transport and communication technology should not be seen as a case of technological determinism. The application of technology is mediated by social trends. Decentralisation and the so-called 'death of distance' and the end of the city are not foregone conclusions. Peter Hall (1998, p. 943) argues that information technology does not drive decentralisation in any

'simple or determinist' way: 'new technology shapes new opportunities, to create new industries and transform old ones, to present new ways of organising firms or entire societies, to transform the potential for living; but it does not compel these changes'. Similarly, Manuel Castells (1989, pp. 1–2) has noted how, despite various prophecies that the need for concentration of population in cities will be removed, 'intensely urban Paris is the success story for the use of home-based telematic systems'. Similarly, Mitchell (1995, p. 169) questions whether: the 'development of national and international information infrastructures and the consequent shift of social and economic activity to cyberspace, mean that existing cities will simply fragment and collapse? Or does Paris have something that telepresence cannot match?'

The next three sections discuss the evolution of urban form from the core-dominated cities of the industrial age to the polycentric and extended urban regions of the post-industrial and informational ages. For the urban designer, it is important to understand this evolution because urban design both contributes to the evolving trends in the development of new urban form and reacts to that left behind by previous patterns of growth.

THE INDUSTRIAL CITY

Before the full emergence of capitalist economies in the eighteenth century, and the advent of the

	SYNCHRONOUS	ASYNCHRONOUS
LOCAL	Example: talking face-to-face. In pre-literate societies, because there was no alternative, activity was limited to the local-synchronous quadrant and the associated costs of communication constrained the size and form of settlements.	Example: leaving a note. With literacy, a significant amount of human interaction shifted to the local-asynchronous quadrant, and cities began to develop into their characteristic modern forms.
REMOTE	Example: talking by telephone. With telecommunications, the remote-synchronous quadrant opened up, the scales of organisations and social units grew, and the process of globalisation began.	Example: sending e-mail. With the development of digital networks, there is a massive shift of activity to the very low cost, remote-asynchronous quadrant.

FIGURE 2.1
Modes of communications (source: adapted from Mitchell, 1999, pp. 136–8)

TABLE 2.1
Impacts of communication technology

TRADITIONAL LOCAL BOOKSHOP	E-TAIL BOOKSELLER
• Provides a place where customers can browse and purchase books • Book purchasing and browsing in public becomes a social interaction • Book purchasing and browsing can only be undertaken during opening hours • Stores a stock of books on the premises • Must be located near to customers. • Bookstore has a 'real' presence, advertising/communicating itself as such within the local environment • The shop is managed, and accounts kept, in offices within the building	• Browsing and purchasing is done at home or anywhere with an internet connection (i.e. these activities are decentralised) • Book purchasing becomes a private activity • Book purchasing can be undertaken 24 hours per day • Storage and distribution of books are centralised where land is cheap and communications good • Retailer is both everywhere and nowhere • Retailer has a virtual presence • Administration undertaken anywhere labour is available

(Source: adapted from Mitchell, 2002, p. 19).

Industrial Revolution in the nineteenth century, cities were essentially small-scale settlements. During the late eighteenth and the nineteenth centuries, initially in England and subsequently in other countries, major social and economic changes took place. As population increased rapidly, changes in farming methods produced a surplus of labour in agricultural districts. At the same time, the increasingly prosperous towns and cities of industrial and mining districts offered the prospect of employment and a perceived higher standard of living. There was a general migration of population into towns. The introduction of steam power enabled a factory system which demanded further concentration of labour. The rapid growth of cities led, however, to severe overcrowding. Without mass public transport, workers had to be within walking distance of factories, and there was relatively indiscriminate development of factories among poorly constructed and designed workers' housing, producing unsanitary and unhealthy conditions. City authorities were inadequately organised for, and experienced in, coping with such rapid growth.

The growth of the urban population was nevertheless spectacular. In 1801 the urban population of England and Wales was three million – about one third of the total population. By 1911, the urban population was thirty-six million – almost 80 per cent of the total population. The modern or industrial city was, therefore, a product of the Industrial Revolution.

For much of the early twentieth century, the most influential ideas about, and explanations of, urban form and structure came from the University of Chicago's urban sociology unit, and constituted what became known as the 'Chicago School'. Chicago was then a new city. It had grown rapidly, owing much of its growth to industrialisation. Several models of urban structure – most famously Burgess's concentric zone model – were based on research there, and inevitably reflected the city's structure and the forces that created it (Figure 2.2). The 'typical' mature industrial city had a dominant, largely commercial, city centre or Central Business District (CBD). Surrounding the centre was a ring of industry which required a large labour force to be housed nearby, leading to the development of a further ring of blue-collar and working-class housing. Beyond this was a ring of mainly middle-class suburbs. The urban structure focused on the CBD as the most accessible point, the hub of the transport network and road system. Competition for sites and the ability of some land uses to outbid others meant land values were at their highest at the city centre. Land values and the intensity of development there declined smoothly with distance from the centre of the city.

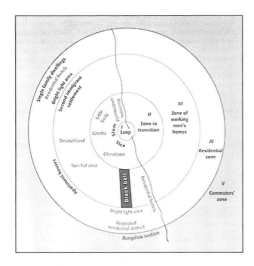

FIGURE 2.2
Burgess's Concentric Zone Model (source: Knox and
Pinch, 2000, p. 216)

POST-INDUSTRIAL URBAN FORM

Since the 1960s, new urban forms have been
emerging that are significantly different to
modern/industrial cities in their form, pattern of
land values, and social geographies. Following the
urbanisation precipitated by the Industrial Revolution, when the main means of transport was by
horse or on foot, the introduction of mass transport
systems broke the necessarily close spatial relation
between workplace and residence. Whereas industrial cities had initially grown in terms of density,
after about 1870, with the development of suburban railway systems, they began to grow in area
too. The early 1900s saw the development of
horse-drawn, and then motorised, trams and
buses, and (in the years before and after the First
World War) of underground railways in the largest
cities. Such developments permitted the decentralisation of residential land uses.

While the initial motivation for living in suburbs
was to escape the industrial city and its pollution,
disease and crime, there were also the attractions
of better quality housing, a garden, healthier living
conditions, and the social status that such locations
conferred. In the 1930s, the steady salaried
employment of the burgeoning middle classes
enabled banks to lend money as mortgages. This
fuelled speculative development, which, together
with the expansion of transport systems – and, in

most countries, ineffective planning systems – led
to further suburbanisation. The post-Second World
War period saw further extension enabled by the
individual mobility afforded by steadily increasing
car ownership, spreading out the previously integrated activities of home, work, business and
leisure.

Rapid urban decentralisation has been a feature
of most Western countries since the Second World
War, and earlier in the US. Breheny (1997 p. 21)
observes how the nature of this decentralisation
has differed. In North America, Japan and Australia,
it has tended to take the form of massive, sprawling suburbanisation. In European countries, by
contrast, it has tended to involve both the suburbanisation of larger cities and towns, and the
growth of smaller towns and villages, partly as a
result of the imposition of green belts around larger
cities.

A suburban population commuting to work in
the city centre created problems of access and
congestion, reducing the CBD's accessibility advantages. In the 1950s and 1960s, road-building
schemes addressed the increasing need for access
from suburbs to city centres, and were supplemented by ring roads, bypasses and connections to
national motorway systems. In time, the transport
pattern was transformed from a 'hub-and-spoke'
configuration where the city centre hub was the
most accessible point, to networks where the most
accessible locations were the junctions in the net.
These transformations materially changed the
pattern of access in the city region, opening up the
potential for scattered growth and removing the
necessity of being close to the centre, which had
kept city form compact and growth patterns
concentric throughout the nineteenth century
(Southworth and Owens, 1993). Suburban densities of jobs and residents might now appear next
to the CBD, while new concentrations of residential, employment and retail development could
sprout on the urban periphery. To describe larger
versions of the latter, Joel Garreau (1991) coined
the term 'edge city'.

Central city decline, and the emergence of less
monocentric city forms, were perhaps inevitable
once the original CBD lost its advantage in terms of
accessibility. In many cases this precipitated its
dissolution as a political economic, social and
symbolic locus – a process termed the 'hollowing
out' of cities. Fishman (1987, p. 17) observes the
creation of 'perimeter cities that are functionally
independent of the urban core', a phenomenon

that has been most prominent in the USA. In Europe, there is usually a still vibrant (though often revitalised and reinvented) core surrounded by a 'shatter zone' and then suburbia, with more prosperous residential developments and a mix of other developments – retail malls, leisure complexes, business parks, and employment centres – surrounding it.

An extensive body of work by scholars based in California defines Los Angeles as the archetypal post-industrial or 'postmodern' city. The 'Los Angeles school' argues that post-industrial 'cities' are increasingly fragmentary in their form and chaotic in their structure, and are generated by different processes of urbanisation than were earlier cities (Box 2.4). A key theme is that of 'fragmentation', both in terms of the urban form and of the associated economic and social geographies (see Figure 2.3). Graham and Marvin (2001, p. 115) describe how:

> complex patchworks of growth and decline, concentration and decentralisation, poverty and extreme wealth are juxtaposed. Whilst downtowns may maintain their dominance of some high level service functions, back offices, corporate plazas, research and development and university campuses, malls, airports and logistics zones, and retail, leisure and residential spaces spread further and further around the metropolitan core.

The prime contributor to this pattern of growth has been the car. Schwarzer's 'market place' urbanists see the car as the 'elixir of city life', enabling dwelling, work and shopping to 'break free from their dependency on rail centres and corridors. Edge cities soar beyond inner-city constraints of land assembly, zoning regulation and high tax rates; they exploit fears of crime through privatised space, and desires for comfort and convenience via car-accessible and climatised space' (Schwarzer, 2000, p. 131). Nevertheless, while cars have enabled cities and their activities to spread out, to operate effectively in such cities, cars become a necessity and both society and our environment become increasingly auto-dependent (Kunstler, 1994; Kay, 1997; Duany et al., 2000). In such environments urban form and transport options are such that choice is limited to car use with an associated range of environmental, economic and social problems (see Table 2.2).

Growing concern about development patterns in the US has led to the emergence of 'smart

BOX 2.4 – THE LOS ANGELES SCHOOL

Much of the value of the Los Angeles School's work lies in its early and clear recognition of emergent processes shaping urban landscapes, economies and cultures. Soja (1995, 1996) identified six 'geographies' or processes of restructuring:

1. A combined process of de-industrialisation and re-industrialisation, resulting in the rise of new flexible forms of economic organisation and production. This represents a shift 'from the tight organisation of mass production and mass consumption around large industrial complexes to more flexible production systems, [which are] vertically disintegrated but geographically clustered in "new industrial spaces" ' (1995, p. 129).
2. The processes of internationalisation, the expansion of globalised capital, and the formation of a global system of 'world cities', combine to 'globalise the local' and 'localise the global'.
3. The emergence of post-industrial urban forms involves a combination of decentralisation and recentralisation, the peripheralisation of the centre, and the centralisation of the periphery. The city is simultaneously being turned inside out and outside in.
4. The development of new patterns of social fragmentation, segregation and polarisation includes increasing inequality and new patterns of spatial segregation. Restructuring has resulted in a widening income gap, and the multiplication of 'blatant contrasts', between wealth and poverty, starkly revealing differences in income, culture, language and lifestyles.
5. The preceding four processes have resulted in the rise of 'carceral architecture' based on protection, surveillance and exclusion. With its 'kaleidoscope complexities', the postmodern city has become both 'increasingly ungovernable' and a 'carceral city' (see Chapter 6).
6. In both a summary of, and a new dimension formed by, the forgoing issues, the increasing presence of simulation within urban landscapes is seen as involving a 'radical change' in 'the ways we relate our images of what is real to empirical reality itself' (1995, p. 134). To explain this restructuring process, Soja utilises Baudrillard's (1989) concept of 'simulacra': imitations of things that never actually existed, copies without originals (see Chapter 5).

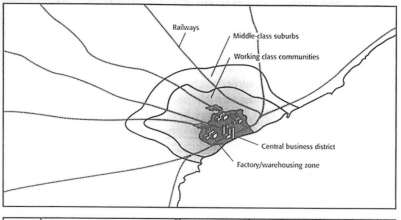

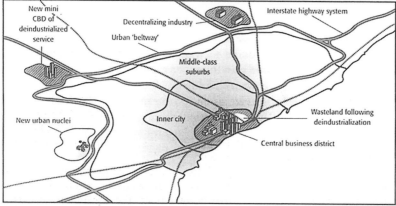

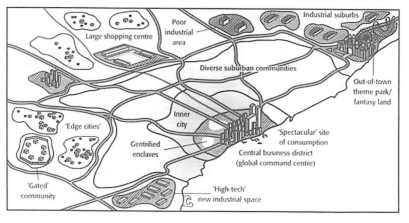

FIGURE 2.3
Transition from the classic industrial city c.1850–1945 (top), to the 'Fordist' city c.1945–1973 and 'post-Fordist' metropolis, c.1975 onwards (source: Knox and Pinch, 2000, p. 69)

growth' (see www.smartgrowth.org). Its advocates unify around the aim of trying to change undesirable impacts of (sub)urban sprawl. They typically question the economic costs of abandoning infrastructure only to rebuild it further out; the social costs of the mismatch between new employment located in the suburbs, and the available workforce in the city; and the environmental costs of abandoning 'brownfield' sites, building on open space and prime agricultural land at the suburban fringe, and thus increasing pollution by necessitating longer commuter journeys (Environmental Protection Agency, 2001). Downs (2001) identifies fourteen basic elements of smart growth (see Box 2.5),

TABLE 2.2
Problems of car dependency

ENVIRONMENTAL	ECONOMIC	SOCIAL
• Oil vulnerability • Petrochemical smog • Toxic emissions such as lead and butane • High greenhouse gas contributions • Urban sprawl • Greater stormwater problems from extra hard surfaces • Traffic problems such as noise and severance	• External costs from accidents and pollution • Congestion costs, despite road building • High infrastructure costs in new sprawling suburbs • Loss of productive rural land • Loss of urban land to bitumen	• Loss of street life • Loss of community • Loss of public safety • Isolation in remote suburbs • Access problems for those without cars and those with disabilities

(Source: Newman and Kenworthy, 2000, p. 109).

and four groups that claim to support it in principle:

1. *Anti- or slow-growth advocates*, aiming for slower urban expansion with reduced car-dependence.
2. *Pro-growth advocates*, aiming for outward expansion to fully accommodate future growth.
3. *Inner-city advocates*, aiming to prevent the draining of resources from the inner city by outward growth processes.
4. *Better-growth advocates*, aiming for reasonable growth with reduced negative impacts.

Restructuring processes are mediated by sociocultural choice, by institutional structures and by pre-existing physical forms. The cities epitomising industrial (Chicago) and post-industrial (Los Angeles) urban form were relatively free from the constraints of earlier patterns. Most cities, particularly European ones, have extensive physical and socio-economic legacies of earlier urbanisation, but not the levels of disinvestment that have plagued many North American cities. Thus, while Los Angeles-style restructuring and urban form may be a future for some cities, it is not necessarily a future for all. Knox and Marston (1998, pp. 449–53) identify distinctive physical, social and economic features of European cities which both distinguish them from those of North America, and provide some form of resistance to Los Angeles-style restructuring:

- *Complex street patterns*, reflecting ancient patterns of settlement and long, slow growth.
- *The presence of plazas and squares* (many of pre-modern foundation) which remain important centres of activity.
- *High density and compact forms*, resulting from high levels of urbanisation, a long history of urban development, the constraints of defensive walls and, more recently, strong planning regulations limiting lateral growth.
- *Low skylines*, constrained by historic materials and technology, and by planning and building codes preserving the dominance of important buildings.
- *Lively downtowns*, due to the relatively late arrival of the suburbanising influence of the car, and because of strong planning controls directed at urban containment.
- *Stable social and physical neighbourhoods*: Europeans move house much less frequently than Americans; and, due to past use of durable construction materials (e.g. brick and stone), the physical life cycle of neighbourhoods tends to be longer.
- *The scars of war*: defensive hill-top sites and city walls limited and shaped the growth of modern cities.
- *Symbolism*: the legacy of a long and varied history includes a rich variety of valued symbols in the built environment and the historic area.
- *A tradition of municipal socialism*: European welfare states generally provide – or have

BOX 2.5 – PRINCIPLES OF SMART GROWTH

(adapted from Downs, 2001)

Elements provoking widespread disagreement among groups supporting smart growth

- Placing limits on the outward extension of further growth
- Financing the additional infrastructure needed to deal with growth and maintain existing systems
- Reducing dependency on private automotive vehicles, especially one-person cars

Elements with less-than-total agreement among groups supporting smart growth

- Promoting compact, mixed-use development
- Creating significant financial incentives for local governments to adopt 'smart growth' planning within ground rules laid out by the state government
- Adopting fiscal sharing among localities
- Deciding who should control land-use decisions
- Adopting faster project application approval processes, providing developers with greater certainty and lower project carrying costs
- Creating more affordable housing in outlying new-growth areas
- Developing a public–private consensus-building process

Elements provoking agreement among groups supporting smart growth

- Preserving large amounts of open space and protecting the quality of the environment
- Redeveloping inner-core areas and developing infill sites
- Removing barriers to urban design innovation in both cities and new suburban areas
- Creating a greater sense of community within localities and neighbourhoods, and greater recognition of regional interdependence and solidarity throughout the metropolitan area

provided – a broad range of municipal services and amenities, including public transit systems and housing.

INFORMATIONAL AGE URBAN FORM

The contemporary restructuring of urban form is not just a consequence of the transition from an industrial to a post-industrial era. As Manual Castells (1989) suggests, it is also part of the transition from an industrial to an 'informational' era. Precisely how cities and urban areas will develop in the informational age is, as yet, unknowable. Nevertheless, it has been argued that 'the very idea of a city is challenged and must eventually be reconceived. Computer networks become as fundamental to urban life as street systems. Memory and screen space become valuable, sought-after sorts of real estate. Much of the economic, social, political and cultural action shifts into cyber-space' (Mitchell, 1995, p. 107).

Another dimension of the development of electronic communications is the increasing potential for telecommuting – the ability to work from home, blurring distinctions between 'home' and 'workplace' – which has been hailed as both revolutionising living and working conditions and allowing greater choice of domicile. Thus, rather than 'urbanity by necessity', it could be a case of 'urbanity by choice'. Telecommuting does not remove the need to design and create places where people want to live, work and play. Telecommuting may also facilitate spatially fluid and complex urban lifestyles. Graham and Marvin (1999, pp. 95–6), for example, note that most teleworking is done in the zones within and around the large cities, allowing people to go to the office on one or two days a week for face-to-face meetings.

The informational age also takes further the ideas of Melvin Webber (1963, 1964) who extolled the freedom offered by the freeway system and the highly decentralised city. Webber conceived the 'non-place urban realm' (where 'place' refers to geographical location) that challenges the real estate orthodoxy of 'location, location, location'. Arguing that spread-out cities such as Los Angeles worked just as well as traditional high-density ones such as New York, he suggested that 'the essential qualities of urbanness are cultural in character not territorial . . . these qualities are not necessarily tied to the conceptions that see the city as a spatial phenomenon' (1963, p. 52). In a celebrated passage, he concluded that:

the values associated with the desired urban structure do not reside in the spatial structure per se. One pattern of settlement is superior to another only as it better serves to accommodate ongoing social processes and to further the non-spatial ends of the political community. I am flatly rejecting the contention that there is an overriding spatial or physical aesthetic of urban form. (Webber, 1963, p. 52)

Electronic communication could mean that future 'cities' are aspatial and ageographic. Mitchell argues that: 'The Net negates geometry . . . it is fundamentally and profoundly aspatial. . . The Net is ambient – nowhere in particular but everywhere at once' (1995, p. 8). As it does not matter where computers are located, merely that they are connected together, the Internet gets much closer to providing universal accessibility (where everywhere is equally accessible) than does the car. A possible implication in terms of urban form is the situation described in Dear and Flusty's concept of Keno Capitalism. Dear and Flusty (1999, p. 77) argue that in 'the absence of conventional and transportation imperatives mandating propinquity, the once-standard Chicago School logic has given way to a seemingly haphazard juxtaposition of land uses scattered over the landscape'. They argue that the result, in terms of urban form, could be a landscape 'not unlike' that formed by a keno gamecard, in which: 'Capital touches down as if by chance on a parcel of land, ignoring the opportunities on intervening lots . . . The relationship between development of one parcel and non-development of another is a disjointed, seemingly unrelated affair.' Here, 'Conventional city form, Chicago-style, is sacrificed in favour of a non-contiguous collage of parcelised, consumption-oriented landscapes devoid of conventional centres yet wired into electronic propinquity and nominally unified by the mythologies of the disinformation super-highway' (1998, p. 81).

'Places' or facilities are nevertheless interdependent assets, and the direct rather than virtual experience of place remains important. If location in space (geographical location) matters less in locational decisions, then the quality of local 'place' may start to matter more. Graham and Marvin (1999) contest the assumption that new communication technologies will 'dissolve' the city, arguing that IT applications are largely metropolitan phenomena. Noting how, as the value added in IT industries is shifting to places that can sustain innovation in software and content – and, crucially, where the employees of such industries want to live and socialise – they cite a study of Manhattan's SoHo and TriBeCa, which found that the raw material for such industries was 'the sort of informal networks, high levels of creativity and skills, tacit knowledge, and intense and continuous innovation processes that become possible in an intensely-localised culture, based on on-going, face-to-face contacts supported by rich, dense and interdependent combinations of meeting places and public spaces' (1999, p. 97). They also note how, despite the growth of e-tailers, a wide range of consumer services – tourism, shopping, visiting museums and leisure attractions, eating and drinking, sport, theatre, cinema and so on – remains embedded in urban locations and seems likely to resist any simple, substantial substitution by 'online' equivalents (1999, p. 95).

Environmental sustainability

Other factors influential in changing urban form include concerns about global warming, about pollution (especially from cars), and about the depletion of fossil fuel reserves. Factors such as increasing fuel prices will change the parameters of locational choices. While some argue that this will lead to more compact and centralised urban forms, there is considerable debate about such predictions.

Breheny (1997, pp. 20–1) suggests that the dominant motive for urban compaction and the compact city is the need to reduce travel by facilitating shorter journeys and the use of public transport (thereby reducing the use of non-renewable fuels and vehicle emissions). Other motives are, that it can support retention of open space and valued habitats; encourage traffic calming and walking and cycling; make the provision of amenities and facilities economically viable, enhance social sustainability; and encourage social interaction.

Central to the argument that more compact cities will result in less travel has been Newman and Kenworthy's work relating petroleum consumption per capita to population density, for a number of large cities (Figure 2.4). Higher densities were found to be consistently associated with lower fuel consumption. Their ideas were criticised for, *inter alia*, their focus on the single variable of density. Hall (1991) argued that travel distances and modal splits depend also on urban structures, Gordon and Richardson (1989) argued that market mechanisms would produce polycentric cities with relatively low energy consumption and congestion, and Gordon and Richardson (1991) found that, despite continuing decentralisation, commuting distances in the US had recently tended to remain stable or to fall, which they attributed to the co-relocation of people and jobs, with most work – and non-work – trips being suburb to suburb, rather than suburb to centre. Jobs and retail had generally moved

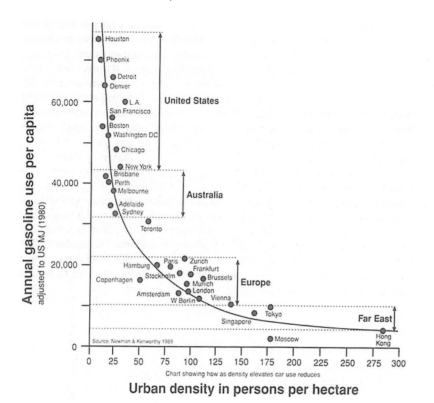

FIGURE 2.4
Newman and Kenworthy's comparison of petroleum consumption per capita to population density (source: Newman and Kenworthy, 1989)

closer to, rather than further from, where people live (Pisarski, 1987).

Various commentators have suggested other sustainable urban forms, such as decentralised but concentrated and compact settlements linked by public transport systems, and concentrated nodes and corridors of high-density development (Frey, 1999). Many such patterns are based on aggregation of relatively small-scale, walkable neighbourhoods. Susan Owens (from Hall, 1998, p. 972) suggests that:

- At regional scale, neighbourhood-sized units (10–15 000 people) might be clustered to form larger settlements, with the units arrayed in a linear or rectangular form along a public transport spine.
- At subregional scale, compact settlements, also in linear or rectangular form, might have employment and commerce dispersed to give a 'heterogeneous' land-use pattern.
- At local scale, subunits at pedestrian and cycle scale, medium to high residential density, and possibly high linear density, might have local employment, commercial and service opportunities clustered to permit multi-purpose trips.

CONCLUSION

This chapter has reviewed the context in which contemporary urban design operates. At the start of the twenty-first century, the old 'certainties' about urban form are challenged. The future will be different from now, in ways we do not yet know. Mitchell (1999, p. 7) contends that the impact of the digital revolution will 'redefine the intellectual and professional agenda of architects, urban designers, and others who care about the spaces and places in which we spend our daily lives'. Pollution, global warming and the depletion of fossil fuels may also provoke radical change. Mitchell suggests that, while future urban environments will retain much that is familiar, there will be a new layer consisting of 'a global construction of high-speed telecommunication links, smart places, and increasingly indispensable software, [which will] shift the functions and values of existing urban elements, and radically remake their relationships'. As a result, he suggests that:

the new urban tissue will be characterised by live/work dwellings, twenty-four hour neigh-

bourhoods, loose-knit, far-flung configurations of electronically mediated meeting places, flexible, decentralised production, marketing and distribution systems, and electronically summoned and delivered services.

Future urban design might, therefore, increasingly be about the design of mixed-use urban neighbourhoods and villages, business and employment parks, leisure and entertainment complexes, offices, shopping malls and home-work units – cheek-to-jowl or widely separated, and with seemingly no overarching logic of land values providing an even transition of intensity and density of development. Terms such as 'city centre', 'suburb' and 'periphery' may become less meaningful, and social and spatial fragmentation may continue, with exclusive enclaves of wealth and privilege, but also areas of intense deprivation and disadvantage.

Urban design is not simply a passive reaction to change. It is – or should be – a positive attempt to shape change and to make better places. The recent UK urban renaissance agenda (Urban Task Force, 1999) and the smart growth movement in the US have highlighted how the ignoring of fundamental urban design considerations such as connections, accessibility and mixed uses, can result in the creation of less sustainable, less socially equitable, and in the long term less economically viable urban forms. While types of urban form may have to be rethought and reconsidered, it is clear that the structure of urban places matters. Furthermore, there is a clear relationship between the spatial and physical characteristics of a city, and its functional, socio-economic and environmental qualities. The need, therefore, is to design cities and urban places to work well, to be people-friendly and to have a positive environmental impact.

3

Contexts for urban design

INTRODUCTION

This chapter discusses a set of broad 'contexts' – local, global, market and regulatory – that constrain and inform all areas of urban design action. Although these contexts change over time, at any particular moment they are relatively fixed and are typically outside the scope of the urban design practitioner's influence. Hence, in relation to individual urban design projects and interventions, they have to be accepted as givens. They also underpin and inform the discussions of the *dimensions of urban design* in the following six chapters. The dimensions constitute the everyday material of urban design, which urban designers have greater scope to manipulate and change. In practice, the boundaries between 'contexts' and 'dimensions' are blurred. In a general sense, however, while urban designers can make decisions about a development's form or visual appearance, they cannot change the fact that it is situated in a particular local and global context, or that it occurs within a market economy that is regulated to a greater or lesser extent. Relating the four contexts and the six dimensions is urban design's essential nature as a problem-solving process. The final part of this chapter, therefore, presents a discussion of the urban design process.

THE LOCAL CONTEXT

Where urban design action involves the preparation of a public realm strategy, the site is itself part of the context. Where urban design action involves a development project, the context can be considered to include the site plus the area immediately outside its boundaries. In general, the larger the project, the greater its scope to control or create its own context. Nevertheless, whatever their scale, all urban design actions are embedded within and contribute to their local context. All acts of urban design are therefore contributions to a greater whole.

Encapsulated in Francis Tibbalds' golden rule that 'places matter most', is the idea that respect for, and informed appreciation of, context are prime components of successful urban design. Each place's unique quality is perhaps its most precious design resource, with urban designers frequently operating within established, generally complex, and often delicate contexts. As discussed in Chapter 2, the ideologically motivated innovation and the 'clean sweep' of comprehensive schemes were largely responsible for the rejection of Modernist ideas of urban space design. As a response, there has been a preference for more incremental development that respects local character and context (Figure 3.1).

Not all contexts or places require the same degree of 'contextual' response. Areas of highly unified character generally require more respectful responses, while areas of low environmental quality offer greater opportunity for the creation of new character. Most areas fall between these extremes. Equally, while not of particular historic or aesthetic quality, they may also be valued for their social or cultural qualities. The concept of context must be considered broadly. Buchanan (1988, p. 33) argued that 'context' was not just the 'immediate surroundings', but the 'whole city and perhaps its surrounding region'. It was not 'narrowly formal', but included 'patterns of land use and land value, topography and microclimate, history and symbolic significance and other socio-cultural realities and aspirations – and of course (and usually especially significant) the location in the larger nets of movement and capital web'.

A study of London's urban environmental quality (Tibbalds *et al.*, 1993) identified eight key factors forming a useful departure point from which to explore the diversity of established urban contexts (Figure 3.2). Lang (1994, p. 19), for example, suggests that all environments can be conceived of in terms of four interlocking components:

1. *Terrestrial environment* – the earth, its structure and processes.
2. *Animate environment* – the living organisms that occupy it.
3. *Social environment* – the relationships among people.
4. *Cultural environment* – the behavioural norms of, and artefacts created by, a society.

Terrestrial and *animate* factors include climate and local microclimates; the established natural environment; underlying geology, land form and topographical features; environmental threats; and sources of food and water. *Social* and *cultural* factors include a settlement's original purpose; changes of purpose and human interventions over time; patterns of land ownership; the culture of the inhabitants; relations with neighbouring populations; and adaptability in changing circumstances. In any one place and time, an 'urban environment' is part of a particular terrestrial context inhabited by a diverse animate community, incorporating multi-layered social interactions producing a distinctive local culture, and forming one among a proliferation of distinctive and complex urban contexts.

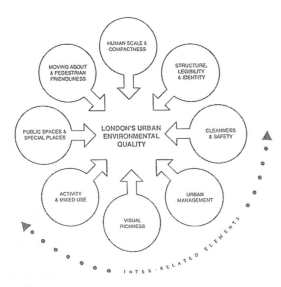

FIGURE 3.1
London's Urban Environmental Quality (source: Tibbalds *et al.*, 1993, p. 22)

FIGURE 3.2
New development in London's Isle of Dogs makes little reference to and is often not connected with its surrounding context. Despite significant investment in the area, the benefits are almost negligible in the areas adjacent to the key developments

It is also clear that considerations of context are not just concerned with 'place' in a physical sense, but also with the people that create, occupy and use the built environment. Understanding local sociocultural contexts and cultural differences allows urban places to be 'read' and understood, revealing much about the culture that created and maintains them.

The relationship between culture and environment is a two-way process. Over time, people's choices create distinctive local cultures that shape and reinforce their environments, and are symbolised within them. Based on prior experience, such choices are motivated by shifting criteria related to goals, values (both individual and societal) and preferences. While people – and the choices they make – collectively create sociocultural contexts, they do not do so in a vacuum. Choices are shaped by, for example, the ability and willingness to pay; the constraints and opportunities offered by the local climate; the availability and cost of technology and resources. The contemporary urban environment in the US, for example, is a product of choices predicated on relatively low motoring costs (and the expectation of their remaining low). In much of Europe, it is a product of choices predicated on relatively high motoring costs.

Technology, especially that of communication and transport, provides new opportunities. Although its impact on social and cultural life can be both dramatic and radical, as change often occurs in incremental and subtle ways, we are less conscious of it while it is actually happening and more aware in retrospect. The impacts of new technology on social, cultural and economic life can be illustrated by the example of the local high street, where, until recently, banks were a ubiquitous presence, often occupying architecturally elaborate buildings and offering face-to-face interaction (Mitchell, 2002, p. 19). Their role was affected by the provision of automatic cash points providing banking facilities 24 hours a day, and as telephone and electronic banking further diminished the need for high street branches, they tended to close, and their buildings found other uses.

Such changes come about through the aggregate effect of individual market choices, based on the availability of new technology. While urban designers must respect and work with the grain of people's sociocultural values and preferences, urban design both responds to cultural change and is itself a means towards such change. Through their involvement in the development process and in creating and managing the built environment, urban designers shape, but do not determine, patterns of social and cultural life and interaction. The last two decades, for example, have seen the emergence of 'cafe society', 'loft living' and a culture of urban living in the centres of many British cities. This is a result of people seeking these lifestyles and of the media and cultural industries presenting positive images of them – but also of developers and designers making such opportunities available.

Given the naivety of assuming that principles of good urban design are universal and transferable between cultures, urban design requires sensitivity to cultural diversity. Furthermore, as processes of globalisation threaten to overwhelm cultural diversity, it is increasingly important to respect that which continues to exist. While the discussion in this book is drawn primarily from a Western (and probably Anglocentric) perspective, Barrie Shelton's *Learning from the Japanese City: West Meets East in Urban Design* offers an important reminder that ideas about urban space are culturally specific. Shelton (1999, p. 9) notes that, to most Western eyes, Japanese cities 'lack civic spaces, sidewalks, squares, parks, vistas, etc.; in other words, they lack those physical components that have come to be viewed as hallmarks of a civilised Western city'. He explains how, behind Japan's urban forms, there are ways of thinking and seeing that are rooted deeply in the wider Japanese culture. Japanese thinking about architectural and urban space, for example, has greater affinity with 'area' – as shown by the importance of the *tatami* mat and the floor in buildings – than that of Western thinking, which focuses on 'line'. There are also debates about, for example, 'European' and 'American' traditions of urban design, usually in attempts to identify a distinctively American, rather than a transplanted and remedial European, tradition (Dyckman, 1962; Attoe and Logan, 1989).

As the economic, social, cultural and technological context continually changes, so does the urban environment. Change is inevitable and often desirable. Prior to the Industrial Revolution, change in the built environment tended to be slow and incremental. Since then, the pace and scale of change has increased, with a corresponding increase in development pressures on particular places, and in the homogenisation of places and contexts (see Chapter 5). Pressures include globalisation and internationalisation; standardisation of building types, styles, and construction methods; loss of vernacular traditions; use of mass-produced materials; decentralisation; estrangement of people from the natural world; pressures for short-term financial returns in the development industry and in the decisions people make about their living environments; the public sector's often unthinking and homogenising regulation of the built environment; and increased personal mobility, and dominance of cars. These pressures, which have both local and global dimensions, provide the link between local and global contexts.

THE GLOBAL CONTEXT

Just as all acts of urban design are embedded in their local context, they are also inextricably embedded in the global context: local actions have global impacts and consequences, while global actions have local impacts and consequences. Given warnings of global warming, climate change, pollution of the natural environment, and the depletion of fossil fuel sources, the need for environmental responsibility is an important consideration for urban designers – one which impacts on design decisions at many levels, including those of:

- The integration of new development with existing built form and infrastructure (e.g. choice of location/site, use of infrastructure, accessibility by various modes of travel).

- The range of uses a development contains (e.g. mixed use, access to facilities/amenities, working from home).
- Site layout and design (e.g. density, landscaping/greening, natural habitats, daylight/sunlight).
- The design of individual buildings (e.g. built form, orientation, microclimate, robust buildings, building reuse, and choice of materials).

The concept of sustainable development includes not only environmental, but also economic and social, sustainability. Urban designers need to have regard to social impacts and long-term economic viability, as well as environmental impacts.

There is often tension between the meeting of human needs, aspirations and desires, and environmental responsibility (Figure 3.3). If human needs are considered to be short-term and 'urgent' and those of the environment long-term and 'important', a balance is needed between short-term and long-term interests. The problem is the tendency to privilege short-term urgent needs at the expense of long-term important ones. Commenting about the short-termism of market behaviour, the economist John Maynard Keynes suggested that in the market's view the long-term did not matter because 'in the long-term, we are all dead'. A different view is expressed in Chief Seattle's wise and poetic words: 'We do not inherit the world from our ancestors; we borrow it from our children.' If future generations are to enjoy the

FIGURE 3.3
Supermarket, Greenwich Peninsula, London, UK. This development shows the all too frequent contradictions inherent in the concept, in this case an 'energy efficient' yet car-dependent development

BOX 3.1 – ENVIRONMENTAL FOOTPRINTS

A development's environmental impact can be likened to a footprint. Initially, the footprint might appear to be small: the site area on which the development sits, together with the destruction of any natural environment that existed there. When the 'invisible' environmental capital inherent in the construction of that development is considered, a second, larger footprint becomes apparent (i.e. the energy and resources expended in the manufacture and transport of materials, the energy required to prepare the site and construct the development, the energy required to extend infrastructure needed to service the site, etc.). When the development is occupied, there is a third, even larger footprint (i.e. the energy and resources expended to sustain the development: the maintenance requirements, the development's energy requirements, the waste disposal requirements, the occupants' travel to and from the development, etc.). Finally, when the development reaches the end of its life, the energy required to alter or demolish it and to deal with the resulting site and materials, completes its lifetime environmental costs, thereby further

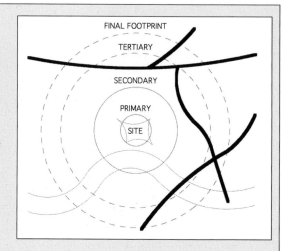

enlarging the footprint. Typically only concerned with the environmental impact of construction (the first and second set of costs), the developer is rarely concerned with the development's subsequent environmental impacts, which typically bear on the investor, the occupants and society at large.

environmental quality and the quality of life enjoyed today, sustainable design and development strategies are of paramount importance.

A key difficulty is that environmental concerns are often marginalised and seen as 'someone else's problem'. Concern for such issues in development is often limited to the extent to which they are financially prudent or are required by public regulation. Financial calculations within development processes often fail – through inability, unwillingness or lack of compulsion – to include the full environmental costs. The developer is typically concerned only with those costs that directly impact on the project's viability and rarely with wider environmental impacts bearing on the investor, the occupants, and society at large.

Developments have a much larger environmental impact than is immediately apparent. This can be visualised by considering a development's environmental footprint (Box 3.1). More sustainable urban design involves reducing the total environmental footprint by, for example, reducing dependence on the wider environment for resources, and reducing pollution of it by waste products. To achieve this, development – in its construction and

throughout its lifetime – should be as self-sufficient as possible. Barton et al. (1995) view developments in terms of a series of spheres of influence (Figure 3.4). For more sustainable and self-sufficient development, the aim is to increase the level of autonomy by reducing the impact of the inner spheres on the outer spheres. Although many urban design actions are relatively small scale, their aggregation results in major effects on the overall natural systems of the neighbourhood, town, city, region, and – eventually – on the earth's biosphere.

Some commentators propose that urban environments should be explicitly viewed as natural ecosystems. In his book *Design with Nature*, for example, Ian McHarg (1969) argues that towns and cities should be considered as part of a wider, functioning ecosystem. Similarly, Hough (1984, p. 25) argues that, just as ecology has become the 'indispensable basis' for environmental planning of the larger landscape, 'an understanding and application of the altered but nonetheless functioning natural processes within cities becomes central to urban design'. Decision-makers need to be aware of, and understand, the natural processes operating within urban areas (Figure 3.5).

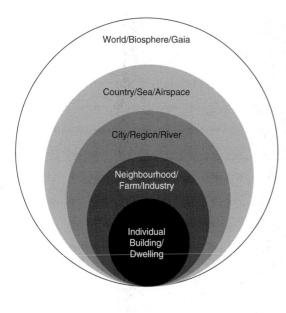

FIGURE 3.4
Nesting spheres of influence (source: Barton, *et al.*, 1995, p. 12)

A number of writers have identified more specific principles of sustainable urban design. Michael Hough (1984) identified, for example, five ecological design principles:

1. Appreciation of process and change: natural processes are unstoppable, and change is inevitable and not always for the worse.
2. Economy of means: deriving the most from the least effort and energy.
3. Diversity: the basis for environmental and social health.
4. Environmental literacy: the basis for wider understanding of ecological issues.
5. Enhancement of the environment: as a consequence of change, not just as damage limitation.

A range of commentators and organisations have also suggested sets of principles for sustainable urban development and/or design (Table 3.1). Of these, Barton *et al.*'s (1995) analysis of sustainable design principles is the most comprehensive. A combined set of criteria can also be created (Table 3.2).

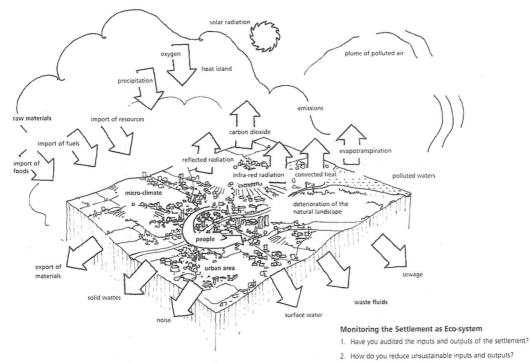

Monitoring the Settlement as Eco-system

1. Have you audited the inputs and outputs of the settlement?
2. How do you reduce unsustainable inputs and outputs?

FIGURE 3.5
The settlement as ecosystem (source: Barton *et al.*, 1995, p. 13)

TABLE 3.1
Strategies for sustainable development design

MICHAEL BREHENY (1992)

- Urban containment policies should be adopted and decentralisation slowed down
- Extreme compact city proposals are unreasonable
- Town centres and inner cities should be rejuvenated
- Urban greening should be encouraged
- Public transport needs to be improved
- Intensification should be supported around transport nodes
- Mixed-use schemes are to be encouraged
- CHP systems should be used more widely

COMMISSION OF THE EUROPEAN COMMUNITY (1990)

- Appropriate open and civic space to improve health and quality of life
- Importance of planting and landscape in ameliorating pollution
- Compact and mixed forms of development
- Reducing travel
- Recycling and energy reduction initiatives
- Maintenance of regional identity
- Integrated planning across disciplines and bureaucracies

EVANS ET AL. (2001)

- Freedom from pollution – minimising waste
- Biotic support – by maintaining biodiversity
- Resource conservation – air, water, topsoil, minerals and energy
- Resilience – a long life for development
- Permeability – providing a choice of routes
- Vitality – making places as safe as possible
- Variety – providing a choice of uses
- Legibility – enabling people to understand the layout and activities of a place
- Distinctiveness – in landscape and culture

URBED (1997)

- Quality space – attractive, human and urban
- A framework of streets and squares – well-observed routes and spaces
- A rich mix of uses and tenures
- A critical mass of activity – to sustain facilities and animate the streets
- Minimal environmental harm – during development and in the ability to adapt and change over time
- Integration and permeability
- A sense of place mixing new with old
- A feeling of stewardship and responsibility

IAN BENTLEY (1990)

- Energy efficiency – minimising the external energy needed to construct and use a place, and maximising the use of

HUGH BARTON (1996)

- Increasing local self-sufficiency – seeing each development as an organism or a mini eco-system in its own right

GRAHAM HAUGHTON AND COLIN HUNTER (1994)

- Variety – multifunctional districts with varied building styles, ages and conditions
- Concentration – sufficient density to maintain variety and activity

RICHARD ROGERS (1997)

- A just city – where justice, food, shelter, education, health and hope are fairly distributed and where all people participate in government

- ambient, particularly, solar energy
- *Resilience* – building to adapt to different uses over time, rather than wastefully tearing down and rebuilding each time human aspirations change (an extension of the earlier robustness principle)
- *Cleanliness* – designing places to minimise pollution output, and where a degree of pollution is unavoidable designing as far as possible to be self-cleansing
- *Wildlife support* – designing places to support and increase the variety of species
- *Permeability* – increasing choice by making places accessible through a variety of alternative routes
- *Vitality* – the presence of other people and 'eyes on the street'
- *Variety* – the choice of experiences
- *Legibility* – understanding the potential for choice

- *Human needs* – matching a concern for sustainable development with the satisfaction of basic human needs
- *Development structured around energy-efficient movement networks* – taking circulation of people on foot and bike and the effectiveness of public transport as a starting point
- *The open space network* – to manage pollution, wildlife, energy, water, and sewage as well as enhancing the local provision of greenspace
- *Linear concentration* – around movement networks while avoiding town cramming
- *An energy strategy* – for every new development to save money; reduce fuel poverty; and reduce resource exploitation and emissions
- *A water strategy* – to decrease water run-off and increase infiltration into the ground

- including people who are resident
- *Democracy* – offering choice in where activities are conducted
- *Permeability* – connecting people with each other and to facilities
- *Security* – through the design of spaces to enhance personal safety
- *Appropriate scale* – developments building on local context and reflecting local conditions
- *Organic design* – respecting historic narrative and local distinctiveness
- *Economy of means* – designing with nature and using local resources
- *Creative relationships* – between buildings, routeways and open spaces
- *Flexibility* – adaptability over time
- *Consultation* – to meet local needs, respect traditions and tap resources
- *Participation* – in the design, maintenance and running of projects

- A *beautiful city* – where art, architecture and landscape spark the imagination and move the spirit
- A *creative city* – where open-mindedness and experimentation mobilise the full potential of its human resources and allows a fast response to change
- An *ecological city* – which minimises its ecological impact, where landscape and built form are balanced and buildings and infrastructures are safe/resource-efficient
- A *city of easy contact* – where the public realm encourages community and mobility and information is exchanged both face-to-face and electronically
- A *compact* and *polycentric city* – which protects the countryside, focuses and integrates communities within neighbourhoods and maximises proximity
- A *diverse city* – where a broad range of activities create animation, inspiration and foster a vital public life

TABLE 3.2
Matrix of sustainable design principles

	Michael Hough (1984)	Ian Bentley (1990)	Commission of the European Community (1990)	Michael Breheny (1990)	Andrew Blowers (1993)	Graham Haughton and Colin Hunter (1994)	Hugh Barton (1996)	URBED (1997)	Richard Rogers (1997)	Evans et al. (2001)	Hildebrand Frey (1999)
STEWARDSHIP	Enhancement through change		Integrated planning	Town centre rejuvenation				A sense of stewardship	A creative city		
RESOURCE EFFICIENCY	Economy of means	Energy efficiency	Reducing travel/energy reduction, recycling	Public transport, CHP systems	Land/minerals/ energy resources, infrastructure and buildings	Economy of means	Energy efficient movement. Energy strategy	Minimal environmental harm	An ecological city	Resource conservation	Public transport, reduce traffic volumes
DIVERSITY AND CHOICE	Diversity	Variety, permeability	Mixed development	Mixed use		Variety. Permeability		Integration. Permeability. A rich mix of uses.	A city of easy contact. A diverse city	Permeability, variety	Mixed-use, hierarchy of services and facilities
HUMAN NEEDS		Legibility			Aesthetics. Human needs	Security. Appropriate scale	Human needs	A framework of safe/legible space	A just city. A beautiful city	Legibility	Low crime. Social mix. Imageability
RESILIENCE	Process and change	Resilience				Flexibility		Ability to adapt and change		Resilience	Adaptability
POLLUTION REDUCTION		Cleanliness	Ameliorating pollution through planting		Climate/water/ air quality		Water strategy			Freedom from pollution	Low pollution and noise
CONCENTRATION		Vitality	Compact development	Containment/ intensification		Concentration	Linear concentration	A critical mass of activity	A compact, polycentric city	Vitality	Containment. Densities to support services
DISTINCTIVENESS			Regional identity		Heritage	Creative relationships. Organic design		Sense of place		Distinctiveness	Sense of centrality. Sense of place
BIOTIC SUPPORT			Open space	Urban greening	Open space. Bio-diversity		Open space networks			Biotic support	Green space – public/private. Symbiotic town/country
SELF-SUFFICIENCY	Environmental literacy				Self-sufficiency	Democracy. Consultation. Participation	Self-sufficiency				Some local autonomy. Some self-sufficiency

(Source: Carmona, 2001, from Layard et al., 2001).

A further overarching principle for environmentally responsible urban design involves building in – or leaving room for – future choice. Proposing a 'pragmatic principle' for urban design, Lang (1994, p. 348) argues that, rather than assuming that technology will always find an answer, urban designers should take an environmentally benign position, designing flexible and robust environments that enable and facilitate choice. For example, there should be choice of means of travel – walking, cycling, public transit – even though, in the short term, people are likely to continue to use their cars. Table 3.3 summarises environmental design issues at various spatial scales.

THE MARKET CONTEXT

The third and fourth contexts – market (economic) and regulatory (governmental) represent different sides of the same (state–market) coin. As most of us live in market economies, most urban design actions occur within a context based on fundamental forces of supply and demand. The necessity of obtaining a reward (or, at least, a return that covers production costs) imposes – at the very least – budgetary constraints. Furthermore, in a market economy, many decisions that have public consequences are made in the private sector. The context for decision-making in the private sector is, however, usually mediated by policy and by regulatory frameworks and controls designed to offset – or, at least, temper – economic power so as to produce better outcomes. Thus, urban design actions typically occur in market economies that are regulated to a greater or lesser extent.

To operate effectively, urban design practitioners need to understand the financial and economic processes by which places and developments come about. Market economies are driven by the search for profit and by the prospect of reward mediated by associated risks. They are often characterised by strategies or regimes of capital accumulation. As the development and redevelopment of the built environment is a means of making profits and accumulating capital, urban design and the production of the built environment are often key components of such strategies (Harvey, 1989b). In discussing architects, but making a more general point that applies to urban designers, Knox (1984, p. 115) argues that, by helping to stimulate consumption and the constant circulation of capital, designers have an instrumental role in the development process in, for example, the constant search for novelty and innovation.

While urban designers need to recognise and appreciate the processes that drive development, two common misconceptions must be noted: that built environment professionals are the main agents in shaping urban space; and that developers make the main decisions, with designers merely providing 'packaging' for those decisions (Madanipour, 1996, p. 119). The first overstates the role of designers and exposes them to criticism for aspects of development that are outside their control; the second understates their role in shaping the urban environment. The overstating of the architect's role – and indeed, those of other professionals in the development process – has been called the 'fetishising of design' (Dickens, 1980) (i.e. focusing on buildings and architects rather than on the broader social processes and relations surrounding the production and meaning of the urban environment).

Urban development is substantially determined by those in control of – or in control of access to – resources. As buildings and urban developments are typically expensive to produce, those financing them do so for their own purposes, usually concerned with making profits. As Bentley (1998, p. 31) observes, most major property developers are not interested in 'art for art's sake', and have shareholders who will invest elsewhere if acceptable profits are not achieved. Economic and market power lies, therefore, in the hands of those groups with the power and resources to initiate development. As Cowan (2000, p. 24) asserts, 'it is markets that lead investment, not design'. Urban design is itself intrinsically limited: while its initiatives and actions can assist trends that are under way, attempts to channel market activity to other than where it wants to be are unlikely to be successful. As Cadman and Austin-Crowe (1991, p. 19) warn: 'No amount of careful design or promotion can totally overcome the disadvantage of a poor location or a lack of demand for the accommodation at an economic price irrespective of location.'

Subject to appropriate considerations of value, cost, risk/reward and uncertainty, development has to be economically viable before it is undertaken. The potential rewards and risks attached to any development opportunity reflect both the complexity of the process, and the wider economic context within which it occurs. At all stages a project is vulnerable to external and internal risks, not least market fluctuations and the need to main-

TABLE 3.3
Sustainable design by spatial scale

	BUILDINGS	SPACES	QUARTERS	SETTLEMENTS
STEWARDSHIP	• Respond to and enhance context • Design for easy maintenance	• Respond to and enhance context • Calm traffic • Allowing personalisation of public space • Manage the public realm	• Design for revitalisation • Developing long-term vision • Invest the necessary resources	• 'Join-up' contributions to quality – design, planning, transport, urban management • Governance that supports stakeholder involvement
RESOURCE EFFICIENCY	• Using passive (and active) solar gain technologies • Design for energy retention • Reduce embodied energy – local materials and low energy materials • Use recycled and renewable materials • Design for natural light and ventilation	• Layouts to allow sun penetration • Spaces that reduce vehicle speeds and restrict vehicle circulation • Design spaces that reduce wind speeds and enhance microclimate • Using local, natural materials	• Reduced parking standards • Create urban block depths that allow sun and natural light penetration and which encourage natural ventilation • Use combined heat and power systems • Provide local access to public transport	• Invest in public transport infrastructure • Utilise more efficiently before extending established capital web (infrastructure)
DIVERSITY AND CHOICE	• Provide opportunities to mix uses within buildings • Mix building types, ages and tenures • Build accessible, lifetime homes and buildings	• Design for mixed uses along streets and in blocks • Design for walking and cycling • Combat privatisation of public realm • Remove barriers to local accessibility	• Design for mixed uses within quarters • Design fine grained street and space network (micro scale) • Support diversity in neighbourhood character • Localise facilities and services	• Integrate travel modes • Connect route networks (macro scale) • Centre hierarchy to boost choice • Variety in services and facilities between centres • Remove barriers to accessibility
HUMAN NEEDS	• Support innovation and artistic expression in design • Design to human scale • Design visually interesting buildings	• Provide high quality, imageable, public spaces • Combat crime through space design and management • Enhance safely by reducing pedestrian/vehicle conflict • Design for social contact and for safe children's play	• Design visually interesting networks of space • Enhance legibility through landmark and space disposition • Socially mix communities	• Enhance legibility through quarter identity and disposition • Promote equity through land-use disposition • Build settlement image to foster sense of belonging
RESILIENCE	• Build extendible buildings • Build adaptable buildings • Build to last • Use resilient materials	• Design robust spaces, usable for many functions • Design spaces able to accommodate above and below ground infrastructure requirements • Design of serviceable space	• Design to allow fine grained changes of use across districts • Design robust urban block layouts	• Build robust capital web – infrastructure to last and adapt • Recognise changing patterns of living and work

POLLUTION REDUCTION	• Reuse and recycle waste water • Insulate for reduced noise transmission – vertically and horizontally • Provide on-site foul water treatment	• Reduce hard surfaces and run-off • Design in recycling facilities • Design well-ventilated space to prevent pollution build-up • Give public transport priority	• Match projected CO_2 emissions with tree planting • Plant trees to reduce pollution • Tackle light pollution	• Challenge 'end-of-pipe' solutions to water/sewerage disposal • Control private motorised transport • Clean and constantly maintain city
CONCENTRATION	• Design compact building forms to reduce heat loss, i.e. terraces • Bring derelict buildings back into use • Consider high buildings where appropriate	• Reduce space given over to roads • Reduce space given over to parking • Increase vitality through activity concentration	• Intensify around transport intersections • Raise density standards and avoid low density building • Build at densities able to support viable range of uses and facilities • Respect privacy and security needs	• Enforce urban containment and reduce expansion • Intensify along transport corridors • Link centres of high activity
DISTINCTIVENESS	• Reflect surrounding architectural character in design • Enhance locally distinctive building settings • Retain important buildings	• Reflect urban form, townscape and site character in design • Retain distinctive site features • Design for sense of place – local distinctiveness • Retain important building groups and spaces	• Reflect morphological patterns and history – incremental or planned • Identify and reflect significant public associations • Consider quarter uses and qualities	• Protect any positive regional identity and landscape character • Utilise topographical setting • Preserve archaeological inheritance
BIOTIC SUPPORT	• Provide opportunities for greening buildings • Consider buildings as habitats	• Design in robust soft landscaping • Plant and renew street trees • Encourage greening and display of private gardens	• Provide minimum public open space standards • Provide private open space • Create new or enhancing existing habitats • Respect natural features	• Link public (and private) open space into network • Green urban fringe locations • Integrate town and country • Support indigenous species
SELF-SUFFICIENCY	• Demonstrate sense of public sector civic responsibility • Encourage private sector civic responsibility • Provide bicycle storage • Connect to internet	• Encourage self-policing through design • Providing space for small-scale trading • Provide bicycle parking facilities	• Build sense of community • Involve communities in decision making • Encourage local food production – allotments, gardens, urban farms • Pay locally for any harm	• Encourage environmental literacy through example and promotion • Consultation and participation in vision making and design

(Source: adapted from Carmona, M., in Layard et al., 2001, pp. 179–81).

tain cash flow (Figure 3.6). In the private sector, viability is considered in terms of the balance between risk and reward, with reward seen primarily in terms of profits. A major barrier to achieving urban design quality is the argument that such development 'does not pay', at least not on the time scale required by investors. In the public sector, viability is considered both in terms of value for public (or taxpayers') money and in terms of the broader objective of achieving and maintaining a healthy economy.

The operation of markets

A market exists when buyers wishing to exchange money for a good or service are in contact with sellers wishing to exchange goods or services for money. Advocates generally claim two main advantages to the market mechanism:

1. *Competition* between producers and suppliers means efficient allocation of goods and services. Prices are determined (largely) by the interaction of supply and demand, with competition on quality and/or price, benefiting consumers by providing goods and services reduced by the benign forces of competition, while ensuring that all producers strive to offer a service as good as that available from other producers, thereby forcing producers to compete or go out of business. Competition also encourages entrepreneurs to innovate and exploit technology to gain advantage.

2. *Choice*, provided by markets, empowers consumers by giving access to competing suppliers, and the opportunity to combine different packages of goods and services according to personal preferences. People are able to maximise their individual welfare, constrained only by their willingness and ability to pay.

As Klosterman (1985, p. 6) explains, the argument is that competitive markets can be relied upon 'to co-ordinate the actions of individuals, provide incentives to individual action, and supply those goods and services which society wants, in the quantities which it desires, at the prices it is willing to pay'. Adam Smith famously referred to this as the 'invisible hand' of competitive market processes. He considered that, although individuals pursued their own advantage, the greatest benefit to society as a whole was achieved by their being free to do so. Each individual was 'led by an invisible hand to promote an end which was no part of his intention'. Hence, as Smith wrote: 'It is not from the benevolence of the butcher, the brewer, or the baker, that we expect our dinner, but from their regard for their own interest.' As Varoufakis (1998, p. 20) suggests, it is 'as if an invisible hand forces on those who act shamelessly a collective outcome fit for saints'.

While in (neo-classical) market theory, the producer supplies precisely what the consumer wants, in practice this 'consumer sovereignty' does not exist because the necessary competition does

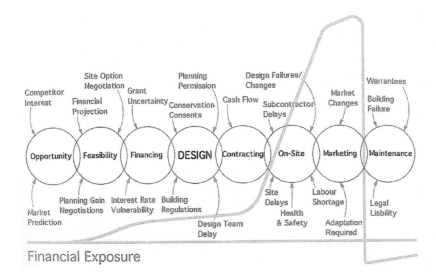

FIGURE 3.6
Risks in the procurement process

not occur. Critics argue that because 'big business' corporate concerns and multinational corporations dominate markets, consumers are inevitably manipulated into buying the products and services offered for sale rather than what they really want. Another problem is that 'big business' typically represents economic interests that are increasingly freed and estranged from allegiance to specific locations. Zukin (1991, p. 15) highlights the fundamental tension between 'global capital' that can move and 'local community' that cannot, while Harvey (1997, p. 20) considers that capital is no longer concerned about place: 'Capital needs fewer workers and much of it can move all over the world, deserting problematic places and populations at will.' As a consequence, the fate of local place is increasingly determined from afar by anonymous and impersonal economic forces.

To work efficiently, markets require 'perfect' competition, which in turn requires all of the following: a large number of buyers and sellers; the quantity of any good from one seller being small relative to the total quantity traded; the goods or services sold by different sellers being identical; all buyers and sellers having perfect information, and perfect freedom of entry to the market. In practice, markets often 'fail' in some way, due, for example, to monopoly or oligopoly conditions; public (or collective consumption) goods; externalities or spill-over effects; 'prisoners' dilemma' conditions where individual actions result in suboptimal collective outcomes; and common pool goods to which there exist common property rights.

Adams (1994, pp. 70–1) argues that market failure in land and property markets results from the intrinsic nature of land as a 'social' rather than a 'private' commodity. Land is a social good because the potential use and value of any land is directly constrained by neighbouring activity, which inevitably spills over. Land is, therefore, an interdependent asset and a substantial proportion of its value (or lack of value) derives from activities beyond its boundaries.

The social costs and benefits of private production and consumption can be considered in terms of spill-over effects. These are not taken into account in the process of voluntary market exchange (i.e. they are external to the price paid). They are illustrated by the social and environmental costs imposed by cars, which pollute the air and add to road congestion (Hodgson, 1999, p. 64). Each driver bears relatively little of the environmental cost, most of which is imposed on others.

Furthermore, because the market does not penalise drivers commensurately with the social cost, decisions to drive are taken with regard to drivers' private costs and benefits rather than those of society as a whole. Negative externalities also derive from landowners who ignore the costs of congestion, noise and loss of privacy that their development imposes on the neighbours. Landowners gain positive externalities through the increased land values associated with new transportation links and other large-scale improvements. Although such gains are sometimes recouped by the state (e.g. through betterment taxes), private landowners mostly benefit without incurring costs. Appreciation of externalities and spill-over effects is a crucial part of urban design, which is often about enhancing positive effects – as in the positive synergy deriving from a mix of uses within a limited geographical area – and minimising negative ones (see Chapter 8).

While land and property markets are well equipped to handle private costs and benefits, they are unable to take account of social costs and benefits (Adams, 1994, p. 70). Given the imperative of profit maximisation (or, more simply, profit-seeking), developers generally minimise 'private' development costs and maximise private benefits, at the expense of 'social' costs and benefits. The individual developer's profit maximisation, therefore, tends to be achieved at the expense of the wider community. As a result, the process and product of development is often flawed because it is essentially concerned with individual developments that ignore their local context, rather than with the creation of places that form an intrinsic part of it. As the social costs can often be ignored, markets often result in highly individualistic behaviour, with a prioritising of individual (private) outcomes that benefit the individual over collective (social) outcomes that benefit society.

Although, once produced, the built environment is usually durable and lasts for many years, the provision of funding for development normally depends on returns on investment, with the returns made over the first few years of a building's life exceeding the development costs sufficiently to ensure the desired profit (Adams, 1994, p. 71). In conventional methods of development appraisal, costs and benefits that occur over longer periods are substantially discounted. A higher priority is, therefore, accorded to short-term rather than long-term concerns, resulting in short-termism and a neglect of the long-term.

Whether a public or private sector activity, urban design always has public outcomes. The exterior of a development, for example, is a public object and both aesthetically and functionally forms part of the public realm. It is a local 'public' (collective) good, simultaneously benefiting many individuals because (ignoring congestion effects) one person's enjoyment does not prohibit that of others. It is a *local* public good, because the benefits are attenuated by distance. Controlling access to such goods is often impossible. By contrast, access to a private good can be restricted, with a price charged for its enjoyment. The benefit individuals receive from a public good depends on the total supply of that good, rather than on their contribution towards its production. In making contributions to pay for a particular good, individuals have an incentive to understate their real preferences, in the hope that others will pay for it. This allows them to be 'free riders', enjoying the good at no personal expense. If everyone did this, however, funds to provide the good would not be available. Thus, as private actors cannot (exclusively) appropriate the benefits and rewards, 'rational' developers contribute to the development of collectively used infrastructure and public realm only to the extent that they can accrue private benefits. The same argument applies to elements of infrastructure used collectively. For these reasons, the private sector tends to lack interest in the creation and supply of such goods. If the private sector under-provides public goods, then either the state must supply them or they are not supplied.

A conclusion often drawn from the above discussion is that there is a case for government intervention to 'correct' market failures. This might nonetheless commit the fallacy of supposing that the alternative to imperfect markets is 'perfect government'. The (often political) choice concerns which imperfect form of organisation is likely to lead to a better outcome (Wolf, 1994). Although sometimes presented as a binary choice between the unfettered play of market forces or state intervention, it is often the case that some intervention makes markets work better. Many urban design actions (particularly in the public sector) are public interventions into land and property markets. The main argument for state intervention in land and property markets is that it produces a better environment and greater efficiency and/or equity in the use of land and environmental resources than would be produced by unfettered markets. Intervening and regulatory agencies must, however, fully appreciate the working of market mechanisms

and be able to predict most of the direct and indirect consequences of intervention/regulation – that is, they must be market-aware. In urban design terms, designers need to appreciate the market-driven and market-led nature of the development process.

THE REGULATORY CONTEXT

The fourth context for urban design is the regulatory context. The concern here is with the 'macro' regulatory (governmental) context, which provides the overall context for the detailed elaboration of public policy, including, in particular, urban design policy and the operation of design control/review (see Chapter 11). Despite having to accept the macro regulatory context as a given, urban designers frequently lobby for change here, typically through professional societies and organisations rather than as individuals.

It is important to distinguish between 'politics' and 'government'/regulation. Politics is essentially an activity where the merits of alternative forms of action to deal with public problems can be debated as a prelude to choice, as individuals and groups put their opinions onto the agenda for government action. It is here that, for example, the balance between 'economic' and 'environmental' objectives is determined. Government, by comparison, is where decisions are made on behalf of all, and where legal and policy frameworks are established. The regulatory context proper is therefore preceded and informed by a political process. Before a policy can be enacted, the political arguments must be won.

In representative democracies, decisions are made by elected politicians who, in principle, first consider and reconcile the varied views and opinions held by the public. Decisions may then be implemented through direct action by government agencies, or by influencing private actors via policy, administrative and legal frameworks, and fiscal measures (taxes, tax breaks and subsidies). In most market economies, the public sector does not act directly on private sector actors (developers, land owners, etc.). Instead it establishes the public policy and regulatory framework for private sector decision-making – influencing the set of incentives and sanctions available, thereby making some actions more likely than others.

While there will inevitably be debates about whether the state should have a greater or lesser direct role, and how much it should intervene in the operation of land and property markets, for many urban design practitioners these are of only academic interest. The reality is that urban design projects must be designed and implemented in accordance with prevailing market conditions and within the regulatory context that exists at the time.

The structure of government and governance

In democracies, members of the various tiers of government are elected for a limited period, after which they must seek re-election. Governments and politicians can therefore be voted out of office. The achievement of significant improvements in urban areas is typically a long-term process, for which relatively short periods of political office, coupled with various economic cycles, do not provide a stable context for long-term investment or for the implementation of strategic visions. Indeed, the short-termism of elected mayors and politicians – whether desiring instant effects or avoiding unpopular decisions – can result in long-term objectives being sacrificed for short-term 'electoral' reasons. Some politicians have, nevertheless, been strong advocates of good design, and influential in raising the quality of development in their cities.

As changes of administration can also result in wavering commitment to particular policies, there is a need to secure commitment to long-term goals and strategies. Achieving long-term change often requires the support of a broad-based coalition of interest groups spanning different administrations and policy eras. Studies of the planning histories of cities with reputations for urban design quality testify to the long-term commitment to and struggle for such quality by a range of local stakeholders (Abbott, 1997; Punter, 1999).

A key element of the (macro) regulatory context is the relationship between the tiers of government and the relative autonomy of each tier, especially with regard to local governments' autonomy to develop responses to local problems, opportunities and contexts. Centre–local relations are a focus for much political science inquiry and debate. In the US, where the Federal Government has little or no role in planning or urban design, individual states and cities have relative freedom to develop their own responses and, depending on local priorities, the result is both poor and high quality urban design. In France, the strong mayoral system facil-

itates local innovation where the mayor values urban design while, at the national level, prestige projects act as design exemplars. In the UK, the relatively strong central government, and correspondingly less autonomous local authorities, provide potential for a more consistent design emphasis, but also – until the mid-1990s – a general undermining of initiative at the local level.

Rather than relatively straightforward, hierarchical systems, more complex systems of governance are emerging, with central government bodies and quasi- and non-governmental organisations (quangos and NGOs) being established at various levels and across different functional sectors and geographical areas. These are complemented by an increasing range of public–private partnerships, also operating within different levels, sectors and areas.

Market–state relations

An important part of the regulatory context is the balance between public and private sectors. Depending on the sectoral viewpoint, development will often be perceived differently. Some basic distinctions can be identified (see Box 3.2).

This provokes consideration of the degree to which the activities of the private sector are or should be regulated, which in turn raises issues regarding the purpose of urban design. The key issue is whose interests does – or should – urban design serve: the maximisation of returns for private sector investment or the interests of the public at large. In practice, each sector depends on the other to achieve its goals and their roles are generally complementary rather than antagonistic, as is shown by the increasing proliferation of public–private partnerships.

In considering market–state relations, distinction must be made between 'mixed' and 'market-led' economies. As both are, in a strict sense, mixed economies, the distinction is between the state playing a more, or a less, significant and direct role in the management of the economy. In mixed economies, the state generally has a more executive, 'hands-on' role, with direct action public agencies. Here, urban design policies and decisions have, in principle, the potential to more fully reflect the public interest, to address context, to reflect urban design as well as architectural concerns, and to incorporate local concerns. In market-led economies, the state has a more facilitative, 'hands-off' role, with direct action being undertaken by

BOX 3.2 – SOME BASIC DISTINCTIONS

Public sector aims
- development that adds to the local tax base
- enhancement of long-term investment opportunities in its area of responsibility
- enhancement of existing, or creation of a new, high quality environment
- development creating or supporting local jobs and for having a social benefit
- to find opportunities to support public sector services
- development to meet local needs

Private sector aims
- good return on investment, mediated by considerations of risk and liquidity (the profit margin)
- investment opportunities, wherever and whenever they arise
- a context supportive of the particular development, which will not undermine its asset value for as long as the investment is held
- basing of investment decisions on local purchasing power and the availability of a ready market
- looking to the cost and availability of financing for development

the private and voluntary sectors. Here, for reasons of economic and construction efficiency, design decisions are based on market analysis, contribution to the wider public interest is rarely a major consideration, and context is not a major concern unless seen as a financial asset, with the qualities and attributes of buildings as individual objects prioritised over their contribution to place.

As direct state intervention often involves public spending, the degree of intervention is often a function of politicians' and political parties' perception of the willingness of the taxpayer to fund public provision and infrastructure. Lang (1994, pp. 459–62) usefully distinguishes between 'paying' and non-paying clients of urban design. In both public and private sectors, paying clients include entrepreneurs and their financial backers. In the public sector, entrepreneurs are government agencies and politicians, and their financial backers are the taxpayers and increasingly also the private sector (for example, through direct payments for planning gain). Traditionally the public sector has acted on behalf of the public interest in the public realm. It has promoted – and often substantially funded – development of the 'Capital Web' (see Chapter 4). It has also been concerned with those elements of the urban environment seen as beneficial to society as a whole, but which would not pay for themselves directly through user fees, or for which it is administratively impossible to collect fees. Such public goods are funded through general taxation.

Taxpayers appear, however, to be increasingly reluctant to fund investment in the public realm and are often considered to be unwilling to fund or

subsidise any activity that does not benefit them directly as individuals. As Lang (1994, p. 459) notes, stereotypical taxpayers want to minimise tax payments: weighed down by self-interest, they are only concerned with public infrastructure and design of the built environment when it directly affects them. Galbraith (1992, p. 21) suggests that expenditure and new investment in public infrastructure is 'powerfully and effectively resisted' because 'present cost and taxation are specific, future advantage is dispersed. Later and different individuals will benefit; why pay for persons unknown?' Alternatively, taxpayers are concerned that the state will not make 'good' use of 'their' money. As a consequence, there are pressures for tax limitation, which imposes budgetary constrains on state action and, as is discussed below, a desire for 'privatism'.

Over the last thirty years or so, debate has increased about the appropriate roles of the private and public sectors, and the relationship between the state and the market. Following critiques of 'big government' and of assumptions that 'more government' was the solution, came arguments that government was actually part of the problem, and that the solution involved freeing market forces through deregulation. The 1970s and 1980s saw neo-liberal and 'New Right' arguments coming to prominence – particularly during the Reagan era in the US and the Thatcher era in the UK – with much effort directed at reducing the state's powers and its role to provide room for market forces to flourish. The result saw a shift towards market-led economies.

From the mid-1980s onwards, 'managerialism' became a key theme in the form of 'reinventing government' where governments should 'steer' rather than 'row' (Osbourne and Gaebler, 1992), and in general operating more like the private sector. The emphasis was on making government work 'better', defined and measured somewhat narrowly in terms of cost (lower rates of personal taxation) and the size of government, rather than in terms of the quality of services provided, and of outcomes. As new political ideologies combined with fiscal constraints on municipal governments to dictate the public sector's dependence on private sector investors and developers, the overall result was a distinct shift towards private provision and privatisation.

'Privatism' became a dominant policy theme, especially in the US and UK, and throughout much of the developed world. A key means of privatism was various forms of privatisation and private provision of what had previously been public services. In the context of urban design, Graham (2001, p. 365) observes how elements of the urban public realm and infrastructure were privatised and sold off to profit-seeking companies or to various types of public–private partnership. Similarly, Loukaitou-Sideris (1991, from Loukaitou-Sideris and Banerjee, 1998, p. 87) attributes the privatisation of public space in US downtowns to three interrelated factors: the public sector's desire to attract private investment and to relieve its financial burdens by utilising private resources; the private sector's responsiveness to development initiatives and its willingness to participate in public–private partnerships and provide (quasi-) public spaces within private development projects; and the existence of a market demand for the facilities and services offered in privately built open spaces. She notes how the desire of office workers, tourists and conventioneers to be separated from 'threatening' groups, provided the market opportunity for spaces produced, maintained, and controlled by the private sector (see Chapter 6).

Against the background of a retreat from proactive public policy direction and direct public sector investment, Loukaitou-Sideris and Banerjee (1998, p. 280) examined the outcomes of market-led urban design in West Coast American cities. In particular, they noted how:

- urban design had been privatised and was mainly dependent on private initiatives;
- to maximise returns on investment, urban design interventions were exclusively designed for tenants rather than for the wider public;
- design initiatives were opportunistic, and public policy reactive rather than proactive;
- as a result, developments were *ad hoc*, disjointed, episodic and incrementalist;
- this new urban design had lost any larger public purpose or vision;
- privatisation had exacerbated polarisation into the rundown, public downtown of indigents, and the glamorous, private downtown of corporate America.

Similar observations can be made in the UK, where throughout much of the 1980s and 1990s, public agencies were often characterised by short-termism, lack of strategic vision and an absence of public sector interest in design quality, resulting in an abandonment of urban design. In commenting on early developments in the London Docklands area and, as he saw it, the folly of not providing an urban design framework to guide development, Michael Wilford (1984, p. 13) argued that: 'Dependence on the capacities of non-regulated capitalism as fairy god-mother has been demonstrated time and again to be a deluding myth and cowardly evasion on the part of those charged with the task of designing our cities' (Figure 3.7). Demonstrating a positive response to the public sector's abandonment of urban design considerations, the Canary Wharf development marked a turning point. To protect their investment's long-term viability, the developer/investors – Olympia and York – insisted on higher design and infrastructure standards which, within its own terms, produced a high quality – albeit introspective, commercial and private – development.

During the 1990s and into the twenty-first century, attempts to go beyond simplistic notions of 'government good, market bad' (or vice versa) have tended to coalesce around the notion of a 'third way' or, more precisely, third ways (Giddens, 2001). Concepts of the third way are based on the argument that contemporary society is undergoing profound and irreversible changes which call established political and policy-making frameworks into question. Third way advocates claim to go beyond the conventional categories of 'left' and 'right' defined in terms of attitudes to the role of the market. In contrast to the 'second way' of neo-liberalism, the third way accepts the need for intervention by government to moderate the impact of market forces, while simultaneously – unlike the 'first

FIGURE 3.7
At the same time as the relatively deregulated
development of the London Docklands, the Broadgate
development was completed within an equally frenzied
development context in the City of London. The
Broadgate development provides a coherent addition to
the City of London, is integrated into its context and
creates a successful and coherent series of 'public'
spaces. It illustrates the potential of the private sector to
innovate and its ability to deliver quality outcomes

way' of social democracy – recognising important
limits to state action. Rather than 'command and
control' models of policy and delivery, local governments are expected to use their powers to provide
leadership, to enable a co-ordinated local approach,
and to seek to harness the creativity, energy and
resources of the private and voluntary sectors.

This discussion of the regulatory context is not
intended to make the case that one or other form
of economy is likely to produce better urban design
outcomes – although this may be implied. It simply
acknowledges that there are different (macro)
regulatory contexts within which urban design
practitioners must operate. It can nevertheless be
argued that there is the need for a regulatory
context that recognises and supports the value and
quality of urban design and that seeks to increase

urban design quality. During the 1990s there have
been positive changes in this context in the UK that
have begun to do so (Carmona, 2001,
pp. 304–19). The desire to improve levels of quality, for example, underpinned the Government's
'Quality in Town and Country Initiative' from 1994
to 1997. Elsewhere, a philosophy that recognises
the role of design in achieving environmental quality was already well established. Urban design was
seen as a means to add and/or ensure quality in the
development of, for example, the Berlin IBA, the
waterfronts of Barcelona and Boston, and, in the
UK, in Birmingham's city centre regeneration
schemes.

THE URBAN DESIGN PROCESS

The notion of urban design as a process is a recurring theme in this book. Through a design process
the four contexts discussed above and the six
dimensions discussed in Part II are related. Part I
will therefore conclude by briefly focusing on the
urban design process. The 'design' in urban design
is not (only) an 'art'-type process, it is also one of
research and decision-making. Design is a creative,
exploratory and problem-solving activity through
which objectives and constraints are weighed and
balanced, the problem and possible solutions
explored, and optimal resolutions derived. It adds
value to the individual component parts, so that
the resulting whole is greater than the sum of the
parts.

All design must satisfy certain criteria. Vitruvius'
'firmness, commodity and delight' can be taken as
criteria of good urban design in a product design
sense: firmness concerns achievement of the necessary technical criteria; commodity concerns the
functional ones; while delight is about aesthetic
appeal. These criteria cannot be placed in a hierarchy of importance: good design must achieve
them simultaneously. In an era of increasing awareness of the scarcity of natural resources, a fourth
criterion of 'economy' should also be added, not
only in the financial sense of respecting budget
constraints, but also in the wider sense of minimising environmental costs.

All 'design' activity follows an essentially similar
process. John Zeisel (1981) characterised this as a
'design spiral', a cyclical and iterative process by
which solutions are gradually refined through a
series of creative leaps or 'conceptual shifts' (Figure
3.8). A problem is identified to which the designer

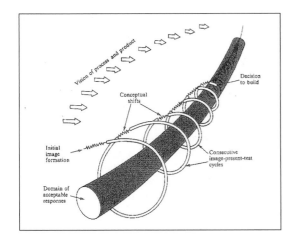

FIGURE 3.8
The design spiral (source: John Zeisel, 1981)

forms a tentative solution, a range of solutions or – more generally – approaches to a solution. These are evaluated in terms of the original problem or set of objectives, and then refined, developed and improved through testing, discovering and purging of errors or inappropriate ideas, or abandoned. Design is therefore a continuous process of trial–test–change, involving imaging (thinking in terms of a solution), presenting, evaluating and re-imaging (reconsidering or developing alternative solutions). The process moves towards a final acceptable solution, until, once within the domain of acceptable responses, the decision is taken to proceed and implement the proposal. The proposal will also be further modified and improved through the implementation process.

As well as seeking solutions, the design process involves exploring and researching the design problem. Von Meiss (1990, p. 202) suggests that those outside the design process (the public, politicians, clients, etc.) often experience difficulty in understanding its essential 'uncertainty'. Karl Popper (1972, p. 260) also stresses the exploratory nature of design:

We start . . . with a problem, a difficulty . . . Whatever it may be when we first encounter the problem we cannot, obviously, know much about it. At best, we have only a vague idea what our problem really consists of. How, then, can we produce an adequate solution? Obviously, we cannot. We must first get better acquainted with the problem. But how?

My answer is very simple: by producing an inadequate solution and by criticising it. Only in this way can we come to understand the problem. For to understand a problem means to understand its difficulties; and to understand its difficulties means to understand why it is not easily soluble – why the more obvious solutions do not work. We must therefore produce these more obvious solutions; and we must criticise them, in order to find out why they do not work. In this way, we become acquainted with the problem, and may proceed from bad solutions to better ones – provided always that we have the creative ability to produce new guesses, and more guesses.

This . . . is what is meant by 'working on a problem'. And if we have worked on a problem long enough, and intensively enough, we begin to know it, to understand it, in the sense that we know what kind of guess or conjecture or hypothesis will not do at all, because it simply misses the point of the problem, and what kind of requirements would have to be met by any serious attempt to solve it. In other words, we begin to see ramifications of the problem, its sub-problems, and its connection with other problems.

At the macro scale, urban design processes take two distinct forms (see Chapter 1):

1. *Unknowing design*: the ongoing accumulation of relatively small-scale, often trial-and-error, decisions and interventions. Many towns developed in this way, slowly and incrementally, never being designed as a whole. The resulting environments that have survived are highly valued today. It also worked because the pace of change was relatively slow and the increments of change relatively small. For better or worse, many contemporary urban environments also happen in this *ad hoc* and piecemeal fashion without express planning or design.
2. *Knowing design*: the process by which different concerns are intentionally shaped, balanced and controlled through development and design proposals, plans and policies.

The latter typically follows four key phases: brief setting; design; implementation; and post-implementation review. In each, the nature of the problem evolves as new information and influences come to bear, resulting in an iterative process with designs – including design policies and other guidance – reconsidered in the light of new objectives, or implemented in part and later adapted as new external influences come to bear.

In each of the four key development phases – particularly that of design – the urban designer's thought processes can be disaggregated into a series of thought stages:

- *Setting goals*: in conjunction with other actors (particularly clients and stakeholders), and having regard to economic and political realities, proposed time scale, and client and stakeholder requirements.
- *Analysis*: gathering and analysing information and ideas that might inform the design solution.
- *Visioning*: generating and developing various possible solutions through an iterative process of imaging and presenting, usually informed by personal experience and design philosophies.
- *Synthesis and prediction*: testing the generated solutions to identify workable alternatives.
- *Decision-making*: determining the alternatives to be discarded, and those for further refinement or promoting as the preferred design solution.

- *Evaluation (appraisal)*: reviewing both the finished product and its success, measured against the identified goals.

Each stage represents a complex set of activities, which, while generally conceptualised as a linear process, is in practice iterative and cyclical, and less mechanistic and more intuitive than the various diagrams of design process appear to indicate.

At this level, urban design parallels similar design processes in urban planning at the city-wide scale, in architectural design of individual buildings, engineering at infrastructure and in landscape design across the range of scales (Figure 3.9). This reiterates both the position of the urban design process within the development and planning processes (see Chapters 10 and 11) and its multi-disciplinary, multi-actor nature.

CONCLUSION

This chapter has presented four fundamental contexts for urban design action. The essence of its argument has been that urban design requires a respect for the local and global contexts and the

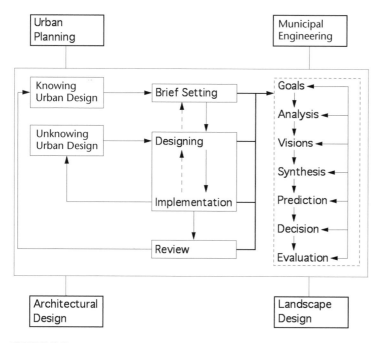

FIGURE 3.9
The integrated urban design process

market and regulatory contexts. It has also emphasised that the nature of urban design – like all forms of design – is a cyclical, iterative process.

The four contexts are subsumed within the definition of urban design given at the start of Chapter 1. This definition – urban design is *the process* of making *better* places for people *than would otherwise be produced* – also asserts the importance of four themes that occur throughout this book. First, urban design is for and about people. It involves considerations of equity, gender, income groups, etc., and generally stresses broader, collective outcomes rather than narrower, individual outcomes. Second, it emphasises the value of place and the need for an explicit concern for issues of place making and responses to both local and global context. Third, it recognises that urban design operates in the 'real' world and that the field of opportunity for urban designers is typically constrained and bounded by forces (market and regulatory) that are beyond its control or influence. This does not, however, prevent urban designers

from attempting to challenge and push the boundaries of their field of opportunity. Fourth, it asserts the importance of design as a process.

Each of the next six chapters discusses a different dimension of urban design – 'morphological', 'perceptual', 'social', 'visual', 'functional' and 'temporal'. As urban design is a joined-up activity, this separation is for the purpose of clarity in exposition and analysis only. Overlapping and interrelated, these dimensions are the 'everyday matter' of urban design. The crosscutting contexts outlined in this chapter relate to and inform all the dimensions. The dimensions and contexts are linked and related by the conception of design as a design process – a process that, for urban design to be effective, must be grounded in an appreciation of and respect for local and global context and prevailing economic (market) and political (regulatory) realities. Without this, urban design is not worthy of the title 'urban design' – it is either just 'development' or simply a fanciful aspiration with little chance of successful implementation.

PART II

THE DIMENSIONS OF URBAN DESIGN

PART II

The morphological dimensions of
THE DIMENSIONS OF
URBAN DESIGN

4

The morphological dimension

INTRODUCTION

This chapter is in three parts and focuses on the 'morphological' dimension of urban design; that is, the layout and configuration of urban form and space. There are essentially two types of urban space system, which, for the purposes of this book, will be referred to as 'traditional' and 'modernist' (Box 4.1). 'Traditional' urban space consists of buildings as constituent parts of urban blocks, where the blocks define and enclose external space. 'Modernist' urban space typically consists of free-standing 'pavilion' buildings in landscape settings. During the modern period, the morphological structure of the public space network has changed in two important ways (Pope, 1996; Bentley, 1998): from buildings as constituent elements in urban blocks (i.e. connected terraced masses) defining 'streets' and 'squares', to buildings as separate free-standing pavilions standing in an amorphous 'space'; and from integrated and connected small-scale finely meshed street grids, to road networks surrounding segregated and introverted 'enclaves'. In each case there is currently a reaction to these changes. The changes are discussed in the first and second parts of this chapter. The final part discusses urban blocks and urban block structures. Before that, it is necessary to present a more general discussion of urban morphology.

URBAN MORPHOLOGY

Urban morphology is the study of the form and shape of settlements. Appreciation of morphology helps urban designers to be aware of local patterns of development and processes of change. Initial work in the field focused on analysing evolution and change in traditional urban space. Morphologists showed that settlements could be seen in terms of several key elements, of which Conzen (1960) considered land uses, building structures, plot pattern and street pattern to be the most important. He emphasised the difference in stability of these elements. Buildings, and particularly the land uses they accommodate, are usually the least resilient elements. Although more enduring, the plot pattern changes over time as individual plots are subdivided or amalgamated. The street plan tends to be the most enduring element. Its stability derives from its being a capital asset not lightly set aside; from ownership structures; and, in particular, from the difficulties of organising and implementing large-scale change. Changes do happen, however, through destruction by war or natural disaster or, in the modern period, through programmes of comprehensive redevelopment.

The following sections expand on Conzen's four morphological elements. The varied patterns and environments that these form can be studied through what Caniggia terms *tessuto urbano* or 'urban tissue' (Caniggia and Maffel, 1979, 1984).

Land uses

Compared with the other key elements, land uses are relatively temporary. Incoming uses often lead to redevelopment and the creation of new buildings, to plot amalgamations and, less often, to subdivisions and changes in the street pattern. By contrast, displaced land uses are more likely to relocate to existing buildings in older areas and, rather than redeveloping them, to adapt and convert them.

BOX 4.1 – TRADITIONAL AND MODERNIST URBAN SPACE

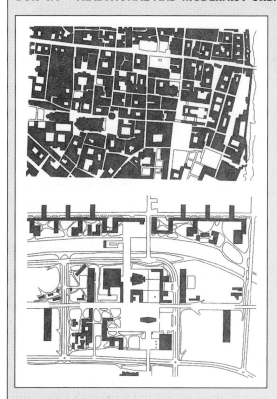

Figure-ground diagrams of Parma and Saint-Die
(source: Rowe and Koetter, 1978, pp. 62–3)

These figure-ground diagrams show the different patterns of traditional and Modernist patterns of urban space. The plan for Parma (top) shows buildings as constituent elements in a generalised, highly connected mass ('urban blocks'), which defines 'streets' and squares' and a small-scale, finely meshed street grid. Buildings are generally low-rise and of similar height. Taller buildings are exceptions, and usually have some civic significance

as religious or major public buildings. The street pattern consists of a grid, the cells of which are relatively small. The plan of Saint-Die (bottom) represents Modernist buildings as separate pavilions freestanding in a more generalised type of 'space' and a coarsely meshed 'road' grid. The buildings are set within a 'super block' system, the cells of which are relatively large (perhaps 2–3 square kilometres in area). The super blocks are typically surrounded by major roads carrying all non-local traffic. Modernist urban space generally appears in its pure form when built on greenfield sites.

	Small block patterns	Super block patterns
Building defining and enclosing space	A	B
Buildings as objects in space	C	D

Each space system consists of two component parts: a two-dimensional pattern ('small blocks' or 'super blocks') and a three-dimensional form ('buildings enclosing space' or 'buildings in space'). In what can be considered 'ideal' systems, they are paired in a particular way: small blocks and buildings enclosing space (i.e. Parma/traditional urban form – type A) and super blocks and buildings in space (i.e. Saint-Die/Modernist urban space – type D). These are rarely seen as ideal systems. Indeed, it is not clear at what point 'space between buildings' becomes 'open space containing buildings'. Other combinations are also possible. These are hybrid or compromised versions of the ideal systems (i.e. types B or C). Tall buildings often spring up from within small block patterns (as in the City of London and central Hong Kong). Type C represents situations where freestanding buildings are located in small block street patterns.

Building structures

Plots have often had a recognisable progression or cycle of building development. In England, this process transformed the medieval 'burgage' plots, which started out as long, narrow fields laid out perpendicular to a street or circulation route (Conzen, 1960) (see Box 4.2). Because the first part of a plot to be developed was that adjoining the street, development generally began in 'perimeter

block' form. Loyer (1988) describes similar development and urban intensification in eighteenth and nineteenth century Paris, and the cycle also holds true for nineteenth century industrial towns and twentieth century suburbs (Whitehead, 1992). With no indigenous tradition of burgage plots, many New World countries witnessed an early focus on grids: Moudon (1986) details the evolution of block, lot and building patterns in San Francisco's Alamo Square neighbourhood.

BOX 4.2 – THE BURGAGE CYCLE

Exploiting proximity to pedestrian traffic and its opportunities for access, trade and commerce, the first building – the 'plot dominant' – is on the street frontage or head of the plot. Through time, as land uses on the plot and in the building change, there is pressure to extend the building upwards or towards the rear of the plot. Exploiting the access at the back, the tail of the plot becomes built up. The intermediate space – perhaps fields or gardens – is developed as freestanding buildings or, more typically, through additions to the initial/existing buildings. New, larger, taller buildings may replace the initial ones. Over time, with continuing development, the open spaces within the plot are reduced to small courts. As greater densities are achieved by creating rooms without direct access to the street or to adequate light and air, development reaches its 'choke point'. When all of

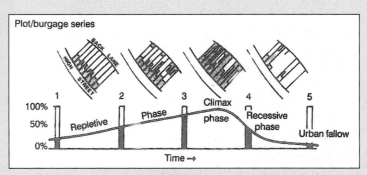

(source of illustration: Larkham, 1996, p. 33).

the plot area is developed, this is the cycle's high point or 'climax phase'. After this may come a partial or complete clearance before total redevelopment. Depending on the development pressure, there might also be changes in the plot pattern as plots are amalgamated to create development sites for larger buildings or truncated by running mid-block alleys through, creating independent plots.

Some buildings – churches, cathedrals, public buildings, etc. – will last longer than others for a variety of reasons, including the greater investment – financial and symbolic – in their design, construction and ornamentation. Such buildings may also become particularly meaningful to residents and visitors, and often symbolically represent the city. In the absence of conservation controls, other buildings survive only if they are able to adapt to new or changing uses: that is, if they have a quality known as robustness (see Chapter 9). Buildings that endure over time often accommodate various uses and/or intensities of use during their lifetime – for example, a townhouse may successively be an upmarket single-family home, then offices, then student bedsits.

The plot pattern

Cadastral units (urban blocks) are typically subdivided or 'platted' into plots or lots (Figure 4.1). These may be 'back to back', each having a frontage onto the street and a shared boundary at the rear. Plots may also face onto main streets at the front with service alleys at the rear. Less common are 'through' plots with a frontage onto

a main street at each end. Over time, as plots are bought and sold, boundaries can change. Large plots may be subdivided, or several may be amalgamated. As plots have been amalgamated to enable the construction of larger buildings, plot sizes have become larger. This process usually occurs in one direction only: plots are often amalgamated, but more rarely subdivided. In extreme cases, such as the construction of shopping centres in central areas, whole urban blocks can be amalgamated, with any intervening streets being privatised and built over. Although plot and block amalgamation removes most of the evidence of earlier forms, in many towns, especially in Europe, evidence of earlier plot patterns persists from that period. As few of these plots have buildings of that period, it also demonstrates that buildings change more rapidly than plot patterns.

The cadastral (street) pattern

The cadastral pattern is the layout of urban blocks and, between them, the public space/movement channels or 'public space network' (see below). The blocks define the space, or the spaces define the blocks. The ground plan of most settlements

FIGURE 4.1
These buildings in central Prague show the evidence of their original long narrow plots fronting onto a public space

can be seen as a series of overlays from different ages. The term 'palimpsest' is used as a metaphor for such processes of change, where current uses overwrite, but do not completely erase, the marks of prior use. Twentieth century roads often cut through the street patterns of older areas, leaving fragmented townscapes. Patterns of streets and spaces have often developed over many hundreds of years, and fragments and 'ghosts' of patterns from different eras can be seen in the ground plans of many cities. In Florence, for example, the Roman street pattern is still evident in the plan of the city's central core (Figure 4.2).

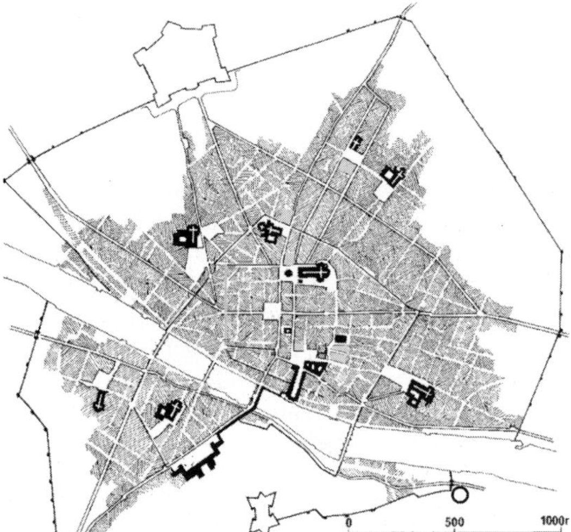

An important urban design quality established by the cadastral pattern is that of 'permeability' – meaning the extent to which an environment allows a choice of routes both through and within it. It is also a measure of the opportunity for movement. A related measure – 'accessibility' – is a measure of what is achieved in practice (i.e. a product of the interaction between the individual and the cadastral system). 'Visual' permeability refers to the ability to see the routes through an environment, while 'physical' permeability refers to the ability to move through an environment. In some cases there may be visual but not physical permeability (and vice versa).

Cadastral patterns composed of many small-sized street blocks have a *fine* urban grain, while patterns with fewer larger blocks have a *coarse* urban grain. An area with smaller blocks offers a greater choice of routes and generally creates a more permeable environment than one with larger blocks (Figure 4.3). Smaller blocks also increase *visual* permeability – the smaller the block, the easier it is to see from one junction to the next –

FIGURE 4.2
The street pattern of central Florence retains the layout of the original Roman settlement (source: adapted from Braunfels, 1988)

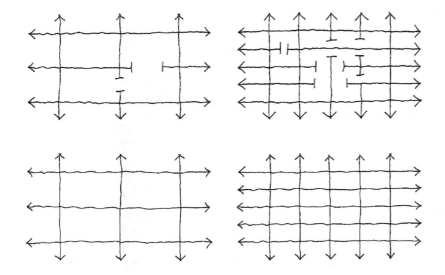

FIGURE 4.3
Permeability. Finely meshed grids offer many different ways to get from place to place within the grid. Coarser grids offer fewer ways. If the grid becomes discontinuous through the severing of connections and the creation of dead ends, permeability is reduced. This has radical impacts within coarsely meshed grids

thereby improving people's *awareness* of the choices available.

A basic distinction in cadastral patterns can be made between regular or 'ideal' grids characterised by geometric regularity and organic or 'deformed' grids characterised by apparent irregularity. Although in terms of physical permeability, the shape of the grid does not matter, deformities may affect potential movement by reducing visual permeability (see Chapter 7).

In countries and regions with a long history of incremental urbanisation, most urban grids are 'deformed' (Figure 4.4). They are often described as 'organic'; their layouts having been, or appearing to have been, generated naturally rather than being consciously manmade. Generally based on pedestrian movement, and strongly influenced by local topography, they were built as integral parts of the immediate area rather than as through routes, and evolved and developed with use. Bill Hillier (1996a, 1996b; Hillier *et al.*, 1993) has extensively theorised the relation between movement and the evolution of the urban grid. His central proposition is that movement largely dictates the configuration of urban space, and is itself largely determined by spatial configuration. The theory's principal generator is that, considered purely as a spatial configuration, the urban grid's structure is the 'most powerful single determinant' of urban movement (Hillier, 1996b, p. 43) (see Chapter 7).

Regular and ideal grids are usually planned and typically have some degree of geometric discipline. Due to the ease of laying out straight streets, the most basic planned layouts have generally been rectilinear. Many European cities have as their foundation Greek or Roman regular or semi-regular grid plan settlements. In Europe, regular grid

FIGURE 4.4
Plan of Rothenburg, Italy. In a 'deformed' grid, the structure of the space is deformed in two ways. First, the shaping and alignment of the islands of buildings (i.e. urban blocks) mean that sight lines do not continue right through the grid from one side to the other but continually strike the surfaces of the building blocks. Second, as one passes along lines, the spaces vary in width. Hillier (1996) argues that 'deformities' in the grid affect visual permeability and are, thereby, an important influence on movement (source: Bentley, 1998)

patterns have frequently been overlaid on, or added alongside, more organic patterns, for example by Cerda in Barcelona. Various cities in the New World are examples of regular, orthogonal grids, by which large, relatively plain tracts of land could be easily divided into manageable plots and sold off.

The grids used to lay out cities in the US became simpler over time. The public squares and diagonal streets that constituted important features of earlier street patterns – in Savannah, Philadelphia, Washington, etc. – were often dropped later in favour of simpler systems of straight streets and rectangular blocks. Noting that few American cities used the grid-iron as 'more than an equitable expedient', Morris (1994, p. 347) regards Savannah as an important exception and suggests that the urban mid-west's geometry might well have been 'less monotonously debasing' under its influence (Figure 4.5).

Some planned street patterns have an important symbolic function written into the overall plan. Traditional Chinese capital cities, for example, were planned as perfect squares, with twelve city gates, three on each side, representing the twelve months of the year; Roman new towns had two intersecting main streets representing the solar axis and the line of the equinox. Such layouts are not always religious or ancient. In Washington DC, for example, the locations of the White House and the Capitol symbolise the separation of executive and legislative powers.

While deformed grids usually have a picturesque character as a result of their changing spatial enclosure, regular grids have often been criticised for their supposed monotony. Camillo Sitte (1889, translated in 1965, p. 93) condemned Mannheim's 'unrelenting thoroughness', where there were no exceptions to 'the arid rule that all streets intersect perpendicularly and that each one runs straight in both directions until it reaches the countryside beyond the town'. Rybczynski (1995, pp. 44–5) argues, however, that such grids do not necessarily lack poetic character: picturesque elements occur where, for example, grids meet the natural landscape, as in the fracturing of the grid by ravines in Los Angeles. Equally grids do not have to be homogeneous and entirely regular. The 1811 plan of midtown Manhattan, for example, had broad, short-block avenues for large buildings, and narrow, long-block streets for smaller row houses, while open squares, wider avenues, and in particular the meander of Broadway, introduced elements of differentiation and interest.

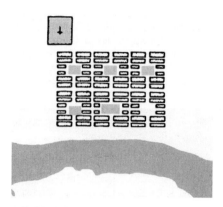

FIGURE 4.5
Savannah was laid out on the basis of cellular units with growth intended to be by repetition of those units. Each unit had an identical layout: four groups of ten house lots and four 'trust lots' (reserved for public or more important buildings) surrounding a public square. The main through traffic was on the streets between cellular units, leaving the public squares to quieter traffic. At intervals, tree-lined boulevards, replaced ordinary streets (source: adapted from Bacon, 1967)

During the late nineteenth and early twentieth centuries, in many countries (especially the USA) the dominance of rectilinear patterns provoked reaction against their use in favour of continuous curvilinear layouts, where wide, shallow plots (in contrast to deep, narrow ones) offered an impression of spaciousness. Curvilinear layouts derived from English picturesque design of the early nineteenth century, such as John Nash's 1823 design for Park Village near Regent's Park, are exemplified in Olmsted and Vaux's 1868 plan for Riverside near Chicago, and Letchworth Garden City (1905). While curves served to enclose views and add visual interest to newly developing neighbourhoods and suburbs, they were also designed to reduce visual permeability and discourage non-residents from entering into the area.

Most of the curvilinear patterns developed from the late nineteenth century through to the 1920s and 1930s were variations of grids. A refinement (introduced by Unwin and Parker at New Earswick, 1898) which became increasingly common during the late 1950s, was the cul-de-sac. Cul-de-sacs sought to retain the aesthetics of curvilinear layouts while militating the nuisances and dangers of cars and other traffic such as the problems of through traffic. As is discussed later in this chapter, widespread use of this road form changed the public space network from a grid to a hierarchical and discontinuous pattern.

THE PUBLIC SPACE NETWORK AND THE CAPITAL WEB

The cadastral pattern establishes an urban area's public space network and is a key element in the broader concept of the capital web (see below). As well as displaying and providing access to the 'public face' of private property, the public space network accommodates the overlapping realms of 'movement space' and 'social' space (i.e. outdoor space for people to engage in economic, social and cultural transaction). This social space is a constituent part of the 'public realm' (see Chapter 6). Pedestrian movement is compatible with the notion of streets as social space. Indeed, there is a symbiotic relationship between pedestrian movement and interpersonal transactions. By contrast, car-based movement is pure circulation. Opportunities for most forms of social interaction and exchange only occur once the car has been parked – prompting a focus on destinations rather than journeys.

When the principal modes of transport were by foot or by horse, the realms of movement and social space had considerable overlap. With the development of new modes of travel, these realms have become increasingly compartmentalised into vehicular movement space and pedestrian movement/social space. At the same time, public space has been colonised by the car and the social aspects of the 'street' suppressed in favour of movement and circulation – the 'road'.

The pattern of blocks and the public space network, plus basic infrastructure and any other relatively permanent elements of an urban area, constitute the above ground, visible elements of David Crane's 'capital web'. For Buchanan (1988a, p. 33), the capital web 'structures a city, its land uses and land values, the density of developments and the intensity of their use, and the way the citizens move through, see and remember the city as well as encounter their fellow citizens'.

In working within the capital web, urban designers need to be aware of patterns of stability within change: that is, to differentiate between elements which either do not change or change slowly (giving a measure of consistency of character and identity) and those that change over much shorter periods of time. Buchanan (1988, p. 32) argued that it was the movement network, the services buried beneath it, and the monuments and civic buildings within and adjacent to it – plus the images these structured in the mind – that formed

the relatively permanent parts of the city. Within this framework, individual buildings, land uses and activities come and go. Hence, even though subject to change, some essence of the city's identity is retained (see Chapter 9).

BUILDINGS DEFINING SPACE AND BUILDINGS IN SPACE

A major transformation in the morphological structure of the public space network was from buildings as constituent elements in urban blocks – i.e. terraced masses, defining 'streets' and 'squares' – towards buildings as freestanding pavilions in amorphous space. According to Modernist 'functionalist' ideas, the convenience of a building's internal spaces was the principal determinant of its external form. Le Corbusier (1927, p. 167), for example, likened a building to a soap bubble: 'This bubble is perfect and harmonious if the breath has been evenly distributed and regulated from the inside. The exterior is the result of interior.' Designed from the inside out, responding only to their functional requirements and to considerations of light, air, hygiene, aspect, prospect, 'movement', 'openness', etc., buildings became sculptures, 'objects in space', their exterior form – and therefore the relationship to public space – merely a by-product of their internal planning.

At the larger scale – and based on ideas of providing healthier living conditions, of aesthetic preference, and of the need to accommodate cars in urban areas – Modernist urban space was intended to flow freely around buildings rather than to be contained by them. Le Corbusier, for example, saw the traditional street as 'no more than a trench, a deep cleft, a narrow passage. And although we have been accustomed to it for more than a thousand years, our hearts are always oppressed by the constriction of the enclosing walls' (quoted in Broadbent, 1990, p. 129). The desire for separation was reinforced by public health and planning standards such as density zoning, road widths, sight lines, the space required for underground services, street by-laws and daylighting angles.

The shift towards freestanding buildings was also fuelled by the desire for them to be distinctive – a consequence of the commercial interests of the development industry and building sponsors. Buildings can stand out in a number of ways, such as by being physically separate or taller than surrounding buildings, and/or architecturally distinctive. Through separation and physical distance, freestanding buildings are insulated from negative (and positive) spill-over effects of the local context.

Before the modern period, only a few building types – churches, town halls, palaces, etc. – used these means of gaining distinction. These were typically 'public' rather than 'private' buildings, whose interiors had some significance for the city and its people. Von Meiss contends that a fundamental problem of twentieth century urbanisation has been the multiplication of 'objects' and the neglect of 'fabrics', 'There are too many buildings which present themselves as "objects", indifferent to the public or hierarchical role they play in the values of our society.' He further complains that contemporary production methods confer an object status on buildings whose 'content and significance are ordinary' (Von Meiss, 1990, p. 77).

When freestanding buildings were built in traditional urban space, they challenged and broke down the urban block system. In traditional space, where buildings are normally sited adjacent to one another and flush with the street, their façades form the 'walls' of open space. As the only part exposed to view, the façade conveys – and is designed to convey – the building's identity and character. Embedded in a dense urban fabric, the building's backs and sides can be more mundane without detriment to the public realm. Furthermore, while complete in itself, the façade is also a constituent part of the larger systems of the 'street' and the 'urban block'.

Urban block systems have an inherent discipline that relies on each individual property owner/developer abiding by certain 'rules' in order to achieve a collective benefit. If a developer cannot rely on others abiding by the rules, more individualistic strategies come into play. If neighbouring buildings are likely to be destroyed, enlarged, or rebuilt in a different configuration, property owners can no longer rely on only their façade to represent their building, nor on neighbouring buildings to protect the privacy and security of their backs. If it can no longer be assumed that adjacent structures will be similar in size and style (i.e. if the stability of the context can no longer be relied upon), owner/developers become motivated to design and build structures that can stand alone.

Applied across a range of building types and within traditional urban space systems, freestanding buildings had major impacts on the character of public space. As a direct consequence, the public space network changed from definite spatial types ('streets' and 'squares') towards an amorphous 'space' that – unless expressly designed and maintained – is residual, accidental and merely 'occupied' by objects standing within it. As such developments became more common during the second half of the twentieth century, cities tended to lose their spatial coherence, becoming a series of unrelated and competing or isolated monuments and small complexes of buildings surrounded by roads, parking and (often disparate) landscaping.

The combination of Modernist ideas with modern construction and development processes resulted in a new kind of city, made up of amorphous spaces 'punctuated with monumental buildings' and 'arbitrary and disconnected individual features' (Brand, 1994, p. 10). In the absence of explicit concern for the spaces between the buildings, environments were simply collections of individual buildings. The unintended outcome was a bastardised version of Modernist ideas of urban space design. As Trancik (1986, p. 21) observes: 'Somehow – without any conscious intention on anyone's part – the ideals of free flowing space and pure architecture have evolved into our present urban situation of individual buildings isolated in parking lots and highways.' Similarly, Lefebvre (1991, p. 303) argues that the outcome was a 'fracturing of space': 'a disordering of elements wrenched from each other in such a way that the urban fabric itself – the street, the city – is also torn apart'.

The apparent choice between 'connected masses' or urban blocks defining space and freestanding pavilions is more than one of aesthetic preference. The resultant space has different social characteristics. As Bentley (1999, p. 125) argues, the concept of buildings as freestanding sculptural objects ignores the socially constructed distinction between front and back which is vital in establishing conditions of privacy, and in the relationship of public and private. Development generally benefits from having a front onto public space, for entrances, social display and 'public' activities, and a back for more private activities. Backs should face onto private space and other backs, while the public fronts should face onto public space and other fronts. The shift away from buildings having distinct fronts and backs has been further emphasised by the denigration in architectural circles of the 'façade' (Bentley, 1999, p. 125).

A related distinction can be made between 'active' and 'passive' fronts. Because social space provides opportunities for interaction and exchange, development facing onto it will tend to be 'socially' active. By contrast, movement space has few opportunities for interaction, and development facing onto it will tend to be 'socially passive'. Thus, although it is public space, movement space will tend to be faced by socially passive fronts with few or no windows and little indication of human presence (see Chapter 8).

Because freestanding pavilion buildings are surrounded by public space, at least some of this must be faced by backs: 'The privacy barriers, which are necessary in these situations, create increasing proportions of inactive, blank edges to public space – edges without windows or doors – as the transition from perimeter blocks to pavilions proceeds' (Bentley, 1999, p. 184). Thus, with a proliferation of freestanding buildings, the interface between buildings and the public spaces adjoining them increasingly shifts from 'socially active' to 'socially passive'.

THE RETURN TO TRADITIONAL URBAN SPACE

Reacting both to Modernist approaches and to contemporary development patterns, recent urban design has seen a new interest in the relationship between built space and urban space. This has led to attempts to organise the parts so that the whole (the public realm) is greater than the sum of its individual buildings and developments. It has also prioritised the need (both functional and aesthetic) to focus on the creation of defined, positive space (see Chapter 7). Such approaches have often taken reference from the traditional urban space of blocks formed by the connected mass of individual 'background' buildings defining, or defined by, 'positive' spaces. As well as being a reaction to the Modernist attitude to the past, this also demonstrated a new interest in, and concern for, the continuity of places, together with a willingness to examine and learn from precedent.

A key figure in the re-evaluation of urban space design was Colin Rowe. Under Rowe's influence, an approach explicitly relating new development to a city's historical structure and to traditional typologies of urban space was explored at Cornell University from the early 1960s. Particularly significant in these studies were figure-ground diagrams which Rowe used to teach architectural students to

consider buildings not just as objects, but also as backgrounds (Figure 4.6). Subsequently in *Collage City*, Rowe and Koetter (1978) described the 'spatial predicament' of the Modernist city as one of 'objects' and 'texture' (pp. 50–85). Objects are sculptural buildings standing freely in space, while texture is the background matrix of built form defining space. Using figure-ground diagrams, Rowe and Koetter showed how traditional cities were the inverse of Modernist ones: one diagram was almost all white (an accumulation of solids in largely unmanipulated void), the other almost all black (an accumulation of voids in largely unmanipulated solid). Nevertheless, rather than privileging the positive space ('space-fixation') or the positive building ('object-fixation'), they recognised situations where one or the other would be appropriate. The situation to be hoped for, therefore, was 'one in which both buildings *and* spaces exist in an equality of sustained debate. A debate in which victory consists in each component emerging undefeated' (Rowe and Koetter, 1978, p. 83). In other words, this would be a state of figure-ground reversal (see Chapter 7).

Another morphological approach to urban space design developed from the ideas of Aldo Rossi and the Italian Rationalist School in the mid-1960s, and subsequently of others such as Rob and Leon Krier. Rossi's book *The Architecture of the City* (1982) resurrected ideas of architectural types and typology. In contrast to building type, which

FIGURE 4.6
Extract of the Nolli plan of Rome

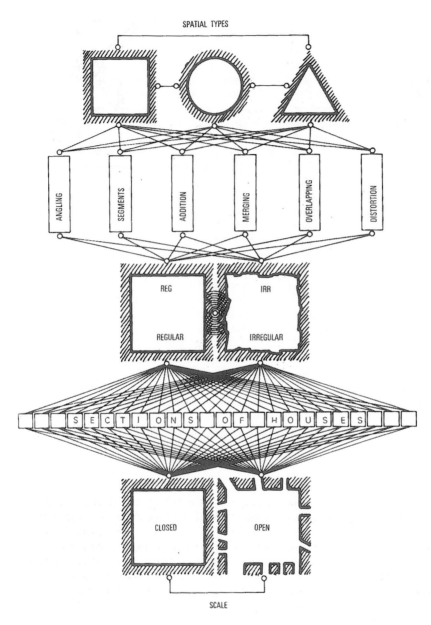

SPATIAL TYPES

ANGLING SEGMENTS ADDITION MERGING OVERLAPPING DISTORTION

REG IRR

REGULAR IRREGULAR

SECTIONS OF HOUSES

CLOSED OPEN

SCALE

FIGURE 4.7
Rob Krier's typology of urban squares. In Krier's analysis, European urban spaces generally fall into three main plan shapes: squares, circles or triangles. These basic shapes can be adapted or modified in a variety of ways: they can occur on their own or in combination with the others; they can be regular or irregular; they can be modulated by altering their angles, dimensions and by adding or subtracting from the basic shape; they can be twisted, divided, penetrated, or overlapped; they can be closed by walls, arcades or colonnades from the streets around them, or they can be open to the environment. Building façades frame the spaces and can take many forms: from solid, unrelieved masonry to masonry with openings of various kinds: windows, doors, arcades, colonnades, to façades that are entirely glazed. The basic shapes can also be modified by a great variety of sections that substantially alter the quality of the space. Each section can also be treated differently in elevation, which in turn influences the quality of the space. Finally, the number and positions of intersecting streets determines the 'closed' or 'open' nature of the square (source: R. Krier, 1990)

generally refers to function, the architectural type is morphological and refers to form. Architectural types are abstractions of basic principles, ideas or forms and, in a sense, are three-dimensional templates that can be repeatedly copied with endless variation (Kelbaugh, 1997, p. 97).

The study of architectural and morphological types effectively formalised and systematised the processes of learning from experience and precedent, and revived a traditional way of looking at function. Typologists asserted that, when designing a building or an urban space, 'tried and tested' architectural types that had evolved over time offered a better point of departure than Modernist functionalism which sought to discover new forms latent in 'programme' or 'technology'. As Kelbaugh

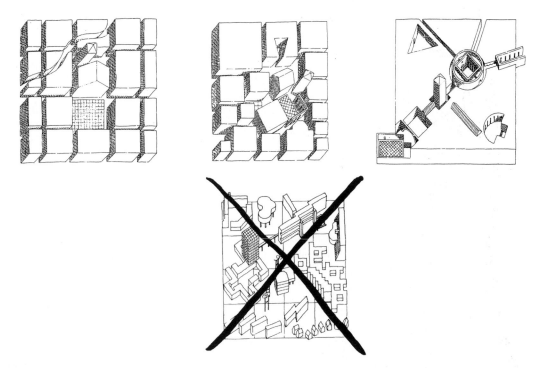

FIGURE 4.8
Leon Krier identified four types of urban space. Three are types of traditional urban space; the fourth is a form of Modernist urban space. (i) The urban blocks are the result of the patterns of streets and squares: the pattern is typologically classifiable. (ii) The pattern of streets and squares is the result of the position of blocks: the blocks are typologically classifiable. (iii) The streets and squares are precise formal types: the public 'rooms' are typologically classifiable. (iv) The buildings are precise formal types: there is a random distribution of buildings standing in space (source: L. Krier, 1990)

(1997, p. 96) explains, while typologists may 'admit that a design can present unprecedented social issues and new technical opportunities . . . they also know that human nature, human needs, and the human body haven't changed; nor has climate (yet) or geography (much)'.

One source of evidently durable morphological types is the historic city itself. As Gosling and Maitland (1984, p. 134) note: 'Until the point at which it was destroyed by the disastrous innovations of the twentieth century, the city is seen as having developed certain "type" elements . . . universal solutions of great simplicity and integrity, arrived at over a period of time by the operation of anonymous forces of selection.' Key urban types include the 'quarter', the 'urban block', and more specific types such as 'streets', 'avenues', 'arcades' and 'colonnades'. In his book *Urban Space* (1979), Rob Krier analysed urban space and developed a typology of urban squares (see Figure 4.7). In contrast

to Camillo Sitte (1889) and Zucker (1959) (see Chapter 8) who concentrated on the aesthetic effect of urban spaces, Krier used elementary geometry as his starting point. Krier's brother Leon also developed a critique of Modernist urban space design, rooted in a preference for traditional urban spatial forms and types, and identifying four systems of urban space (L. Krier, 1978a, 1978b, 1979) (Figure 4.8).

Although much contemporary urban space design has been informed by a reaction to Modernism's stance on history and tradition and has a strong historicist dimension, many remain sceptical of such approaches. Read (1982) warned that while we are far enough removed from the Modern Movement to recognise its limitations, we should also recognise that the industrial city's problems were real problems and that 'while it may be reasonable now to reject the forms which Modernists evolved in their response to the problems of the industrial city, those problems will not be removed simply by looking further back to the pre-industrial city'. Equally, it can be argued that the pioneer Modernists sought to emphasise what was new and different by downplaying what was essentially the same: Aldo Van Eyck (see Smithson, 1962, p. 560), for example, criticised Modernist architects for continually 'harping' about 'what is different in our time to such an extent that they have lost touch with what is not different, with what is essentially the same'.

While learning from experience demands awareness and involves recognition of what changes over time and what stays the same, there are two particular areas of difficulty:

First, while morphological approaches to urban design tend to be premised on patterns of urban form rather than on economic, social or functional arguments that generate form (the Modernist approach), prescription about particular forms can invite accusations of environmental determinism (see Chapter 6). Although it is naive to say that spatial forms will create particular social behaviour, such spaces may offer potential for certain activities. Furthermore, while certain forms have been 'tried' in the past and 'tested' in the intervening period, their suitability for the future is unknown. It is also debatable whether particular types and patterns can be applied in differing cultures, climates and social conditions. This does not, however, preclude the identification of regional or locally appropriate types.

Second, there is tension in the design process between the value placed on 'originality' and 'creativity', and the role of types. On the one hand, as Bentley (1999, p. 55) argues, pre-existing types cannot be seen as a product of the individual designer's creativity. On the other hand, designers competing in the market have to be able to claim originality in their work – a claim undermined by the notion that they 'are "merely" selecting and manipulating socially-sanctioned types' (Bentley, 1999, p. 55). Although many design theorists regard the idea of type as a problem (see Lawson, 1980, p. 110), Bentley counters the suggestion that the 'type' approach denies potential for 'individual genius', by arguing that types change over time and that how they change is a function of individual human action. More generally, the ideological imperative for originality, creativity and endless novelty is often misplaced: rather than being valued as ends in themselves, they should more usefully be seen as means to create better buildings and environments.

'STREET/BLOCK' STRUCTURES AND 'ROAD' NETWORKS

The other major transformation in the public space network's morphological structure – from finely meshed grids to road networks surrounding super blocks and segregated enclaves – was a product of the need to accommodate fast-moving vehicular traffic. When the dominant modes of travel were walking and travel by horse, there were relatively few conflicts between the needs of movement space and social space. Arrangements for different forms of travel started with the special needs of canals and railways. While these involved mostly separated systems of infrastructure, horse-drawn carriages, and then cars, shared space with pedestrians, exacerbating the tension between the competing demands of movement space and social space. Thus, provision for vehicular traffic initially evolved by usurping pedestrians from large parts of the public space network. The separation of pedestrian from vehicular movement in conventional streets occurred in many cities during the eighteenth and nineteenth centuries, through the introduction of pavements (sidewalks) which left the centre of the street for vehicles, where pedestrians had to beware. Pavements also served to separate pedestrians from the new side channels and cambered roads designed to improve health through more efficient disposal of sewage and run-off (Taylor, 2002, p. 28).

During the early twentieth century, more radical ideas evolved. The best way to accommodate the growing numbers of cars seemed to be to give them their own dedicated movement network. Noting Le Corbusier's well-known dislike of the 'hurly-burly' of streets, Boddy (1992, p. 132) argues that formulating a 'more rationalised alternative' was the generative idea of his urbanism. Le Corbusier's city plans featured both the radical separation of modes of travel and their equally radical reintegration in vast transport interchanges. Ideas for separating different modes of traffic were further developed, from the late 1920s to the 1940s, in works such as Alker Tripp's *Road Traffic and its Control* (1938) and *Town Planning and Road Traffic* (1942). The intention was to distribute traffic through a hierarchy of routes closely matched to traffic flows.

The introduction of hierarchical road systems meant that some roads in the network would be expressly designed or designated for higher traffic loads. Traffic flow on such roads was assisted by

BOX 4.3 – TRANSFORMATION OF TRADITIONAL GRID INTO SUPER BLOCK

Rather than a single movement or travel system, there are often different systems, each with its own network or grid, overlying one another. The layers may be distinguished by mode of travel or, where there is a single mode of travel, in response to considerations such as speed, traffic flow and efficiency. A hierarchical road system consists of a series of layers. Major highways form a layer of their own. Access points from layers lower in the hierarchy are limited to enable faster traffic flow on those higher up the hierarchy: for example, the number of pedestrian crossings is reduced; the number of connecting roads is limited; and private driveways are prohibited from opening into them. While there may be various reasons for reducing the links between networks or layers (including safety and traffic flow), the absence of links introduces discontinuities into the movement system, reducing its permeability.

In his book, *Ladders*, Albert Pope (1996, p. 109) argues that the introduction of freeways with restricted access disrupted and severed the 'continuities of gridded space' and eliminated choice 'by enforcing a strict hierarchical movement along a primary route of transportation, dramatically coarsening the urban fabric'. While a grid allows movement in a variety of directions and through a variety of paths, a 'ladder' only allows movement from A to B and vice versa. Pope also discusses the phenomenon of 'grid erosion' – the process by which traditional grids are transformed into super block systems and, in particular, into 'pod' systems. In Pope's terms, the process involves open gridded street systems giving way to 'laddered' street systems where every destination has an exclusive highway entrance/exit (see diagrams). Many contemporary developments on greenfield sites start with laddered rather than gridded layouts.

As each road termination or residential cul-de-sac becomes an exclusive destination, it becomes only a place to go to rather than a place that might also be passed through on the way to somewhere else. This greatly diminishes what Hillier (1996) terms the 'by-product' of movement – that is, the potential for other (optional) activities in addition to the basic activity of travelling from origin to destination. Hillier argues that the by-product of movement is a critical element of urbanity (see Chapter 8). Pope also considers that 'ladders' have supported broader desires for exclusivity, isolation and separation, creating what he terms 'xenophobic enclaves'. While such enclaves may also be justified by the argument that defining discrete areas of territory

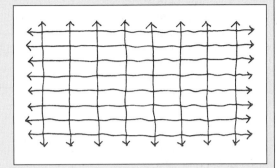

Gridded street system

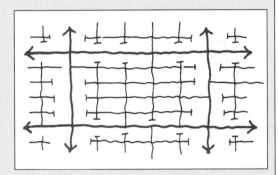

Process of grid erosion

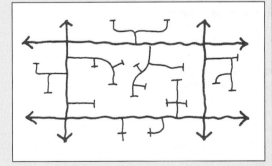

Laddered street system

helps variously to generate a sense of identity, a sense of community and a sense of safety and security for those living in the area, their ultimate development is the gated community (see Chapter 6).

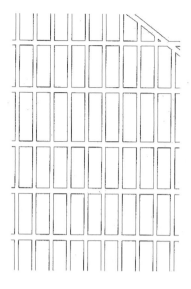

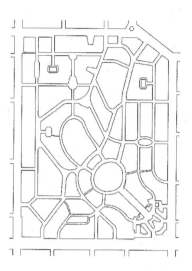

FIGURE 4.9
Street pattern of Clarence Perry's Neighbourhood Unit compared with grid layout. Perry proposed that arterial roads would bypass rather than penetrate the unit, thereby protecting the unit from through traffic. The hierarchy of relatively poorly connected streets deters traffic from 'rat running' through the unit

reducing the number of pedestrian crossings, limiting the number of other roads connecting into them, and prohibiting private driveways from opening onto them. The idea continues today: in England, for example, government guidance in *Design Bulletin 32: Residential Roads and Footpaths* (DETR, 1998, p. 15) suggests a four-level hierarchy: primary distributor roads; district distributor roads; local distributor roads and residential access roads.

Where a new hierarchical road system was created within a traditional street grid, certain streets were designated and equipped as major roads, with access onto them limited to allow traffic to move more freely and quickly. To enable a wider road to be built, buildings on one or both sides might be demolished. The 'super block' surrounded by major roads would be many times larger than the traditional urban block. Pope (1996, p. 189) describes this process as 'grid erosion', with open gridded streets giving way to 'laddered' streets where every destination has an exclusive highway entrance/exit (see Box 4.3).

More often, a hierarchical road layout would be laid out on previously undeveloped land, providing access to the major road network at widely spaced intervals between relatively large cells. The coarse-grained major road network would carry non-local traffic, allowing the streets/roads within each cell to carry local traffic only. The area within the super block – the cell of the major road

Before

After

FIGURE 4.10
Buchanan's concept of 'environmental areas' (source: Scoffham, 1984)

FIGURE 4.11
Chicago, USA. Major roads create problems of severance in urban areas

network – also needed to be designed to prevent or deter traffic from taking short cuts ('rat running') through streets intended to carry lighter traffic loads. One option was to make the local road network relatively discontinuous (i.e. through the use of cul-de-sacs) or at least poorly connected. Clarence Perry's neighbourhood unit of 1929, for example, was a super block surrounded by major arterial roads. Within the unit there was a hierarchy of roads, each sized according to the intended traffic load, and deliberately less well integrated than in a grid layout where opportunities for rat runs are maximised (Figure 4.9). Perry also saw through traffic as an obstacle to community formation, and busy traffic routes as obvious boundaries for residential areas.

Similarly, within his hierarchical road network, Tripp (1942) advocated a 'precinct principle' – effectively a super block – from which extraneous traffic would be excluded. Given the ideas of his day, Tripp saw the precincts as specialised, single land-use areas. In the early 1960s, a similar idea appeared in the highly influential Buchanan report, *Traffic in Towns* (1964). Buchanan proposed the division of the city into 'environmental' areas – a mixed-use rather than a specialised single-use super block concept – each bounded by major roads and kept free from through-traffic (Figure 4.10). Although often taken as an argument for road

building, Buchanan's report was much subtler. A road engineer as well as an architect, Buchanan recognised the conflict between providing for easy traffic flow and preserving the residential and architectural fabric of the street – and the related need to strike a balance between accommodating traffic and sustaining the quality of urban life.

A particular problem in this regard is the tendency for major roads to act as barriers to movement across them, creating severance and fragmenting urban areas (Figure 4.11). Lefebvre (1991, p. 359), for example, describes how urban space is 'sliced up, degraded, and eventually destroyed by . . . the proliferation of fast roads'. Movement between the fragments becomes a purely movement experience rather than a movement and social experience. Containing both social space and movement space, walkable streets connect buildings and activities across space. Containing only movement space, roads divide and separate areas. In a well-known piece of research, Appleyard and Lintell (1972) compared three San Francisco streets which, while similar in many ways, varied in the amount of traffic on them and in their social use (Figure 4.12). Where roads present obstacles to movement, subways and pedestrian bridges are often used to reconnect the areas either side (Figure 4.13). These often cause significant inconvenience to pedestrians, however, and

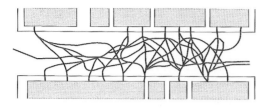

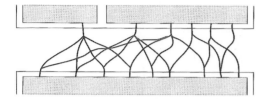

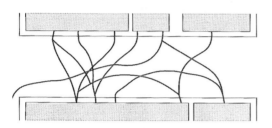

FIGURE 4.12
Appleyard and Lintell (1972) compared three San Francisco streets that, while similar in many ways, varied in the amount of traffic travelling along them. On the heavily trafficked street, people tended to use the sidewalk only as a pathway between home and final destination. On the lightly trafficked street, there was an active social life: people used the sidewalks and the corner stores as places to meet and initiate interaction. The high-volume street was seen as a less friendly place to live than the lightly trafficked street

FIGURE 4.13
Furnival Gate, Sheffield, UK. To avoid slowing cars down, pedestrians are often severely inconvenienced

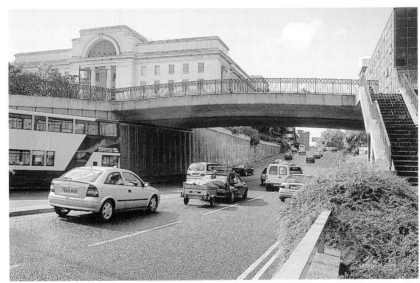

FIGURES 4.14 and 4.15
As an explicit strategy of 'breaking the concrete collar' of the inner ring road and making a more pedestrian-friendly environment, a section of Birmingham's inner ring road was lowered and a wide pedestrian bridge created to link the existing city centre with a new public space at Centenary Square. Pedestrians now barely notice they are crossing the busy inner ring road

in many cities there are now plans to remove subways and replace them with surface crossings (Figures 4.14 and 4.15).

POD DEVELOPMENTS

A further transformation in the morphological structure of urban areas is that from outward-facing urban blocks to inward-focused complexes of buildings, often referred to as 'pods' (Ford, 2000). In 'pod' developments, each use – shopping mall, fast-food outlet, office park, apartments, hotel, housing cluster, etc. – is conceived as a separate element, surrounded by its associated parking and usually with its own access onto a collector or main distributor road. As Ford (2000, p. 21) comments: 'The idea is to separate – often to the point of walling off – land uses into distinctive social and functional worlds.'

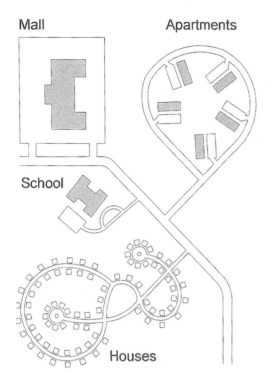

Mall Apartments

School

Houses

FIGURE 4.16
Each development is a self-contained pod, unrelated to other pods and having its own exclusive connection to the collector road (after Duany *et al.*, 2000, p. 23)

While individual pods may be more or less well designed, they tend to be introverted and separated from adjacent developments by main roads and by hectares of car parking. Often deliberately turning their back on their surroundings, pods may be geographically proximate but otherwise have very little relation. Indeed, apart from a road link, there is little need for connection because almost everyone drives between them. Thus, instead of a system of blocks defining space, urban areas become conceived of in terms of routes surrounding individual buildings or inward-focused complexes of buildings in space, sometimes in landscaped settings, but more often amid car parks (Figure 4.16). Furthermore, many pod schemes are entirely standardised and repetitive – Duany *et al.* (2000) refer to them as 'cookie cutter' developments – imposed on a location 'from above', with little regard for local context, topography or landscape. Pod development is also the characteristic form of out-of-centre complexes and edge cities (Garreau, 1991).

With no pedestrian flow, only vehicular flow, pods do not generally front onto main traffic distribution roads. Instead, development is introverted, focused on the road/street network within the super block, and the points where people can park their cars. As an alternative pattern, 'large lump' developments such as shopping centres, office complexes, multi-screen cinemas or hotel complexes, occupy the centre of the block, surrounded by car parking.

Although some pod developments have pedestrian-oriented spaces where buildings enclose or define spaces, they are usually private spaces, with access and behaviour closely controlled and regulated (see Chapter 6). In their book, *Splintered Urbanism*, Graham and Marvin (2001, pp. 120–1) observe how urban spaces are increasingly being reconfigured 'as inward-looking "islands" or "enclaves", surrounded by the physical highways, connections and services to support motor access, parking and use'. Similarly, Bentley (1999, p. 88) observes how the city as a whole becomes 'transformed into a series of islands, with spectacular interiors, set in a "left over" sea'.

A particular kind of pod development (first introduced in the late nineteenth century) is the residential cul-de-sac, a relatively short dead-end street with a turning hammerhead or circle, serving perhaps twenty or thirty dwellings. Its advantages included savings in road construction costs – having a lighter traffic load, cul-de-sacs could be built with a lower specification. Their use increased from the mid-1950s onwards as traffic engineers began to address the safety problems associated with through traffic in residential streets, by means of hierarchical road networks and discontinuous road patterns. Many contemporary residential areas are designed with 'dendritic' (tree-like) street patterns, in which a curvilinear collector road loops off a major highway, with a number of cul-de-sacs branching off it. In its most extreme form all the houses are situated on cul-de-sacs with none on the busier loop road. Due to their shape on plan, these are sometimes contemptuously referred to as 'lollipops' and the system as 'loops and lollipops'.

Southworth and Ben-Joseph (1997, pp. 120–1) note that among many architects and planners, the term cul-de-sac has become pejorative because 'it represents the essence of suburbia today: the isolated, insular, private enclave, set in a formless sprawl of similar enclaves, separated socially and physically from the larger world, and dependent upon the automobile for its survival'. New Urbanists (e.g. Duany *et al.*, 2000) have strongly criticised

BOX 4.4 – CUL-DE-SACS

(adapted from Southworth and Ben-Joseph, 1997, pp. 121–5)

Arguments for cul-de-sacs

- *Provides quieter and safer streets*: For residents, the pattern offers quiet and safe streets, where children can play with minimal fear of the hazards of fast-moving traffic.
- *Promotes resident interaction*: A discontinuous short street system, unlike the grid, may promote neighbouring, familiarity and interaction.
- *Provides a local sense of identity*: The scale of the cul-de-sac provides a local sense of identity.
- *Reduces opportunities for crime*: Compared with traditional street layouts, hierarchical discontinuous layouts deter burglaries because criminals avoid street patterns where they might get trapped (Mayo, 1979; Newman, 1995) (see Chapter 6).

Arguments against cul-de-sacs

- *Lack of interconnectedness*: Isolation from through traffic may simultaneously result in isolation from nearly everything else. To go anywhere, one must always leave the cul-de-sac and travel on a collector road. Furthermore, designed for access by cars, cul-de-sac layouts often have poorly developed networks of pedestrian routes. Having to follow the vehicular routes, pedestrian walks are often long and inconvenient.
- *Creates car-dependency*: Going almost anywhere beyond the cul-de-sac means going out to a major road, virtually necessitating a car journey, thus isolating and excluding those too young, old or poor to drive, and sentencing the rest to a life ferrying themselves and their dependants around.
- *Generates traffic congestion*: As every trip from one component to another must enter the collector road, the area's traffic relies on a single road. As a result, it is generally congested during much of the day, while any major accident on the collector road will block the entire system.
- *Enhances opportunities for crime*: Cul-de-sac patterns interrupt the through movement of people and, thereby, reduce the policing effect of people presence (see Chapter 6).
- *Lack of identity and character*: The sense of being part of a neighbourhood or town, with a clear structure and identity, is often lost because through streets connecting places are missing. There is a sense of identity within the cul-de-sac, but not beyond it.

the use of cul-de-sacs and are committed advocates of interconnected and grid street patterns. Though disparaged by professionals, the cul-de-sac seems to be much loved by suburban residents and developers (see Box 4.4). Nevertheless, Southworth and Ben-Joseph (1997, p. 126) argue that it is possible to design new residential districts – and, perhaps less easily, to retrofit old ones – with interconnected pedestrian networks as well as limited access vehicular systems.

THE RETURN TO 'STREETS'

As discussed above, for reasons of safety and traffic flow, accommodating the car in traditional streets has typically led to an effacement of social space by movement space. As Buchanan (1988a, p. 32) observed, it is only in recent times that movement is separated spatially and functionally in the city: 'Before that . . . movement [was] always inextricably linked with – and indeed usually generates – other activities, both adjacent and within the same external space.' Sustainable urban design, nevertheless, requires patterns of development able to accommodate and integrate the demands of the various movement systems, while supporting social interaction and exchange. Hence, while there are inexorable tensions and conflicts between the public space network's roles as movement space and as social space, a multi-purpose public space network is needed where the two are separated if absolutely necessary, but otherwise have considerable overlap.

Alexander (1965) uses the separation of pedestrians from moving vehicles as an example of what he terms a 'tree' structure, arguing that while this is often a good idea, there are times when the 'ecology of a situation' demands the opposite – as in the case of taxis, which can only function when pedestrians and vehicles are not strictly separated: the 'prowling taxi' needs a fast stream of traffic so that it can cover a large area to find passengers, while the pedestrian needs to be able to hail the taxi from any point, and then to be taken to any other point in the 'pedestrian world'. The system containing taxis, therefore, needs to overlap both the vehicular traffic system and the pedestrian circulation system.

While there will always be a need for 'roads', many commentators advocate rediscovering 'streets' as both social space and as connecting –

rather than dividing – elements within cities. Various authors (e.g. Appleyard, 1981; Moudon, 1987; Hass-Klau, 1990; Jacobs, 1993; Loukaitou-Sideris and Banerjee, 1998; Hass-Klau et al., 1999; Banerjee, 2001) highlight the role of streets in contributing to the quality of public life and emphasise how streets and sidewalks can be captured for social purposes. Noting how the contemporary downtown in many Californian cities has been fragmented into a series of unrelated and spatially limited realms, Loukaitou-Sideris and Banerjee (1998, p. 304) argue that instead of – or perhaps in addition to – treating the street as a 'channel for efficient movement' (as in the Modernist era) or as an 'aesthetic visual element' (as in the City Beautiful era), urban design 'should rediscover the social role of the street as a connector that stitches together and sometimes penetrates the disparate downtown realms'.

The problem is not only that demand for movement diminishes the potential of streets to function as social space, but also that greater concern is given to traffic than to pedestrians. Buchanan (1988, p. 32) complains that public space has lost its social function and purpose and is often considered solely in terms of movement. In this respect, the car is often uniquely privileged. Sheller and Urry (2000, p. 745) argue that car travel 'rudely interrupts' the use of urban space by others 'whose daily routines are merely obstacles to the high-speed traffic that cuts mercilessly through slower-moving pathways and dwellings'. Research in central Aberdeen, for example, showed that while the ratio of pedestrian to vehicular movement was 4:1, the space available for this movement was 1:4. The figures were used to support arguments for increasing the area of pedestrianised space in the city centre.

Careful design is needed to reconcile the demands of different forms of movement. In practice, this generally involves protecting social space from the impacts of cars and the creation of areas that, while accessible by cars, are pedestrian-dominant (see Moudon, 1987; Hass-Klau, 1990; Southworth and Ben-Joseph, 1997). Such ideas are epitomised by the concepts of 'shared streets', Home Zones (in the UK) and 'woonerfs', all of which integrate pedestrian activity and vehicular movement on a shared surface. In the late 1960s, a professor at Delft University of Technology, Niek De Boer designed streets, which he named woonerfs, wherein 'motorists would feel as if they were driving in a "garden" setting, forcing drivers

to consider other road users' (Southworth and Ben-Joseph, 1997, p. 112). The shared street layout gives pedestrians primary rights, so that, sensing they are intruding into a pedestrian zone, motorists drive more cautiously.

Writing about residential areas, David Engwicht (1999) refers to the process of recapturing social space as 'Street Reclaiming' – a conceptual step beyond traffic calming, which typically involves speed bumps and chicanes. He argues that 'the more space a city devotes to movement, the more the exchange space becomes diluted and scattered. The more diluted and scattered the exchange opportunities, the more the city begins to lose the very thing that makes a city: a concentration of exchange opportunities' (Engwicht, 1999, p. 19). Comparing streets with houses, he suggests that the latter are designed to reduce movement space (corridors) while maximising exchange space (rooms). He, therefore, proposes 'Five Rs' of traffic reduction: *replace* car trips with other travel modes; *remove* unnecessary trips by combining purposes; *reduce* trip lengths; *reuse* saved space; and *reciprocate* by acting collectively for mutual benefit. The first three are strategies for households, who, he argues, through simple strategies can reduce their car use by 25–50 per cent without significant impact on lifestyle. The last two are for streets, neighbourhoods and cities, as individual actions are of little value if other drivers quickly fill the space freed. Such actions are only really possible where choice is available: they are not possible in car-dependant environments.

URBAN BLOCK PATTERNS

Reaction to the two major transformations of the morphological structure of public space networks has led to a shift towards a new appreciation of the qualities of traditional urban space. Many contemporary urban design projects are conceived in terms of urban blocks defining space rather than individual buildings in space (Figure 4.17).

The layout and configuration of urban block structure is important both in determining the pattern of movement and in setting parameters for subsequent development. Conceived as a public space network, such structures open up possibilities and – in conjunction with basic typologies/codes/rules about physical parameters – can provide coherence and 'good' urban form, without necessarily being deterministic about architectural form

FIGURE 4.17
Many contemporary
urban development
schemes use urban block
structures. Master plan
for Granton, Edinburgh,
Scotland (source:
Llewelyn Davies)

or content. This is akin to designing cities without designing buildings (Barnett, 1982). As the block pattern forms a basic element of the capital web, the pattern and configuration of blocks should be based on appreciation of the different rates of change of different morphological elements. As the street pattern is generally the most resilient part of the infrastructure, it is important to give it a configuration and dimensions that allow it to be robust and enduring.

The size and shape of urban blocks contribute significantly to an environment's character. Micro-climate, wind and sun penetration also need to be considered. Tall, narrow streets in northerly or southerly climes, for example, will have limited sunlight penetration for much of the year. In establishing new patterns of urban development – or in 'healing' established ones – a balance needs to be

struck between providing sufficient area for development to make it commercially viable and providing sufficient space for efficient and convenient circulation and social space. A balance also needs to be struck between arguments for smaller blocks, pedestrian permeability and social use of space and those for larger blocks and an optimum distribution of built form and open space (see below). A range of block sizes (including, in particular, small blocks) may encourage diversity of building types and land uses.

Block sizes can be determined by the local context (Figure 4.18). In undertaking development in established contexts or on brownfield sites, block sizes may be inferred by an 'urban healing' approach – that is, working with the existing fabric and remnant patterns of previous urbanisations, reintegrating isolated fragments, and re-establishing –

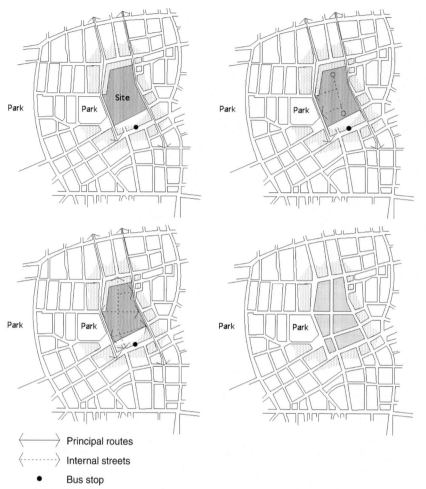

Principal routes

Internal streets

• Bus stop

FIGURE 4.18
Block sizes can be established by considering existing linkages and connections and working within the grain of the local context. The diagrams shown here from the *Urban Design Compendium* start by considering how the site can be connected with nearby main routes and public transport facilities. The second diagram shows how cul-de-sac layouts would create an introverted layout that failed to integrate with the surroundings. The third diagram suggests a more pedestrian-friendly approach that integrates with the surrounding context, and links existing and proposed streets. The street pattern then forms the basis for urban blocks – shown in the fourth diagram. This approach can be seen as 'urban healing' or 'urban weaving' (source: Llewelyn-Davis, 2000, p. 36)

and/or creating new – linkages with the wider context that facilitate movement and integration of the new development with its surrounding context. On greenfield sites there are usually fewer contextual cues to suggest appropriate block sizes. Block sizes could be determined by analysing the requirements of particular land uses (e.g. offices, housing, shops, industry) or through the use of historical precedents – that is, patterns that have endured and accommodated growth and change over time. Noting that ideal block size cannot be established any more precisely than the ideal height of a human body, Leon Krier (1990, p. 197) argued that through 'comparison and experience', sizes of urban blocks 'more apt' to form a 'complex urban pattern' can be deduced. Krier observed that, in most European cities that have evolved organically, the smallest and typologically most complex blocks are generally

found at the urban centre, with blocks tending to grow larger and simpler towards the periphery, before finally dissolving into single freestanding objects.

Small block sizes are often advocated for reasons such as urban vitality, permeability, visual interest and legibility. Jane Jacobs (1961, pp. 191–9), for example, devoted a chapter of *The Death and Life of Great American Cities*, to 'The Need for Small Blocks', because of the increased vitality and choice such layouts offer. Krier (1990, p. 198) also prefers small blocks, for their greater urbanity: 'If the main cause for small blocks and a dense pattern is primarily economic, it is this very same reason which has created the intimate character of a highly urban environment. Such an environment is the basis of urban culture, of intense *social*, *cultural* and *economic* exchange.'

FIGURE 4.19
Perimeter blocks in central Paris, France. Perimeter block development has a number of advantageous characteristics/features: explicit public and private sides; the capacity to accommodate different densities of development; and a public façade that both physically defines and 'socially' addresses an urban space

Small urban blocks may be a single building, with perhaps a central light well or atrium. Akin to freestanding buildings, such blocks raise problems of 'fronts' and 'backs'. Larger urban blocks are often perimeter blocks, with the ribbon of buildings around the edge providing the public front and private or semi-private space in the interior (Figure 4.19). Because the depth of the perimeter ribbon is limited to the depth of building that can be naturally lit and ventilated, the size of the central space increases as the dimensions of the block get larger. Depending on its size, this space can be used for various purposes – residents' car parking, private or communal gardens, sports facilities, etc. Larger

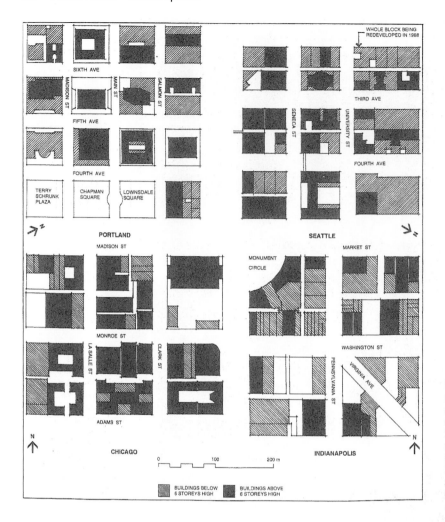

FIGURE 4.20
CBD block structures
and sizes in four US
cities – Portland and
Seattle (small square and
rectangular block cities)
and Chicago and
Indianapolis (medium
square block cities)
(source: Siskna, 1998)

perimeter blocks provide greater opportunities for bio-diversity: Llewelyn-Davies (2000, p. 58) recommends that blocks of external dimensions of about 90 m × 90 m, containing private or communal gardens, provide a good trade-off between bio-diversity and other considerations.

Larger block structures may, however, be more efficient in terms of the distribution of built form and open space. Examining the densities and land-use intensities of different development patterns, Martin and March (1972) provided mathematical arguments both for larger block sizes, and for perimeter rather than pavilion development. Looking at housing layouts in particular, they showed that, subject to certain environmental criteria, courtyard layouts (perimeter blocks) had a higher land-use intensity than pavilions (tower blocks). Investigating the area of central Manhattan

between Park and Eighth Avenues and 42nd and 57th Streets, Martin (1972, pp. 21–2) demonstrated how the same volume of development could be organised in radically different ways. Imagining the area developed as 36-storey 'Seagram'-type buildings, he calculated the amount of floor space achieved. Replacing the Seagram buildings with perimeter blocks and enlarging the street block by omitting some of the cross streets, he showed how the same amount of floor space could be accommodated in buildings of eight storeys. The spaces inside the perimeter blocks would each be equivalent in area to Washington Square and, furthermore there would be twenty-eight such spaces. For Martin, this both showed the range of choices available and raised 'far-reaching questions' about the relationship between built form and open space. The open

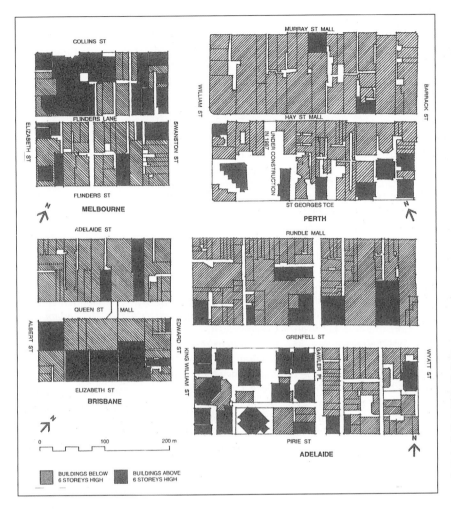

FIGURE 4.21
CBD block structures
and sizes in four
Australian cities –
Melbourne and
Brisbane (medium
rectangular block
cities) and Perth and
Adelaide (large
rectangular block
cities) (source: Siskna,
1998)

space provided in the Seagram layout was in the form of traffic corridors – within the perimeter blocks it was traffic-free courts. While this example provides support for larger, coarser, less permeable block structures, it also demonstrates the need to consider the layout of the urban framework in three dimensions rather than two (i.e. in terms of the possible configurations of urban form).

To examine the development and sustainability of urban patterns, particularly block sizes and circulation meshes, Siksna (1998) studied the CBDs of four American cities – Portland and Seattle (small square and rectangular block cities) and Chicago and Indianapolis (medium square block cities) – and four Australian cities, Melbourne and Brisbane (medium rectangular block cities) and Perth and Adelaide (large rectangular block cities) (Figures 4.20 and 4.21). Laid out in the first half of the nine-

teenth century (before the onset of the automobile age), each city plan had had more than a century and a half of growth and evolution.

Two interrelated characteristics of the evolution of the block and street patterns were of particular interest: the persistence of the block and street patterns, and the size of the circulation meshes.

1. *Persistence of the block and street pattern*: Demonstrating their durability in changing circumstances, the original block and street patterns of the small block cities were substantially intact. Similarly, the patterns of the medium block cities were largely intact – albeit with some insertion and/or deletion of alleys and arcades – more so in Melbourne and Brisbane. Although the original street patterns of the large block cities were also largely intact, the blocks and streets had changed considerably, the

original blocks having been broken down into smaller ones, and the street patterns altered significantly by the insertion of alleys and arcades. In Adelaide, for example, all blocks had been divided, typically into four or five smaller blocks or sub-blocks; in Perth, they had been subdivided into two or three blocks. In both cities, the original large blocks now approached the dimensions of those in the other cities.

2. *Circulation mesh*: Regarding the area available for circulation, Siksna concluded that a good proportion was one where circulation occupied 30 to 40 per cent of the total area. All the American examples attained or exceeded this in their initial layouts and needed few additional streets or alleyways. Layouts where streets and alleys initially occupied less than 30 per cent of the area needed additional routes. Layouts with small and medium blocks, where streets and alleys initially occupied more than 40 per cent of the area, could be seen as too generous. Siksna concluded that a circulation mesh of between 80 m and 110 m gave optimal provision. In some cases a finer pedestrian mesh (from 50 m to 70 m spacing) had evolved in intensively used retail areas, through the insertion of additional streets, alleys, arcades, and other routes. Although the vehicular mesh of most cities in the study had coarsened in recent years, primarily as a result of one-way systems, cities with small blocks had retained a convenient mesh size (i.e. below 200 m), while in medium and large block cities the mesh size generally exceeded 300 m, which was considered inconvenient for local traffic movement.

Although his research suggests an evolution towards optimum blocks sizes, Siksna concluded that processes of incremental change generally overcame, or at least reduced, the deficiencies of the initial layout. He also noted that, in practice, these changes had generally emerged through the initiative of individual or adjacent owners rather than through direct public intervention. The initial pattern nevertheless played an important role, with certain block forms and sizes proving more robust or more amenable to adaptation over time.

CONCLUSION

This chapter has discussed the morphological dimension of urban design, focusing on two key issues of urban form and urban layout. In general terms, it has showed and discussed the contemporary preferences for urban block patterns and gridded, permeable street layouts. While such preference is clear, it is necessary to appreciate why hierarchical, segregated and introverted layouts have come about. Given the prevalence of such layouts, active resistance is needed to reductions in permeability. If a high level of permeability is initially provided, segregation can usually be achieved later, if necessary, through design or management: the layout is robust and capable of adaptation. Conversely, it is difficult, even impossible, to turn an environment designed for segregation into one for integration. To ensure permeability, all streets should lead somewhere and terminate in other streets or space rather than in dead ends. Such a principle would tend to create permeable grids.

The chapter also reveals that a key issue in contemporary urban space design is how to accommodate the car. By colonising public space networks, subordinating other forms of mobility, and reorganising the distribution of activities in space, automobility both undermines other forms of mobility (walking, cycling, rail travel, etc.) and has a disabling effect on those who do not have access to cars. Furthermore, by monopolising resources – leading to inadequate public transport, and to transformations of the city landscape such that important services become inaccessible to non-car uses – the car system discriminates against non-car users (Lohan and Wickham, 2001, p. 43). A solution may be to prioritise and provide for other forms of movement, and then to accommodate the car.

5

The perceptual dimension

INTRODUCTION

Awareness and appreciation of environmental perception, and, in particular, of perception and experience of 'place', is an essential dimension of urban design. Since the early 1960s an interdisciplinary field of environmental perception has developed, and there now exists a significant body of research on people's perception of their urban environment. An initial concern with environmental images has been supplemented by work on symbolism and meaning in the built environment. The interest in environmental perception has also been reinforced by a body of work focusing on the experiential 'sense of place' and 'lived-in' experiences associated with urban environments. Exploring how people perceive environments and experience places, this chapter is in two main parts. In the first, environmental perception is discussed, and in the second, the construction of place, in terms of sense of place, placelessness, and the phenomenon of 'invented' places is explored.

ENVIRONMENTAL PERCEPTION

We affect the environment and are affected by it. For this interaction to happen, we must *perceive* – that is, be stimulated by sight, sound, smell or touch that offer clues about the world around us (Bell *et al.*, 1990, p. 27). Perception involves the gathering, organising and making sense of information about the environment. A distinction is generally made between two processes that gather and interpret environmental stimuli – 'sensation' and 'perception'. These are not discrete processes:

in practice, it is not clear where sensation ends and perception begins.

Sensation refers to human sensory systems reacting to environmental stimuli. The four most valuable senses in interpreting and sensing the environment are vision, hearing, smell and touch.

- *Vision*: The dominant sense, vision provides more information than the other senses combined. Orientation in space is achieved visually. As Porteous (1996, p. 3) observes, vision is active and searching: 'We look; smells and sounds come to us.' Visual perception is highly complex, relying on distance, colour, shape, textural and contrast gradients, etc.
- *Hearing*: While visual space involves what lies before us and concerns objects in space, 'acoustic' space is all-surrounding, has no obvious boundaries, and emphasises space itself (Porteous, 1996, p. 33). Hearing is information poor, but emotionally rich. We are strongly aroused by, for example, screams, music, thunder, and soothed by the flow of water or the wind in the leaves (Porteous, 1996, p. 35).
- *Smell*: As with hearing, the human sense of smell is not well developed. Nevertheless, while even more information poor than sound, smell is probably emotionally richer.
- *Touch*: In the urban context, as Porteous (1996, p. 36) notes, much of our experience of texture comes through our feet, and through our buttocks when we sit down, rather than through our hands.

These sensory stimuli are usually perceived and appreciated as an interconnected whole. The individual dimensions can only be separated out by deliberate actions (closing one's eyes, blocking one's nose or ears) or by selective attention. While vision is the dominant sense, the urban environment is not only perceived visually. Bacon (1974, p. 20), for example, argued that the 'changing visual picture' was 'only the beginning of the sensory experience; the changes from light to shade, from hot to cold, from noise to silence, the flow of smells associated with open spaces, and the tactile quality of the surface under foot, are all important in the cumulative effect'.

Although contributing to the richness of experience, non-visual dimensions of sensation and perception are often underdeveloped and underexploited. Lang argues that concern for the 'sonic environment' should – in specific settings – focus on increasing the positive, e.g. birdsong, children's voices, the crunching of autumn leaves. He argues that an environment's 'soundscape' 'can be orchestrated in much the same way as its visual qualities by the choice of materials used for the surfaces of the environment and the nature of objects within it' (1994, p. 227). Positive sounds – waterfalls, fountains, etc. – can mask negative sounds like traffic noise.

Perception (sometimes, confusingly referred to as 'cognition') concerns more than just seeing or sensing the urban environment. It refers to the more complex processing or understanding of stimuli. Ittelson (1978, from Bell *et al.*, 1990, p. 29) identifies four dimensions of perception, which operate simultaneously:

- *Cognitive*: involves thinking about, organising and keeping information. In essence, it enables us to *make sense* of the environment.
- *Affective*: involves our feelings, which influence perception of the environment – equally, perception of the environment influences our feelings.
- *Interpretative*: encompasses meaning or associations derived from the environment. In interpreting information, we rely on memory for points of comparison with newly experienced stimuli.
- *Evaluative*: incorporates values and preferences and the determination of 'good' or 'bad'.

The 'environment' can be considered as a mental construct, an environmental image, created and valued differently by each individual. Images are the result of processes through which personal experiences and values filter the barrage of environmental stimuli. For Kevin Lynch (1960, p. 6) environmental images resulted from a two-way process in which the environment suggested distinctions and relations, from which observers selected, organised, and endowed with meaning what they saw. Similarly, Montgomery (1998, p. 100) distinguished between 'identity', what a place is actually like, and 'image', a combination of this identity with perception of the place by the individual with their own set of feelings about, and impressions of, it. Pocock and Hudson (1978, p. 33) suggest that the overall mental image of an urban environment will be:

- *Partial*: not covering the whole city;
- *Simplified*: omitting a great deal of information;
- *Idiosyncratic*: every individual's urban image being unique;
- *Distorted*: based on subjective, rather than real, distance and direction.

Relph (1976, p. 106) argues that environmental images are 'not just selective abstractions of an objective reality but are intentional interpretations of what is or what is not believed to be'. As is discussed later, this is the basis of 'intentionality' and 'phenomenology'.

Rather than being simply a biological process, perception is also socially and culturally 'learnt'. While sensations may be similar for everyone, how individuals filter, react to, organise and value those sensations differs. Differences in environmental perception depend on factors such as age, gender, ethnicity, lifestyle, length of residence in an area, and on the physical, social and cultural environment in which a person lives and was raised. Despite everyone effectively living in their 'own world', similarities in socialisation, past experience and the present urban environment mean that certain aspects of imagery will be held in common by large groups of people (Knox and Pinch, 2000, p. 295). Mental 'maps' and images of places and environments, particularly shared images, are central to studies of environmental perception in urban design.

The key work in the field of urban imagery is Kevin Lynch's *The Image of the City* (1960) based on cognitive (mental) mapping techniques, and interviews with residents of Boston, Jersey City and Los Angeles. Initially interested in legibility (how people orientate themselves and navigate within cities), Lynch argued that the ease with which we mentally organise the environment into a coherent pattern or 'image' relates to our ability to navigate through it. A clear image enables one to 'move about easily and quickly', and an 'ordered environment' can 'serve as a broad frame of reference, an organiser of activity or belief or knowledge' (p. 4).

Through his research, Lynch found that the minor theme of city orientation grew into the major theme of the city's mental image. Observation of cities with districts, landmarks and pathways that were easily identifiable and easily grouped into an overall pattern, led to the definition of what Lynch called 'imageability', 'that quality in a physical object which gives it a high probability of evoking a strong image in any given observer' (p. 9). Although aware that images could vary significantly between different observers, Lynch sought to identify the city's public, collective image, or its key components.

He argued that 'workable' environmental images required three attributes:

- *Identity*: an object's distinction from other things, as a separable entity (e.g. a door);
- *Structure*: the object's spatial relation to the observer and other objects (e.g. the door's position);
- *Meaning*: the object's meaning (practical and/or emotional) for the observer (e.g. the door as a hole for getting out) (p. 8).

Since meaning was less likely to be consistent at the city level and across disparate groups of people, Lynch separated meaning from form, exploring imageability in terms of physical qualities relating to identity and structure. Through mental mapping (cognitive geography) exercises, he aimed to identify aspects of the environment that left a strong image in observers' minds. Aggregation of individual images would define a public or city image. From his research, Lynch derived five key physical elements:

1. *Paths*: Paths are the channels along which observers move (streets, transit lines, canals, etc.). Lynch noted that paths were often the predominant elements in people's images, with other elements arranged and related along them. Where major paths lacked identity or were easily confused with each other, the whole image would be less clear. Paths could be important features in city images for several reasons, including regular use, concentration of special uses, characteristic spatial qualities,

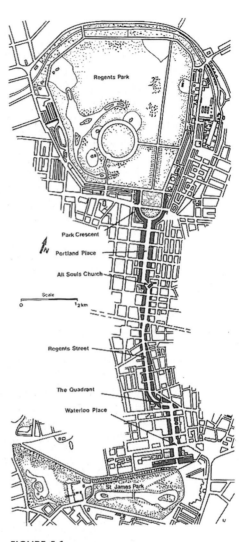

FIGURE 5.1
Certain paths are significant in supporting clear mental maps of cities or parts of cities. The mental maps of Londoners locate various other parts of London – such as The Mall, Piccadilly Circus, and Oxford Street – in relation to Regent Street (source: Moughtin, 1992, p. 163)

façade characteristics, proximity to special features in the city, visual prominence, or by virtue of their position in the overall path structure or topography (Figure 5.1).

2. *Edges*: Edges are linear elements that are either not used or considered as paths and often form boundaries between areas or linear breaks in continuity (e.g. shores, railroad cuts, edges of development, walls). As Lynch (p. 47) notes:

'edges may be barriers, more or less penetrable, which close one region off from another; or they may be seams, lines along which two regions are related and joined together'. The strongest edges are visually prominent, continuous in form, and often impenetrable to cross movement. Edges are important organising features, particularly when they hold together generalised areas, as in the outline of a city by water or a wall. Most cities have very clearly identified edges. The image of Istanbul, for example, is structured by the River Bosphorus which forms an edge for both the European and Asian sides of the city. Water forms an important edge for many cities located on coasts (e.g. Chicago, Hong Kong, Stockholm) or rivers (e.g. Paris, London, Budapest).

3. *Districts*: Districts are the medium-to-large parts of a city which observers mentally 'enter', and/or which have the identifying physical character of 'thematic continuities' in terms of texture, space, form, detail, symbol, uses, inhabitants, maintenance, topography, etc. (p. 47). Given some distinctive elements, but not enough to create a 'full thematic unit', a district will be recognisable as such only to someone familiar with the city. Reinforcement of clues may be needed to produce a stronger image. Districts may have hard, precise boundaries, or soft uncertain ones gradually fading away into surrounding areas (Figure 5.2).

4. *Nodes*: Nodes are point references: 'the strategic spots in a city into which an observer can enter, and which are the intensive foci to and from which [s/he] is travelling' (p. 47). Nodes may be primarily junctions, or simply 'thematic concentrations' of a particular use or physical character. As decisions are made and attention heightened, junctions and changes of travel mode make nodes more significant. Dominant nodes, however, tend to be both 'concentrations' and 'junctions', with both functional and physical significance, for example, public squares. While not essential, distinctive physical form is more likely to make the node more memorable (pp. 72–6).

5. *Landmarks*: Landmarks are point-references external to the observer. Some – towers, spires, hills – are distant, typically seen from many angles and distances over the tops of smaller elements. Others – sculpture, signs, trees – are local, visible in restricted localities and from certain approaches. Landmarks with a clear

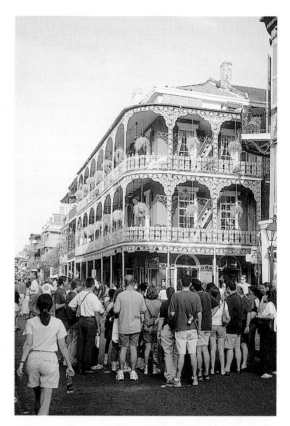

FIGURE 5.2
New Orleans' French Quarter has a strong identity as a district

form contrasting with their background, and a prominent spatial location, are more easily identifiable and likely to be significant to the observer. Lynch (pp. 78–9) argued that a landmark's key physical characteristic was 'singularity': 'some aspect that is unique or memorable in the context', and that 'spatial prominence' can establish elements as landmarks by making them visible from many locations and/or creating contrast with nearby elements. How an environment is used may also strengthen a landmark's significance: for example, its location at a junction involving path decisions (Figures 5.3 and 5.4).

None of Lynch's elements exists in isolation: all combine to provide the overall image: 'districts are structured with nodes, defined by edges, penetrated by paths, and sprinkled with landmarks . . . elements regularly overlap and pierce one another'

FIGURE 5.3
Whatever one thinks of its design, the prominently sited Haas Haus in central Vienna (Austria) provides a notable local landmark

FIGURE 5.4
The Grand Arch at La Defense, Paris, provides a powerful distant landmark that can be seen across the city

(pp. 48–9). Sets of images often overlap and inter-relate in a series of levels reflecting the scale of the area. Thus, observers move as necessary from images at street level to those of the neighbourhood, the city and beyond.

BEYOND THE IMAGE OF THE CITY

Lynch's original study, based on a small sample of people, has been replicated in various contexts. Lynch (1984, p. 249) argued that in 'every case' the basic ideas held, 'with the important proviso that images are much modified by culture and familiarity'. He noted that basic elements of the city image 'seem astonishingly similar in some very diverse cultures and places. We were lucky.' From various studies in the Lynch tradition, there is a wealth of information about the way different groups in different places structure their city images. De Jonge (1962), for example, found that Amsterdam was more legible to its inhabitants than were Rotterdam and The Hague to theirs. Comparing Milan and Rome, Francescato and Mebane (1973) found that, while both cities were highly legible, they were legible in different ways. The mental maps of the Milanese were structured by a clearly connected set of paths relating to their city's radial street pattern, whereas Romans' mental maps exhibited a greater diversity of content and tended to be structured around the landmarks and edges associated with the city's historic buildings, its hills and the River Tiber.

Some work has been highly critical of Lynch's findings and methods. To some extent this is unfair, because Lynch explicitly offered it as a 'first initial sketch'. Three areas of criticism are of particular note:

1. *Observer variation:* The validity of aggregating the environmental images of people with different backgrounds and experience has been questioned. While finding that common city images could be identified, arising from common human cognition strategies, culture, experience and city form, Lynch (1984, p. 251) acknowledged the 'deliberate and explicit' neglect of observer variation in his original study. Francescate and Mebane's study of Milan and Rome (1973) and Appleyard's study of Ciudad Guyana (1976), showed how, as a result of social class and habitual use, people's city images differed.

2. *Legibility and imageability*: In *Good City Form*, Lynch (1981, pp. 139–41) reduced the emphasis on legibility, seeing it as one kind of 'sense' within just one dimension of city experience. Further downplaying its significance in 'Reconsidering *The Image of the City*', he accepted way-finding as a 'secondary problem for most people', 'If lost in a city, one can always ask the way or consult a map' (Lynch, 1984, p. 250). He questioned the value of legible environments: 'What do people care if they have a vivid image of their locality? And aren't they delighted by surprise and mystery' (p. 250). This raised the issue (discussed below) of the distinction between environments that are imageable and those that are liked. De Jonge's (1962) study in Holland suggested that people liked 'illegible' environments, while Kaplan and Kaplan (1982) highlighted the need for environmental 'surprise' and 'mystery' (see Chapter 7).

3. *Meaning and symbolism*: It has also been argued that attention should be paid to what the urban environment meant to people, and how they felt about it (the 'affective' dimension), as well as to the structuring of mental images. Cognitive mapping techniques tend to neglect those issues. Appleyard (1980) extended Lynch's work by identifying four ways in which buildings and other elements in the urban environment were known:
   - by their imageability or distinctiveness of form;
   - by their visibility as people move around the city;
   - by their role as a setting for activity;
   - by the significance of a building's role in society.

Gottdiener and Lagopoulos (1986, p. 7) argued that, in the Lynchian tradition, 'signification' – the process whereby places, people and things are given representational meaning – is reduced to a perceptual knowledge of physical form, at the expense of the important elements, such as the 'meaning' of an environment and whether people liked it or not. Although he had sought to set aside issues of meaning, Lynch (1984, p. 252) considered that they had 'always' crept in because 'people could not help connecting their surroundings with the rest of their lives'. The conclusion was drawn that the social and emotional meanings attached to, or evoked by, the elements of the urban environment were at least as important –

often more so – than the structural and physical aspects of people's imagery (Knox and Pinch, 2000, p. 302). Environments could be memorable or forgettable, liked or disliked: Lynch's method tended only to record the first options. Issues of meaning and symbolism are in fact important components of environmental images.

ENVIRONMENTAL MEANING AND SYMBOLISM

All urban environments contain symbols, meanings and values. The study of 'signs' and their meanings is known as semiology or semiotics. As Eco (1968, pp. 56–7) explains, semiotics studies '*all* cultural phenomena *as* if they were systems of signs'. The world is replete with 'signs', interpreted and understood as a function of society, culture and ideology. Following Ferdinand de Saussure, the process of creating meaning is called 'signification': 'signifieds' are what are referred to, 'signifiers' are the things that refer to them, and 'signs' establish the association between them. A sign represents something else: in a language, for example, a word represents a concept. Different types of sign are identified:

- *Iconic signs*: have a direct similarity with the object, e.g. a portrait represents the sitter;
- *Indexical signs*: have a material relationship with the object, e.g. smoke indicates fire;
- *Symbolic signs*: have a more arbitrary relationship with the object, and are essentially constructed through social and cultural systems, e.g. classical columns represent 'grandeur' (from Lane, 2000, p. 111).

Just as the words of a formally codified language have agreed-upon meanings, the meaning of non-verbal signs also arises from social and cultural conventions. There is greater flexibility, however, in interpreting the latter. As society changes, so does signification. Meanings attached to the built environment become modified as social values evolve in response to changing patterns of socio-economic organisation and lifestyles (Knox, 1984, p. 112).

A key idea in semiotics is the layering of meaning. The first layer or 'first-order' sign is that of *denotation*, meaning the object's 'primary function' or the function it makes possible (Eco, 1968). The 'second-order' sign or 'secondary function' is that

of *connotation*, and is of a symbolic nature. Layering enables distinction to be made between the use of objects for their immediate function, and the socially sustained understanding of them. Thus, structures or building elements have second-order, connotative, meaning: for example, a porch (primary function, providing shelter from the weather) made of Italian marble with Doric columns, connotes a different 'symbolic function' or meaning from one made of roughly sawn timber (Figure 5.5).

Eco shows that the secondary function can be more important than the primary one. For example, a chair denotes the function of being able to sit down. If it is a throne, however, it should be sat on with a certain dignity. The connotation can become so functionally important as to distort the basic function: in connoting 'regalness', a throne 'often demands that the person sitting on it sits rigidly and uncomfortably . . . and therefore seats one "poorly" with respect to the primary *utilitas*' (1968, p. 64). The second-order meaning enables differentiation to be made between objects. It can thereby stimulate consumption: commodities consist of more than their material qualities, we also consume the 'idea' of them and what they will allow us to become. The 'idea' can become more important than the commodity itself – rather than selling houses, for example, developers sell images of desirable 'lifestyles' (Dovey, 1999). Economic and commercial forces are, therefore, highly influential in creating the symbolism of the built environment.

Because meanings in environments and landscapes are both interpreted and produced, there is debate about the extent to which meaning resides in the object or in the mind of the beholder. It is clear that certain elements have relatively stable meanings to most people. Knox and Pinch (2000, p. 273) note the difference between 'intended' messages sent by owners/producers via architects, planners, etc., and the 'received' messages of 'environmental consumers'. The 'gap' between the intended and the perceived meaning of architecture and architectural symbolism can be related to Barthes' (1968) discussion of the 'death of the author' – that is, the figurative death of those authors who proposed a system of meaning based upon 'mimesis' – the belief that an image, word or object (or work of architecture) carries a fixed message determined by the author (architect, sponsor). For Barthes, the reader inexorably constructs a new text in the act of reading. Thus,

FIGURE 5.5
Seaside, Florida, USA. In their ideas and claims, New Urbanists are often accused of architectural determinism. Huxtable (1997, p. 42), for example, contends that the New Urbanist developments are based on a 'past ideal of community', which has become part of the 'mythology of the American dream'. She argues that by reducing 'the definition of community to a romantic social aesthetic emphasising front porches, historic styles, and walking distance to stores and schools as an answer to suburban sprawl . . . they have avoided the questions of urbanisation to become part of the problem' (Huxtable, 1997, p. 42). Nevertheless, while the porches may symbolise or connote 'community', they also have a practical function (i.e. a use value) which may – or, equally, may not – assist the creation of contacts between neighbours (see Chapter 6)

reading an environment involves understanding how it comes to mean different things to different people and how meanings change. Accordingly, much of the built environment's social meaning depends on the *audience*, and on the concepts of 'audience' held by developers, architects and managers of the built environment (Knox, 1984, p. 112) (see Figure 5.6).

The symbolic role of buildings and environments is a key part of the relationship between society and environment. Much attention has focused on how environments represent, communicate and embody patterns of power and dominance. According to Lasswell (1979, from Knox, 1987, p. 367), the 'signature of power' is manifested in two ways: through 'strategies of awe', which 'intimidate' the audience with 'majestic displays of power', and through 'strategies of admiration', which 'divert' the audience with 'spectacular' design effects. While, as Knox (1984, p. 110) argues, the source of this symbolisation has changed over time – from royalty and aristocracy, through industrial capital, to present-

day 'big government' and 'big business' – the purpose has always been the same: 'to legitimise a particular ideology or power system by providing a physical focus to which sentiments could be attached'. As it may not always be desirable to display power, symbolism may 'involve "modest" or "low profile" architectural motifs; or carry deliberately misleading messages for the purposes of maintaining social harmony' (Knox, 1987, p. 367). There may, however, be competing associations and interpretations: for some, large office blocks symbolise financial strength and influence; for others they symbolise 'corporate greed' (Knox and Pinch, 2000, p. 55). Political and economic power is not the only message conveyed, as elements of counter-ideology generate their own symbolic structures and environments. The symbolic content of the contemporary built environment is multi-layered and often ambiguous.

All manmade environments symbolise the power to make or change the environment. Knox (1984, p. 107) argues that the built environment is not

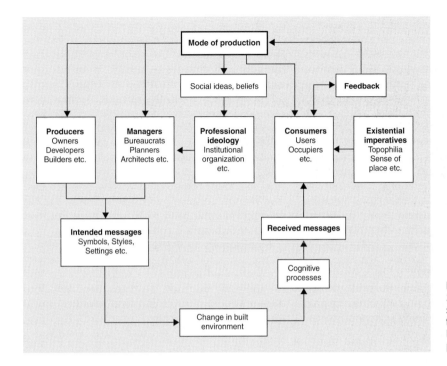

FIGURE 5.6
Signs, symbols and
settings: A framework
for analysis (source:
Knox and Pinch, 2000,
p. 273)

simply an expression of the power exerted at different times by individuals, groups and governments, but also a means by which the prevailing system of power is maintained. Dovey (1999, p. 2) observes how: 'The more that the structures and the presentations of power can be embedded in the framework of everyday life, the less questionable they become and the more effectively they can work.' He argues that: 'the exercise of power is slippery and ever-changing. Power naturalises and camouflages itself, chameleon-like within its context. The choice of the mask is a dimension of power' (p. 16). At other times, the expression of power is more overt. Indeed, many totalitarian or imperial/colonial regimes have used the built environment to symbolise political power (see Saoud, 1995).

Acknowledging the impact of symbolism in the built environment, architectural Modernists rejected its display in the form of applied ornament or decoration. As Ward (1997, p. 21) argues, Modernist buildings were to carry no associations beyond their own 'magnificent declaration of modernity'. Their universally applicable 'modern style' transcended national and local cultures, and was capable of reproduction anywhere – Hitchcock and Johnson (1922) introduced it to America as 'The International Style'.

However, in rejecting one form of symbolism, Modernists were unable to avoid it altogether. All elements of the built environment are inescapably symbols. In his highly influential book, *Complexity and Contradiction in Architecture* (1966), Robert Venturi challenged the minimalism and elitism of the International Style, and the role of symbolism and meaning in Modernist architecture. In their-subsequent book, *Learning from Las Vegas*, Venturi *et al.* (1972) identified three ways of externally expressing a building's function or meaning:

- *the 'Las Vegas way'*: placing a 'Big Sign' in front of a 'Little Building';
- *the 'decorated shed'*: designing an efficient building, and covering the façade with signs;
- *the 'duck'*: making the building's overall form express or symbolise its function (i.e. an iconic sign).

Venturi *et al.*, point out that while most pre-twentieth century buildings were decorated sheds, Modernist buildings, designed to express their internal functions, were ducks (see Chapter 4). Influenced by Venturi's arguments, new 'postmodern' ideas about architecture emerged, emphasising stylistic pluralism and scenographic, decorative and contextual properties with architects exploring the variety of ways in which people gain meanings from the environment. From the 1970s onwards, there was a greater interest in and use of architectural symbolism. Thus many postmodern buildings are collages of different visual styles, languages or codes, and make allusions to popular culture, technology, local traditions and context.

In contrast to Modernism's 'univalent' single, universal meaning, Jencks (1987) argued that postmodernism was 'multivalent', open to many different meanings and interpretations. This shift has elicited much debate in the architectural literature.

Because it uses pre-existing forms of explicit symbolism, much postmodern architecture is characterised as 'historicist'. Jameson (1984) suggested a two-part categorisation: 'parody', the mimicry of old styles, which, Ward (1997, p. 24) suggests, has a critical edge and 'mocks rather than merely plunders from tradition'; and 'pastiche', a 'neutral practice' possessing none of 'parody's ulterior motives', but instead being 'speech in a dead language' (Jameson, 1984, p. 65). Jencks (1987) distinguished between 'straight revivalism' – problematic because it simply repeated rather than challenged tradition – and 'radical eclecticism', the ironic mixing of styles and references expressing a more critical attitude to tradition and architecture (Ward, 1997, pp. 23–4). While the historicist influence can be ironic or earnest, Doug Davis (1987, p. 21, from Ellin, 1999, p. 160) argues that, in ignoring the ideological or religious implications of the periods quoted, supposedly historicist architects and urbanists are, in fact, anti-historicist: 'they prefer history-as-arcadian-symbol, not history-as-reality'.

THE CONSTRUCTION OF PLACE

Having discussed environmental perception/cognition and the generation of meaning in the urban environment, the second part of this chapter discusses one kind of meaning that is particularly important in urban design – that of 'sense of place'. Sense of place is often discussed in terms of the Latin concept of 'genius loci', which suggests that people experience something beyond the physical or sensory properties of places, and can feel an attachment to a spirit of place (Jackson, 1994, p. 157).

The genius loci or spirit of place often persists in spite of profound changes. Many cities and countries have retained their identities in the face of significant social, cultural and technological change (Dubos, 1972, p. 7, from Relph, 1976, p. 98). For Relph (1976, p. 99), the spirit of place retained through such changes is 'subtle', 'nebulous', not easily analysed in 'formal and conceptual terms', but nonetheless 'extremely obvious'. From a more commercial perspective, Sircus (2001, p. 31) likens the sense or spirit of place to a brand that connotes certain expectations of quality, consistency and reliability: 'Every place is potentially a brand. In every way as much as Disneyland and Las Vegas, cities like Paris, Edinburgh and New York are their own brands, because a consistent, clear image has emerged of what each place looks, feels like, and the story or history it conveys.'

Montgomery (1998, p. 94) highlights the nub of the issue for urban designers: it is relatively straightforward to think of a successful place, and to experience it as such; it is much more difficult to discern why it is successful, and whether similar success can be generated elsewhere. The next section discusses the sense of place. Providing a wider frame of reference, the final sections discuss the concept of placelessness and the phenomenon of 'invented' places.

Sense of place

The period since the 1970s has seen increasing interest in examination of people's ties to, and conceptions of, places. This has often drawn on 'phenomenology', which, based on Edmund Husserl's notion of 'intentionality', aims to describe and understand phenomena as experiences wherein human consciousness takes in 'information' and makes it into 'the world' (Pepper, 1984, p. 120). Thus, while the meanings of places are rooted in their physical setting and activities, they are not a property of them, but of 'human intentions and experiences' (Relph, 1976, p. 47). Hence, what 'the environment' represents is a function of our own subjective construction of it.

Dovey (1999, p. 44) sees phenomenology as a 'necessary but limited' approach to the understanding of place, since the focus on the lived-in experience involves a 'certain blindness' to the effects of social structure and ideology on everyday experience. Jurgen Habermas makes a useful distinction between the 'life-world', the everyday world of place experience, social integration and 'communicative action' and the 'system', the social and economic structures of the state and the market (Dovey, 1999, pp. 51–2). Phenomenology tends to focus on the former to the exclusion of the latter.

Edward Relph's *Place and Placelessness* (1976) was one of the earliest works drawing on phenomenology and focused on the psychological and experiential 'sense of place'. Relph (1976, p. 8) argued that, however 'amorphous' and 'intangible', whenever we feel or know space, it is typically associated with a concept of 'place'. For Relph, places were essentially centres of meaning constructed out of lived-experience. By imbuing them with meaning, individuals, groups or societies change 'spaces' into 'places': for example, as the epicentre of the Velvet Revolution, Wenceslas Square is particularly meaningful to the citizens of Prague.

Concepts of 'place' often emphasise the importance of a sense of 'belonging', of emotional attachment to place (see Chapter 6). Place can be considered in terms of 'rootedness' and a conscious sense of association or identity with a particular place. Rootedness refers to a generally unconscious sense of place: Arefi (1999, p. 184) suggests it is 'the most natural, pristine, unmediated kind of people-place tie'. For Relph (1976, p. 38) it meant having 'a secure point from which to look out on the world, a firm grasp of one's own position in the order of things, and a significant spiritual and psychological attachment to somewhere in particular'.

It is often argued that people need a sense of identity, of belonging to a specific territory and/or group. Crang (1998, p. 103) suggested that 'places provide an anchor of shared experiences between people and continuity over time'. Individuals need to express a sense of belonging to a collective entity or place, and of individual identity, which may be achieved by physical separation or distinctiveness, and/or a sense of entering into a particular area. Design strategies can emphasise these themes (see Chapter 6). Norberg-Schulz (1971, p. 25) argued that 'to be inside' was 'the primary intention behind the place concept'. Similarly, for Relph (1976, pp. 111–12) the 'essence of place' lay in the, occasionally unconscious, experience of an 'inside' as distinct from an 'outside'. He distinguished types of place-identity based on notions of 'insiders' and 'outsiders' (see Box 5.1).

Territoriality and personalisation

The concept of inside–outside is most easily understood in terms of 'territoriality', people's definition and defence of themselves – physically and psychologically – by the creation of a bounded, often

---

BOX 5.1 – TYPES OF IDENTITY OF PLACE

(source: adapted from Relph, 1976, pp. 111–12)

Existential insideness	Where place is lived and dynamic, full with known meanings and experienced without reflection.
Empathetic insideness	Where place records and expresses the cultural values and experiences of those who create and live in it.
Behavioural insideness	Where place is an ambient environment possessing qualities of landscape or townscape that constitute a primary basis for public or consensus knowledge of that place.
Incidental outsideness	Where the selected functions of a place are what is important, and its identity is little more than the background for those functions.
Objective outsider	Where place is effectively reduced either to the single dimension of location, or to a space of located objects and activities.
Mass identity of place	Where an identity is provided more or less ready-made by the mass media, and remote from direct experience. It is a superficial and manipulated identity, which undermines both individual experiences and the symbolic properties of the identity of place.
Existential outsideness	Where identity of place represents a lost and now unattainable involvement; places are always incidental, for existence itself is incidental.

exclusive, domain (Ardrey, 1967). Suggesting that people structure groups and define each other by distinguishing between 'insiders' and 'outsiders', territoriality is frequently the basis for the 'development of distinctive social milieus' that 'mould the attitudes and shape the behaviour of their inhabitants' (Knox and Pinch, 2000, pp. 8–9).

Individual identity is associated with 'personalisation', the putting of a distinctive stamp on one's environment. Typically this occurs at, and makes explicit, the threshold or transition between public (group) and private (individual) domains, where small-scale design details contribute to the symbolism or delimitation of space. Personalisation of private space expresses tastes and values, and has little outside impact. Personalisation of elements visible from the public realm communicates these tastes to the wider community. Although generally designed and built by someone else, individuals adapt and modify their given environment – rearranging furniture, changing the decoration, planting the garden.

Von Meiss (1990, p. 162) identified three design strategies to assist a sense of identity for people and groups:

- Creation of an environment responsive to, and based on, designers' deep understanding of the values and behaviour of the people and groups concerned, and the environmental features crucial to their identity. This requires recognition of difficulties posed by the designer–user gap (see Chapter 12).
- Participation of future users in the design of their environment. This, too, requires understanding of the designer–user gap.
- Creation of environments that users can modify and adapt. Herman Hertzberger (from Von Meiss, 1990, p. 162) advocated an 'architecture of hospitality' reconciling mass production with our need for individual identity. This involves issues of robustness, and of the differing time frames of change for relatively permanent, and for shorter-term, urban environmental elements (see Chapter 9). It also demands that the potential for group and individual personalisation be considered within the design process (see Bentley *et al.*, 1985, pp. 99–105).

Personal or group engagement with space gives it meaning as 'place', at least to the extent of differentiating it from other places. Sense of place is, however, more than this. Lynch (1960, p. 6) defines 'identity of place' simply as that which provides 'individuality or distinction from other places . . . the basis for its recognition as a separable entity'. For Relph (1976, p. 45) this merely acknowledges that each place has a 'unique address', without explaining *how* it becomes identifiable. He argues that 'physical setting', 'activities', and 'meanings' constitute the three basic elements of the identity of places. Sense of place does not, however, reside in these elements but in the human interaction with these elements. The Dutch architect Aldo Van Eyck emphasised this in his famous description of place: 'Whatever space and time mean, place and occasion mean more. For space in the image of man is place, and time in the image of man is occasion.' The impact of occasion on place is dramatically demonstrated by contrasting a sports stadium full of people at a sporting event, with the same stadium empty (Lawson, 2001, p. 23).

Drawing on Relph's work, Canter (1977) saw places as functions of 'activities' plus 'physical attributes' plus 'conceptions'. Building on Relph and Canter's ideas, Punter (1991) and Montgomery (1998) located the components of a sense of place within urban design thought (Figure 5.7). These diagrams illustrate how urban design actions can contribute to and enhance sense of place.

Any individual's conception of place will have its own variation of Relph's components. The significance of the physicality of places is often overstated: activities and meanings may be as, or more, important in creating a sense of place. Jackson (1994, pp. 158–9) makes the general observation that sense of place in Europe is grounded more in the physicality of space than in America, arguing that 'the average American still associates a sense of place not so much with architecture or a monument or a designed space, as with some event, some daily or weekly or seasonal occurrence which we look forward to or remember and which we share with others'. Seen from a temporal perspective, the physical dimensions of places are most salient in the short-term, being displaced in the longer-term by sociocultural dimensions.

Successful places typically have animation and vitality, an 'urban buzz'. Jacobs (1961) argued that bringing people onto the street created animation and vitality:

we may fancifully call it the art form of the city and liken it to a dance – not to a simple-minded

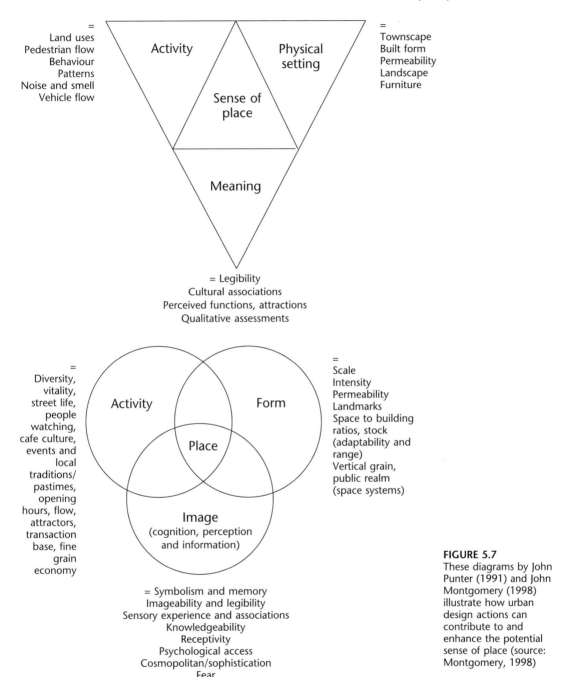

= Land uses
Pedestrian flow
Behaviour
Patterns
Noise and smell
Vehicle flow

Activity

Physical setting

Sense of place

= Townscape
Built form
Permeability
Landscape
Furniture

Meaning

= Legibility
Cultural associations
Perceived functions, attractions
Qualitative assessments

= Diversity,
vitality,
street life,
people
watching,
cafe culture,
events and
local
traditions/
pastimes,
opening
hours, flow,
attractors,
transaction
base, fine
grain
economy

Activity

Form

Place

= Scale
Intensity
Permeability
Landmarks
Space to building
ratios, stock
(adaptability and
range)
Vertical grain,
public realm
(space systems)

Image
(cognition, perception
and information)

= Symbolism and memory
Imageability and legibility
Sensory experience and associations
Knowledgeability
Receptivity
Psychological access
Cosmopolitan/sophistication
Fear

FIGURE 5.7
These diagrams by John Punter (1991) and John Montgomery (1998) illustrate how urban design actions can contribute to and enhance the potential sense of place (source: Montgomery, 1998)

precision dance with everyone kicking up at the same time, twirling in unison and bowing off en masse, but to an intricate ballet in which individual dancers and ensembles all have distinctive parts which miraculously reinforce one another and compose an orderly whole.

Successful public spaces are characterised by the presence of people, in an often self-reinforcing process. Public spaces are essentially discretionary environments: people have to use them and conceivably could choose to go elsewhere. If they are to become peopled and animated, they must offer what people want, in an attractive and safe environment. The Project for Public Space (1999) identified four key attributes of successful places: comfort and image; access and linkage; uses and activity; and sociability (see Table 5.1).

For Montgomery (1998, p. 99), the key to a successful public realm is the 'transaction base', which should be 'as complex as possible', 'without a transaction base of economic activity at many different levels and layers, it will not be possible to create a good urban place'. As not all transactions are economic, urban areas and cities must also provide space for social and cultural transactions. Montgomery lists a number of key indicators of vitality:

- The extent of variety in primary land uses, including residential;
- The proportion of locally owned or independent businesses, particularly shops;
- Patterns of opening hours, and the existence of evening and night-time activity;

- The presence, size and specialisms of street markets;
- Availability of cinemas, theatres, wine bars, pubs, restaurants and other cultural/meeting places, offering service of different kinds, prices and quality;
- Availability of spaces, including gardens, squares and corners, enabling people-watching and activities such as cultural animation programmes;
- Patterns of mixed land use enabling self-improvement and small-scale investment in property;
- Availability of differing unit sizes and costs of property;
- The degree of innovation and confidence in new architecture, providing a variety of building types, styles and designs;
- The presence of an active street life and street frontages.

TABLE 5.1
Key attributes of successful places

KEY ATTRIBUTES	INTANGIBLES		MEASUREMENTS
COMFORT AND IMAGE	safety charm history attractiveness spirituality	sittability walkability greenness cleanliness	crime statistics sanitation rating building conditions environmental data
ACCESS AND LINKAGE	readability walkability reliability continuity	proximity connectedness convenience accessibility	traffic data mode split transit usage pedestrian activity parking usage patterns
USES AND ACTIVITY	realness sustainability specialness uniqueness affordability fun	activity usefulness celebration vitality indigenousness 'homegrown' quality	property values rent levels land-use patterns retail sales local business ownership
SOCIABILITY	co-operation neighbourliness stewardship pride welcoming	gossip diversity storytelling friendliness interactivity	street life social networks evening use volunteerism number of women, children and elderly

(Source: adapted from Project for Public Space, 1999).

While urban designers cannot make places in any simplistic or deterministic manner, they can increase 'place potential' – the likelihood that people will consider the space a significant and meaningful place. The social and functional dimensions of place are discussed in Chapters 6 and 8.

Placelessness

Whereas constituting a sense of place tends to be associated with something of intrinsic value, placelessness is generally viewed negatively. Gertrude Stein's dismissal of Oakland, 'There's no there there', aptly captures this. Nonetheless, appreciation of the concept of 'placelessness' can provide a frame of reference for urban design. Relph (1976, p. ii) considered investigation of place 'unrealistic' without consideration of 'placelessness', which he defined as the 'casual eradication of distinctive places' and the 'making of standardised landscapes'.

Placelessness tends to signify absence or loss of meaning. Embedded within a 'narrative of loss' (e.g. Arefi, 1999; Banerjee, 2001), there has been growing concern about its consequences. Various factors are considered to contribute to the contemporary phenomenon of placelessness, including the market and regulatory approaches (see Chapters 3, 10 and 11). Three interrelated processes will be discussed here: globalisation; the emergence of mass culture; and the loss of the social and cultural relations embedded in specific places/territories.

(i) Globalisation
Many trends towards homogenisation of, and loss of, meaning in places relate to processes of globalisation and the creation of global space, through improved communications (both physical and electronic). Globalisation is a multi-faceted process in which the world is becoming increasingly interconnected, with centralised decision-making exploiting economies of scale and standardisation. The changing, and problematising, of relationships between local and global has significant implications for what constitutes the meaning of place. Castells (1989, p. 6) described the effects of information technology in the creation of a 'space of flows' which 'dominates the historically constructed space of places'. For Zukin (1991, p. 15), there is a fundamental tension between 'global capital' that can move and 'local community' that cannot, while Harvey (1997, p. 20) observes that capital is no longer concerned about place: 'Capital needs fewer workers and much of it

can move all over the world, deserting problematic places and populations at will.' The fate of local place is increasingly determined from afar, by anonymous and impersonal economic forces.

Globalisation has differing effects. Entrikin (1991) suggests two possible scenarios: 'convergence', where sameness through the standardisation of landscapes is emerging, and 'divergence' where disparate elements maintain cultural and spatial distinctiveness. The situation is perhaps more complex: King (2000, p. 23) argues that because it is embedded in local context, urban design is 'torn between the representation, and even celebration, of the global and the enhancement and often rescue of the local'. He further notes how global trade depends on 'the riches of local culture that it threatens to commercialise, degrade, swamp, and eventually destroy' (King, 2000, p. 23). Dovey (1999, pp. 158–9), however, argues that, because local differences of urban culture are attractive to global marketing strategies, globalisation 'does not simply iron out differences between cities, it also stimulates them'.

(ii) Mass culture
With globalisation has come 'mass' culture, emerging from the processes of mass production, marketing and consumption, which homogenise and standardise cultures and places, transcending, crowding out, even destroying, local cultures. According to Crang (1998, p. 115), much of the worry over placelessness can be interpreted as fear that local, supposedly 'authentic' forms of culture – made from, and making, local distinctiveness – are being displaced by mass-produced commercial forms imposed on the locality. In Relph's (1976, p. 92) view, these 'are formulated by manufacturers, governments, and professional designers, and are guided and communicated through mass media. They are not developed and formulated by the people. Uniform products and places are created for people of supposedly uniform needs and tastes, or perhaps vice versa.'

(iii) Loss of (attachment to) territory
Placelessness is also a reaction to the loss, or absence, of environments we care about. Such deterritorialised places promote what Relph termed 'existential outsideness': because people do not feel they belong, they no longer care for their environment (Crang, 1998, p. 112). Auge (1995, p. 94) contrasts 'non-places' dominated by 'contractual solitariness' – where individuals or

small groups relate to wider society through specific, limited interactions – with 'places' where there is 'organic sociality', where people have long-term relationships and interactions serving more than immediate functional purposes.

In considering the development of a 'placeless' society, Meyrowitz (1985) highlighted the shift from cultures inhabiting specific areas, to a more mobile society. Mobility and communication technology have unprecedented implications for concepts of 'place' and 'community', as communities of 'interest' supplant place-based ones (see Chapter 6). Crang (1998, p. 114) suggests that few cultures today remain 'place-bound', and that past geographic links may have been due more to limitations of communications and transport than to any more fundamental connection. If this is the case, he concludes, 'loss of place' does not really matter.

The influence of theme parks and invented places is widespread and pervasive. The manufacture of 'places' and place values, drawing on the techniques of theme parks – usually to further the purposes of consumption – occurs in a variety of settings, including shopping malls, historic districts, urban entertainment districts, central city redevelopments and tourist destinations (see Relph, 1976; Zukin, 1991; Hannigan, 1998). Crang (1998, p. 126) argues that, while shopping malls may destroy sense of place through their 'replication of anonymous, universal patterns' and by isolating consumers from the outside world, many have specific place references in their design. West Edmonton Mall, for example, has parts themed on 'Old Orleans' and on simulated Parisian boulevards. It is nevertheless all manufactured and contrived, which, Shields (1989) suggests, actually creates a sense of 'elsewhereness'.

'Invented' places

One response to the standardisation of place is a deliberate 'manufacturing' of difference – in terms more specific to urban design, the 'invention', sometimes 'reinvention', of places. Crang (1998, pp. 116–17) notes an industry 'that sets out to "imagineer" places, to create "uniqueness" in order to attract attention, visitors and – in the end – money. Landscapes can be engineered, their culture commodified for financial gain. If places are becoming increasingly alike, the rewards for standing out are increasing.' Invented places spring from the creative minds of authors, artists, architects, designers and imaginers (Figure 5.8). 'Reinvented places' start from a basis in reality, but generally involve a significant degree of change, distortion and loss of authenticity (see below and Figure 9.1). For Sircus (2001, p. 30), Disneyland is the quintessential invented place:

It creates reality out of fantasy in ways that are often symbolic and subliminal; digging deep into the user's psyche, connecting with cross-cultural images and multi-generational, hard-wired memories. It is successful because it adheres to certain principles of sequential experience and storytelling, creating an appropriate and meaningful sense of place in which both activities and memories are individual and shared.

FIGURE 5.8
Universal Studio's *CityWalk,* Los Angeles (USA), is a quintessentially invented place

In their purest forms, invented places depend on a high degree of control – particularly of context – and on a certain scale of operation. Graham and Marvin (2001, p. 264) refer to the contemporary phenomenon of 'bundled' urban environments – 'invented street' systems within shopping malls, theme parks and urban resorts, often with strong tie-ins to leading transnationals (Disney, Time-Warner, Nike, etc.), to exploit merchandising spin-offs. Such developments cover increasingly large 'footprints' as developers attempt to bundle together the maximum number of 'synergistic' uses within single complexes – retailing, cinemas, IMAX screens, sports facilities, restaurants, hotels, entertainment facilities, casinos, simulated historic scenes, virtual reality complexes, museums, zoos, bowling alleys, artificial ski-slopes, etc.

In his book *Fantasy City: Pleasure and profit in the postmodern metropolis* (1998), John Hannigan discusses a particular kind of bundled or invented place – the urban entertainment destination (UED). He states that the typical UED or 'Fantasy City' is:

- theme-o-centre: 'everything from individual entertainment venues to the image of the city itself conforms to a scripted theme, normally drawn from sports, history or popular entertainment';
- 'aggressively branded': 'Urban entertainment destinations are not financed and marketed exclusively on the basis of their ability to deliver a high degree of consumer satisfaction and fun but also on their potential for selling licensed merchandise on site';
- open day and night, reflecting 'its intended market of "baby boomer" and "generation X" adults in search of leisure, sociability and entertainment';
- modular, 'mixing and matching an increasingly standard array of components in various configurations';
- solipsistic: 'isolated from surrounding neighbourhoods, physically, economically and socially';
- postmodern: 'insomuch as it is constructed around technologies of simulation, virtual reality and the thrill of the spectacle'.

While there has been much criticism of invented places (Harvey, 1989; Sorkin, 1992; Crawford, 1992; Boyer, 1992, 1993; Huxtable, 1997), they provide opportunities for urban design and the creation of people places. The concept, therefore, raises a number of urban design issues.

(i) Superficiality

There are various criticisms of the apparent superficiality and 'depthlessness' of much postmodern architecture and urban development. The attention postmodernism pays to place is (say some critics) superficial, undermining the real, or unique identity of places. Dovey (1999, p. 44) observes how the 'currency and intangibility' of 'sense of place' has been 'widely exploited by the market to legitimise design projects ... [but in so doing, it] ... is reduced to scenographic and rhetorical effect as a cover for place destruction'. Huxtable (1997, p. 3) complains that 'themed parodies pass for places ... even as real places with their full freight of art and memories are devalued and destroyed'.

Similarly, in his polemic introduction to *Variations on a Theme Park: The American City and the End of Public Space*, Sorkin (1992, p. xiii) argues that contemporary urban developments have replaced the 'anomaly and delight' of real places with 'a universal particular, a generic urbanism inflected only by appliqué', and that the profession of 'urban design' is almost wholly preoccupied with the 'creation of urbane disguises':

> Whether in its master incarnation at the ersatz Main Street of Disneyland, in the phoney history of a Rouse market place, or the gentrified architecture of the 'reborn' Lower East Side, this elaborate apparatus is at pains to assert its ties to the kind of city life it is in the process of obliterating ... The architecture of this city is almost purely semiotic, playing the game of grafted signification, theme-park building. Whether it represents generic historicity or generic modernity, such design is based on the same calculus as advertising, the idea of pure imageability, oblivious to the real needs and traditions of those who inhabit it. (p. xiv)

Crang (1998, pp. 116–17) comments on 'manufactured difference', which 'takes the form of façades placed over standardised substructures – designed to tone in with an area or to distinguish an otherwise ordinary building'. A significant implication of Venturi's 'decorated shed' was that a standard box could be 'wallpapered' to take on a variety of meanings. Dovey (1999, p. 34) notes how the 'detachment of form from social life' allows a 'commodification of meaning under the aesthetic guise of a revival of meaning'. Some see this 'superficiality' as a defining characteristic of postmodernism. Jameson (1984), for example, criticises the 'depthlessness' of postmodern architecture – indeed, of postmodern culture generally. In some respects, this becomes a form of architectural 'fetishism', which, Harvey (1989a, p. 77) suggests, involves a 'direct concern with surface appearances that conceal underlying meanings'.

(ii) Other-directedness – created from without rather than from within

As their symbolism tends to come from outside rather than 'inside', invented places are, in Relph's term, 'other-directed'. Rather than autonomous expressions of the local culture, meanings and place associations are 'outside inventions'. In Habermas' terms, they are instances of the system invading and colonising the life-world, whereby, as Dovey (1999, pp. 51–2) explains, 'places of everyday life become increasingly subject to the system imperatives of the market and its distorted communications, advertising and constructions of meaning'. Here, 'economic space' invades 'lived space', and the life-world is less an end in itself and increasingly becomes a means to the system's ends. This 'commodification of place', making its exchange value its primary quality, has attracted many comments (for example, Harvey, 1989; Zukin, 1991; Sorkin, 1992; Crawford, 1992; Boyer, 1992, 1993; Huxtable, 1997; Dovey, 1999).

(iii) Lacking authenticity

Relph (1976, p. 113) recognised that sense of place may be 'authentic' and 'genuine' or 'inauthentic', 'contrived' or 'artificial'. Use of the terms 'authentic' and 'inauthentic' is often slippery and contingent – authentic being what particular critics like. Nonetheless, many critics regard contemporary urban development that copies or draws explicit reference from historical precedent as 'false' and lacking 'authenticity'. For Boyer (1992, p. 188), recent development at New York's Union Square, Times Square and Battery Park City involve 'the reiteration and recycling of already-known symbolic codes and historic forms to the point of cliché'. She argues that historic preservations and 'retro urban designs' are literal representations of the past designed for 'inattentive viewers'. Similarly, Ellin (1999, p. 83) argues that, although ostensibly 'preserving' the past, both preservationists and gentrifiers could 'be more accurately described as rewriting or inventing the past since buildings and districts are "renovated", "restored",

or "rehabilitated" to correspond to ideal visions of the past and to satisfy contemporary needs and tastes'. However, she notes that this may also represent 'a welcome corrective to Modernism's obsession with forgetting the past and starting over on a clean slate' (Ellin, 2000, p. 104).

Discussing the 'real' and the 'simulation', Baudrillard (1983, from Lane, 2000, pp. 86–7) argues that there are three levels of simulation:

- First-order simulations are obvious copies of reality.
- Second-order simulations are copies that blur the boundaries between reality and representation.
- Third-order simulations – 'simulacra' – are imitations of things that never actually existed.

Third-order simulation generates what Baudrillard called 'hyper-reality' – a world without a real origin. He argues that hyper-reality will eventually be the dominant way of experiencing the world. In first-order and second-order simulation, the real still exists and the success (or otherwise) of simulation can be measured against – or, at least, distinguished from – it. With third-order simulation, the real does not exist. Baudrillard regards Disneyland as a third-order simulation. While Disneyland's 'Main Street USA' is meant to evoke a typical main street anywhere in the USA, it is not actually from anywhere: 'It mobilises images people already have about what typical America was like' (Crang, 1998, p. 126).

In his review of Huxtable's *The Unreal America* (1997), Rybczynski (1997, p. 13) comments that her analysis presumes the public cannot distinguish between what is real and what is not. He contends that people watching the erupting lava outside the Mirage in Las Vegas do not mistake it for a real volcano, just as commuters using the neo-classical concourse of the old Pennsylvania Station knew they were not in ancient Rome. He asserts that 'the relationship between reality and illusion has always been blurred; Pennsylvania Station was simultaneously a surrogate Baths of Caracalla and a real place' (Rybczynski, 1997, p. 13). While it is of concern that Disney's Main Street USA may be mistaken for a 'real' main street, the danger is that, increasingly, people do not have a real main street – or, indeed, real places – to compare it against.

For Fainstein (1994, p. 231), Disney World, 'is an *authentic* reflection of underlying economic and social processes . . . It *is* the genuine.' Commenting on the 'exaltation of authenticity', she notes difficulties of the 'implied definition' of authenticity used to denounce new projects: 'Although the critical literature is replete with accusations of fakery, the nature of the authentic, late twentieth-century design is rarely specified' (p. 230). The dismissal as inauthentic presupposes that there was, is, or can be, a more authentic urbanity, but she goes on to argue that authenticity is not the appropriate value to apply because 'deconstruction of the urban environment reveals a reasonably accurate portrayal of the social forces underlying it' (p. 232). Fainstein argues that, while a 'deeper critique' of supposedly artificial environments should demonstrate how they fail to satisfy important human needs, critics seem reluctant to do this because it puts them on the 'thorny ground of explicating exactly what activities afford genuine as opposed to false satisfaction'. Similarly, Ellin (2000, p. 103) argues that although themed environments are criticised for being contrived and 'artificial', these might be the qualities people actually like:

> Accused of distracting people from the injustices and ugliness of their lives, of placating them, and of being places of 'spectacle and surveillance', themed environments might also be applauded for the diversion they offer, for simply providing places in which people can relax and have fun in the company of family and friends.

Criticism of invented places provokes the question: Why shouldn't urban design produce places that people like and enjoy? Fainstein (1994, p. 232) observes that the popularity of many out-of-centre shopping complexes and revitalised areas appears to drive 'the cultural critics into paroxysms of annoyance as they attempt to show that people ought to be continually exposed to the realities of life at the lower depths'. Ultimately, people make places and imbue them with meaning and value. Furthermore, most places are discretionary environments and people must actively choose to use them for them to be successful. Urban designers need to learn how to make places by observing existing places and by establishing a dialogue with their users and stakeholders (see Chapters 8 and 12).

CONCLUSION

This chapter has discussed the perceptual dimension of urban design, focusing on environmental perception and on the construction of place. The value of this dimension of urban design is the stress on people and how they perceive, value, draw meaning from, and add meaning to, the urban environment. Places that are 'real' to people, invite and reward involvement – intellectual and/or emotional – and provide a sense of psychological connectedness. Although urban design as a process inexorably invents and reinvents places, with a greater or lesser degree of finesse, contrivance and authenticity, it is people who make places and give them meaning. Thus, just as messages are 'sent', they are also 'received' and interpreted: it is for individual users to determine whether a place is authentic or not, and the quality and meaning of their experience there. Rather than a duality of 'authentic' and 'inauthentic', it is necessary to consider degrees of authenticity.

Contrary to what some critics may suggest, people are not necessarily concerned about authenticity – at least, they care less about it than whether or not they like a place. It is people's perceptions that are important. Nasar (1998, p. 69) asserts that: 'Historical content may be authentic or not. If observers consider a place historical, it has historical content to them.' Thus, as Sircus (2001, p. 31) argues:

> Place is not good or bad simply because it is real versus surrogate, authentic versus pastiche. People enjoy both, whether it is a place created over centuries, or created instantly. A successful place, like a novel or a movie, engages us actively in an emotional experience orchestrated and organised to communicate purpose and story.

6

The social dimension

INTRODUCTION

This chapter discusses the social dimension of urban design. Space and society are clearly related: it is difficult to conceive of 'space' without social content and, equally, to conceive of society without a spatial component. As is discussed in this chapter, the relationship is best conceived as a continuous two-way process in which people (and societies) create and modify spaces while at the same time being influenced by them in various ways. Dear and Wolch (1989) argue that social relations can be: *constituted through space* (e.g. where site characteristics influence settlement form); *constrained by space* (e.g. where the physical environment facilitates or obstructs human activity); and *mediated by space* (e.g. where the 'friction of distance' facilitates or inhibits the development of various social practices). Hence, by shaping that built environment, urban designers influence patterns of human activity and social life.

This chapter focuses on five key aspects of urban design's social dimension. The first is the relationship between people and space. The second is the interrelated concepts of the 'public realm' and 'public life'. The third concerns the notion of neighbourhoods. The fourth concerns issues of safety and security. The fifth is the issue of accessibility.

PEOPLE AND SPACE

An understanding of the relationship between people ('society') and their environment ('space') is essential in urban design. The first idea to be considered here is that of architectural or environmental determinism, where the claim is that the physical environment has a determining influence on human behaviour. By negating the role of human agency, it assumes that environment-people interaction is a one-way process. People are not passive, however; they influence and change the environment, as it influences and changes them. It is, therefore, a two-way process. While physical factors are neither the exclusive nor necessarily the dominant influence on behaviour, environmental opportunities clearly affect what people can and cannot do: a window in an otherwise solid wall allows one to see out, while a continuous wall does not afford that opportunity. Human behaviour is therefore inherently 'situational': it is embedded in physical – and also in 'social', 'cultural' and 'perceptual' – contexts and settings.

In addition to determinism, there are two other main viewpoints on the degree of environmental influence on people's actions: 'environmental possibilism' (i.e. people choose among the environmental opportunities available to them) and 'environmental probabilism' (i.e. in a given physical setting some choices are more likely than others) (Porteous, 1977; Bell *et al.*, 1990). The latter is illustrated by a simple example (from Bell *et al.*, 1990, p. 365). At a seminar involving a few people in a large room with a formal layout of chairs and tables, there is minimal discussion. When the chairs and tables are arranged differently, there is more discussion – that is, when the environment is changed, behaviour also changes. This outcome is not inevitable: had the seminar been scheduled late in the day, or the convenor failed to motivate participants, the rearrangement might have been no more successful than the original layout. The example shows that *design matters* but not absolutely. What happens in any particular environment depends on those using it.

In this respect, Gans (1968, p. 5) drew a valuable distinction between 'potential' environments, which provide a range of environmental opportunities; and the 'resultant' or 'effective' environments created by what people actually do within that setting. Hence, while urban designers might create potential environments, people create effective environments. Rather than determining human actions or behaviour, urban design can be seen as a means of manipulating the probabilities of certain actions or behaviours occurring. Taking a probabilist or possibilist perspective, it can credibly be argued that environments with, for example, a high concentration of street-level doors, are more conducive to social interaction than those characterised by fortress-like structures with blank walls; similarly, residential neighbourhoods where houses have front porches present a more gregarious setting than those where three-car garage doors face onto public space (Ford, 2000, p. 13). Hence, as discussed in the previous chapter, while urban designers cannot 'make' places, they can create more 'place potential' (see Box 6.1).

The choices made in any particular setting depend partly on each individual's own situation and characteristics (their ego, personality, goals and values, available resources, past experiences, life stage, etc.): in an analogy with computer science, these characteristics are 'hard wired'. Despite the seemingly individualistic and complex demands of human values, goals and aspirations, the existance of an overarching hierarchy of human needs has been proposed by several authors. Such hierarchies often follow the original work on human motivation by Maslow (1968), who identified a five-stage hierarchy of basic human needs:

- physiological needs: for warmth and comfort;
- safety and security needs: to feel safe from harm;
- affiliation needs: to belong – to a community, for example;
- esteem needs: to feel valued by others;
- self-actualisation needs: for artistic expression and fulfilment.

The most basic physiological needs must be satisfied before progress can be made to the higher-order ones; for example, self-actualisation. However, although there is a hierarchy, the different needs are related in a complex series of inter-linked relationships (Figure 6.1). Furthermore, it might be argued that the true test of a 'civilised'

BOX 6.1 – GEHL'S NECESSARY, OPTIONAL AND SOCIAL ACTIVITIES

In his book *Life Between Buildings*, Jan Gehl (1996) adopts a probabilistic approach to understanding how design influences behaviour. He argues that through design, and within certain limits – regional, climatic, societal – it is possible to influence *how many* people use public spaces, *how long* individual activities last, and *which* activity types can develop. 'Greatly simplified' outdoor activities in public spaces can be divided into three categories:

- *Necessary activities* are more or less compulsory (e.g. going to school or work, shopping, waiting for a bus). As participants have no choice, the incidence is only slightly influenced by the physical setting.
- *Optional activities* are undertaken voluntarily, if time and place allow, and weather and setting invite them (e.g. taking a walk to get a breath of fresh air, stopping for a coffee in a street cafe, people-watching, etc.).
- *Social activities* depend on the presence of others in public space (e.g. greetings and conversations, communal activities, passive contacts such as simply seeing and hearing other people). They occur spontaneously as a direct consequence of people moving about and being in the same spaces at the same time. This implies that such activities are supported whenever necessary and optional activities are given better environmental conditions.

The crux of Gehl's argument is that in poor quality public spaces, only strictly necessary activities occur. In higher quality public spaces, necessary activities take place with approximately the same frequency – although people choose to spend longer doing them – but, more importantly, a wide range of optional (social) activities also tend to occur.

---

society is one that attempts to meet all the human needs concurrently.

The choices people make in any given setting are also influenced by 'society' and 'culture', involving characteristics which are learnt or, continuing the computer science analogy, 'soft-wired'. Society can be considered to be as any self-perpetuating human grouping occupying a relatively bounded territory, interacting in a systematic way, and possessing its own more or less distinctive culture and institutions. Culture is probably best understood in an 'anthro-

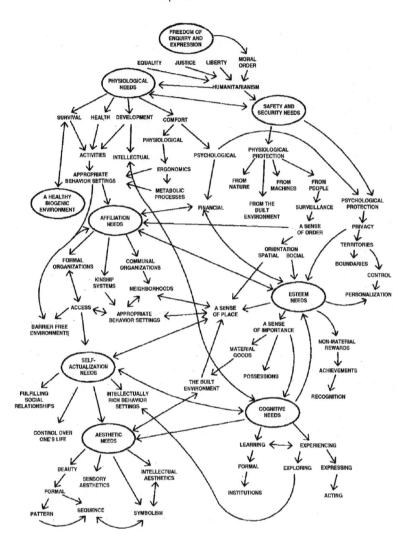

FIGURE 6.1
Hierarchy of human needs (source: Lang, 1987, p. 10)

pological' sense, as a 'particular way of life, which expresses certain meanings and values not only in art and learning, but also in institutions and ordinary behaviour' (Williams, 1961, p. 41).

Lawson (2001, pp. 2–3) argues that people collectively inhabiting an area tend to make 'rules' governing their use of space. While some rules are a matter of local social and cultural convention, many reflect deep-seated needs of the psyche and characteristics of human beings. He suggests (pp. 7–8) that the queue typifies conventionalised behaviour triggered by signals from the designed environment:

> When someone pushes in front of you in a queue, you feel offended not just because you are one place further back but also because they failed to respect the rules. In most situa-

tions where we queue there are also token signals from the physical environment that we should behave in this highly artificial way. The rope barriers sometimes used to form queues in public places are hardly able to contain a crowd physically, and yet without them the crowd would probably push and shove in a chaotic and possibly aggressive manner. Our civilisation and our culture enables us to be remarkably co-operative, even when we are actually competing for limited tickets at the theatre or sale bargains in a shop (pp. 7–8).

Recent years have, however, witnessed a decline in the apparent civility of public space, and in respectful behaviour towards other space users. Although this suggests a 'golden age' when public order was of a higher order, it is also an extremely common observation (see Lofland, 1973; Milgram, 1977; Davis, 1990; Carter, 1998; Fyfe, 1998). While designers can attempt to manipulate functional and cognitive cues to increase the probability of better behaviour in public spaces, there are limits to what they can achieve. Many urban design practitioners are, nevertheless, optimistic about the probability of particular behaviours in certain environments and advocate good design as a means to achieve certain desirable outcomes. As Ford (2000, p. 199) argues, writers such as Jane Jacobs and William H. Whyte believed that: 'Good streets, sidewalks, parks, and other public spaces bring out the best in human nature and provide the settings for a civil and courteous society. Everything will be fine if we can just get the design right.' Others, holding a much more pessimistic view of contemporary urban society, argue that, for example, small parks will inevitably attract undesirables, front porches will attract nosy neighbours, grid street patterns will invite strangers into the neighbourhood, and benches in public spaces will encourage vagrants. Such pessimistic attitudes – combined with problems of liability and responsibility for anything that may happen in a public place – often translate into highly risk-averse approaches that discourage all activity rather than risk anti-social behaviour. Such attitudes frequently result in hostile and anti-social environments that paradoxically seem to encourage anti-social behaviour.

While needing to counter pessimistic views and attitudes, overoptimistic claims by urban designers invite accusations of environmental determinism. Claims, for example, that if houses have front porches, then residents will be more neighbourly and eventually form communities, may be borne out, or, equally, may not. In fact, both optimistic and pessimistic views stray into architectural determinism: if public benches are provided, vagrants may sleep on them, but this is not inevitable and if they are not provided, the problem is avoided at the expense of people not having somewhere to sit down. As urban design should be an activity that provides people with choices rather than denying them choice, it is preferable to provide the opportunity, and then to manage its use.

THE PUBLIC REALM

Frequently evoked in discussions of urban design, the 'public realm' – and the related and overlap-ping concept of 'public life' – require further consideration. 'Public' must be understood vis-à-vis 'private': in broad terms, as Loukaitou-Sideris and Banerjee (1998, p. 175) observe: 'Public life involves relatively open and universal social contexts, in contrast to private life, which is intimate, familiar, shielded, controlled by the individual, and shared only with family and friends.'

The public realm has 'physical' (space) and 'social' (activity) dimensions. The *physical* public realm is understood here to mean the spaces and settings – publicly or privately owned – that support or facilitate public life and social interaction. The activities and events occurring in those spaces and settings can be termed the *sociocultural* public realm.

The function of the public realm

Defined as the sites and settings of public life, and including some notion of 'public space', the public realm ideally functions as a forum for political action and representation; as a 'neutral' or common ground for social interaction, intermingling, and communication; and as a stage for social learning, personal development, and information exchange (Loukaitou-Sideris and Banerjee, 1998, p. 175). Although these functions are rarely (if ever) wholly attained in practice, their definition provides a measure of the degree to which 'real' public realms fall short of the ideal state. The second and third of these dimensions are discussed later; the first requires further explanation here.

As a political stage, the public realm (sometimes referred to as the 'democratic' public realm) involves and symbolises activities important to 'citizenship' and the existence of a civil society (i.e. social relations and public participation, as against the narrower operations of the state or the market) (Figure 6.2). Although not necessarily predicated on the existence of public space, the concept of a 'political' public realm has interested many writers. Hannah Arendt (1958) conceived of the city as a 'polis', a self-governing political community whose citizens deliberate, debate and resolve issues. She saw the public realm as satisfying three criteria: by outlasting mortal lives, it memorialised the society and thereby conveyed a sense of its history; it was an arena for diverse groups of people to engage in debate and oppositional struggles; and it was accessible to, and used by, all (from Ellin, 1996, p. 126). Existing between the domain of the state

FIGURE 6.2
Old Market Square, Nottingham, UK. Public space offers the opportunity for political display and canvassing – activities rarely allowed in quasi-public space

or government, and the private domain of the individual and the family, Habermas' (1962) concept of the 'public sphere' relates to the discussion of public affairs. His ideas are based on the development of various spaces – coffee houses, salons, etc. – together with newspapers and periodicals in eighteenth century Europe, which encouraged new forms of reasoned argumentation. In contemporary society, rather than a 'unitary' polis or public sphere, it may be better to conceive of a series of separate yet overlapping spheres involving, for example, different social-economic, gender and ethnic groups (Calhoun, 1992; Boyer, 1993; Sandercock, 1997; Featherstone and Lash, 1999). Boyer (1993, p. 118), for example, argues that: 'Any contemporary references to the "public" is by nature a universalising construct that assumes a collective whole, while in reality the public is fragmented into marginalized groups, many of whom have no voice, position or representation in the public sphere.'

The decline of the public realm

Many commentators have observed the declining significance of the public realm, attributed in part to the reduced availability of, and significance attached to, public space and public life. Ellin (1996, p. 149) observes that many social and civic functions that traditionally occurred in public spaces have been transferred to private realms – leisure activities, entertainment, gaining information, and consumption, for example, can increasingly be undertaken at home through television and the Internet. Activities that were once only available in collective and public forms have increasingly become available in individualised and private forms, while the use of public space has been challenged by various developments and changes, such as increased personal mobility – initially through the car and subsequently through the internet (see Chapter 2). As discussed in Chapter 4, social interaction today is also affected by conflict within public space between the demands of social space and those of mechanised movement. Cars also facilitate an essentially private control over public space.

More generally, the disengagement from public space and public facilities has been both a cause and a consequence of the trend towards privatisation. In *The Fall of Public Man*, for example, Sennett (1977) documented the social, political and economic factors leading to the privatisation of people's lives and the 'end of public culture'. Similarly, Ellin (1999, pp. 167–8) observed how, as the public realm has grown increasingly impoverished, 'there has been a corresponding decline in meaningful space, and a desire to control one's space, or to privatise'. For Ellin, the 'privatisation impulse' is epitomised by the appropriation of public space by private agencies such as 'the inward-turning shopping mall which has abandoned the central city for the suburbs and which turns its back entirely on its surroundings with its fortress-like exterior surrounded by a moat-like car park'. Observing the process of privatising and selling off standardised infrastructural systems, Graham (2001, p. 365) suggests that this is most familiar and widespread in the domain of public streets: 'The municipally-controlled street systems, that once acted as effective monopolies of the public realm in many cities, are being paralleled by the growth of a set of shadow, privatised street spaces.'

Nevertheless, some commentators (e.g. Brill, 1989; Krieger, 1995) argue that the public realm's apparent decline is based on a false notion and that, in reality, it has never been 'as diverse, dense, classless, or democratic as is now imagined' (Loukaitou-Sideris and Banerjee, 1998, p. 182). Others note resurgence in the use of public space and see it in a process of sociocultural transformation. Carr et al. (1992, p. 343) argue, for example, that the relationship of public space to public life is dynamic and reciprocal and that new forms of public life require new spaces. Use of the public realm is also a function of its quality as a supportive and conducive environment (Gehl, 1996). There is, nevertheless, the possibility of a vicious spiral: if people use public space less, then there is less incentive to provide new spaces and maintain existing ones. With a decline in their maintenance and quality, public spaces are less likely to be used, thereby exacerbating the vicious spiral of decline.

The physical and sociocultural public realms

In broad terms, the public realm includes all the spaces accessible to and used by the public, including:

- *External public space*: pieces of land that lie between private landholdings. In urban areas, these are public squares, streets, highways, parks, parking lots, etc., and in rural areas they are stretches of coastline, forests, lakes, rivers, etc. Accessible to all, these spaces constitute public space in its purest form (Figure 6.3).
- *Internal 'public' space*: public institutions such as libraries, museums, town halls, etc., plus public transport facilities such as train or bus stations, airports, etc.

- *External* and *internal quasi-'public' space*: although legally private, places such as university campuses, sports grounds, restaurants, cinemas, shopping malls, also form part of the public realm. This category also includes what are commonly described as 'privatised' (often but not exclusively external) public spaces. As the owners and operators of all these spaces retain rights to regulate access and behaviour there, they are only nominally public. Sorkin (1992) refers to this pejoratively as 'pseudo-public' space.

It is clear that there is a spectrum of 'public-ness' with regard to the public realm. As well as issues of space, issues of access and accessibility, and of whether – and in what sense – the setting constitutes 'neutral' ground, must be considered. While, in urban design terms, 'accessibility' is the capacity to enter and use a space – as is discussed later in

FIGURE 6.3
Public space is used for a variety of different activities. In Dolgellau, North Wales, UK, the public space is occasionally used for a livestock market

FIGURE 6.4
Castlefields, Manchester, UK. Street cafes provide an example of informal public life

FIGURE 6.5
Informal use of space on the banks of the Seine, Paris, France

BOX 6.2 – OLDENBURG'S 'THIRD PLACE'

Plaza Mayor, Salamanca. Piazzas provide an illustration of Oldenburg's third place

In Oldenburg's book, *The Great Good Place: Cafes, coffee shops, bookstores, bars, hair salons and the other hangouts at the heart of a community* (1989, 1999), the central thesis is that, to be 'relaxed and fulfilling', daily life must find its balance in three realms of experience: 'domestic', 'work' and 'social'. Contemporary domestic life typically consists of isolated nuclear families or single people living alone, while the work environment may be essentially solitary (e.g. telecommuters whose work contacts are through the Internet and telephone) or conspicuously anti-social and competitive. Drawing on contemporary US society, Oldenburg argues that because expectations of family and work have 'escalated beyond the capacity of those institutions to meet them', people need the release and stimulation that more sociable realms can provide.

Oldenburg argues that, while seemingly 'amorphous and scattered', informal public life is actually highly focused, emerging in 'core settings'. His term 'third place' signifies the 'great variety of public places that host the regular, voluntary, informal, and happily anticipated gatherings of individuals beyond the realms of home and work' (1999, p. 16). Representing 'fundamental institutions of mediation' between the individual and the larger society, third places are often specific to cultures and to historical eras: Paris has its sidewalk cafes, Vienna its coffee houses, Germany its

beer gardens. Such places emerge and decline, are sustained or neglected, and replaced or usurped by new 'third' places. Banerjee (2001, p. 14), for example, suggests that, in many American cities, Starbuck's coffee shops, Borders bookstores, and health clubs and video rental stores have become 'major icons' of the third place.

For Oldenburg, the core qualities of third places, which could also be regarded as core qualities of the public realm, include:

- being 'neutral ground', where individuals can come and go as they please;
- being highly inclusive, accessible and without formal criteria of membership;
- their 'taken-for-granted-ness' and low profile;
- being open during, and outside, office hours;
- being characterised by a 'playful mood';
- providing psychological comfort and support;
- with conversation their 'cardinal and sustaining' activity, providing 'political fora of great importance'.

The last quality highlights the overlap between third places and the 'democratic' public realm. Oldenburg (1999, p. xxiv) argues that it is easy to understand why at various points in history coffee houses 'came under attack by government leaders . . . It was in the coffee-houses where people congregated and often, in their discussion, found fault with the countries' rulers.'

this chapter, not all public spaces are 'open' to everyone.

Given that public space, quasi-public space, and the boundary between them, are often difficult to define precisely, Banerjee (2001, p. 19) recommends that urban designers focus on the broader concept of 'public life' (i.e. the sociocultural public realm of people and activities), rather than the narrower one of physical 'public spaces' (Figures 6.4 and 6.5). He argues that, while planners have traditionally associated it with public spaces, increasingly public life is 'flourishing in private places, not just in corporate theme parks, but also in small businesses such as coffee shops, bookstores and other such third places' (Banerjee, 2001, pp. 19–20). The concern in urban design is therefore usually with 'social space' (i.e. spaces that support, enable or facilitate social and cultural interaction and public life) regardless of whether it is genuinely 'public' space or private space that is publicly accessible.

Public life can be broadly grouped into two interrelated types: 'formal' and 'informal'. Of most interest in urban design is informal public life, which occurs beyond the realm of formal institutions and entails choice. Many parts of the public realm are discretionary environments, which people choose whether or not to use: for example, there are often alternative routes for getting from one point to another, with choice made on interrelated grounds of convenience, interest, delight, safety, etc. Oldenburg's concept of the 'third place' provides a useful way of enhancing understanding of informal public life and its relation to the public realm (see Box 6.2).

NEIGHBOURHOODS

The essence of neighbourhood design is that, as successful and desirable neighbourhoods already exist, it should – in principle – be possible to create similar ones. There is a well-developed tradition of neighbourhood design. The most significant idea was Clarence Perry's neighbourhood unit, developed in the US during the 1920s (Box 6.3), as a means of systematically organising and developing city areas. Incorporated within the physical design and layout of the neighbourhood were social objectives such as neighbour interaction, the creation of a sense of community, neighbourhood identity, and social balance.

In the UK, the first generation of post-war new towns (e.g. Stevenage) drew on Perry's ideas.

However, the concept went out of favour in the mid-1950s with the plan for Cumbernauld, for example, delivering increased 'urbanity' through higher densities and centralisation. Subsequent new towns returned to a limited notion of the neighbourhood concept. Thus, the network road grid at Milton Keynes enclosed (approximately) one-kilometre squares, each incorporating a 'village' which, while no longer regarded as the prime social focus, provided an area of identity.

Three interrelated strands of thinking have informed neighbourhood design. First, neighbourhoods are seen as providing identity and character, creating or enhancing a sense of place. While this may be a relatively superficial sense of identity with the area's physical character, it may also provide a deeper and more meaningful sense of identity with the place's sociocultural character (i.e. through time-thickened experience of that place).

Second, neighbourhoods provide a relatively pragmatic way of planning urban areas (with or without associated social objectives). Rather than a highly atomised development, there are attempts to contribute to something larger – a mixed-use or 'balanced' area rather than a mono-functional housing estate. Increasingly the pursuit of more sustainable modes of development has justified such approaches: neighbourhoods can, for example, be designed to be more self-sufficient, reducing the need to travel by encouraging opportunities for work and recreation closer to home.

Third, and somewhat more controversially, neighbourhoods can be seen as a means of creating areas of greater social interaction. Neighbourhood design has often been associated with the environmentally determinist idea that certain layouts, forms and land uses assist the creation of 'communities'. The fallacy of conflating the idea of 'physical' neighbourhoods (defined by territory or boundaries) with 'social' communities (defined by relationships, associations, etc.) has, however, been increasingly exposed. Blowers (1973) identified five types of neighbourhood. While each is recognisable as such, only the final one has the attributes of a community:

- 'Arbitrary' neighbourhoods, where the only common feature is spatial proximity.
- 'Ecological' and/or 'ethnological' neighbourhoods, with a common environment and identity.
- 'Homogeneous' neighbourhoods, inhabited by particular socio-economic or ethnic groups.
- 'Functional' neighbourhoods, derived from the geographical mapping of service provision.
- 'Community neighbourhoods', in which a close-knit, socially homogeneous group engages in primary contacts.

While some critics presume that all attempts to design better neighbourhoods *ipso facto* aim to create communities, some advocates of neighbourhood planning expose themselves to criticism by claiming that certain design strategies will inexorably create a sense of community. In making such claims, for example, some New Urbanists have overreached themselves.

Talen (2000, p. 179) advises 'steering away' from the term community in connection with physical design and suggests that using specific elements of community makes better sense in the context of urban design. 'Resident interaction', for example, can be influenced by provision of opportunities for increased visual and eye contacts. Visual contacts, however, stimulate a relatively superficial form of social interaction. For more in-depth, enduring interaction, those involved must have 'something in common'. As Gans (1961a; 1961b) noted in his studies of residential environments, while propinquity may initiate social relationships and maintain less intensive ones, friendships required social homogeneity.

Recent developments of the concept of neighbourhood design have consistently emphasised the principle of mixed use, which is considered valuable for environmental and social sustainability purposes (Figure 6.6). Leon Krier (1990), for example, argued that zoning resulted in mechanical segregation of urban functions rather than their organic integration (see also Chapter 8). Based on his proposals for the reconstruction of the 'European city', he argued that there should only be mixed-use urban quarters, integrating all the daily functions of urban life (dwelling, working, leisure) within a territory not exceeding 35 hectares and 15 000 inhabitants.

Originating with the Birmingham BUDS plan (Tibbalds et al., 1990), and drawing upon precedents in US cities such as Seattle and Portland, the concept of mixed-use 'urban quarters' and distinctive neighbourhoods has influenced a series of city centre urban design plans in the UK (including those for Glasgow, Leeds, Sheffield and Leicester). These aim to identify and reinforce areas of existing character and highlight opportunities to introduce new character. The concept of urban quarters also resonated with the Urban Villages Forum in the UK, established to promote the development of 'urban villages' (Aldous, 1992), while traditional neighbourhood development (TND) has been a key element of the US-based New Urbanism (see Chapter 2) (Box 6.4).

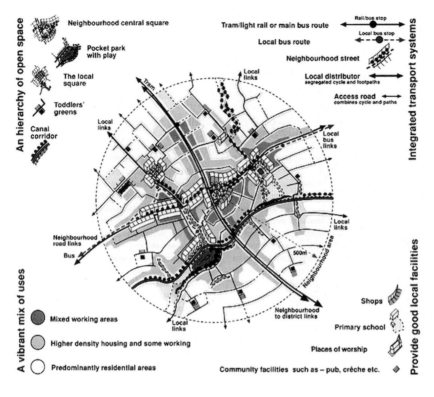

An hierarchy of open space

Neighbourhood central square

Pocket park with play

The local square

Toddlers' greens

Canal corridor

A vibrant mix of uses

● Mixed working areas

◔ Higher density housing and some working

○ Predominantly residential areas

Integrated transport systems

Tram/light rail or main bus route

Local bus route

Neighbourhood street

Local distributor
segregated cycle and footpaths

Access road
combines cycle and paths

Rail/bus stop

Local bus stop

Provide good local facilities

Shops

Primary school

Places of worship

Community facilities such as – pub, crèche etc.

FIGURE 6.6
Mixed-use neighbourhood (source: Urban Task Force, 1999, p. 66)

Some central issues regarding neighbourhood design concepts can usefully be discussed under the headings of size, boundaries, social relevance, and social mix.

(i) Size

There has been considerable debate over the optimal neighbourhood size. The concept is usually expressed in terms of population (sometimes that of a school's catchment area); of area (often what is seen as comfortable walking distance); of a combination of both; or as a derivation of – supposedly more social – communities found in small towns and villages. Jane Jacobs (1961), however, highlighted the fallacy of trying to establish a rigid threshold population, one of 10 000 in a large city, for example, would lack the innate cross-connections occurring among the same population in a small town. She argued that only three kinds of neighbourhood were useful: the city as a whole; city districts of 100 000 or more (i.e. large enough to be politically significant); and the street-neighbourhood.

Research has shown that identifiable neighbourhoods do not necessarily correspond with people's social relations, nor do residents necessarily perceive a neighbourhood unit as such. Conceptions of neighbourhood and community are often top-down constructions, with little meaning when viewed from the bottom up. Gans (1962, p. 11), for example, found that patterns of activity within his Boston West End neighbourhood were so diverse that only outsiders ever considered it a single neighbourhood. Lee (1965) identified three neighbourhoods that residents themselves perceive: the 'social acquaintance' neighbourhood; the 'homogeneous' neighbourhood (i.e. people in homes like ours); and the 'social provision', or unit, neighbourhood. Most congruent with people's social relations was the social acquaintance neighbourhood: 'The schema includes a small physical area, perhaps half-a-dozen streets containing only houses, apart from the few corner shops and pubs that invariably go with them. Sheer propinquity produces a state of affairs in which the family knows everyone else.'

(ii) Boundaries

Another prevalent idea has been that clear boundaries defining a distinct territory enhance the devel-

BOX 6.4 – CHARACTERISTICS OF URBAN VILLAGES AND NEIGHBOURHOODS

(source: Aldous, 1992, pp. 27–37; CNU, 1998)

Poundbury Farm, Dorchester – one of the UK's first urban village projects

Urban villages

- *Size* – small enough for all places to be within walking distance of each other and for people to know each other.
- *Size* – large enough to support a wide range of activities and facilities and to be able to stand up for itself if its interests come under threat.
- *A range of uses* – mixed within street blocks as well as within the village as a whole.
- *A balance of houses and flats and workspaces* – such that there is a theoretical one-to-one ratio between jobs and residents able and willing to work.
- *A pedestrian friendly environment* – catering for the car without encouraging its use.
- *A mixture of different building types and sizes*, including some degree of mixed use with buildings.
- *Robust building types.*
- *Mixed tenure* – both for residential and employment uses.

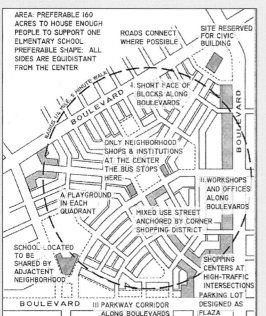

Duany and Plater-Zyberk's neighbourhood concept
(source: Leccese and McCormick, 2000, p. 76)

New urbanist neighbourhoods

- Compact, pedestrian-friendly, mixed-use and identifiable areas that encourage citizens to take responsibility for their maintenance and evolution.
- Daily living activities within walking distance, allowing independence to those who do not drive.
- Appropriate building densities and land uses within walking distance of transit stops, permitting public transit to become a viable alternative to the automobile.
- Interconnected networks of streets, encouraging walking, reducing the number and length of automobile trips, and conserving energy.
- A broad range of housing types and price levels, bringing people of diverse ages, races, and incomes into daily interaction.
- Concentrations of civic, institutional, and commercial activity.
- Schools sized and located to enable children to walk or bicycle to them.
- A range of parks.

opment of functional and social interaction, a sense of community, and identification with the area. However, Jacobs (1961) argued that neighbourhoods that worked best had no beginnings or ends – a major part of their success depended on their overlapping and interweaving. In his seminal essay 'A City is Not a Tree', Christopher Alexander (1965) criticised the definition of neighbourhoods as discrete units within the city. His argument concerns the properties of 'tree' and 'semi-lattice' structures as ways of combining a number of small systems into larger and more complex ones. While tree structures consist of separate systems organised into hierarchies, in semi-lattice structures – Alexander's preferred structure – systems are complexly related and overlapped. Accordingly, Alexander condemned city plans that established bounded neighbourhoods and/or functionally zoned areas. Similarly, Lynch (1981, p. 401) argued that planning a city as a series of neighbourhoods was either 'futile' or would 'support social segregation', because 'any good city has a continuous fabric, rather than a cellular one'.

(iii) Social relevance and meaning
The idea of self-sufficient neighbourhoods has also been criticised for its limited relevance to contemporary society, particularly considering increased (especially car-based) mobility, and electronic communications. While communities of place still exist, they have been supplemented, often supplanted, by 'communities of interest' detached from any specific geographic locale. Common territory is, therefore, no longer a prerequisite of community and social interaction. In a highly mobile age, it is argued that people no longer want or need the previous sense of community and neighbourliness: they can now choose from the entire city (and beyond) for jobs, recreation, friends, shops, entertainment, etc. – and in the process form communities of choice. The issue, though, is not one of an either/or choice between mobility with spatially diffuse contact networks or spatially proximate contact networks. Instead, it is one of providing opportunities for both, and allowing people to find their own balance.

(iv) Social mix and 'balanced' communities
While a general criticism of all attempts at creating neighbourhoods/communities, the charge of social engineering has particularly been levelled at attempts to create socially 'balanced' neighbour-

hoods and communities (Banerjee and Baer, 1984). Some element of social mix is, nevertheless, generally desirable, and various benefits stem from mixed and (better) balanced neighbourhoods. Both the Urban Villages Forum and the New Urbanists emphasise the need for variety in house prices and tenures. English planning guidance (DTLR/CABE, 2001, p. 34) lists the following advantages:

- providing a better balance of demand for community services and facilities (e.g. schools, recreation facilities, care for elderly people);
- providing opportunities for 'lifetime' communities, where people can move home within a neighbourhood;
- making neighbourhoods more robust, by avoiding concentrations of housing of the same type;
- enabling community self-help (e.g. with arrangements for childcare, shopping, gardening, or coping with a winter freeze);
- assisting surveillance, by people coming and going throughout the day and evening.

Mixed neighbourhoods also provide greater diversity of building form and scale, making the area (potentially) more visually interesting, with greater scope for local distinctiveness and character.

Achieving social mix is often problematic. Given a relatively free property market, and contemporary desires to live with people 'like us', it is difficult for adverse social mix to be achieved or sustained: neighbourhoods that start out diverse will evolve towards greater social homogeneity. The tendency is nevertheless exacerbated by certain development patterns and design strategies. In residential development, a high degree of market segmentation can be obtained by dividing developments into separate 'pods', each designated for one type of dwelling, occupant and price bracket (see Chapter 4). Observing a suburban landscape composed of such pods, Duany et al. (2000, p. 43) commented on the 'ruthless segregation by minute graduations of income': 'There have always been better or worse neighbourhoods, and the rich have often taken refuge from the poor, but never with such precision.'

Conversely, certain patterns of development can provide an element of exclusivity without resulting in strict separation. In traditional neighbourhoods, house prices and types may vary considerably from street to street, with the transition typically occurring mid-block, where backyards and gardens meet. Recent research on mixed tenure development in the UK (Jupp, 1999) has shown, however, that it is only by mixing tenures within streets, rather than street by street or block by block, that benefits in terms of cross-tenure social networks occur – indicating, *inter alia*, that the street is the strongest social unit.

These criticisms do not negate the value of neighbourhood design patterns, but merely qualify their use. Most principles of neighbourhood design (such as those advocated by the Urban Villages Forum and the New Urbanists) also support sustainable design. Whether neighbourhoods have certain social characteristics or not, they are places with distinct characters that residents can identify with, and that offer a sense of belonging. Problems often stem from over-rigid application of principles of better neighbourhood design. Lynch (1981, p. 250), for example, concluded that it was 'the concept of the large, autonomous, sharply defined, and rigid neighbourhood unit of a standard size, to which all physical and social relations are keyed, that seems to be inappropriate for our society'. Rather than dogma, neighbourhoods are merely a set of generally desirable design principles to be adapted in the light of local context and prevailing social, economic and political realities.

SAFETY AND SECURITY

People face a variety of threats in the urban environment: crime, terrorism, fast-moving vehicles, air pollution, water contamination, and so forth. In some places the threat of natural disasters is an everyday fear to be faced in the design of buildings and settlements. In most Western societies, although many 'natural' threats are now adequately managed, other 'human' threats – real or imagined – are seemingly on the increase. These include road safety and fear of crime. As the issue of road/pedestrian safety was discussed in Chapter 4, this section deals principally with crime, safety and security, and their relationship to the public realm.

Security relates to the 'protection' of oneself, one's family and friends, and individual and communal property. Lack of security, perceptions of danger, and fear of victimisation, threaten both the use of the public realm and the creation of successful urban environments. A sense of security and safety is, therefore, an essential prerequisite of successful urban design. Increased security has, however, often been attained by privatisation, and retreat from the public realm. In urban design terms, privatisation usually entails the control of certain territories or spaces by means of segregation (such as physical distance, walls, gates and less visible barriers to exclude the outside world and its perceived threats and challenges) and also by means of policing strategies and the use of surveillance cameras.

Privatisation is akin to 'voluntary exclusion' – an activity described as the 'succession of the successful' and explored in Christopher Lasch's book, *The Revolt of the Elites and the Betrayal of Democracy* (1995). Generally involving affluent groups choosing to live separately from the rest of society, it can be manifested in a variety of ways, including opting out of public education and health systems. This withdrawal often turns otherwise – or originally – 'public goods', into 'club goods'.

Gated communities provide an explicit example of voluntary exclusion. In their book *Fortress America* (1997), Blakely and Snyder chronicle how, in attempting to find like-minded neighbours, secure property values, and escape crime, communities erect walls and gates controlling who can – and, more importantly, who cannot – enter. In contrast to apartment blocks with entry control systems preventing public access to lobbies, halls and parking lots, the gated community prevents public access to streets, parks, beaches, trails, etc., which would otherwise be shared by all local citizens. Rather than being public or 'quasi-public' goods, they become private 'club' goods, with explicit criteria of membership (usually the ability to pay) determining their use. Their gates form a dramatic and highly visible manifestation of social fragmentation and polarisation.

Gating, however, does little to address the cause of the problems it is a response to: the neighbourhood remains embedded within a wider society, which it cannot wholly escape or insulate itself from. Blakely and Snyder (1997, p. 173) argue that the entire public realm should be considered when gating. Furthermore, the supposed safety advantages of gating are gained at the expense of those left outside 'the relatively influential and law-abiding citizens on the inside are no longer motivated or, probably, even able to make any contribution to the safety, or the sense of safety of conditions outside' (Bentley, 1999, p. 163). The gates are, in fact, a private solution that imposes significant public and social costs.

Fear of victimisation

Fear of victimisation is a major factor in the creation of the contemporary urban environment (see Ellin, 1997; Oc and Tiesdell, 1997). If people do not use a place because they feel uncomfortable or afraid there, the public realm is impoverished. Such avoidance is often due to fear of certain environments – dark alleys, deserted areas, or ones crowded with the 'wrong kind of people' – as well as of particular incidents. Many people dislike situations that offer no alternatives, for example, subways as the only means of crossing busy roads, or narrow pavements and entrances, particularly those obstructed by 'people who create anxiety' such as winos, beggars, or rowdy youths. Similarly, signs of physical and social disorder, such as graffiti, litter, or vandalised public property, suggest an environment out of control and unpredictable.

Considerations of safety are related to – but distinct from – concerns about crime. Crime is about offenders and offences; safety is about victims and the fear of victimisation. Distinction should also be made between 'crime' and 'incivilities': whereas crime generally involves transgression of a formally constituted law, much of the behaviour which provokes anxiety and apprehension and deters people from using the public realm is not technically crime. It is, however, usually termed incivilities or, sometimes, 'quality of life' crime: Jane Jacobs (1961, p. 39) aptly referred to it as 'street barbarism'.

Distinction should also be made between 'fear' and 'risk', the difference between 'feeling safe' and actually 'being safe'. In general, women are more fearful of victimisation than men (though the gap narrows somewhat with increasing age). Fear of victimisation may be disproportionate with risk: in the UK, for example, young males are, statistically, most at risk, while those who exhibit most fear are women, the elderly and ethnic minorities. There is, however, a convincing explanation. Being more risk averse, vulnerable people take precautionary measures and are therefore less likely to be victimised.

In terms of the impact of crime, perception of it (i.e. fear) is as important as its actuality (i.e. statistical risk). Perceptions come from many sources: press reports of crime, for example, can sustain mis- or half-truths in the popular imagination. Responding to fears of victimisation, many people take precautionary actions to avoid risk, or at least to reduce their exposure through risk manage-ment: hence, fear of victimisation can cause exclusion not just from particular places, but from much of the public realm.

Approaches to crime prevention

The two main approaches to crime prevention are the 'dispositional' – removing or reducing an individual's motivation to commit crimes, through education and moral guidance, sanctions and penalties, and/or social and economic development – and the 'situational' approach, whereby *once* an offender has made the *initial decision* to offend, certain techniques make the commission of *that* crime in that *particular place* more difficult.

Principally developed and codified by Ron Clarke (1992, 1997), the situational approach focuses attention on the opportunity for crime. As Clarke (1997, p. 4) explains: 'Proceeding from an analysis of the circumstances giving rise to specific kinds of crime, situational crime prevention introduces discrete managerial and environmental change to reduce the opportunity for those crimes to occur. Thus, it is focused on the settings for crime, rather than upon those committing criminal acts.' It is, therefore, not necessary to understand precisely what motivates an individual, merely to recognise that some people are criminally motivated. Situational measures manipulate the physical, social and psychological setting for crime, using four overarching opportunity reduction strategies:

- Increasing the perceived effort of the offence;
- Increasing the perceived risk of the offence;
- Reducing the reward from the offence; and
- Removing excuses for the offence. (Clarke, 1997)

There is continuing debate regarding which approach is most effective. In theory, reducing the motivation to offend is innately superior, but, because this is often difficult to effect, opportunity reduction measures are justified on practical grounds. While design may affect crime and/or perceptions of safety, it can only create the preconditions for a safer environment: it is not a substitute for changing the conduct or reducing the underlying motivation of offending individuals.

Dispositional and situational approaches may produce radically different environments. Bottoms (1990, p. 7) uses an analogy with child-raising: 'some parents might lock cupboards or drawers to prevent their children from helping themselves to loose cash, chocolates and so forth (opportunity reduction); others will prefer . . . not to lock up anything in the house but so to socialise their children that they will not steal even if the opportunities are available'. Dispositional approaches are, however, generally outside the scope of urban design action, and hence outside the remit of this book.

Opportunity reduction methods developed within the mainstream urban design literature and involve key themes of activity, surveillance and territorial definition and control (see Table 6.1). Originating with Jane Jacobs (1961), these ideas were developed through Newman's ideas of 'defensible space' and the CPTED approach. More recently, Bill Hillier has offered a perspective on crime and safety that re-engages with Jacobs.

TABLE 6.1
Situational approaches

	JANE JACOBS	OSCAR NEWMAN	CPTED	BILL HILLIER
CONTROL OF SPACE/ TERRITORIALITY	Clear demarcation between public and private space.	*Territoriality –* capacity of the physical environment to create perceived zones of territorial influence (including mechanisms symbolising boundaries and defining a hierarchy of increasingly private zones).	*Natural access control* aimed at reducing opportunities by denying access to the crime target. *Territorial reinforcement –* physical design strategies creating or extending a sphere of influence so that users of a property develop a sense of proprietorship.	Spaces integrated with other spaces, so that pedestrians are encouraged to see into and move through them.
SURVEILLANCE	Need for 'eyes upon the street' belonging to street's 'natural proprietors' (both residents and users). Enhanced by a diversity of activities and functions that naturally create peopled places.	*Surveillance –* capacity of physical design to provide surveillance opportunities for residents and their agents.	*Natural surveillance* as a result of the routine use of property.	Surveillance provided by people moving through spaces.
ACTIVITY	Sidewalks need 'users on it fairly continuously, both to add to the number of effective eyes on the street and to induce people in buildings along the street to watch the sidewalks in sufficient number'.	Rejects the argument that more activity on the street and the presence of commercial uses necessarily reduces street crime.	Argues for reduced through-movement and hence reduced levels of activity.	As feeling safe depends on areas being in continuous occupation and use, areas should be designed to enable this (e.g. by making them better integrated with regard to the movement system).

Jacobs stressed the need for activity to provide surveillance, and for territorial definition to distinguish between 'private' and 'public' space. For Jacobs (1961, p. 40), a prerequisite of a successful neighbourhood was that 'a person must feel personally safe and secure on the street among all these strangers'. Rather than by the police, she argued that the 'public peace' was kept by an intricate network of voluntary controls and standards, with sidewalks, adjacent uses and their users becoming 'active participants' in the 'drama of civilisation versus barbarism'. Jacobs (1961, p. 45) argued that 'the streets of a city must do most of the job of handling strangers, for this is where strangers come and go. The streets must not only defend the city against predatory strangers, they must protect the many, many peaceable and well-meaning strangers who use them ensuring their safety too as they pass through.'

Oscar Newman developed some of Jacobs' ideas further, emphasising surveillance and territorial definition. Based on a study of the locations of crimes in housing projects in New York, Newman, in his book *Defensible Space: People and Design in the Violent City* (1973), proposed restructuring urban environments 'so that they can again become liveable and controlled not by police but by a community of people sharing a common terrain'. Newman identified three factors associated with increases in the rate of crime in residential blocks: *anonymity* (people did not know their neighbours); a *general lack of surveillance* within the building, making it easier for crimes to be committed unseen; and the *availability of escape routes*, enabling criminals to disappear from the scene. From these he developed his concept of 'defensible space': 'the range of mechanisms – real and symbolic barriers, strongly defined areas of influence, and improved opportunities for surveillance – that combine to bring an environment under the control of its residents' (Newman, 1973).

The Crime Prevention Through Environment Design (CPTED) approach has many elements in common with Newman's concept. The main idea is that the physical environment can be manipulated to reduce the incidence and fear of crime, by reducing the support it provides for criminal behaviour (Crowe, 1991, pp. 28–9). 'Secured by Design' approaches, widely adopted by police agencies around the world, are similar to those of CPTED. In the UK, for example, most police authorities ensure that such principles are adopted in new developments. Analysis of these approaches in the UK (BRE, 1999) and the US (Sherman *et al.*, 2001) provides a strong basis for place-specific physical interventions, including defensible space principles.

The emphasis on territorial definition in Newman's and the CPTED approaches has tended to support hierarchical (i.e. segregated) and discontinuous road layouts such as cul-de-sacs. These deter burglary because (it is argued) criminals avoid streets where they might get trapped (Mayo, 1979). Segregated residential areas include two broad groups: those where the means of segregation are relatively implicit (i.e. 'strangers' are passively deterred from entering, perhaps because they feel conspicuous) and those where it is explicit and physical (i.e. strangers are actively prevented from entering, such as gated developments).

Hillier (1988, 1996a) criticised defensible enclaves that prevent the natural movement of people by excluding all strangers, regardless of whether they are predatory or peaceable. He argued that the presence of people enhances the feeling of safety in public space and provides the primary means by which a space is naturally policed. The more the natural presence of people is eliminated, the greater the danger. In his studies of the relationship between spatial configuration and movement, Hillier (1996a, 1996b) argued that certain spatial characteristics increase the likely presence of people, and thus enhance feelings of safety (see Chapter 8). Research has also shown that burglary rates for locations that are 'less integrated' are higher than for dwellings in 'more integrated' locations (Chih-Feng Shu, 2000).

There is a basic contradiction therefore between design strategies advocating people presence and 'eyes on the street' to ensure the safety of people and property and design strategies restricting access and permeability in order to ensure the safety of people and property within defined areas. While both ideas have their merits and applications, the crucial issue concerns the density of pedestrian movement. To act as a deterrent, sufficient surveillance is needed. Integrated layouts require a certain density of movement to increase surveillance, which high density, mixed-use urban areas may provide. If this level of pedestrian movement is unlikely, as in low-density mainly residential 'dormitory' communities, then defensible space design may be more useful. It should also be noted that these strategies are not necessarily mutually exclusive.

Related debates concern the relative merits of surveillance strategies and of strategies that prevent or obstruct access. Although often considered unneighbourly, high, impermeable fences reduce access to the private space surrounding a dwelling, and thus to the dwelling itself. Fences around such private spaces are common in Europe, where typically they are much higher at the rear than to the front, allowing interaction, including 'eyes on the street', between the dwelling and the street. However, because they hide suspicious activity, fences can hinder policing. Where private spaces are open and unfenced – an approach common in parts of the US – break-in attempts are open to view. This approach, however, reduces the privacy of the backyard through exposing all façades of the dwelling. As well as security issues, there may also be aesthetic preferences for one type of arrangement or the other.

Opportunity reduction approaches are criticised on two main grounds. First, express concerns for security and protection have resulted in some highly defensive urbanisms. Sorkin (1992, pp. xiii–xiv) notes an 'obsession with "security", with rising levels of manipulation and surveillance over its citizenry and with a proliferation of new modes of segregation'. The features of what Soja termed the 'carceral city' (see Chapter 2) are explored in Mike Davis' *City of Quartz* (1990) and include panopticon-like shopping centres with advanced forms of spatial surveillance; 'smart' office buildings impenetrable to outsiders; 'bunker' and 'paranoid' architecture; armed police and home owners; and 'sadistic' streets with razor-protected trash bins, and park benches designed to prevent indigents sleeping on them. Public spaces that are made safe, but intimidate potential users, defeat their very *raison d'être*, while expressly policed environments may reassure some, but be oppressive to others.

Opportunity reduction methods can be subtler in their application. It is instructive to consider the controls that operate in theme parks. Disneyworld, for example, handles 100 000 visitors per day in an orderly fashion enhanced by constant instruction and direction, by physical barriers that severely limit the choice of available actions, and by the surveillance of 'omnipresent employees who detect and rectify the slightest deviation' (Shearing and Stenning, 1985, p. 419). The control strategies are embedded in both the environmental design and its management: every Disney Productions employee, for example, 'while visibly and primarily engaged in other functions, is also engaged in the maintenance of order'. The overall effect is to embed the control functions into the 'woodwork'. Shearing and Stenning argue that Disney Productions' power rests both in the physical coercion it can bring to bear – if and when it needs to – and in its capacity to induce co-operation by depriving visitors of a resource they value. As a consequence, control becomes consensual.

Second, it is argued that restricting opportunities for crime in one location may simply redistribute it. Displacement may take different forms:

- *geographical displacement*: the crime is moved from one location to another;
- *temporal displacement*: the crime is moved from one time to another;
- *target displacement*: the crime is moved from one target to another;
- *tactical displacement*: one method of crime is substituted for another;
- *crime type displacement*: one kind of crime is substituted for another (Felson and Clarke, 1998, p. 25).

As displacement takes place in various ways, conclusive demonstrations of its absence are extremely elusive, and the possibility of displacement can never be precluded by research. Equally, it is probable that the frictional effect of displacement dissipates at least some criminal energies and that motivation, and the degree of displacement correlates with the availability of alternative targets, and with the offender's strength of motivation. Displacement does not, however, provide a compelling argument against opportunity reduction measures. Barr and Pease (1992) usefully distinguish between 'benign' displacement, which involves a less serious offence being committed, and 'malign' displacement involving a shift to a more serious offence or to offences that have worse consequences. Though the aim is crime reduction, benign is generally preferable to malign displacement. Evidence indicates that integrated approaches to crime prevention through design can reduce displacement to neighbouring areas, and improve residents' perceptions of their areas (Ekblom *et al.*, 1996).

Synthesising opportunity reduction approaches with more general urban design ideas, Oc and Tiesdell (1999, 2000) identify four urban design approaches to creating safer environments:

- *The fortress approach* involves walls, barriers, gates, physical segregation, privatisation and control of territory, and strategies of exclusion.
- *The panoptic approach* (or 'police state') involves explicit control and/or privatisation of public space, the presence of explicit police/security guards, CCTV systems as tools of control, covert surveillance systems, and exclusion.
- *The management or regulatory approach* (or 'policed state') involves the management of public space, explicit rules and regulations, temporal and spatial regulations, CCTV as a management tool, and city centre representatives in public space.
- *The animation or 'peopling' approach* involves people presence, people generators, activities, a welcoming ambience, accessibility and inclusion.

These are not exclusive approaches: in any particular situation, the approach adopted depends on the local context and may combine different elements of all four. The appeal of fortress and panoptic approaches is that they are positive actions, something is being seen to be done. Essentially private-minded, however, they result in increased safety for some, but possibly decreased safety for others. In effect, individual solutions of this nature inhibit collective solutions and may result in situations that are less good for everyone. While elements of these strategies may have their place, there are more positive ways of making urban places feel safer. The management and animation approaches, for example, offer inherently more expansive and positive notions of urban areas and public spaces.

ACCESSIBILITY AND EXCLUSION

A key element of any discussion of the public realm is accessibility. While by definition, the public realm should be accessible to all, some environments are – intentionally or unintentionally – less accessible to certain sections of society. Exclusion often establishes or reinforces connotations of 'exclusivity' or (as discussed in the previous section) 'security'. In essence, it is a manifestation of power through the control of space and access to it. Various forces in society purposefully reduce accessibility in order to control particular environments, often to protect investments. Nevertheless, if access control is practised explicitly and widely, the public realm's

public-ness is compromised. While design strategies can enable and enhance both exclusion and inclusion, the idea that environments should increase choice and be inclusive is central to much urban design thinking.

Carr *et al.* (1992, p. 138) identify three forms of access:

- *Visual access* (visibility): if people can see into a space before they enter it, they can judge whether they would feel comfortable, welcome and safe there.
- *Symbolic access*: cues (symbols) can be animate or inanimate. For example, individuals and groups perceived either as threatening, or as comforting or inviting, may affect entry into a public space, while elements such as particular kinds of shops may signal the type of people that are welcome there.
- *Physical access* concerns whether the space is physically available to the public. Physical exclusion is the inability to get into or to use the environment, regardless of whether or not it can be seen into.

Accessibility and exclusion can be discussed in terms of management of the public realm (i.e. prevention or exclusion of undesirable/undesired social behaviour). Managers and owners of quasi-public space have various motives for controlling activity, such as their responsibility for maintenance, liability for what may happen within the space, and concern for marketability. Exclusion of certain behaviours/activities can be a function – even an objective – of the management or control regime. Murphy (2001, p. 24) highlights the proliferation of 'exclusion' zones designed to be free of undesirable social characteristics. This is a broad phenomenon: it includes zones free from, for example, smoke, political campaigning, skateboards, mobile phones, alcohol, cars, and so forth.

Management and the public realm

The public realm often needs to be managed to balance collective and individual interests. This inevitably involves finding a balance between freedom and control. Discussing accessibility in the sense of being 'open', Lynch (1972a, p. 396) argued that this meant 'open to the freely chosen and spontaneous actions of people'. He subsequently argued that, while the free use of open space may 'offend us, endanger us, or even threaten the seat of power', it was also one of our 'essential values': 'We prize the right to speak and act as we wish. When others act more freely, we learn about them, and thus about ourselves. The pleasure of an urban space freely used is the spectacle of those peculiar ways, and the chance of an interesting encounter' (Lynch and Carr, 1979, p. 415). Freedom of action in public space is, nevertheless, necessarily a 'responsible freedom'. According to Carr *et al.* (1992, p. 152), it involves 'the ability to carry out the activities that one desires, to use a place as one wishes but with the recognition that a public space is a shared space'.

Even benign management of public space is complex. Lynch and Carr (1979, p. 415) argue that it involves:

- Distinguishing between 'harmful' and 'harmless' activities, and controlling the former without constraining the latter.
- Increasing general tolerance toward free use, while stabilising a broad consensus of what is permissible.
- Separating – in time and space – the activities of those groups with a low tolerance for each other.
- Providing 'marginal places' where extremely free behaviour can go on with little damage.

Although public spaces may be regulated through bylaws, etc, explicit controls on behaviour and activity are more pronounced and evident in quasi-public space (Figure 6.7). Ellin (1999, pp. 168–9) illustrates the potential intensity of regulation by reference to a sign that used to hang at the entry to Universal Studio's CityWalk, Los Angeles, warning visitors against:

obscene language or gestures, noisy or boisterous behaviour, singing, playing of musical instruments, unnecessary staring, running, skating, roller-blading, bringing pets, 'non-commercial expressive activity', distributing commercial advertising, 'failing to be fully clothed', or 'sitting on the ground more than five minutes'. (Figure 6.7)

Loukaitou-Sideris and Banerjee (1999, pp. 183–5) note two types of control:

- 'Hard' (active) control uses private security officers, surveillance cameras, and regulations either prohibiting certain activities, or allowing

FIGURE 6.7
Restrictions in quasi-public space illustrating its compromised nature

them subject to the issue of permits, programming, scheduling or leasing.
- 'Soft' (passive) control focuses on 'symbolic restrictions' that passively discourage undesirable activities, and on *not* providing certain facilities (e.g. public toilets).

Whatever the control strategy, if public spaces are to be successful as people places, they must be attractive (Figure 6.8). Equally, control strategies are part of the appeal. The common reality, however, is that many open spaces are not designed as public places, and are often intended (merely) to show off a building or to appeal to a select group of people. In public realm management, it is important to note the often subtle distinction between the creation of a socially authoritarian 'police state', and a more tolerant 'policed state' that protects the freedoms of its citi-

FIGURE 6.8
The recently redeveloped Peace Gardens in Sheffield, UK, provide a lively and vibrant place for people. On the first sunny weekend after its opening Sheffield people used it more like a beach than a traditional European square. Management staff considered how to regulate its uses but quickly appreciated that provided the square was not being damaged such free behaviour suggested a feeling of ownership and affinity with the space

zens. While many may favour greater regulation of the public realm in the interest of public order and safety, the danger exists of progression from rules enacted in the wider public interest, to rules prohibiting behaviours objectionable to dominant groups, for reasons such as profitability or marketability. The latter provides much of the rationale for reduced accessibility within the public realm.

Exclusion and the public realm

Rather than particular behaviours, some strategies seek to exclude particular individuals or social groups. A principal right of private ownership is that of excluding and/or preventing access. Unless a special order has been created, one cannot – in principle – legally be excluded from true public space. The public realm, however, includes spaces that are publicly accessible but privately owned; for example, those given as a public contribution (e.g. through density bonuses, or direct financial subsidies) on condition that they are publicly accessible. Commenting on the design of such spaces, Banerjee (2001, p. 12) observes that, while the public is welcome as patrons of shops and restaurants or as business workers or clients, access to and use of the space remains a privilege rather than a right.

Hence, 'undesirable' individuals or groups, such as those whose mere presence creates anxiety in others, may be excluded both for the well-being and security of others, and to further profit-making. Access control of this nature is usually risk-averse, tending to exclude too many rather than too few. Seen positively, such strategies are based on 'profiling', on identification of the characteristics of groups or individuals deemed likely to contravene desired behaviours, so that attention can be concentrated there; seen negatively, it amounts to stereotyping and even discrimination.

Exclusion can be practised through physical design strategies. Based on observations in Los Angeles, Flusty (1997, pp. 48–9) distinguished five types of space designed to exclude by a combination of their function and cognitive sensibilities:

- 'Stealthy' space cannot be found, it is camouflaged or obscured by intervening objects or level changes.
- 'Slippery' space cannot be reached due to contorted, protracted or missing paths of approach.
- 'Crusty' space cannot be accessed, due to obstructions such as walls, gates, and checkpoints.

- 'Prickly' space cannot be comfortably occupied (e.g. ledges sloped to inhibit sitting).
- 'Jittery' space cannot be utilised unobserved due to active monitoring by roving patrols and/or surveillance technologies.

In evaluating Security Pacific, Noguchi and Citicorp plazas in central Los Angeles, Loukaitou-Sideris and Banerjee (1998, pp. 96–7) found 'introversion' and a 'deliberate fragmentation' of the public realm. Each plaza was designed to inhibit visual access and, thereby, to be exclusive (stealthy space). The exteriors give few clues to the space within, while certain design strategies – isolation from the street, de-emphasis of street-level access, major entrances through parking structures, etc. – achieved an inward orientation of the spaces: 'These defensive design postures insulate the space from the outside environment, thereby fragmenting and disconnecting the space from the surrounding city fabric.'

A different form of direct exclusion is effected by charging an entry fee, where the entrance ticket contains an undertaking to obey the rules (or be ejected from the place). While common in some parts of quasi-public space (cinemas, theatres, etc.), this is less common in other parts, such as public parks and civic space. Nevertheless, Disney's proposed redesign of a civic centre in Seattle would have made an entrance fee inevitable (Warren, 1994).

A subtler form of exclusion is practised through visual cues symbolising and communicating the *ability* to pay (or, more precisely, to consume). Those lacking appropriate cues may be treated with suspicion, made to feel unwelcome, or refused entry, while a sufficiently prosperous appearance ensures access. As people conform to the expected behaviour and dress norms, the regulation is self-enforcing. Observing the 'spatial apartheid' in Detroit's Renaissance Centre, for example, Boddy (1992, p. 141) highlights 'the very conservative and very expensive clothes worn by young black men, even those who are clerks, messengers, and trainees. One soon starts to wonder whether the overdressing is a survival strategy, the entrance ticket to the new fortified urban encampments.'

EQUITABLE ENVIRONMENTS

The design of the urban environment can also be considered in terms of the ways in which it reduces the choices available to certain social groups, such as those with disabilities, women and the elderly, and those without access to cars and reliant on walking or public transport.

Disability, accessibility and exclusion

For the disabled, the elderly, those with young children in pushchairs, pregnant women, etc., various physical barriers inhibit their use of the public realm. Hall and Imrie (1999, p. 409) observe that disabled people tend to experience the built environment as a series of obstacle courses:

> *Most buildings are not wheelchair accessible and few contain sufficient tactile colouring or colour contrasts to enable vision-impaired people to navigate with ease. The design of specific items, such as doors, handles, and toilets, are also standardised to the point whereby many people with a range of physiological and/or mental impairments, find them impossible to use.*

There are two main models of disability. The 'medical model' defines it in terms of a medical condition (e.g. a person is 'arthritic' or 'epileptic'): the disabling factors are placed on the individual, without reference to social context. The 'social model' focuses on the barriers imposed by a *disabling* society/environment unable to make adjustments: this, rather than personal impairment, is the disability factor. In this model, people have impairments, environments are disabling.

Imrie and Hall (2001, p. 10) argue that design and development processes are both disabling and disabilist and that inclusive design is about attitudes and processes as much as about products. Most built environment professionals have little awareness of disabled people's needs, reacting to them only when forced to do so by legislation. In such a context, features for the less able-bodied in society are regarded as 'add-ons', an extra cost to be resisted. Unsurprisingly, people with disabilities are often alienated from the built environment, as well as from the social and developmental processes underlying it.

In practice, narrow perceptions of disability and the needs of disabled people often mean that 'disabled provision' is geared only to the needs of wheelchair users. The UK 1995 *Disability Discrimination Act* contains a much broader definition: 'a physical or mental impairment which has a substantial and long-term adverse effect on a person's ability to carry out day-to-day activities'. To be regarded as disabled for the purpose of the Act, a person must be affected in at least one of the following respects: mobility; manual dexterity; physical co-ordination; continence; ability to lift, carry or otherwise move everyday objects; speech, hearing or eyesight; memory or ability to concentrate, learn or understand; and/or perception of risk of physical danger. Recognition of this range expands our appreciation of ways in which the built environment is disabling: for example, just 4 per cent of the population with disabilities in the UK are wheelchair users, yet the stereotypical disabled person is a wheelchair user (Imrie and Hall, 2001, p. 43).

In an urban design context, addressing environmental disability involves:

- understanding social disability and the ways in which the environment is disabling;
- designing for inclusion rather than for exclusion or segregation; and
- ensuring proactive and integrated consideration, rather than reactive 'tacked-on' provision.

Attention specifically to disability can, however, obscure the fact that good access and design features make buildings easier to use for everyone. The overarching argument, therefore, is that the needs of those with disabilities should be considered an integral part of the design process, since barrier-free buildings and environments will then perform better for all users.

Mobility, accessibility and exclusion

Accessibility can also be discussed in terms of transport. Environments are inaccessible if their use depends on private (usually car) travel. Inclusive urban design relies partly on spatial concentration of different land uses, making places and facilities accessible, and public transport viable.

Accessibility is related to mobility: women and lower income groups, for example, tend to have reduced mobility and access because they rely on public transport. Today, 'automobility' – meaning car-based mobility plus the economic and political systems supporting car-based society – is especially privileged, resulting in a prevalence of car-dependent environments. On the positive side, as Sheller and Urry (2000, p. 743) argue, automobility is a 'source of freedom', enabling car users to travel fast, at any time, anywhere. Cars also provide secu-

rity and in some respects, 'women's "emancipation" has been predicated on the automobile. Cars afford many women a sense of personal freedom and a relatively secure form of travel in which families and objects can be safely transported, and fragmented time-schedules successfully intermeshed' (p. 749). This flexibility and freedom is, nevertheless, itself necessitated by automobility: many people's work and private lives could not be undertaken without the car and its 24-hour availability (p. 744). Urry (1999, pp. 13–14) contends that, in reality, the flexibility of the car is 'coerced', because automobility supports an ever-increasing spatial separation of uses, necessitating ever greater use of the car to recombine the separated facilities. Thus, despite the 'widespread depiction in advertising and the media of cars as "harbingers of unproblematic liberation" ', mass mobility does not generate mass accessibility.

While the particular advantage of car use is the making of (virtually) 'seamless' journeys with, in principle, a high degree of personal safety, provision for the car has often interrupted and/or severed linkages that made other forms of transport possible. Compared to seamless car journeys other modes of travel seem fragmented and inconvenient – gaps occur, for example, in the walk to the bus stop; the wait there; the walk from the bus station to the train station; the wait on the station platform; etc. (Sheller and Urry, 2000, p. 745). Each gap is a source of uncertainty, inconvenience, perhaps danger. Although gaps exist in car journeys (e.g. in using a multi-storey car park), they are 'much less endemic' than in other travel modes.

Social segregation and fragmentation

With widespread prevalence, strategies of exclusion lead to social segregation and fragmentation. While there is considerable debate about the merits of 'integration' versus 'segregation' in the layout of urban areas (see below and Chapter 4), the trend today is towards segregation.

Segregation compromises the public realm's third function, that of social learning, personal development and information exchange. It begets ignorance, and thus fear, regarding social differences (Ellin, 1996, pp. 145–6). Within the urban design literature – especially that of the US – the social segregation of urban space, and the damaging effects of exclusion, are receiving increasing attention.

Social segregation has been central to Richard Sennett's work (1970, 1977, 1990). Sennett (1990, p. 20) argues that people living in 'sealed communities' are 'diminished in their development': 'The wounds of past experience, the stereotypes which have become rooted in memory, are not confronted. Recognition scenes that might occur at borders are the only chance people have to confront fixed, sociological pictures routinised in time.' Echoing Sennett's arguments, Duany *et al.* (2000, pp. 45–6) argue that the segregationist pattern is self-perpetuating: children raised in homogeneous environments are 'less likely to develop a sense of empathy for people from other walks of life and [are] ill-prepared to live in a diverse society. The *other* becomes alien to the child's experience, witnessed only through the sensationalising eye of the television.'

Desire for a more inclusive public realm can be thwarted in various ways, not least by the demand for exclusive spaces. Discussing public space in southern California, Loukaitou-Sideris and Banerjee (1998, p. 299) argue that such spaces reflect a 'collective apathy and reluctance' to create inclusion:

> The introverted, enclosed, controlled, escapist, commercial, and exclusive nature of these settings cannot be attributed simply to the whims of private enterprise or to the collective imagination of architects, planners, and urban designers. There is clearly a demand for the settings of the new downtown from the parts of the public sector that are threatened by the presence of other groups and are willing to pay for more privacy and seclusion.

What is witnessed here is both express desires for exclusiveness and segregation, and the ability of urban design – and urban designers – to respond to those needs. This raises important ethical issues in urban design, concerning, in particular, the need to balance collective and individual interests.

CONCLUSION

More than any other dimension of urban design, the social dimension raises issues concerning values, and difficult choices with regard to the effects of design decisions on individuals and groups in society. Furthermore, the role of design is delivering particular social goals, which is inevitably limited (although important), and urban designers will need to work with a wide range of other public and private stakeholders to effect significant sound benefits. Although 'public space' has never been truly 'public', the 'public' space network of many cities is giving way to

> instrumental quasi-public spaces geared overwhelmingly to consumption and paid recreation by those who can afford it and who are deemed to warrant unfettered access . . . In many cases 'public space' is now under the direct or indirect control, of corporate, real estate or retailer groups, which carefully work with private and public police and security forces to manage and desire out any groups or behaviour seen as threatening . . . This generally amounts to the recreation, consumption and spectacle of middle-class shoppers, office workers and tourists.
> (Graham and Marvin, 2001, p. 232)

Don Mitchell (1995, p. 110) asks whether, as a result, we have reached the 'end of public space': 'Have we created a society that expects and desires only private interactions, private communications, and private politics, that reserves public spaces, solely for commodified recreation and spectacle?' It is clear that the social dimension involves some difficult and challenging questions for urban designers. While arguably the aim should be the provision of an accessible, safe and secure, equitable public realm for all, economic and social trends in many parts of the world are making this increasingly difficult to deliver.

7

The visual dimension

INTRODUCTION

In this chapter, the visual – or, more precisely, the visual–aesthetic – dimension of urban design is discussed. Architecture and urban design are often described as the only truly inescapable, and therefore public, art forms. Nasar (1998, p. 28) notes that while observers can choose whether or not to experience art, literature and music, urban design does not afford such a choice: 'In their daily activities, people must pass through and experience the public parts of the city environment.' Thus, while we may 'accept the idea of "high" visual arts that appeal to a narrow audience who choose to visit a museum, city form and appearance must satisfy the broader public who regularly experiences it' (p. 2).

The chapter focuses on four key issues. The first part concerns aesthetic preferences. The second concerns the appreciation of space and the aesthetic qualities of urban spaces and townscape. The third and fourth concern the design of elements that define and occupy urban space – the architecture, and the hard and soft landscaping.

AESTHETIC PREFERENCES

Aesthetic appreciation of the urban environment is primarily visual and kinaesthetic (i.e. involving awareness of movement of all parts of the body). Experiencing urban environments nevertheless involves all our senses and in some situations, hearing, smelling and tactility can be more important than vision. As Von Meiss (1990, p. 15) urges designers: 'Let us try to imagine the echo in the spaces that we are designing, the smells that will be given off by the materials or the activities that will take place there, the tactile experience that they will arouse.'

Visual appreciation of urban environments is also a product of perception and cognition – that is, what stimuli we perceive, how we perceive them, how we process, interpret and judge the information gathered, and how it appeals to our mind and emotions (see Chapter 5). Such information is inseparable from, and significantly influenced by, how we feel about the particular environment (whether we care about it) and what it means to us (how we value it). As well as a significant personal component, aesthetic appreciation also has socially and culturally learnt components that go beyond simple expressions of individual taste. As notions of 'beauty' are socially and culturally constructed (at least in the aggregate), then beauty must reside – at least in part – in the object, rather than simply in the mind of the beholder.

Although this chapter focuses on the visual dimension of urban design, it is important to recognise that the general public's liking for particular environments is much broader than aesthetic criteria. Jack Nasar (1998) identified five attributes of 'liked' environments. Disliked environments tended to have the opposites of these. In each case, it was the observer's perception of the attribute that was important. The attributes translate into a series of very generalised preferences:

- *Naturalness*: environments that are natural or where there is a predominance of natural over built elements.
- *Upkeep/civilities*: environments that appear to be looked after and cared for.

- *Openness and defined space*: the blending of defined open space with panoramas and vistas of pleasant elements.
- *Historical significance/content*: environments that provoke favourable associations.
- *Order*: in terms of organisation, coherence, congruity, legibility, clarity (see Nasar, 1998, pp. 62–73).

PATTERNS AND AESTHETIC ORDER

As we always experience the 'whole' rather than any single part in isolation, we appreciate environments as ensembles. To make them more ordered, visually coherent and harmonious, however, we select and choose some features. Gestalt psychologists have argued that aesthetic order and coherence comes from the grouping and recognition of patterns, and that to make environments more coherent visually we use principles of organisation or grouping to create 'good' form from the parts (Arnheim, 1977; Von Meiss, 1990). Based on Gestalt theory, Von Meiss (1990, p. 32) argues that: 'Part of the pleasures and difficulties we experience with the built environment can be explained by our ease or difficulty in mentally grouping different elements from the visual field into synoptic units.' Some fundamental 'factors of coherence' or principles of grouping have been identified (see Figure 7.1). As pure situations are rare, in most environments several principles come into play simultaneously, although sometimes one principle is dominant.

More generally, Smith (1980, p. 74) argues that our intuitive capacity for aesthetic appreciation has four distinct components that transcend time and culture:

1. *Sense of rhyme and pattern*: Rhyme involves some similarity in the elements, and presupposes the simultaneous existence of complexity (i.e. a mass of visual detail and information) and patterns. Over time, as the mind 'organises' and makes sense of the information, the patterns become more dominant, in subtle ways. Smith (1980, p. 74) argues that, rather than simple repetition (as in wallpaper), these rhyme patterns comprise a system in which there is 'substantial affinity' rather than 'point-to-point correspondence' (Figure 7.2).
2. *Appreciation of rhythm*: Differing from rhyme, rhythm relies for its impact on a stricter repetition. Visual pleasure, for example, derives from rhythmic elements varying from the simple binary kind to more complex repeated subsystems (Smith, 1980, p. 78). Rhythm is produced by the grouping of elements to create emphasis, interval, accent and/or direction, etc. (Figure 7.3). To avoid monotony, contrast and variety are essential in achieving interesting rhythms.
3. *Recognition of balance*: While we can generally conceive visual 'balance', it is difficult to define precisely. Balance is a form of order generally related to 'harmony' among the parts of a visual scene or environment. It can also be recognised in scenes that are complex and seemingly chaotic – in some cases, it is rarely immediately obvious and may only become apparent over time. Smith (1980, p. 79) suggests that a major attraction of historic towns is the discovery of views where everything suddenly seems to cohere into perfect balance – an important aspect of this is the surprise element. Although symmetry can be a powerful tool in achieving balance, symmetrical compositions can appear mechanical and leaden. Asymmetrical compositions may also use elements of symmetry to achieve visual balance but in more complex and potentially interesting ways. Balance can also be perceived in highly complex organisations of colours, textures, and shapes, which cohere into a state of balance. Different types of balance also exist: in Georgian neo-classical townscapes, for example, there is usually a 'static' form, where all elements contribute and are subservient to the greater whole. In Victorian neo-Gothic townscapes, the elements often compete, giving a more 'dynamic' balance.
4. *Sensitivity to harmonic relationships*: Harmony concerns the relationships between different parts, and how they fit together to form a coherent whole. Certain relationships, such as those of the Golden Section, also contribute to the quality of harmony. Gifted designers often manipulate proportions to achieve more harmonious results. Perspective effects, for example, may be used to suggest that building elements are taller, more slender, or more elegant than they actually are, while deliberate strategies of distraction may concentrate attention on some aspects of the design rather than others.

(i) *The principle of similarity*, which enables recognition of similar or identical elements amid others – repetition of forms or of common characteristics (e.g. window shapes).

(ii) *The principle of proximity*, which enables elements that are spatially closer together to be read as a group and to be distinguished from those that are further apart.

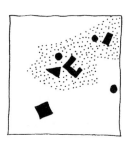

(iii) *The principle of common ground and common enclosure*, whereby an enclosure or a ground defines a field or group. Those elements within the field or ground are distinguished from what lies outside.

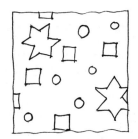

(iv) *The principle of orientation*, whereby elements are grouped through their common orientation, either through parallelism or convergence towards a void or solid.

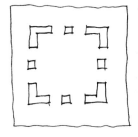

(v) *The principle of closure*, which enables recognition of incomplete or partial elements as wholes.

(vi) *The principle of continuity*, which enables recognition of patterns that may not have been intended that way.

FIGURE 7.1
Principles of organisation and coherence (source: adapted and extended from Von Meiss, 1990, pp. 36–8)

One of the overarching issues in the work of Gestalt psychologists and in Smith's four components, is the apparent need for a balance between order and complexity in environments – a balance that changes over time and with familiarity. There is, however, often a fine line between the richness of diversity and the bewilderment of visual chaos. As Cold (2000, p. 207) observes, we desire 'an environment with a richness of detail that is larger than our immediate ability to process it'. Similarly, Nasar (1998, p. 75) observes that, while *interest* increases with the complexity of an environment, our *prefer-* ence increases only up to a point, beyond which it decreases.

Discussing issues of 'surprise' and 'mystery' in environments, Kaplan and Kaplan (1982) devised an 'environmental preference framework' that relates issues of 'making sense' (i.e. order) and 'involvement' (i.e. complexity) with a time dimension (Box 7.1). They argue that making sense of environments is not sufficient: over time, we also seek to expand our horizons, cherishing the potential for involvement and engagement. Similarly, reflecting on the limitations of his concept of legi-

FIGURE 7.2
Colonnades provide
rhyme and pattern,
contributing to character
and identity, in Central
Bologna

FIGURE 7.3
Façade rhythms in San
Marco's Piazza, Venice,
Italy. Rhythm requires a
stricter repetition than
rhyme

BOX 7.1 – ENVIRONMENTAL PREFERENCE FRAMEWORK

(source: Kaplan and Kaplan, 1982, p. 81)

	MAKING SENSE	INVOLVEMENT
PRESENT OR IMMEDIATE	**COHERENCE** Environments easy to organise or structure.	**COMPLEXITY** Environments with enough in the present scene to keep one occupied.
FUTURE OR PROMISED	**LEGIBILITY** Environments suggesting they could be explored extensively without getting lost.	**MYSTERY** Environments suggesting that, if they were explored further, new information could be acquired.

Kaplan and Kaplan (1982, pp. 82–7) suggest 'coherence', 'legibility', 'complexity', and 'mystery' as 'informational' qualities of environments that contribute to people's preferences for particular physical environments. For immediate appreciation of environments, understanding is supported by environmental 'coherence' (i.e. to make sense) and 'complexity' (i.e. to encourage involvement). In the longer term, qualities of 'legibility' and 'mystery' encourage exploration of the environment.

bility, and noting that we are 'pattern makers' not 'pattern worshippers', Kevin Lynch (1984, p. 252) argued that the 'valuable' city was not an ordered one, but one that could be ordered: while 'some overarching, patent order' was necessary for the 'bewildered newcomer', there should also be an 'unfolding order': 'a pattern that one progressively grasps, making deeper and richer connections. Hence our delight . . . in ambiguity, mystery and surprise, as long as they are contained within a basic order, and as long as we can be confident of weaving the puzzle into some new, more intricate pattern.'

THE KINAESTHETIC EXPERIENCE

As our experience of urban environments is a dynamic activity involving movement and time, the kinaesthetic experience of moving through space is an important part of the visual dimension of urban design. Environments are experienced as a dynamic, emerging, unfolding temporal sequence – to describe the visual aspect of townscape Gordon Cullen (1961) conceived the concept of 'serial vision' (Figure 7.4). Cullen argued that the experience is typically one of a series of jerks or revelations, with delight and interest being stimulated by contrasts, by the 'drama of juxtaposition'. In addition to the immediately present 'existing view', there are also hints of a different 'emerging view'. As well as a sense of being in a particular place ('here'), there may also be an equally strong sense that around and outside it are other places ('there'). Cullen saw particular significance in the tension between 'hereness' and 'thereness' (Figure 7.5). He considered that the urban environment should be designed from the point of view of the moving person, for whom 'the whole city becomes a plastic experience, a journey through pressures and vacuums, a sequence of exposures and enclosures, of constraint and relief' (1961, p. 12).

The development of new modes of travel has provided additional ways of seeing, engaging with and forming mental images of urban environments, seen at different speeds and with different levels of engagement and focus. The pedestrian viewpoint is accompanied by the freedom to stop and engage with one's surroundings. Drivers see the urban environment at speed and through a windscreen, while concentrating on the road, traffic, and any signs or directions. Although they also view at speed and generally through glass, passengers have greater scope to observe the environment than the driver but, equally, are unable to fully engage with it. By viewing the process on film in slow motion, Donald Appleyard, Kevin Lynch and Richard Myer explored and described the motorist's visual experience in their book *The View*

FIGURE 7.4
Gordon Cullen's serial vision (source: Cullen, 1961, p. 17)

from the Road (1964). Played at faster projection speed, some passages of the film stood out, showing a rhythmic spacing of bridges and overpasses. Based on the experience of driving along the 'strip' with its billboards and neon signs, Robert Venturi *et al.*, in their book *Learning from Las Vegas* (1972), highlighted how that environment was designed to suit car-based observers (e.g. quickly read signs). The overarching lesson, however, is that, while environments seen only from cars can – and perhaps should – be designed to suit motorists and passengers, those seen by both motorists and pedestrians should be designed for the pedestrian's more discerning and prolonged attention.

Noting Cullen's (1961) and Bacon's (1974) work showing how movement can be read as a pictorial sequence, Bosselmann (1998, pp. 49–60) described the rich and varied experience of a walk – measuring 350 m and taking about four minutes – from the Calle Lunga de Barnaba to the Rio de la Frescada in Venice. He showed how our perception of time passing and distance travelled differs from reality, and is partly a function of the visual and experiential qualities of the environment we are

FIGURE 7.5
The juxtaposition of 'here' and there' in Budapest, Hungary

moving through. Noting that the walk in Venice seemed to be longer and take more time than it actually did, he assessed the aesthetic experience of the same length of walk in fourteen other cities (Figure 7.6). In most, the same distance appeared to take less time; in a few it appeared almost the same. Bosselmann (1998, p. 90) argued that people measure their walks in terms of 'rhythmic spacing' related to visual and spatial experiences. The Venice walk had frequent and different types of rhythmic spacing, while other environments had fewer types, and their visible information engaged walkers less frequently. The walk in Venice needed

thirty-nine drawings of unequal spacing to explain it; most of the other walks required far less.

James (1892, p. 150, from Isaacs, 2001, p. 110) identifies a similar paradox to that of the Venice walk: 'a time filled with varied and interesting experiences seems short in passing, but long as we look back. [Equally] . . . a tract of time empty of experiences seems long in passing, but in retrospect short.' Isaacs (2001, p. 110) explains this paradox: when walking through an environment that engages the mind, one is less aware of the passing of time, but when one reflects on that experience and the variety of sensations contained within it,

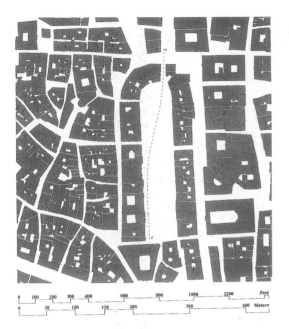

(i) Rome

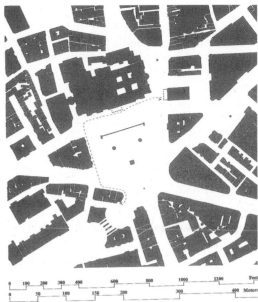

(ii) London

(iii) Copenhagen

(iv) Kyoto

FIGURE 7.6
Four of Bosselmann's walks in (i) Rome, Italy; (ii) London, UK; (iii) Copenhagen, Denmark; and (iv) Kyoto, Japan. The walks illustrated are the same length in terms of distance but the perception of time taken and the experience of the walk vary. Drawn at a consistent scale and read as a set, these diagrams are tissue studies illustrating the different textures; block size and urban grains of each city (source: Bosselmann, 1998, pp. 70, 76, 79 and 81)

one assumes more time must have passed. Conversely, in an environment that does not engage the mind one is more aware of the passing of time, but in retrospect the absence of sensations leads to the belief that less time passed.

Having discussed some of the different aspects of our general visual–aesthetic appreciation of urban environments, the following parts of the chapter concern components of the urban environment.

URBAN SPACE

Positive and negative space

Outdoor space can be considered in terms of 'positive' and 'negative' spaces:

- Positive, relatively enclosed, outdoor space has a definite and distinctive shape. It is 'conceivable', can be measured, and has definite boundaries – we could imagine it being filled with water, which subsequently runs out relatively slowly. It is discontinuous (in principle), closed, static, but serial in composition. Its shape is as important as that of the buildings surrounding it.
- Negative space is shapeless, e.g. the amorphous residue left over around buildings which are generally viewed as positive. It is 'inconceivable' – continuous and lacking in perceivable edges or form. It is difficult to imagine such space being filled with water because – quite simply – it is difficult to conceive of the space (Alexander *et al.*, 1977, p. 518; Paterson, 1984, from Trancik, 1986, p. 60) (Figure 7.7).

The difference between 'positive' and 'negative' outdoor spaces can also be considered in terms of their 'convexity' (Figure 7.8).

In discussing urban space, Trancik (1986, p. 60) makes a useful distinction between 'hard space', principally bounded by architectural walls, and the 'soft space' of parks, gardens and linear greenways, which have less enclosure or defined boundary and are dominated by the natural environment. This section primarily discusses hard space.

Creating positive space

For all 'hard' urban spaces, three major space-defining elements exist: the surrounding structures;

FIGURE 7.7
This diagram illustrates the principle of figure-ground reversal. Depending on which is the 'figure' and which is the 'ground', the image is either a vase or two faces. 'Positive' and 'negative' types of space can be distinguished through figure-ground *reversal*. Where outdoor spaces are negative, the buildings are the figure and outdoor space is the ground, but it is not possible to see the outdoor space as figure and the buildings as ground. Where outdoor spaces are positive, figure-ground reversal is possible and the buildings can be considered as figure or ground

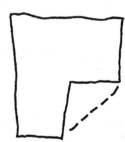

FIGURE 7.8
A space is 'convex' when a line joining any two points inside the space lies totally within the space. The irregular rectangular space (left) is convex and, therefore, positive. The L-shaped space (right) is not convex because a line joining two points cuts across the corner and therefore goes outside the space. According to Alexander *et al.* (1977, p. 518), 'positive' spaces are enclosed – at least to the extent that their areas *seem* bounded (i.e. the 'virtual' area is convex). The L-shaped space, therefore, contains two large virtual spaces (thereby, adding to its interest). 'Negative' spaces are often so poorly defined that it may not be possible to identify their boundaries

the floor; and the imaginary sphere of the sky over-head; which Zucker (1959) argues is usually perceived at three to four times the height of the tallest building. Enclosure and spatial containment must therefore be considered in both plan and vertical section.

The amount of enclosure, and the resulting degree of containment, partially depends on the ratio of the width of the space to the height of the enclosing walls. The most comfortable viewing distance for a building is from a distance of about twice its height, but although not all buildings are – or should be – designed to be seen in a single view. Greater variety in visual experience can be created by spaces that, in different ways, restrict views of the surrounding structures.

The plan arrangement is important in creating a sense of spatial containment. Booth (1983) discusses the quality of enclosure through a series of simple diagrams. A single building of relatively simple form does not define or create space, but is simply an object in space (Figure 7.9a). The weakest definition of space typically occurs when buildings are organised in a long row or sited indiscriminately with no effort to co-ordinate relationships between them (Figure 7.9b). In these situations, the buildings are individual, unrelated elements surrounded by 'negative' space without containment or focus.

One of the simplest and most commonly used means of achieving compositional order is the siting of buildings at right angles to one another. If overused, however, this easily becomes monotonous (Figure 7.9c). Building-to-building association can be strengthened by relating built forms and lines: for example, by extending imaginary lines from the edge of a building and aligning them with the edge of one nearby (Figure 7.9d), though this also risks appearing contrived. An alternative to the rigidity of a rectilinear layout is where some of the building masses are at varying angles to each other, introducing a degree of variety into the layout.

When several buildings or urban blocks are clustered together in a more organised manner, 'positive' spaces can be created. The most straightforward means of creating a sense of spatial containment is to group buildings around a central space, enclosing it within a wall of façades. Where the corners of the space are open, forming street intersections or a gap between two buildings, space leaks out through the corner openings. To better contain it, façades can be overlapped,

preventing or limiting views into or out of the space (Figure 7.9e). When the building walls turn the corner, keeping views within the central space, a much stronger sensation of enclosure is created (Figure 7.9f).

If the whole space can be easily observed, it does not invite further involvement. It may also lack subspaces and implied movement. Given a more varied and complex perimeter, with indentations and projections in the building façades, the resulting space can have a richer quality, with a number of hidden or partially disguised subspaces creating a sense of 'mystery' or 'intrigue' (Figure 7.9g). However, as a simple urban space becomes more complex, there is a danger of it perceptually breaking apart into a disjointed series of separate spaces (Figure 7.9h). A dominant spatial volume helps establish a focus for the composition, the smaller subspaces being unable to compete with the major space. Alternatively, the spaces might be organised on an axis, or by a single dominant building.

A further key factor in creating a strong sense of enclosure is the design of openings into the space. Booth (1983, p. 142) refers to the 'windmill' or 'whirling' square, while Camillo Sitte (1889) refers to a 'turbine' plan: here, as the streets do not pass directly through the space, it has a strong sense of containment. Not only does this organisation contribute to strengthening the enclosure of the spaces, it also forces pedestrians entering to experience the space, since they are encouraged to walk through – rather than by – it (Figure 7.9i).

The ideas set out here are schematic. Real squares have a high degree of complexity and subtlety. Geoffrey Baker's splendidly illustrated book, *Design Strategies in Architecture* (1996), for example, provides a thorough analysis of the spatial qualities of the Piazza San Marco, Venice, and the Campo in Siena.

While it is commonly argued that people prefer a sense of enclosure, the value of enclosure must be discussed further. Questioning why people feel comfortable in a space that is at least partly enclosed, Alexander et al. (1977, pp. 520–1) noted this is not always true: for example, people feel comfortable on an open beach. Nevertheless, in smaller outdoor spaces – gardens, parks, walks, plazas – enclosure seems to create a feeling of security: 'when a person looks for a place to sit down outdoors, he rarely chooses to sit exposed in the middle of an open space – he usually looks for a tree to put his back against; a hollow in the ground, a natural cleft which will partly enclose

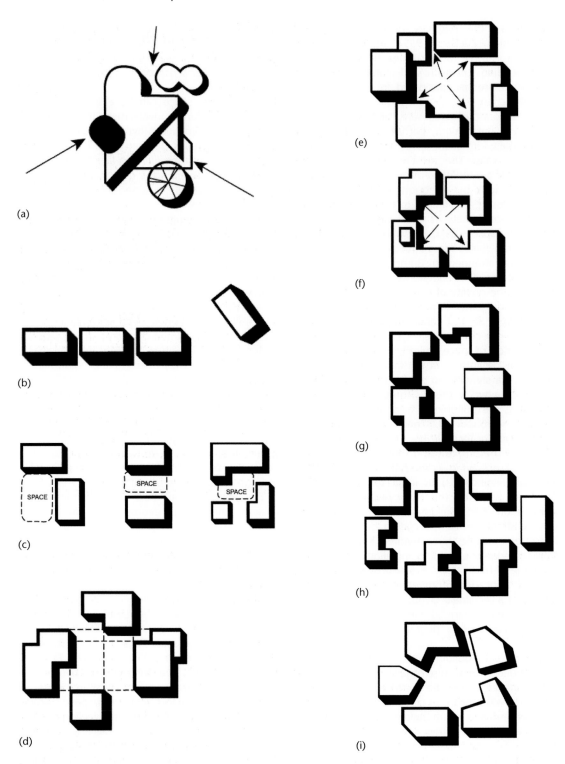

FIGURE 7.9a–i
Principles of spatial containment and enclosure (source: adapted from Booth, 1983)

and shelter him'. While noting people's apparent environmental preference for openness, Nasar (1998, p. 68) cites research that indicates preferences for 'defined openness', in other words for 'open *but* bounded spaces'.

In his book, *City Planning According to Artistic Principles*, Camillo Sitte (1889; Collins and Collins, 1965, p. 61) argued that: 'The ideal street must form a completely enclosed unit! The more one's impressions are confined within it, the more perfect will be its tableau: one feels at ease in a space where the gaze cannot be lost in infinity.' Drawing on his analysis of a number of European squares, however, he showed that those that were well used tended to be partly enclosed, but also open to one another so that each led into the next.

Suggesting that Sitte made a 'highly selective reading of the pre-capitalist city', Bentley (1998, p. 14) argues that while Sitte considered a sense of enclosure to be the most important quality of public space and stressed the medieval street system's spatial enclosure, its more valuable quality was actually its 'integrated continuity'. In this respect, Cullen (1961, p. 106) made a valuable distinction between 'enclosure' and 'closure'. Enclosure, he argued, provided a complete 'private world' that is inward-looking, static and self-sufficient. By contrast, closure involved the division of the urban environment into a series of visually digestible and coherent 'episodes' retaining a sense of progression. Each episode is effectively – sometimes surprisingly – linked to others, making progress on foot more interesting. The conclusion is that a degree of, rather than complete, enclosure is required. A balance must also be struck between achieving enclosure, and considerations such as permeability and legibility, which importantly influence how well the space is used (see Chapter 8).

Streets and squares

Although positive urban spaces come in a variety of different sizes and shapes, there are two main types: 'streets' (roads, paths, avenues, lanes, boulevards, alleys, malls, etc.) and 'squares' (plazas, circuses, piazzas, places, courts, etc.). In principle, streets are 'dynamic' spaces with a sense of movement, while squares are static spaces with less sense of movement. Width-to-length ratios on plan of greater than 1:3 begin to suggest dynamic movement as one axis begins to dominate. This

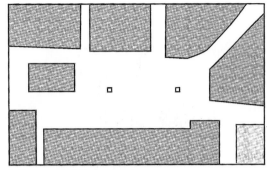

Ratio approx. 1:3

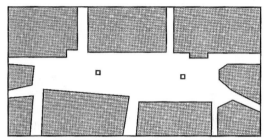

Ratio approx. 1:5

FIGURE 7.10
Width-to-length ratios help distinguish between 'street' spaces and 'square' spaces. If the ratio of width-to-length is 2:3 neither axis dominates. Ratios of about 1:3 begin to form the transition between 'street' and 'square', as one axis begins to dominate. Where the ratio of width-to-length is 1:5, one axis clearly dominates and movement is suggested along that axis. Width-to-length proportions of more than 1:5 suggest a street (i.e. a dynamic space that implies movement)

ratio defines the upper limit for the proportions of a square and, by inference, the lower limit for a street (Figure 7.10).

Streets and squares can be characterised as either 'formal' or 'informal' (Figure 7.11). Formal spaces typically have a strong sense of enclosure; orderly floorscape and arrangement of street furniture; surrounding buildings that enhance the formality; and often a symmetrical layout. Informal squares typically have a more relaxed character, a wide variety of surrounding architecture, and an asymmetric layout. Neither is necessarily more appropriate than the other. A definite geometrical discipline to a space is, however, less ambiguous; for example, on sites surrounding such spaces, developers and their designers are more likely to respect, or be required to respect, the boundary.

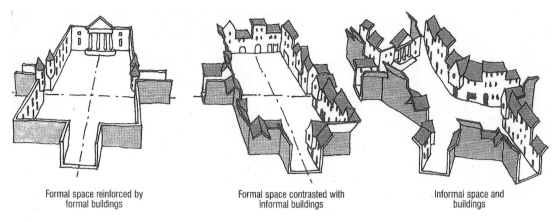

Formal space reinforced by formal buildings   Formal space contrasted with informal buildings   Informal space and buildings

FIGURE 7.11
Formal and informal spaces (source: EPOA, 1997, p. 24)

The square

A 'square' usually refers to an area framed by build-ings. Distinction should be made between squares primarily designed for grandeur and/or to exhibit a particular building, and those designed as 'people places' (i.e. settings for informal public life) (see Chapter 8). This distinction is not absolute: many public spaces function as both, though if we judge one type in terms of the other, difficulties may arise. Spaces designed to show off a particular building or for certain civic functions, for example, may be unsuccessful as people places, but success-ful in their more formal roles.

To better appreciate the aesthetic qualities of squares, the ideas of Camillo Sitte and Paul Zucker are of particular value. Rob Krier's typology of urban spaces (see Chapter 4) is also useful. While Krier's was a morphological structuring based on geometric patterns, both Sitte and Zucker focused on aesthetic effect.

Camillo Sitte

Camillo Sitte (1889) advocated a 'picturesque' approach to urban space design. Collins and Collins (1965, p. xii) contend that Sitte meant 'picturesque' in a pictorial rather than romantic sense: that is, 'structured like a picture and possess-ing the formal values of an organised canvas'. From analysis of the visual and aesthetic character of the squares of a range of European towns, particularly – although not exclusively – those resulting from incremental or 'organic' city growth, Sitte derived a series of artistic principles (Figure 7.12):

- *Enclosure*: For Sitte, enclosure was the primary feeling of urbanity, and his overarching princi-ple was that 'public squares should be enclosed entities' (Figure 7.13). Design of the intersec-tion between side streets and square was one of the most important elements: it should not be possible to see out of the square along more than one street at a time. One means for achieving this was the 'turbine' plan.
- *Freestanding sculptural mass*: Sitte rejected the concept of buildings as freestanding sculptural objects. For Sitte, a building's principal aesthetic was the manner in which its façade defined space, and was seen from within that space. In most squares, observers can stand sufficiently far back to appreciate a façade as a whole, and to appreciate its relation – or lack of relation – with its neighbours. To create a better sense of enclosure, Sitte argued that buildings should be joined to one another rather than being freestanding.
- *Shape*: Arguing that squares should be in proportion to their major building, Sitte identi-fied 'deep' and 'wide' types, depending on whether the main building was long and low or tall and narrow. The depth of a square was best related to the need to appreciate the main building (i.e. between one and two times the main building's height), while the correspond-ing width depended on the perspective effect. In terms of plan shape, Sitte recommended that no relationship should be more than three to one. Sitte also favoured irregular layouts, rejoicing in the variety of combinations found in medieval and renaissance towns. His obser-

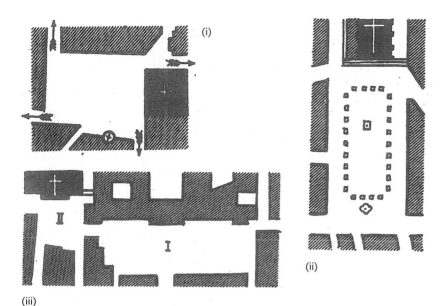

FIGURE 7.12
Camillo Sitte's principles:
(i) the turbine plan
(Piazza del Dumo,
Ravenna); (ii) the 'deep'
type (Piazza Santa
Croce, Florence), and
(iii) the 'broad' type
(Piazza Reale, Modena)
(source: Collins and
Collins, 1965, pp. 34, 39
and 40)

FIGURE 7.13
A good sense of
contained and enclosed
space – Piazza Santa
Croce, Florence, Italy

vations relate to Von Meiss's concept of object-façades projecting a sense of 'radiance' that helps create a sense of space.

- *Monuments*: Although Sitte's general principle was that the centre of the square should be kept free, he recommended supplying a focus, preferably off-centre or along the edge. Collins and Collins (1965, p. ix) note that concern with the proper placement of public statues and

monuments was his book's *raison d'être*. With regard to placement, Sitte made an analogy between children's siting of snowmen on the islands left by paths through the snow and the placing of monuments so as to avoid the natural routes through the space. While such positioning of monuments had an underlying functional logic, he argued that it was also aesthetically pleasing.

Paul Zucker

In *Town and Square* (1959), Paul Zucker discussed 'artistically relevant' squares which represented 'organised' and contained space. He argued that many squares – for example, Piazza San Pietro, Rome, and Piazza San Marco, Venice – were 'undoubtedly art', because the 'unique relationship between the open area of the square, the surrounding buildings, and the sky above creates a genuine emotional experience comparable to the impact of any other work of art' (p. 1). For Zucker, the visual and kinaesthethic relations determined whether a square was a 'whole' or merely a 'hole'.

Zucker outlined five basic types of 'artistically relevant' urban squares (see Figure 7.14):

1. *The closed square – space self-contained*: A closed square is a complete enclosure, interrupted only by the streets leading into it and exhibiting regular geometric forms and,

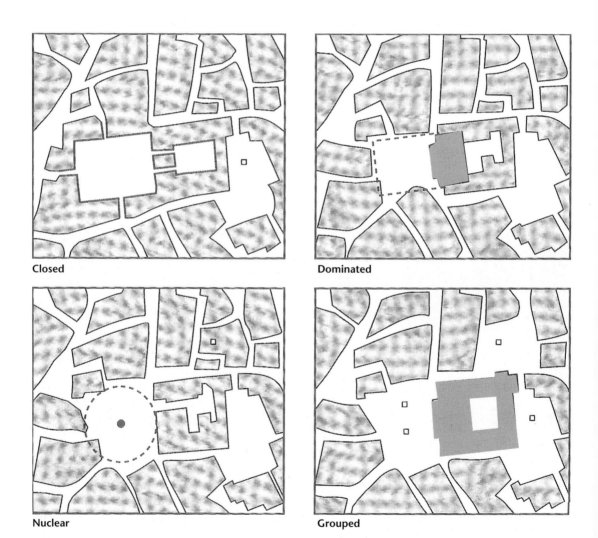

Closed

Dominated

Nuclear

Grouped

FIGURE 7.14
Zucker's typology of urban squares. Note that it is not possible to convey the key attributes of Zucker's amorphous square through a simple sketch. Note also that the surrounding enclosure for the nuclear and dominated types is shown as a broken line. Although the continuity of the enclosing elements may have weaknesses, Zucker (1959, pp. 2–3) argues that, when considered as a work of art, it is not important whether the boundaries of the 'space' are tangible or partially imagined (i.e. there is a virtual space)

usually, repetition of architectural elements around the periphery (e.g. Place des Vosges, Paris). This represents 'the purest and most immediate expression of man's fight against being lost in a gelatinous world, in a disorderly mass of urban dwellings'. Important elements are the layout on plan and the repetition of similar buildings or façade-types (Figure 7.15). Often a rhythmic alternation of two or more types is employed, with richer treatments concentrated on the corners or at the centre of each side (e.g. Place Vendôme, Paris), or framing the streets entering the square (e.g. Place des Victoires, Paris).

2. *The dominated square – space directed*: Recognising that some buildings create a 'sense of space' (Von Meiss's 'radiance') in front of them, Zucker's dominated square is characterised by a building or group of buildings towards which the space is directed, and to which all surrounding structures are related. Although typically the dominant feature is a building, it could, for example, be a view (as in the Piazza del Campidoglio, Rome) or an architecturally

developed fountain (Piazza di Trevi, Rome), provided a sufficiently strong sense of space was created.

3. *The nuclear square – space formed around a centre*: Here a central feature – a vertical nucleus – is sufficiently powerful to create a sense of space (radiance) around itself, charging the space with a tension that keeps the whole together. The force exerted by the nucleus governs the effective size of such spaces.

4. *Grouped squares – space units combined*: Zucker compared the visual impact of a group of aesthetically related squares with the effect of successive rooms inside a Baroque palace, where the first room prepares for the second; the second for third; etc., with each being both a meaningful link in the chain and having additional significance because of it. Provided the successive mental images can be integrated into a greater whole, individual squares can be linked organically or aesthetically, for example by means of an axis (e.g. the Place Royale, Place de la Carriere and the Hemicycle in

FIGURE 7.15
The Place des Vosges, Paris, France, provides a good illustration of Zucker's closed square

Nancy) or by being grouped around a dominant building (e.g. Piazza San Marco, Venice).

5. *The amorphous square – space unlimited*: Amorphous squares do not fall into one of the above categories, but display at least some of their necessary qualities, even if – on further analysis – they appear unorganised or formless. For example, in London's Trafalgar Square, neither the nuclear character suggested by Nelson's column nor the apparently dominating effect of the National Gallery, are sufficient to create a sense of space that relates to the size of the square, while the façades of the surrounding buildings fail to provide a sufficient sense of closure.

Squares rarely represent one pure type, and frequently bear the characteristics of two or more. Zucker (p. 8), for example, noted how Piazza San Marco in Venice might be regarded as primarily a closed square or, equally, as one element of a set of grouped squares. He also noted that the specific function of a square did not automatically produce a definite spatial form, and that each function could be expressed in many different shapes.

The street

Streets are linear three-dimensional spaces enclosed on opposite sides by buildings. They may or may not contain roads. As discussed in Chapter 4, a 'street' is distinct from a 'road': the primary purpose of the latter being a thoroughfare for vehicular traffic. Street form can be analysed in terms of polar qualities, the combination of which gives scope for great diversity: visually dynamic or static; enclosed or open; long or short; wide or narrow; straight or curved; and with regard to the formality or informality of the architectural treatment. To these might be added considerations such as scale, proportion, architectural rhythm, and connections to other streets and squares. Allan Jacobs' book *Great Streets* (1993) provides useful illustrations of different streets types, including scale drawings.

Unlike urban squares – where the degree and nature of enclosure usually gives a visually static character – most streets are visually dynamic, with a strong sense of movement. As horizontal lines are visually faster than vertical lines, the character of streets (as of squares) can be modified to make them more or less dynamic: for example, vertical emphasis in the street wall checks the horizontal flow of space (horizontal emphasis tends to increase it); irregular skylines slow eye incidents; setbacks break down converging perspectives; space may be modulated into a number of discrete sections or 'episodes', or given elements (e.g. street termination features) that punctuate the flow of space.

In streets with strong physical character, their volume generally takes a positive form and possesses a strong sense of enclosure. The continuity of the street wall and the height-to-width ratio determine the sense of spatial enclosure, while the width determines how the surrounding architecture is seen (Box 7.2). In narrow streets, vertical features become more prominent, projections are exaggerated, and eye-level details more important. The observer sees façades at acute angles and, when facing along the street, only sees parts of them. In broad streets, the observer is sufficiently removed to see the surrounding façades as wholes, and their relationship – or lack of it – becomes evident, while the floorscape and skyline become important elements contributing to the street's character.

Streets that wind or have irregular frontages enhance their sense of enclosure, and provide a constantly changing prospect for the moving observer. Many commentators (e.g. Sitte, 1889; Cullen, 1961) express a preference for such streets, arguing that while straight ones have their place, their selection is often made without sufficient consideration of the terrain, circumstances, townscape effect, and the potential for visual delight and interest in the local context.

For Le Corbusier (1929, p. 5), straight roads were the 'way of man' because man had a purpose and therefore took the shortest route. By contrast, the winding way was the 'way of the pack-donkey' who 'zigzags to avoid the larger stones, or to ease the climb, or to gain a little shade; he takes the line of least resistance'. Le Corbusier, therefore, dismissed Sitte's book as a 'most wilful piece of work', a 'glorification of the curved line' and a 'specious demonstration of its unrivalled beauty' (p. 13). As Broadbent (1990, p. 130) comments, however, Corbusean man would clearly 'hack away the stones, scrambling upwards in a straight line, whatever the gradient whilst eschewing any shade to lighten his physical labours!'

The (in visual terms) successful design of straight streets generally depends on such factors as good proportions between length and width; the kind of

(i) Unlike a square, a street has only two walls to
define space. If the walls are low in relation to
the street width, outward views are not
sufficiently contained to provide a sense of
enclosed space. In a street with a 1:4 ratio, there
is three times as much sky as wall within the
range of vision, giving a weak sense of enclosure.
(ii) If the ratio is 1:2 the peripheral glimpses of
sky equal the amount of visual field devoted to
the street wall. The view of the sky is in the less
dominant peripheral vision, so increasing the
three-dimensional sense of enclosure. A ratio of
between 1:2 and 1:2.5 provides a good sense of
enclosure in a street.
(iii) A street wall height that equals the street
width severely limits any sky view and gives a
strong sense of enclosure. A ratio of 1:1 is often
considered the minimum for comfortable urban
streets.
(iv) If the surrounding building height exceeds
the width of the space then the tops of buildings
will no longer be visible without looking up. Such
ratios may lead to feelings of claustrophobia and
will reduce light penetration into the space. In
combination with other street profiles, however,
they can create dramatic contrast.

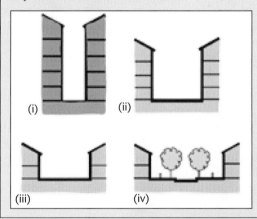

structures of which they are composed; and their
visual termination on a building or other feature
that brings the eye to rest.

Townscape

As well as with the spatial properties and qualities
of streets and squares, urban designers are

concerned with their connection to form social
space and movement systems. The public space
network (see Chapter 4) creates a series of townscape effects, involving, for example, changing
views and vistas; the interplay of landmarks, visual
incidents and design features; and changes and
contrasts of enclosure. In broad terms, townscape
results from the weaving together of buildings and
all the other elements of the urban fabric and street
scene (trees, nature, water, traffic, advertisements,
etc.) so that – in Gordon Cullen's phrase – visual
drama is released.

Although the term 'townscape' was first used in
Thomas Sharpe's 1948 study of Oxford, a self-
consciously 'picturesque' approach to townscape
had already been evident in the work of John Nash
in the early nineteenth century and in the views of
Camillo Sitte at the century's end. Sitte's lead was
developed in the work of Barry Parker and Ray
Unwin, Clough Williams-Ellis and others in the early
twentieth century. While a number of writers have
made significant contributions to contemporary
townscape theory (e.g. Gibberd, 1953; Worskett,
1969; Tugnutt and Robertson, 1987), the modern
'townscape' philosophy has always been closely
associated with Gordon Cullen. His beautifully illustrated essays on the subject appeared in the *Architectural Review* during the mid- and late 1950s, and
were published in book form as *Townscape* (1961),
republished in amended form as *The Concise Townscape* (1971).

Cullen's (1961, p. 10) main contention was that
buildings seen together gave a 'visual pleasure
which none can give separately'. One building
standing alone is experienced as architecture, but
several together make possible an 'art other than
architecture', an 'art of relationship'. Cullen's argument was essentially a contextualist one: each
building should be seen as a contribution to a
larger whole. He also suggested a vocabulary of
terms to describe particular aspects of townscape,
a selection of which is illustrated (Figures
7.16–7.19).

Cullen argued that townscape could not be
appreciated in a technical manner, but needed an
aesthetic sensibility. Although primarily visual, it
also evoked memories, experiences and an
emotional response. As most towns are of old foundation, their fabric shows evidence of differing periods in their architectural styles, 'accidents of
layout', and mixture of materials and scales. He
argued that if we could start again, we might think
of getting rid of this 'hotchpotch' and making all

FIGURE 7.16
Cullen's 'closed vista': 'which puts a building down and then invites you to stand back and admire it'. Vienna, Austria

FIGURE 7.17
Cullen's 'deflection': 'in which the object building is deflected away from the right angle, thus arousing the expectation that it is doing this to some purpose'

FIGURE 7.18
Cullen's 'projection and recession': 'Instead of the eye taking in the street in a single glance, as it would in a street with perfectly straight façades, it is caught up in the intricacy of the meander.' Shrewsbury, UK

FIGURE 7.19
Cullen's 'narrows': 'The crowding together of buildings forms a pressure, an unavoidable nearness of detail, which is in direct contrast to the wide piazza.' Shad Thames, London, UK

'new and fine and perfect': 'We would create an orderly scene with straight roads and with buildings that conformed in height and style. Given a freehand that is what we might do . . . create symmetry, balance, perfection and conformity' (p. 13). Questioning what 'conformity' meant, Cullen suggested an analogy with a private party of half a dozen people who are strangers to each other. At first, polite conversation on general subjects provides an 'exhibition of manners', of how 'one ought to behave'. For Cullen, this was boring conformity. Later, however, as the ice begins to break, out of the 'straitjacket of orthodox manners and conformity real human beings begin to emerge'. Miss X's sharp but good-natured wit is the ideal foil for Major Y's somewhat simple exuberance; and so on. It begins to be fun: 'Conformity gives way to the agreement to differ within a recognised tolerance of behaviour' (p. 14).

While Cullen's concept of townscape is a useful means of analysis and appraisal, it is difficult to translate into a design method. Indeed, it might be better not to attempt that translation. Townscape was primarily criticised for its tendency to isolate, even to overemphasise, the visual dimension of urban design. This trivialises Cullen's ideas. Nevertheless, in his 'Introduction' to *The Concise Townscape*, Cullen himself lamented that it had resulted in 'a superficial civic style of bollards and cobblestones'. The essence of Cullen's argument was that, as well as aiding appreciation of established townscapes, his ideas could also inform the design of new, and interventions into existing, townscapes.

URBAN ARCHITECTURE

The visual–aesthetic character of the urban environment derives not only from its spatial qualities, but also from the colour, texture and detailing of its defining surfaces. For example, warm colours seem to advance into a space, which thus tends to feel smaller, while cool colours retreat, giving a more spacious feel. A space can also feel harsh and inhuman if its surfaces lack fine detail and interest at human scale. Activities occurring within and around a space also contribute to its character and sense of place (see Chapters 6 and 8). This and the following section consider the main elements contributing to the visual–aesthetic character of urban space: its architecture and its landscaping.

For the purpose of this discussion, 'urban' architecture means architecture that responds and contributes positively to its context and to the definition of the public realm. This excludes freestanding buildings, except as an occasional element. The issue of 'object buildings' and 'textures/fabrics' (i.e. building mass) was discussed in Chapter 4. Von Meiss (1990, p. 75) suggests that, while the building fabric gives an 'image of continuity, of expansiveness, stretching to infinity', the object is 'a closed element, finite, comprehensible as an entity'. Standing out against a background, it concentrates visual attention. Where buildings are embedded within urban blocks, the front façade may take on an object role, forming an object-façade. Von Meiss (p. 93) used the concept of 'radiance' to discuss spatial impact: 'A freestanding sculpture or buildings exerts a radiance which defines a more or less precise field around it. To enter the field of influence of an object is the beginning of a spatial experience.' While the object-façade has a radiance onto public space, the building's other (three) sides are embedded in the general fabric. The extent of radiance depends on the nature and size of the object or façade; the context; and/or the design of the surrounding space.

Freestanding buildings are also more difficult to design successfully than buildings which present only their main façade to public space, since they are viewed, and therefore subject to aesthetic critique, from many points. Rejecting the concept of buildings as freestanding sculptural objects, Sitte saw a building's principal aesthetic concern as the manner in which its façade defined the limits to a space and how it was seen from within the space. Since freestanding buildings would inevitably be overexposed, like a 'cake on a serving-platter', and, moreover, would involve the additional 'expense of finishing lengthy façades', he argued that it was greatly to the client's advantage for the building to be embedded within an urban block, since its main façade 'could then be carried out in marble from top to bottom' (Sitte, from Collins and Collins, 1965, p. 28). As the aesthetic effect of object buildings works by contrast with the fabric (i.e. the object needs a ground to stand out against), the design of buildings as freestanding objects in space should therefore properly be occasional exceptions.

This section concentrates on the design of façades – some of which, depending on their radiance or purpose, can be seen as object-façades. Recognising the problem of 'repetitive, boring elevations, prefabricated for speedy erection', Buchanan (1988b, pp. 25–7) argued that they should:

- Create a sense of place.
- Mediate between inside and out and between private and public space, providing gradations between the two.
- Have windows that suggest the potential presence of people and that reveal and 'frame' internal life.
- Have character and coherence that acknowledge conventions and enter into a dialogue with adjacent buildings.
- Have compositions that create rhythm and repose and hold the eye.
- Have a sense of mass and materials expressive of the form of construction.
- Have substantial, tactile and decorative natural materials, which weather gracefully.

- Have decoration that distracts, delights and intrigues.

Attempting to understand what makes a 'good building', the Royal Fine Art Commission (RFAC) identified six criteria (Cantacuzino, 1994). In this area, there is a particular need to avoid turning desirable principles into dogmatic imperatives as strict adherence to 'the rules' often leads to mediocrity and uniformity. The RFAC, for example, was careful to stress that a building could embody every criterion and still not be 'good', and vice versa. Moreover, 'good' designers may successfully break 'the rules' and still create good architecture. The criteria discussed below are therefore best understood as a means of structuring and informing an appreciation of urban architecture.

1. *Order and unity*: The first criterion was the 'satisfying and indivisible unity', created as a consequence of the 'search for order'. In terms of building elements and façade design, order is manifested through such means as symmetry, balance, repetition, the grid, the bay, the structural frame, etc. At street level, unity may come from repetition of an architectural 'style', or, less formally, from common underlying design patterns or motifs, or unifying elements such as building silhouette; consistent plot widths; fenestration patterns; proportions; massing; the treatment of entrances; materials; details; etc.

2. *Expression*: The second criterion was 'the apt expression of the function of a building which enables us to recognise a building for what it is' (Cantacuzino, 1994, p. 70). While subject to debate, symbolic appropriateness is often considered a key requisite of good architecture: a house or church, for example, should communicate its function. Symbolic differentiation produces a hierarchy of building types which increases the legibility of urban areas. Public buildings have traditionally proclaimed their significance through increased scale, contrasting style, lavish detail and high quality materials, providing 'landmarks' in the street scene: to aid this, most private buildings in a townscape should be 'backcloth' buildings. At a different scale, we need clues not only to a building's function, but also in terms of its functionality (e.g. locating its main entrance).

3. *Integrity*: Integrity results from 'a strict adherence to principles of design, not in the sense of rules which may determine the design of a

classical façade, but in the sense that Gothic architecture embodies principles of construction which are quite different to the principles of Classical architecture' (Cantacuzino, 1994, p. 71). Through their form and construction, buildings should express the functions they and their individual parts fulfil; spaces should reflect their purpose and express the structure and construction methods. Buildings should be visually appropriate in their form and construction. This principle can, however, be taken too far – see David Watkin's *Morality and Architecture* (1984). Brolin (1980, pp. 5–6), for example, argues that 'no virtue or higher morality is served by expressing interior uses "honestly" on the exterior. This is one moral preoccupation of Modernism which should be less important than the visual relationship between the building's exterior and its architectural context.'

4. *Plan and section*: This criterion concerns the building as a whole, and the need to consider not only its elevations but also its plan and section. Interest merely in façades relegates the design of buildings (and spaces) to the level of two-dimensional stage set design – while stage sets are a kind of architecture, architecture is more than a stage set (Von Meiss, 1990). There should be a positive relationship between a building's façade and its plan and section (i.e. between interior and exterior) for two main reasons. First, a building is designed as a totality in which the façade addresses – indeed, reconciles – the street in front and the plan and section that lie behind. Second, the relationship of section, plan and local context is fundamental in terms of the volume of development a site can accommodate (i.e. the plot ratio). Instances where this relation is false or weak are usually known as façadism, displayed where there is a functional and structural 'dishonesty' between a building's interior and exterior (Figure 7.20), or where there is new building behind a retained historic façade (see Figures 7.21 and 7.22). This is often a controversial issue in urban design and conservation.

5. *Detail*: As detail is what holds the eye, lack of detail 'impoverishes architecture and deprives us of a layer of experience that brings us into close contact with a building where we can admire the beauty of the materials and the skill of the craftsman or engineer' (Cantacuzino, 1994, p. 76). Façades can be appreciated in terms of their visual 'richness' (the interest and complexity that holds the eye) and 'elegance' (a function of the proportions that the eye finds pleasing and harmonious). Although some façades have both, on elegant façades detail is normally used sparingly – this does not, however, necessarily hold the eye, and can be seen as lacking visual interest, even boring. Detail and visual interest help humanise environments. As buildings are seen in different ways – near and far, straight on or obliquely –

FIGURE 7.20
Richmond Riverside, London. Although the façade suggests a number of separate buildings, this development actually consists of a few large office buildings with open office floors extending across what we are led to assume are party walls

FIGURES 7.21 and 7.22
These examples of façadism in Toronto, Canada, and Hong Kong raise serious questions about the value of retaining the façade of an older building. Where new buildings are placed behind retained façades, the new building's height generally needs to be similar to that of the building being replaced

detail is required at varying scales, depending on their position in the townscape. Small-scale detail is especially important at ground floor level to provide visual interest for pedestrians, while larger-scale detail is important for viewing over longer distances (Figures 7.23, 7.24 and 7.25). Typically, detail intensifies about windows and doorways and at building corners, while appropriate emphasis of entrances allows users to 'read' the façade, facilitating movement from the public to private realm (Figure 7.26).

6. *Integration*: Integration involves the harmonisation of a building with its surroundings, and the qualities needed for this. It is a more problematic area of urban design. During the late 1980s, HRH, the Prince of Wales (1988, p. 84) famously described a proposal for extending the National Gallery in London's Trafalgar

Square as a 'monstrous carbuncle' on the face of a 'much-loved friend'. Stressing his own basic principle that 'places matter most', Francis Tibbalds (1992, p. 16) argued that, in most instances, individual buildings should be subservient to the needs and character of the place as a whole: 'If every building screams for attention, the result is likely to be discordant chaos. A few buildings can, quite legitimately, be soloists, but the majority need simply to be sound, reliable members of the chorus.' While there are occasional needs for a 'prima donna', 'the greater need is for a better vocabulary of well-designed, interesting "back cloth" buildings'.

Integration – sometimes disparagingly (and incorrectly) called 'fitting in' – does not require slavish

FIGURES 7.23, 7.24 and 7.25
This building in central Edinburgh, UK, is richly detailed at a series of different levels. At a distance only the main elements of the façade are apparent. Coming closer other major elements, including the fenestration pattern, become apparent. Closer still, materials and constructional detailing are apparent with additional detail at ground level and at higher levels

adherence to an architectural style. The stylistic dimension is only one aspect of fitting in. Too much emphasis on this element denies the opportunity of innovation and excitement: visual criteria such as scale and rhythm are often more important. Many of the most successful groups of buildings are of dramatically different materials and styles (e.g. those around the Piazza San Marco, Venice).

A continuum of three basic approaches to creating harmony with the existing context can be identified. Each represents a different design philosophy. At one extreme, stylistic *uniformity* involves imitating the local architectural character – and in the process, possibly diluting the qualities desired to be retained. At the other extreme, *juxtaposition* or *contrast* involves new designs, making few concessions to the existing architectural character (Figure 7.27 and 7.28). While this can produce vibrant and successful contrast, the

approach is eminently capable of 'a disastrous result in the form of arrogant exhibitionism' (Wells-Thorpe, 1998, p. 113). Between these two positions lies that of *continuity*, involving interpretation – rather than simply imitation – of local visual character. Typifying postmodern architectural design, this approach reflects a desire for new development to reflect and develop the existing sense of place.

Wells-Thorpe (1998, p. 113) suggests that when a *more* contextualist approach is appropriate, the following qualities of the 'old surroundings' should be considered: (i) the extent; (ii) the worth/quality; (iii) the consistency/homogeneity; (iv) the uniqueness/rarity; (v) the proximity (i.e. whether seen in a single sweep of the eye). Whether or not a building harmonises with its context is, however, ultimately a matter of personal judgement. Pearce (1989, p. 166) succinctly encapsulates the challenge: 'All that is required for the rewarding addition of a new building in an old setting is the genius of the place

FIGURE 7.26
Glasgow, UK. Many traditional urban façades are organised into three elements (i.e. 'base', 'middle' and 'top'). The ground floor is often more richly decorated as this is the part that pedestrians are better able to see and appreciate; the middle is often more visually restrained, while the top and skyline are again more visually complex to detain the eye. Although this practice is rarely followed in contemporary development, this building has been designed in the traditional manner

FIGURE 7.27
The Glass Pyramid at Le Louvre, Paris, France, represents an excellent example of the integration of a new building into an established historical context. The juxtaposition of old and new enhances both

FIGURE 7.28
Contextual juxtaposition – 'Ginger Rogers and Fred Astaire building', Prague, Czech Republic

to be complemented by the genius of the architect.' By definition, however, genius is rare.

Given that areas of homogeneous architectural character are unusual, most contexts, being already varied, allow for contemporary design. Nevertheless, while variety has particular value in the creation of visually interesting street scenes, certain principles apply that enable new buildings to harmonise better with the existing context. The RFAC (Cantacuzino, 1994, pp. 76–9) identify six criteria for the harmonious integration of new buildings into existing contexts (see Box 7.3).

BOX 7.3 – CRITERIA FOR HARMONIOUS INTEGRATION

(source: adapted from Cantacuzino, 1994, pp. 76–9)

(i) *Siting*: Siting concerns the way a building occupies its site and how it relates to other buildings and to the street or other spaces. Respect for existing street patterns and block/plot sizes helps harmonious integration: plot amalgamation, for example, alters the scale of city buildings and breaks down the traditional urban grain. Respect for the established building line and street frontage is important in ensuring the continuity and definition of external space: breaks in the street line should be deliberate – rather than arbitrary or accidental – and should create positive space or incident. Highly sculptural buildings – objects in space – should be exceptions and major incidents in the townscape; their impact being all the more significant for their relative scarcity.

(ii) *Massing*: Massing is the three-dimensional disposition of the building volume. The impact of new development needs to be considered from a range of viewing points and angles. Although sometimes used to control the volume of development on a particular site, plot ratios (gross floor area divided by site area) and floor area ratios (FARs) are a rather crude tool, as a given volume of development can be organised in various different ways (see Chapter 8). Plot ratios should, therefore, usually be accompanied by some form of indicative massing.

(iii) *Scale*: Scale is different from size: size represents the literal dimensions of an object; scale is the perception of that object relative to other objects around it, and to our perception of those objects. Scale concerns, first, the building's dimensions and all its parts relative to the dimensions of a human being (i.e. human scale) and, second, its dimensions relative to those of its setting (i.e. generic scale) (Figure 7.29). Hence, a building can be understood to be of a human scale or not and, separately, to be in or out of scale with its surroundings (Figure 7.30). Scale-giving elements such as windows, doors and construction materials, are particularly important because we often have a clear perception of their size (Figure 7.31). Although the height of buildings is not necessarily significant in achieving a human scale, the articulation of façades and the visual interest at pedestrian level is. The term 'human scale' is also used in a more general sense to refer to a sense of 'human presence'.

(iv) *Proportion*: Proportion is the relation between, for example, the different parts of a building, and between any one part and the whole. It may relate to the ratio of solid-to-void in a building's façade, or

FIGURE 7.29
Mansion House, London, UK. It is difficult to read the scale of this building. It is initially read as a three-storey building, until the clues given by the traffic signs and the cars are noted and it is realised that it is a much larger building than initially suspected

to the way window openings are arranged in relation to solid wall elements. Traditional streets with a series of different buildings tend to have a remarkably consistent ratio of window-to-wall area. Figure-ground studies of the street elevation in which each façade is reduced to solid (white) and void (black) are a means of investigating fenestration proportions and rhythms (see below). By removing extraneous detail, this technique permits a clearer focus on the rhythms of solid-to-void along the street. New buildings in established contexts may be more harmoniously integrated if their proportions are complementary with those of existing buildings.

(v) *Rhythm*: Rhythm is the arrangement and size of the constituent parts of a building's façade (e.g. its windows or bays), which is normally repeated. Of particular significance for rhythm are the proportion of wall to window (i.e. solid-to-void) in a façade; the

FIGURE 7.30
This statue in London's Trafalgar Square deliberately exploits ideas of scale. The statue is human scale but is out of scale with the plinth. To be in scale with the plinth, the statue would need to be much larger. In this case, the sculptor used scale to make the point that in life Christ had been a man not a god

FIGURE 7.31
Scale derives not just from the elements of the building or the façade but also the intrinsic size of building materials. In the past, the limitations of the human body dictated the size of materials used in construction. Where the individual unit can be seen, such elements gave the building scale. With mechanised building techniques, the need for construction units that could be easily handled was less important and many buildings and urban spaces do not have the benefit of such scale-giving elements. In this street scene in Savannah, Georgia, US, there are sufficient cues to give a sense of human scale without people being present

horizontal or vertical emphasis of the fenestration; and the expression of structure in the building façade. One means of integrating a large building into a street scene is by the division of its façade into a series of bays. Although most façades have both vertical and horizontal elements, one or the other tends to dominate, giving vertical or horizontal emphasis (Figures 7.32 and 7.33). As the constituent parts of a building's façade traditionally had a vertical emphasis, buildings with a strong horizontal emphasis tend to disrupt the visual rhythm of traditional streets. Furthermore, as the combination of buildings with horizontal emphasis and the horizontality of streets tends to result in a surfeit of

horizontality, a general principle is that urban buildings have a vertical emphasis to which the street provides a balancing horizontality. An additional argument for verticality in urban architecture is that horizontal lines are visually faster than vertical lines (i.e. the eye runs more quickly along them). As the eye is detained for a shorter period of time, strong horizontal lines are less interesting.

(vi) *Materials*: Materials provide a building with colour and texture. The choice of materials also affects weathering; detailing; visual interest at various distances; and façade patterning. The judicious use of materials can sharpen or soften differences between

BOX 7.3 – CONTINUED

the various parts of the building, and the relation between it and its neighbours. With appropriate modelling, incidents of shade and shadow on a façade are important in giving a sense of visual depth and solidity, and can dramatically alter perception of materials. Materials also help establish local distinctiveness. The UK's exceptional geological diversity has, for example, led to a diverse range of vernacular building traditions, styles and material and, thereby, to significant local distinctiveness, which is often manifested through colour. Consistent use of local building materials can give a town or city a strong sense of unity and place, while their use in a new development helps it to integrate visually (see Porter, 1982; Lange, 1997; Moughtin et al., 1995, pp. 133–44).

FIGURES 7.32 and 7.33
Although most façades have both vertical and horizontal elements, one or the other tends to dominate. The emphasis is shown by the tendency to look *up and down* or *along* the façade. This pair of buildings at Brindleyplace, Birmingham, UK, illustrate this principle. Individual windows or the fenestration pattern as a whole is often a key element in determining the emphasis. For structural reasons, buildings in load-bearing masonry tend to have a vertical emphasis. In framed buildings, the façade is simply a cladding or skin. Openings in that skin can be made in any shape or form. To emphasise the potential of the new construction methods, many Modernist architects design buildings with a horizontal emphasis

HARD AND SOFT LANDSCAPING

With a narrower meaning than 'landscape', 'land-scaping' is used here rather than 'landscape' because of its more limited visual connotations. Landscaping is frequently an afterthought in urban design – something to be added if the budget allows and once the major decisions have been taken, to hide poor quality architecture; and/or as a way of filling left-over space. While well-designed landscaping adds quality, visual interest and colour, poorly designed landscaping detracts from otherwise well-designed developments.

The broader landscape – and, by inference, landscape design – involves not only visual aspects, but also fundamental concerns for ecology, hydrology and geology. Although not discussed here, it is important to reiterate that urban designers should be concerned with underlying natural processes as much as with the problems and opportunities of particular sites (see Chapter 3). The 'greening' of towns and cities represents a key sustainability objective. Trees and other vegetation can be particularly effective in reducing carbon dioxide build-up and restoring oxygen; reducing wind speeds in urban spaces; acting as shelterbelts; and filtering dust and pollution. A positive approach to landscaping is therefore needed, in which its contribution to the totality of the urban environment is considered. Hence, landscape design strategies should be developed before or in parallel with the building design process and play an integral part in an overarching urban design framework.

Floorscape

Floorscape is an important part of a harmonious and integrated whole. There are two main types of flooring in urban areas – 'hard' pavement and 'soft' landscaped areas: the focus here is on the former. A floorscape's character is substantially determined by the materials used (e.g. brick, stone slabs, cobbles, concrete, macadam), the way they are used, and how they interrelate with other materials and landscape features (Figure 7.34). Edging detail is important in visually linking with the façades defining the space, aiding the transition from the horizontal to the vertical plane. Requiring careful consideration, this transition is often an indicator of the quality of a paving design.

The patterning of the floor of urban spaces results from utilitarian considerations, which may also have an aesthetic effect, and/or from attempts to organise the space aesthetically. The primary function of any paved area is to provide a hard, dry, non-slip surface to carry the traffic load. Different traffic loads can be reflected in different flooring materials and construction methods, which also indicate where different types of traffic should go. The junctions between materials are often articulated. In traffic-calmed environments, tarmac is usually used to indicate where cars may go, and

FIGURE 7.34
Telc, Czech Republic. Unity of materials and design between the floorscape and the surrounding architecture adds to a more harmonious townscape

brick or stone for pedestrian areas. The most common edge between vehicular and pedestrian traffic is the ubiquitous granite or concrete kerb with a shallow step from pavement to road. Using materials to add further parallel lines gives greater definition to the change of function, and has a decorative effect.

A change of flooring material can indicate a change of ownership (e.g. from public to private space), indicate potential hazards, or provide a warning. Textured pavements at road crossing points, for example, assist those with sight impairments, while lines across otherwise monolithic surfaces give strong directional qualities. Directional paving may also have a purely aesthetic function, being used simply to reinforce a linear form and thus enhance the sense of movement.

Floorscape can be expressly designed to enhance the aesthetic character of a space – for example, introducing scale (both human and generic), modulating the space by organising it into a series of hierarchical elements, reinforcing existing character, or aesthetically organising and unifying it. A sense of scale in floorscape can derive from the scale of the materials used, from the patterning of different materials, or from a combination of both. Sized to permit easy handling, stone paving slabs generally give a human scale to urban spaces. In smaller spaces, often no additional patterning is required: larger spaces generally need some form of pattern to provide a sense of scale.

Floorscape patterns often perform the important aesthetic function of breaking down the scale of large, hard surfaces into more manageable, human proportions. Floorscape (like façades) can be enriched by repeating and echoing particular motifs or themes, by emphasising changes of materials, and/or by dramatising the edge of an area. In the Piazza San Marco, Venice, for example, the scale of the space is modulated and humanised by a simple grid of white travertine and black basalt. Floorscape patterns can also be used to manipulate the apparent size of the space: the addition of detail and modulation tends to make a big space seem smaller, while a simple and relatively unadorned treatment has the reverse effect.

Floorscape patterns can reinforce the linear character of a street, emphasising its character as a 'path' by providing a sense of direction with a visually dynamic pattern. Alternatively, they can check the flow of space by emphasising its character as a 'place', or by suggesting a feeling of repose with a visually static or contained pattern (Figure 7.35).

FIGURE 7.35
A vibrant street floor pattern in Macao

Parallel lines following the length of the street reinforce the sense of movement, while non-linear paving tends to slow the visual pace and to reinforce qualities of a place to stop or linger. Interplay between floor patterns alternating between movement and rest brings qualities of rhythm and scale to the urban scene.

Floorscapes designed to provide a sense of repose are usually associated with areas where people stop and rest (i.e. with urban squares). The floorscape pattern of squares can perform a number of functions: providing a sense of scale; unifying the space by linking and relating the centre and edges; and bringing order to what might otherwise be a disparate group of buildings. In the latter case, a strong and simple geometric figure (rectangle, circle or oval) might organise the centre of the space, allowing the irregular line of surrounding buildings to form localised relations with the edge (Figure 7.36); thus helping to organise the square

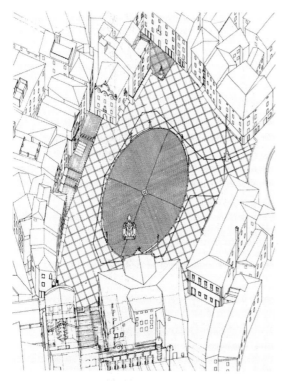

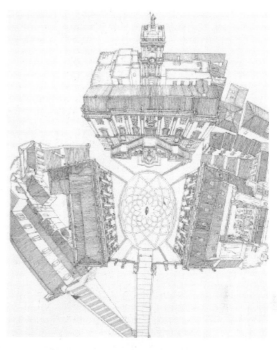

FIGURE 7.36
A simple geometric floorscape unifies and organises the irregular trapezoidal space of the Piazza Giuseppe Tartini, Pirano, Slovenia (source: Favole, 1997)

FIGURE 7.37
Campidoglio, Rome, Italy. The Campidoglio's floor pattern consists of a pattern expanding out from the base of the equestrian statue. The sunken oval containing the pattern reinforces the centrality of the space while the expanding ripples of the central pattern emphasise movement to the edge. As the pattern constantly and repeatedly links the centre and the edge, it unifies the spaces and its enclosing elements (source: Bacon, 1978, p. 119)

into a single aesthetic whole. Michelangelo's floorscape design for the Campidoglio in Rome achieves all of these functions (Figure 7.37).

Street furniture

Street furniture includes hard landscape elements other than floorscape: telegraph poles, lighting standards, telephone boxes, benches, planters, traffic signs, direction signs, CCTV cameras, police boxes, bollards, boundary walls, railings, fountains, bus shelters, statues, monuments, etc. Public art is also a form of street furniture (Figures 7.38 and 7.39). In addition to contributing to identity and character, the quality and organisation of street furniture are prime indicators of the quality of an urban space. Frequently the result of unknowing urban design, it is often the clutter of

street furniture and other paraphernalia that detracts from an urban scene. Street furniture can also set quality standards and expectations for development in an area.

Although integral – and mostly necessary – to the public realm, the myriad items of street furniture are often distributed with little concern for their overall effect, resulting in a visually and functionally cluttered urban scene. In their *Glasgow City Centre Public Realm, Strategy and Guidelines*, Gillespies (1995, p. 65) offers a set of six general principles:

- Design to incorporate the minimum of street furniture.
- Wherever possible, integrate elements into a single unit.
- Remove all superfluous street furniture.

FIGURE 7.38
Jonathan Borofsky's *Hammering Man*, Seattle Art Museum, Seattle, Washington, USA

- Consider street furniture as a family of items, suiting the quality of the environment and helping to give it a coherent identity.
- Position street furniture to help create and delineate space.
- Locate street furniture so as not to impede pedestrians, vehicles or desire lines.

The most basic street furniture comes 'off-the-peg', selected from manufacturers' catalogues. Standard items may be customised to give some degree of local identity, and identity can be further developed by the design of a suite of items specific to a particular locality. For locations where a particularly strong design character is desired, artists might be invited to design a range of street furniture (Gillespies, 1995, p. 67).

Soft landscaping

Soft landscaping can be a decisive element in creating character and identity. 'Oak Street', for example, has a different character to 'Pine Street'. Trees and other vegetation express the changing seasons, enhancing the temporal legibility of urban environments. Thus, if deciduous trees are used, the containment and character of the space will change with the seasons. Landscaping also often plays an important aesthetic role in adding coherence and

FIGURE 7.39
Public art in Bratislava, Slovakia. Humour is a feature of much public art

structure to otherwise disparate environments. Much of the appeal of mature 'garden' suburbs, for example, derives from the continuity of the landscape structure, which enables a diversity of architectural treatments to work harmoniously. In this context, the landscaping plays a crucial role in 'joining up' the environment.

Trees and other vegetation provide a contrast with, and a foil to, hard urban landscapes, and add a sense of human scale. In some streets, trees reinforce or provide a sense of enclosure and continuity, but in all urban environments trees need to be sited positively. Robinson (1992, pp. 41–81), for example, outlines a theory of visual composition

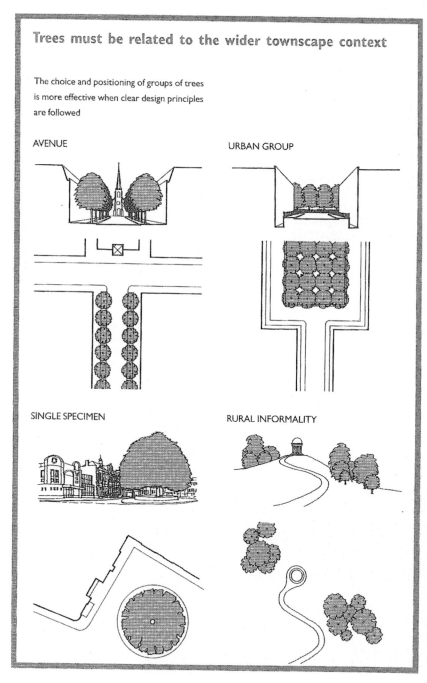

Trees must be related to the wider townscape context

The choice and positioning of groups of trees is more effective when clear design principles are followed

AVENUE

URBAN GROUP

SINGLE SPECIMEN

RURAL INFORMALITY

FIGURE 7.40
Design strategies for street trees. Trees are not always appropriate in urban areas and, where used, should be chosen and located in relation to the overall townscape effect (source: English Heritage, 2000, p. 49)

and making spaces with plants that is as sophisticated as that associated with buildings and urban space. Given a formal setting, siting may involve a degree of regimentation, with trees planted in straight lines or formal geometric patterns rather than picturesque groups.

Much of the floorscape pattern – and, indeed, the three-dimensional effect of urban space – can be enhanced by tree planting, which may reinforce or complete a sense of spatial containment, or create a 'space within a space'. Street trees can, however, be overdone. In order to give a greater emphasis to the landscaped garden squares, Georgian streets rarely contained trees, while Camillo Sitte calculated that the boulevards of nineteenth century Vienna contained enough trees to form an entire forest, and, in his view, they would have been better deployed in two or three parks. Similarly, in their publication *Streets for All*, aimed at guiding the management of London's streets, English Heritage (2000, p. 48) argue that soft landscaping in urban areas is not always appropriate and that where used, it should be chosen and located in relation to the overall townscape effect (Figure 7.40). For all landscape schemes – hard or soft – English Heritage suggest an eight-part strategy:

- Appearance: have regard for historic context and local distinctiveness.
- Consider the suitability of materials and their combination for the tasks they perform.
- Design for robustness in terms of long-term maintenance.
- Cleansing: consider ease of refuse collection, sweeping, washing, and specialist cleansing of graffiti and gum.

- Avoid clutter, by keeping signage to a minimum and using existing posts or wall mountings.
- Have a concern for pedestrians: through a welcoming atmosphere and clear directional signage.
- Have a concern for people with disabilities: for safety, convenience and removal of obstacles.
- Traffic and related matters: consider public transport, cyclists, and the comfort and safety of pedestrians crossing the carriageways.

CONCLUSION

This chapter has emphasised the necessity for urban designers to consider the whole context in which they approach the visual aspect of additions to the urban environment. It is important to avoid overstating the importance of architecture and architectural considerations in creating successful urban places. However, while stressing that urban design is not a question of architectural style, Montgomery (1998, pp. 112–13) accepts that architectural style is 'not unimportant', for it conveys meaning, identity and image. Furthermore, urban designers must be careful to avoid equating consideration of the visual dimension of urban design with considerations of architectural design. Such an equation would emphasise a part to the probable detriment of the whole, neglecting Tibbalds' golden rule for urban design – 'places matter most'. Buildings, streets and spaces, hard and soft landscaping and street furniture should be considered together, to create drama and visual interest and to reinforce or enhance the sense of place.

8

The functional dimension

INTRODUCTION

This chapter focuses on the functional dimension of urban design, which involves how places work and how urban designers can make 'better' places. The 'social usage' and 'visual' traditions of urban design thought each had a 'functionalist' perspective. That of the former concerned the functioning of the environment in terms of how people used it, while in the latter, the human dimension was often abstracted out and reduced to aesthetic or technical criteria such as traffic flow, access or circulation. This chapter is concerned with these two sets of functional considerations, taking the former first. The chapter is in four parts. The first part concerns the use of public spaces, the second concerns mixed uses and density considerations, the third environmental design, and the fourth aspects of the capital web.

PUBLIC SPACE AND THE PUBLIC/PRIVATE INTERFACE

As successful places support and facilitate activities, the design of urban spaces should be informed by awareness of how people use them. Accomplished urban designers generally develop a detailed knowledge of urban spaces, places and environments, based upon first-hand experience. Bacon (1974, p. 20), for example, asserted that only through 'endless walking' could designers 'absorb into their being' the true experience of urban space. Many of the best commentaries on the use of the public realm are based on first-hand observations: Jane Jacobs' (*Death and Life of Great Amer-* ican Cities, 1961) in North American cities; Jan Gehl's (*Life Between Buildings*, 1971) in Scandinavia; and William H Whyte's (*The Social Life of Small Urban Spaces*, 1980) in New York. To these can be added Clare Copper Marcus and Wendy Sarkissian's *Housing As If People Mattered* (1986) and the Project for Public Space's *How to Turn a Place Around: A Handbook for Creating Successful Public Places* (1999). These works are all rooted in observations of the relationship between activities and spaces. As the Project for Public Space (PPS, 1999, p. 51) advise: 'When you observe a space you learn about how it is actually used, rather than how you think it is used.'

Based on a synthesis of research and ideas on the use and design of public space, Carr *et al.* (1992) argued that, as well as being 'meaningful' (i.e. allowing people to make strong connections between the place, their personal lives, and the larger world) (see Chapter 5), and being 'democratic' (i.e. protecting the rights of user groups, being accessible to all groups and providing for freedom of action) (see Chapter 6), public spaces should also be 'responsive' – that is, designed and managed to serve the needs of their users. They identify five primary needs that people seek to satisfy in public space: 'comfort'; 'relaxation'; 'passive engagement with the environment'; 'active engagement with the environment'; and 'discovery'. Good places frequently serve more than one purpose.

(i) Comfort
Comfort is a prerequisite of successful public spaces. The length of time people stay in a public space is a function and an indicator of its comfort. The dimensions of a sense of comfort include environmental

factors (e.g. relief from sun, wind, etc.) (this is discussed later in this chapter); physical comfort (e.g. comfortable and sufficient seating, etc.); and social and psychological comfort. The latter is dependent on the character and ambience of the space. Carr *et al.* (1992, p. 97) argued that this is 'a deep and pervasive need that extends to people's experiences in public places. It is a sense of security, a feeling that one's person and possessions are not vulnerable.' The sense of comfort may also be enhanced by the physical design of the space and/or by its management strategies (see Chapter 6).

(ii) Relaxation
While a sense of psychological comfort may be a prerequisite of relaxation, relaxation is a more developed state with the 'body and mind at ease' (Carr *et al.*, 1992, p. 98). In urban settings, natural elements – trees, greenery, water features – and separation from vehicular traffic help accentuate the contrast with the immediate surroundings and make it easier to be relaxed. The features that make a pleasant sanctuary may, however, also obstruct visual access (visual permeability), creating safety problems and discouraging use. As in all aspects of design, it is necessary to achieve a balanced whole.

(iii) Passive engagement
While passive engagement with the environment can lead to a sense of relaxation, it also involves 'the need for an encounter with the setting, albeit without becoming actively involved' (Carr *et al.*, 1992, p. 103). Perhaps the prime form of passive engagement is people-watching: Whyte (1980, p. 13), for example, found that what attracts people is other people and the life and activity that they bring. The most used sitting places are generally adjacent to the pedestrian flow, allowing observers to watch people while avoiding eye contact (Figure 8.1). Opportunities for passive engagement are also provided by fountains, views, public art, performances, and so forth (Figure 8.2).

(iv) Active engagement
Active engagement involves a more direct experience with a place and the people within it. Carr *et al.* (1992, p. 119) noted that, although some people find sufficient satisfaction in people-watching, others desire more direct contact, whether with friends, family or strangers. Although urban designers may imagine otherwise, the simple proximity of people does not mean spontaneous interaction. Whyte (1980, p. 19) found that public spaces were 'not ideal places' for 'striking up acquaintances', and that, even in the most sociable of them, there was 'not much mingling'. The coincidence of people in space and time does, nevertheless, provide opportunities for contact and social interaction. In his discussion of how the design of public space supports interaction, Gehl (1996, p. 19) refers to the 'varied transitional forms between being

FIGURE 8.1
Wenceslas Square, Prague, Czech Republic. Street entertainment can enhance the animation and vitality of public spaces

alone and being together' and suggests a scale of 'intensity of contact' ranging from 'close friendships' to 'friends', 'acquaintances', 'chance contacts' and 'passive contacts'. If activity in the spaces between buildings is missing, then the lower end of this contact scale also disappears: 'The boundaries between isolation and contact become sharper – people are either alone or else with others on a relatively demanding and exacting level' (Gehl, 1996, p. 19). Successful public spaces provide opportunities for varying degrees of engagement, and also for disengagement from contact.

Design of the public realm can create or inhibit opportunities for contact. Unusual features or occurrences can result in what Whyte (1980, p. 94) calls 'triangulation': 'the process by which some external stimulus provides a linkage between people and prompts strangers to talk to other strangers as if they knew each other'. In public spaces, the arrangement of different elements – benches, telephones, fountains, sculptures, coffee carts – can be made more, or less, conducive to social interaction (Figure 8.3). The Project for Public Space (1999, p. 63) observes

FIGURE 8.2
Piazza SS Annunziata, Florence, Italy. Steps and other sitting places provide opportunities for passive engagement in public space

FIGURE 8.3
Government Square, Boston, Massachusetts, USA. The design of some public spaces does not help their function as people places

FIGURE 8.4
Chicago, Illinois, USA.
Public art helps the
process of triangulation
in public space

how triangulation occurs spontaneously where there is something of interest, such as the life-size fibreglass cows painted by artists and set up on Chicago streets as public art: 'The cows created an excuse for people who didn't know each other to talk to one another' (Figure 8.4).

(v) Discovery

Representing desire for new spectacles and pleasurable experiences, 'discovery' depends on variety and change. While these may simply come with the 'march of time' and the cycle of the seasons, they may also result from the management and animation of public space. Involving a break from the routine and the expected, discovery may require some sense of unpredictability, and even (real or imagined) danger. Lovatt and O'Connor (1995), Zukin (1995), and others, have written about 'liminal' spaces – those formed in the interstices of everyday life and outside 'normal' rules – where different cultures meet and interact. Discovery might also involve programmes of animation, involving, for example, lunch-time concerts, art exhibitions, street theatre, festivals, parades, markets, society events and/or trade promotions, across a range of times and venues. Such programmes of animation may also include annual events, such as the Edinburgh Festival, London's Notting Hill Carnival, and New Orleans' Mardi-Gras.

The social use of space

The work of William H. Whyte (1980, 1988) is of particular interest with regard to how people use public spaces. Using photographic studies of a range of New York's open spaces, Whyte noted that many such spaces appeared little used, apparently failing to justify the extra floorspace given to developers as part of the city's incentive zoning regulations. Initially published as *The Social Life of Small Urban Spaces* (1980), Whyte's work was reissued as a more substantial book, *City: Rediscovering the Centre* (1988). The Project for Public Space, established in 1975, has continued his work (see www.pps.org), and has pioneered the use of video cameras to analyse patterns of space usage over time.

Whyte considered off-peak use provided the best clues to people's preferences. When a place was crowded, people sat where they could rather than where they most wanted to. Later, some parts emptied while others continued to be used. He also found that most spaces contained well-defined subplaces – often around the edge – where people preferred to be, and arranged to meet. Whyte noted that, in general, women were more discriminating in their choice of space and, therefore, that a low proportion of women generally indicated that something was wrong. Women also sought a greater degree of privacy than men, who tended to prefer more prominent seating.

Whyte noted that the most sociable spaces usually possessed the following features:

- A good location, preferably on a busy route and both physically and visually accessible.
- Streets being part of the 'social' space – fencing off a space from the street isolated it and reduced its use.
- Being level or almost level with the pavement (spaces significantly above or below this were less used).
- Places to sit – both integral (e.g. steps, low walls); and explicit (e.g. benches, seats, etc.).
- Movable seats, enabling choice, and the communication of character and personality.

Less important factors included sun penetration, the aesthetics of the space (what mattered was how people used it), and the shape and size of spaces.

Movement

Movement through public space is at the heart of the urban experience, an important factor in generating life and activity (Figure 8.5). As discussed previously, where people choose to sit or linger in public space is often based on opportunities for people watching, and therefore related to desire lines and an appreciation of the activity and through-movement within the space. Similarly, definition of prime retail locations in urban areas (as opposed to out-of-town locations) is based on assessments of pedestrian footfall, a function of pedestrian movement between places. Duany *et al.* (2000, p. 64) assert that, 'pedestrian life cannot exist in the absence of worthwhile destinations that are easily accessible on foot . . . Otherwise, there is no reason to walk, and the streets are empty.' While there is a basic truth to this assertion, it is actually more complex than this (see below).

To design successful public spaces, it is essential to understand movement, especially that of pedestrians; however, origin-destination studies, used to trace car movement, are less appropriate for pedestrian movement. Because interrupting a journey is a major inconvenience for car drivers, the social experience of getting from A to B is less important and most car-based movement is pure circulation (Lefebvre, 1991, pp. 312–13). Opportunities for social interaction only occur once the car has been parked. As breaking a journey can be inconvenient and time-consuming, direct journeys to a single

FIGURE 8.5
Chester, UK. Pedestrian flows and movement through public space are both at the heart of the urban experience and important factors in generating life and activity

destination are preferred (i.e. a 'park once' strategy). Furthermore, trips may often involve climbing into a car at home, travelling, then getting out in the secure car park of the final destination (i.e. transferring from the sanctuary of the personal private realm, to that of private, self-contained attractions – malls, theme parks, multiplex cinemas, sports stadia, etc.). As the urban experience is essentially discontinuous, primarily involving arrival at – rather than the experience of travel between – particular destinations, the continuity of urban space is less important for car drivers.

For pedestrians, the connection between 'places' is important and successful public spaces are generally integrated within local movement systems. Used to study pedestrian movement, origin-destination surveys ignore an essential component of the

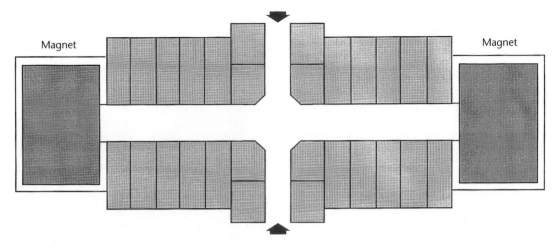

FIGURE 8.6
Retail developers and designers are skilled in exploiting shopper psychology and manipulating shopper movements within shopping centres. In the simplest form of centres, the 'magnet' stores are located at either end of a central mall lined with smaller stores. The magnet stores attract shoppers to the mall. As shoppers enter the mall, they are drawn towards the magnet stores and in the process pass the smaller stores, thereby, generating footfall and potential trade for those smaller stores. If shoppers enter through one of the magnet stores, the other magnet stores provide the stimulus for movement along the mall. This is admittedly a simplified account of movement. The magnet stores attract people in the aggregate; they may not attract any particular individual. Equally, it may be the ambience and character of the mall's 'public' spaces that are the real attraction

experience. In an urban setting, a pedestrian journey is rarely single purpose: on the way to somewhere else, we stop to buy a newspaper, talk to a friend, enjoy a view or watch the 'world go by'. Bill Hillier (1996a, 1996b) terms the potential for such optional activities the 'by-product' of movement – that is, the potential for other (optional) activities in addition to the basic activity of travelling from origin to destination. Thus, as Hillier (1996b, p. 59) argues, by ensuring that origin-destination trips take place past outward-facing building blocks, the traditional 'urban grid' represents a 'mechanism for generating contact', allowing maximisation of the by-product effect. The impact and value of the by-product of movement can be illustrated through its exploitation in the design of shopping centres (Figures 8.6 and 8.7).

FIGURE 8.7
San Diego's Horton Plaza is an excellent example of the notion of public spaces as discretionary environments. Although the public spaces of shopping malls may be considered to be a by-product of the retail offer, it may also be that the supposed by-product is actually the primary attraction – although the public spaces do not produce revenue directly, they attract people to the retail on offer

With colleagues at University College London's Space Syntax Laboratory (www.spacesyntax.com), Hillier (Hillier and Hanson, 1984; Hillier, 1988, 1996a, 1996b; Hillier *et al.*, 1993) has extensively explored and theorised the relationship between (mainly pedestrian) movement and the configuration of urban space and also between pedestrian densities and land uses. He argues that the configuration of space, particularly its effect on visual permeability, is important in determining movement densities and encounter rates. His work challenges urban designers to think critically about the relationship between space configuration, movement and land uses. Although his work is a form of urban morphology (see Chapter 4), it is discussed here because it concerns how people use urban space.

Hillier's empirical research supports his idea that movement densities can accurately be predicted from analysis of the structure of the urban grid. The analytic process involves what Hillier terms 'natural movement' – the proportion of movement determined by the structure of the urban grid rather than by, for example, magnet land uses. Using complex mapping and mathematical techniques, Hillier's analysis is based on key geometric properties of the spatial configuration (i.e. network/grid of spaces) of urban areas. These are conceptualised as a series of 'convex' spaces linked by straight 'axial' lines (Figures 8.8 and 8.9). From the network of axial lines, each line's 'integration value' (its position with respect to the system as a whole) can be calculated. The integration value is regarded as a good predictor of natural movement: the more integrated the line, the more movement along it, the less integrated, the less that route is used.

Hillier argues that the reason why his analysis gives a 'true-to-life functional picture' of movement

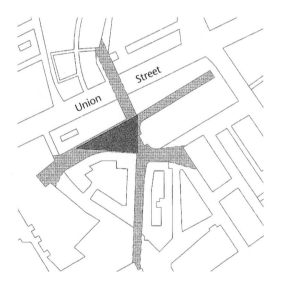

FIGURE 8.8
A shape is convex if all points within the shape can be seen from all other points within that shape (i.e. a straight line drawn between any two points within the shape lies wholly within the shape). Related to this is the 'convex isovist' – the shape defined by all the points that can be seen from any point within the convex space. As sight lines are considered to be important in terms of influencing movement, the convex isovist represents the opportunity space that a pedestrian in the convex space can see and could move to. The diagram shows the convex element (the darker shading) and the strategic isovist (the lighter shading) for *The Green* – an historic but underused space in the centre of Aberdeen. Close to the main pedestrian thoroughfare of Union Street, it is not visually linked to it

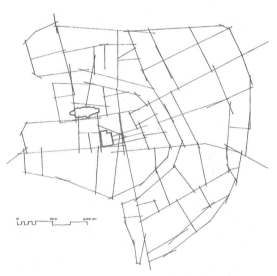

FIGURE 8.9
Axial map of Rothenburg. In an axial map, the plan view of the study area is drawn with axial lines ensuring that all the convex spaces are linked (i.e. integrated). Straight or axial lines are important because, for Hillier, people move along lines and, furthermore, need to be able to see along lines in order to know where they can go. Hillier notes that longer lines tend to strike façades at an open angle (i.e. suggesting further movement), while shorter lines tend to strike them at angles closer to a right angle, thereby, reducing the potential for movement in that direction. He also notes that patterns of land uses generally change slowly along lines of movement and more sharply with the increasing angle of turn onto different lines

densities is due to the influence that natural movement has had on the evolution of urban patterns
and distribution of land uses. The by-product
concept also enables Hillier to explain how the
land-use pattern derives from that of natural movement, rather than – as might intuitively be
expected – the other way round. Hillier argues that
every trip in an urban system has three elements:
an origin (A), a destination (B), and a series of
spaces passed through on the way from one to
another (the 'by-product'). Regardless of the
specific locations of A and B, some routes have
more potential to generate contact than others,
because they have more by-product. Hence, spaces
prioritised by the grid configuration for through-
movement are – and have been – selected as good
locations for 'passing trade' land uses.

Hillier acknowledges the potential for confusion,
between the effects of spatial configuration and of
particular land uses on movement. While accepting
that particular uses can attract people, he argues that
this is actually a multiplier effect: uses cannot change
the line's integration value. In other words, patterns
of natural movement and of space come before land
uses; land uses merely reinforce the basic movement
pattern. Hillier (1996a, p. 169), argues that:

> It is this positive feedback loop built on a foun-
> dation of the relation between the grid struc-
> ture and movement which gives rise to the
> urban buzz, which we prefer to be romantic or
> mystical about – but which arises from the co-
> incidence in certain locations of large numbers
> of different activities involving people going
> about their business in different ways.

Hillier (1996a, p. 169) suggests that this may be
illustrated by London's South Bank, where despite
the co-existence in a small area of many functions,
there is little 'urban buzz'. Hillier attributes this to
the configuration of space, which fails to bring the
different groups of space users into patterns of
movement that prioritise the same spaces – groups
move through the area like 'ships in the night'.

There are two key areas of difficulty in Hillier's
work. First, his method is based on the deformed
grid of the 'organic city', which evolved through
pedestrian movement. It is debatable whether the
method works as well for planned urban areas, or
for those designed from the outset to accommodate vehicular travel, where pedestrian freedom of
movement is restricted and path dependent.
Restrictions on the freedom of various modes of
travel can have major effects on movement densi-

ties: for example, closing streets to cars results in
their more intensive use by greater numbers of
pedestrians. Hillier's theory also does not consider
the design of space as involving more than spatial
configuration. Issues of accessibility and of the
character of urban places are also important: for
example, an unfriendly environment's pedestrian
flow may be increased significantly if the space
becomes more pedestrian friendly (Hass-Klau et al.,
1999; Gehl and Gemzoe, 2000).

Second, although movement comes first in
Hillier's system, it is unrelated to specific purpose.
The assumption is that movement between any two
points is as likely as movement between any other
two. This ignores the purpose of the movement (i.e.
the importance of the destination), which is usually
related to land use: movement is more likely in
connection with some destinations (e.g. public
buildings) than others (e.g. a private house).
Although Hillier considers the configuration of
space to be more important than land uses in the
generation of movement, land uses (particularly
'people attractors' or magnet land uses) will affect
movement through, within and to a public place.
Destination, as well as by-product, ought – at least
in theory – to matter. Hillier's analysis therefore
potentially understates the significance of destinations. As well as being animated through the by-
product of movement to other places, many spaces
are destinations in their own right. Hillier's argument is that, initially and over time, the by-product
of movement is more important than its origin or
destination. Nevertheless, as land uses and the
purpose of movement are entwined, the deterministic role ascribed to configuration and natural
movement remains problematic as land uses give
purpose for movement, changing their location
changes the pattern of movement. Over time, this
will also change the land use pattern in a two-way
interactive process. It must, however, be acknowledged that although Hillier's theory might be based
on a rather mechanistic view of people and their
behaviour, it supports predictions that correlate
highly with observed patterns of movement.

Space syntax has nonetheless been widely
accepted as a useful tool for analysing places. In
particular, it reminds urban designers of the importance of permeability, and of the overarching need
to consider movement (especially pedestrian movement) in the design of urban areas. The key
message is that well-connected places are more
likely to encourage pedestrian movement and to
support a vital and viable range of uses.

The shape, centre and edge of public spaces

As well as ideas about the aesthetically desirable shape and configuration of public spaces (see Chapter 7), consideration of how design features support use and activity is also important. In particular, and as discussed above, Hillier (1996a, 1996b) contends that various functional considerations related to movement need to be taken into account. He argues that attempts to account for the pattern of well- and poorly used informal spaces in the City of London, which have failed to acknowledge the role of movement, have been singularly unsuccessful. Thus, spaces hemmed in by the traffic are often better used than adjacent spaces; exposed spaces often perform better than enclosed spaces (Hillier, 1996b, p. 52). Hillier argues that the only variable that correlates consistently with the degree of use is what he calls the 'strategic value' of the isovist (a measure of the visual permeability of a space, calculated by summing the integration values of all the axial lines that pass through it). He argues that this makes intuitive sense – if the primary activity of those who stop to sit in urban spaces is people-watching, then 'strategic spaces with areas close to – but not actually lying on – the main lines of movement are optimal' (1996b, p. 52).

For Hillier (1996a, p. 161), the main fault in many contemporary public spaces is the prioritising of a sense of enclosure over visual permeability into them. The key quality with respect to pedestrian use of public spaces is their 'connectedness' – in Hillier's term, integration. Hillier (1996a, p. 161) argues that if design is overlocalised (i.e. not well integrated), the natural movement pattern is disrupted, and the space tends to be underused. His essential point is that urban designers must understand movement and design 'movement systems' – and therefore places – that are connected: 'Places are not local things. They are moments in large-scale things, the large-scale things we call cities. Places do not make cities. It is cities that make places. The distinction is vital. We cannot make places without understanding cities' (1996b, p. 42).

The design and use of public space can also usefully be considered in terms of the 'centre' and the 'edge'. Alexander et al. (1977, p. 606) assert that a public space 'without a middle is quite likely to stay empty'. They recommend that between 'the natural paths which cross a public square . . .

choose something to stand roughly in the middle: a fountain, a tree, a statue, a clock-tower with seats, a windmill, a bandstand . . . Leave it exactly where it falls, between the paths; resist the impulse to put it exactly in the middle' (Alexander et al., 1977, pp. 606–8). As well as providing a sense of identity and character, such features can also prompt triangulation.

Design of the edge is, however, the most important element for a successful urban place. Alexander et al. (1977, p. 600) argue that the life of a public square forms naturally around its edge, to which people gravitate rather than linger out in the open. 'If the edge fails, then the space never becomes lively . . . the space becomes a place to walk through, not a place to stop.' They recommend that, rather than treating the edge of a space as a 'line or interface with no thickness', it should be conceived of 'as a "thing", a "place", a zone with volume to it' (p. 753). As a support for people-watching, the edge of a space can be enhanced through the provision of formal or informal places to sit. If these are at a slightly higher level than the space, and partly protected from the weather (e.g. by an arcade), then both the prospect and the potential for people-watching are enhanced. Alexander et al. (1977, pp. 604–5), for example, observe that the most inviting spots are those high enough to provide a vantage point, but low enough to be used.

Building façades should be designed so that buildings reach out to the street and offer an 'active' frontage onto public space, adding interest and vitality to the public realm. As windows and doorways suggest a human presence, the more doors and windows onto public space the better. The interface needs to enable indoor and 'private' activities to exist in close physical proximity with outdoor and 'public' ones. Views into buildings provide interest to passers-by, while views out put 'eyes on the street' and contribute to its safety. The number of doors/entrances generating activity directly visible from public space is a good indicator of the potential for street life. Llewelyn-Davies (2000, p. 89), for example, provide a scale to judge the performance of designs according to the intensity of active frontage (Box 8.1).

The antithesis of active frontage is blank frontage. Whyte (1988) railed against the blank walls, designed as such, which he felt were becoming the dominant townscape feature of US cities: 'They are a declaration of distrust of the city and its streets and the undesirables who might be on

BOX 8.1 – SCALE OF ACTIVE FRONTAGES

(source: adapted from Llewelyn-Davies, 2000, p. 89)

GRADE A
- More than fifteen premises every 100 m
- A large range of functions/land uses
- More than twenty-five doors and windows every 100 m
- No blind/blank facades and few passive ones
- Much depth and relief in the building surface
- High quality materials and refined details

GRADE B
- Ten to fifteen premises every 100 m
- More than fifteen doors and windows every 100 m
- A moderate range of functions/land uses
- A blind/blank or few passive façades
- Some depth and modelling in the building surface
- Good quality materials and refined details

GRADE C
- Six to ten premises every 100 m
- Some range of functions/land uses
- Less than half blind/blank or passive façades
- Very little depth and modelling in the building surface
- Standard materials and few details

GRADE D
- Three to five premises every 100 m
- Little or no range of functions/land uses
- Predominantly blind/blank or passive façades
- Flat building surfaces
- Few or no details

GRADE E
- One or two premises every 100 m
- No range of functions/land uses
- Predominantly blind/blank or passive façades
- Flat building surfaces
- No details and nothing to look at

them.' While a 'technical explanation' (e.g. the need for consistent light levels) might be offered, this is rarely the real reason – blank walls are an end in themselves: 'They proclaim the power of the institution, the inconsequence of the individual, whom they are clearly meant to put down, if not intimidate.' Blank frontages not only deaden part of the street, they also break the continuity of experience that is vital for the rest of it (Figures 8.10 and 8.11).

Issues of active and blank façades also feature in residential design. Southworth and Owens (1993,

FIGURE 8.10
Although residential uses bring life and activity to city centres, the configuration and integration of such developments affect the public realm's vitality. This residential development in Denver consists of a parking structure providing the street edge and frontage with a residential tower block above. Presenting a blank frontage to much of the public realm, the parking structure has a deadening effect on the city centre. A spatial concentration of such developments would undermine both activity and vitality and safety and security in the city centre

FIGURE 8.11
This house in East London, UK, was deliberately designed with no windows facing onto the street. The façade is regularly covered in graffiti

pp. 282–3) note how, in the US, the role and position of the garage usurped that of the porch, in a transformation highlighting social changes and symbolising the primacy of the car in residential environmental design. Originally, the porch enabled and symbolised 'entry', contributing formally and functionally to a human scale street, while the garage was a small structure towards the back of the plot. Gradually the garage came forward to a position of prominence next to the house, and expanded from one to two or even three bays. As lots narrowed, it moved in front of the house, displacing the front porch from its traditional dominant position, and becoming a primary streetscape element and place of access. As lots narrowed further, front entry and porches disappeared, relegating pedestrian access to the house to a narrow alley along the garage to a side door. Southworth and Owens also note how – somewhat ironically – some residents had begun to use their garages as social spaces, equipping them with lawn chairs, radios and televisions, and treating them in

FIGURE 8.12
The garage door has become a dominant feature of the street scene of many residential developments. During the winter or the heat of the summer, the garage is undeniably a useful covered space for unloading groceries and for children's play space

FIGURE 8.13
Seaside, Florida: New Urbanists have both reasserted the importance of the front porch and have returned the garage to the rear of the plot serviced from alleys. Unless the porch reclaims its functional role as the point of entry and of the transition between public and private realms, however, this may simply be a symbolic gesture

a manner analogous to the old front porch. Unlike the porch, however, these 'human' qualities are only conveyed when the garage door is open. When closed, it becomes a blank façade. (Figures 8.12 and 8.13).

The public edge of buildings should also house activities that benefit from interaction with the public realm and contribute to vitality there. Richard MacCormac (1983) discussed the 'osmotic' properties of streets: the way activities within buildings percolate through and infuse the street with life. Some land uses have very little relation to people in the street, while others involve and engage people. MacCormac characterised the activity generated by different land uses as their 'transactional' quality, and distinguished between 'local transactions', which are peculiar to place, sensitive to change, have active frontages and significant impact on street life, and generate many comings and goings; and 'foreign transactions', which can locate anywhere since they are carried out on a regional or national scale, and have frontages with very little impact on street life because their activity is internalised. This does not suggest that some uses have no place within an urban area, merely that they should have less claim to key street frontage and public space. To ensure busier, livelier spaces, more interactive uses must be adjacent to them. MacCormac established a spectrum of uses supportive of an animated public realm. At the greater interaction end of the spectrum were street markets; restaurants, cafes, bars, pubs; housing;

small-scale offices and shops; and small-scale industry. At the other end were car parking; warehouses; large-scale industry; large-scale offices; blocks of flats and supermarkets (Figure 8.14).

FIGURE 8.14
Prague, Czech Republic. Street markets provide an intense series of local transactions

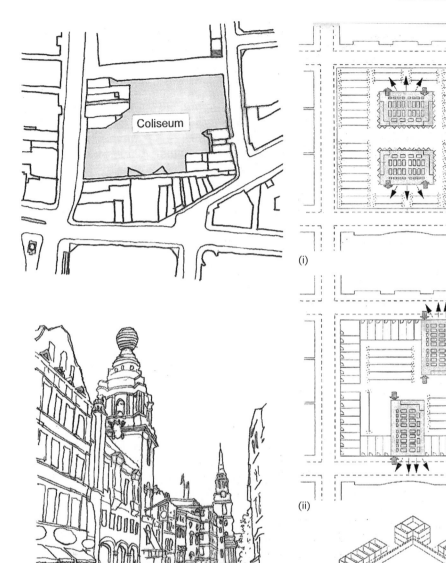

FIGURE 8.15
Although a foreign transaction, London's Coliseum Theatre avoids causing a deadening effect on local street life by being embedded in the core of the street block, and partly surrounded by a perimeter of local transactions. The foreign transaction attains civic presence by appearing emblematically on the skyline. While the theatre is a foreign transaction, the front of house, box office and bar are all potentially local transactions that will benefit the street edge

FIGURE 8.16
Designing for 'big box' retail. (i) Where big box sheds are surrounded by parking, the potentially active frontage is projected into the car park, rear elevations are exposed and the streetscape is undermined; (ii) by turning the sales floor through 90 degrees and inserting the building into a perimeter block, access is provided from both sides, while creating active street frontage; and (iii) to create active frontage, big box sheds can be surrounded by smaller units (source: adapted from Llewelyn-Davies, 2000, p. 43)

Large buildings utilising a single entrance can have a particularly deadening impact on streets. In many urban environments, large firms and offices have usurped smaller traders and obtained prestigious locations on the street frontage, where they often offer little sense of activity relevant to the public outside. In traditional urban environments, large buildings with little to contribute to street life – such as law courts, churches and theatres – were often embedded in the urban fabric, with a limited presence on the street frontage (MacCormac, 1987). Appearing emblematically on the skyline, such buildings freed the frontage for uses that interacted better with the street (Figure 8.15). This traditional development pattern suggests a way of incorporating foreign transactions – e.g. 'big box' retail developments, which often stand alone with exposed 'dead' frontages – into urban settings, without having a deadening effect on local street life: the core of the development contains the foreign transaction, while the perimeter houses local ones (Figure 8.16). For office buildings, locating active uses at the ground floor level can overcome their deadening effect on the street.

PRIVACY

The edge of the public space network provides the interface between public and private realms and needs to both enable interaction and protect privacy. As discussed in Chapter 4 and based on the public/private interface, all developments should have a 'front' onto public space. In terms of layout, the public fronts should face onto other fronts and onto public space, while the private 'backs' should face onto private space and other backs. Used consistently, such a strategy reduces the need for blank walls (i.e. instances where private uses front onto public space).

Privacy is a complex concept. Westin (1967, from Mazumdar, 2000, p. 161) distinguished four types: (1) 'solitude' (being alone); (2) 'intimacy' (when a small number of people are together, undisturbed); (3) 'anonymity' (interaction with others without being identifiable or accountable); and (4) 'reserve' (the limiting of communication about oneself). Mazumdar (2000, p. 161) added three further types: (5) 'seclusion' (being out of the way and difficult to find); (6) 'not neighbouring' (avoiding contact with neighbours); and (7) 'isolation' (being away from others). Some of these types of privacy are based on physical distance,

others on the control of interaction. Each may require its own design response or support.

In urban design terms, 'privacy' is usually defined in terms of selective control of access (to individual or group) and of interaction (especially that which is unwanted). Need for privacy and interaction varies among individuals, with respect to personality, life stage, etc., and across different cultures and societies. In many eastern cultures, concern for privacy has often been a major structuring element of urban areas.

Privacy can be attained in a number of ways, including behavioural/management mechanisms and strategies involving physical distance or the use of visual or sonic 'screens'. Built-form influences on privacy take two forms: more or less permanent 'barriers' and 'filters' which allow individual control of privacy/interaction. In functional terms, privacy can usefully be discussed in terms of 'visual' and 'aural' privacy.

Visual privacy

Issues of visual privacy typically relate to the interface between the public and private realms and, in particular, the physical and visual 'permeability' between these realms. Rather than a simple duality of privacy/no privacy, there is a spectrum of privacy needs. Chermayeff and Alexander (1963, p. 37), for example, argued that 'to develop both privacy and the true advantages of living in a community, an entirely new anatomy of urbanism is needed, built of many hierarchies of clearly anticipated domains'. Designers must enable the requirements of each privacy domain, while balancing these with opportunities for interaction. In domestic space, privacy levels typically structure the position of rooms, grading from the most accessible public spaces such as the entrance hall, to the least accessible and most private spaces (e.g. bedrooms and bathrooms) an ordering which relates to the position of outdoor public space and access to the dwelling (Figure 8.17).

Rather than a hard and impermeable interface between public and private realms, a softer and more permeable one is often desirable. Activities in private space are not all equally private, and 'softer' interfaces may create important interstitial or transitional spaces (e.g. pavement cafes, or places where internal activities can be seen from outside). While visual permeability can enrich the public realm, if used wrongly, it can confuse the vital public/private distinction. The permeability of the

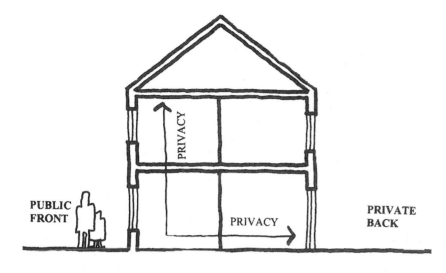

PUBLIC
FRONT

PRIVACY

PRIVACY

PRIVATE
BACK

FIGURE 8.17
Positive privacy
gradients maintain and
respect the public/
private distinction
(source: Bentley, 1999)

public/private interface should be controlled by private users. In practice, however, the necessary degree of control is often absent: instead of enabling users to choose how much privacy they want through the use of adjustable 'filters', by making permanent physical and visual barriers, designers often decide for them.

At a development-wide scale, the overly-rigid use by planners of 'space between dwellings' standards to ensure privacy is also to be avoided because of the tendency to deliver both regimented and monotonous layouts and low densities with high land take. Designers should therefore balance distance with designed-in privacy strategies.

Aural privacy

Undesired sounds – usually termed 'noise' – can disturb and invade privacy and activities. Although noise can be considered to be 'unwanted' sound, it raises issues of unwanted by whom: one person's music is another's 'unwanted sound'. Lang (1994, p. 226) notes that 'sonic comfort' depends not only on the decibel level of sound, but also on its pitch, its source, and perceptions of the degree to which hearers have control over it. While people can adapt to extraordinarily noisy environments, sonic pollution is an increasing concern. Noise disturbance also has a temporal dimension: a given type and level of sound is more acceptable at some times of the day or week than at others.

Glass and Singer (1972, from Krupat, 1985, p. 114) found that, rather than the physical characteristics of noise, it was the social and cognitive

contexts in which it occurred that determined whether it was intrusive. Furthermore, rather than the inability of people to adapt, psychic costs are the major source of noise-induced problems. Research, for example, has indicated that continual exposure to background noise such as that found in relatively noisy neighbourhoods, can lead to raised blood pressure, heart rates and stress in children, reducing maturation and leading to 'learned helplessness syndrome' (Evans *et al.*, 2001).

Design strategies can combat noise nuisance. A broad distinction can be made between noise-generating activities (cafes, bars, night-clubs, traffic, amplified music, etc.) and noise-sensitive uses such as housing. Measures can be taken to prevent or reduce the 'breakout' of noise, and/or separate it from noise-sensitive uses, by physical distance, sound insulation, or the use of screens and barriers. Within buildings, noise-sensitive uses can be located away from noise sources, for example. As change may be unpredictable and impossible to control, a necessary precautionary principle should be to ensure that appropriate insulation is provided for noise-sensitive uses from the start. As physical distance from the noise source is often impractical, the other main means to obstruct the sound path is by solid screening (i.e. solid fencing) or earth-bunds (trees and tree belts have very little effect).

MIXED USE AND DENSITY

A sufficient density of activity and people has often been regarded as a prerequisite of vitality, and for creating and sustaining viable mixed use. Jane Jacobs (1961, p. 163) argued that city life has much to do with density. For her, New York's Greenwich Village, with densities ranging from 310 to 500 dwellings per net hectare, was the optimum environment (p. 216). Similarly, the UK's Urban Task Force (1999, p. 59) noted that Barcelona – described as the 'most compact and vibrant European city' – has an average density of about 400 dwellings per hectare.

Another key aspect of creating a lively and well-used public realm is the spatial and temporal concentration of different land uses and activities. In response to the sterility produced by the functional zoning policies and practices of much post-war planning and urban development, the mixing of uses has become a widely accepted urban design objective. Areas may have mixed uses in either or both of two ways: by having a mix of single-use buildings or by having buildings which each contain a mix of uses (e.g. living over the shop). The latter is generally preferable.

Mixed uses

Although a fundamental part of Modernist urban design (see Chapter 2), functional zoning approaches have been much criticised. Jacobs (1961, p. 155), for example, argued that the vitality of city neighbourhoods depends on the overlapping and interweaving of activities, and that understanding cities requires dealing with combinations or mixtures of uses as the 'essential phenomena'. She outlined four conditions indispensable to the generation of 'exuberant diversity' in a city's streets and districts:

- The district . . . must serve more than one primary function; preferably more than two . . .
- Most blocks must be short; that is, streets and opportunities to turn corners must be frequent.
- The district must mingle buildings that vary in age and condition . . .
- There must be a sufficiently dense concentration of people, for whatever purposes that may be there. (Jacobs, 1961, pp. 162–3) (Figure 8.18).

It is not necessarily zoning *per se* that is problematic, but the type of zoning and how it is applied. Leon Krier (1990, pp. 208–9) illustrates two types: 'inclusive' zoning, where 'all is permitted and promoted that is not strictly forbidden'; exclusion

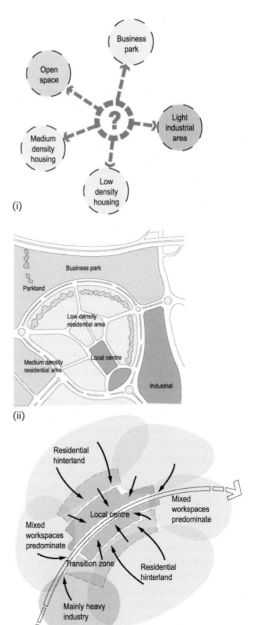

FIGURE 8.18
Designing for mixed uses. (i) If all the potential 'mixed-use elements' are located at the edge of the development, it undermines the role of the centre; (ii) although geographically proximate, the uses are still zoned with roads forming the boundaries between uses; and (iii) more vibrant and sustainable neighbourhoods and areas result from the complex interweaving of uses and by blurring the distinctions between uses (source: adapted from Llewelyn-Davies, 2000, p. 39)

is based on environmental 'nuisance' or incompatibility ('bad neighbours') and – in principle – various uses can occupy the same area. By contrast, in the case of 'exclusive' zoning, 'all that is not specifically obligatory is strictly forbidden'. This is often zoning for its own sake, a routine and largely unquestioned process of mechanical separation of differing land uses and functions for no real purpose other than a misguided sense of order.

Criticisms of functional zoning do not, however, invalidate the mechanism of zoning. Kropf (1996, p. 723) argues that, rather than the general principle of defining areas controlled by particular regulations, what is important is the specific content of zoning ordinance. Some commentators suggest shifting the emphasis from 'use' to 'form' (e.g. from functional to 'typo-morphological' zoning) (Moudon, 1994). In practice, however, conventional systems of land use zoning have often regulated form as well as use. Over the past decade a more explicit use of form-based zoning has been used in some urban design work, notably that of the New Urbanists (Figure 8.19).

In many countries, post-war functional zoning policies have increasingly been abandoned. Nevertheless, although the original need – to separate noxious industries from housing – has now largely gone, the mindset that uses should be neatly separated has proved more enduring. Social, institutional, financial and political conservatism, together with interests such as discrimination, market segmentation, product differentiation, and protection of property prices, also perpetuate and support functional zoning. In many parts of the US, for example, strict segregation is now applied to every use, with typical zoning codes having several dozen land-use designations, and producing an extremely segregated environment – both physically and socially – which both derives from, and appeals to, the self-interest of many local property owners.

Market factors may also result in mono-functional areas. Because all developers and property owners seek to develop or utilise their property in its 'highest and best' possible use, there is a tendency for areas to be mono-functional. This tendency is reduced where secondary uses have a symbiotic relation with the area's dominant one. Where it has sufficient powers, the public sector can intervene to limit the area that can be developed for the primary use, and/or to protect certain sites for other uses.

Llewelyn-Davies (2000, p. 39) identifies the following benefits of mixed-use development:

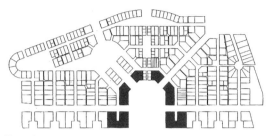

Type I

Type II

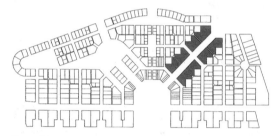

Type IV

FIGURE 8.19
Duany and Plater-Zybeck (DPZ) developed the master plan and the urban and architectural codes for Seaside (Florida, US) – a seminal New Urbanist project. The development is typologically rather than functionally zoned and trades 'uniformity of function within a zone' for a 'variety of building types within a neighbourhood' (Kelbaugh, 1997, p. 106). Nine different types of development were defined. Within an overall conception of the desired three-dimensional form, the master plan allocates each development site a particular development type. The diagrams show the location of Types I, II and IV (source: Mohney and Easterling, 1991, pp. 101–2)

- More convenient access to facilities.
- Minimising travel-to-work congestion.
- Greater opportunities for social interaction.
- Socially diverse communities.
- A greater feeling of safety through more 'eyes on the street'.

- Greater energy efficiency and more efficient use of space and buildings.
- More consumer choice of lifestyle, location and building type.
- Greater urban vitality and street life.
- Increased viability of urban facilities and support for small business.

While functional zoning and mono-functional development often create or exacerbate car-dependency and reduce choice, mixed-use developments generally enable walking or, at least, choice in travel mode, and are therefore more sustainable. They also offer more lifestyle choices. Duany *et al.* (2000, p. 25) argue, for example, that because one can live above the store, next to the store, five minutes from the store, or nowhere near the store, the traditional neighbourhood provides for an array of lifestyles. By contrast, they argue that suburbia offers only one lifestyle – to own a car and to need it for everything.

Despite general support for the principle of mixed-use buildings, developments and areas, the property industry in general, developers, investors and some occupiers, are averse to mixed uses within the same building. Several interrelated factors account for this:

- *Development*: the additional costs of developing mixed-use buildings (for different fire escape requirements, etc.); and the institutional structure of the development industry, with developers tending to specialise in a particular development type (residential, commercial, etc.).
- *Management*: occupiers not wanting certain other users of the building for reasons of incompatibility or security; and additional costs involved in having multiple users, due to different leasing, safety or environmental health requirements.
- *Investment*: different leasing periods reduce the liquidity, and therefore the value, of the development.

There may also be physical, legal or financial obstacles that prohibit or increase the cost of accommodating different land uses within one building. The need, therefore, is to find ways of providing or enabling mixed uses through persuasion, regulation, or financial incentives. Planning policies, master plans, or urban design frameworks could require an element of mixed uses in developments or even within buildings – although, equally, such requirements might make development unviable.

Market volatility provides a rationale for mixed-use developments. Primary office locations are likely always to be fully let. In secondary locations, however, office property markets are more volatile and the effects of recessions and downturns are keenly felt. All or part of office buildings in these locations may periodically be vacant, and it may produce a better overall return to have a mix of office and residential uses, because the building may be let more readily for residential use (albeit at a lower return). Thus, in a secondary location, a mixed-use building with flexibility between land uses may spread the risk of vacancy.

Although the mixing of uses may occur spontaneously through market action, appropriate physical provision of robust buildings or development patterns increases the possibility of a mix emerging over time. If no provision is made, this is unlikely to occur. The need, therefore, is to design for the possibility. Creation of mixed uses in existing areas often involves introducing residential uses into non-residential areas (e.g. the CBD or city centre) or non-residential uses into residential areas (e.g. suburbs). The design challenge is to gain the synergy and benefits of mixed uses, while avoiding bad neighbour situations. In examining the land-use pattern of traditional urban neighbourhoods, MacCormac (1987) noted the tendency for symmetry of land uses across spaces, and asymmetry across blocks. This suggests ways of incorporating different uses into an area while reducing the potential for negative or bad neighbour effects. There might, for example, be a grading of uses across a series of blocks, with intermediary uses between any that would be incompatible as direct neighbours. Another useful development pattern is that of perimeter blocks, which can accommodate a mix of uses in a number of different ways: for example, by insertion of managed workspaces or compatible employment uses into the backland or block interior; introduction of a mews line through the block accommodating single-aspect offices, workshops or studios; and/or placing a residential mews within a commercial block (Llewelyn-Davies, 2000, p. 96).

Density

Recent debates about the creation of more sustainable and compact towns and cities have led to a renewed focus on issues of density, especially residential density (e.g. Urban Task Force, 1999). The argument is that compact cities can offer a high quality of life while minimising resource and energy consumption. Achieving higher densities than has been the norm in the latter part of the twentieth century in the UK and the US, for example, is regarded as fundamental to the creation of more sustainable environments – as discussed in Chapter 2, the study by Newman and Kenworthy (1989) showed the relationship between density and gasoline consumption for several cities throughout the world. Llewelyn-Davies (2000, p. 46) suggests a range of benefits from higher densities of development:

- *Social*: encouraging positive interaction and diversity; improving viability of and access to community services.
- *Economic*: enhancing the economic viability of development and providing economies of infrastructure (e.g. basement car parking).
- *Transport*: supporting public transport and reducing car travel and parking demand.
- *Environmental*: increasing energy efficiency; decreasing resource consumption; creating less pollution; preserving, and helping fund the maintenance of, public open space; reducing overall demand for development land.

BOX 8.2 – DENSITY AND URBAN FORM

(source: adapted from Urban Task Force, 1999, pp. 62–3)

High-rise development standing in open space
- No private gardens, poor amenities directly available to the inhabitants.
- No direct relationship between the buildings and the surrounding streets.
- Large area of open space requires management and maintenance.

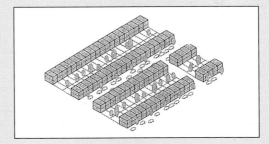

Street layout with 2–3 storey houses
- Front and back gardens.
- Continuous street frontages define the public space.
- Streets form a clear pattern of public space.
- High site coverage minimises potential for communal spaces.

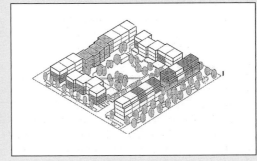

Urban perimeter block
- Surrounding buildings can be of different heights and configuration.
- Buildings are arranged around a landscaped open space.
- Open space can contain a community-based facility.
- Commercial and public facilities can be distributed along the ground floor, maintaining an active street frontage.
- Space is available for use as, for example, rear gardens, communal areas or a park.

Although more compact and higher density development is currently encouraged, it often conflicts with sociocultural preferences for lower density environments and for car-based mobility (see Breheny, 1995, 1997). While lower density was initially a response to conditions within the industrial cities of the nineteenth century, during the twentieth century it became an objective in its own right, backed by various regulations that effectively prohibited higher density development, and thus virtually mandated suburban sprawl. In his review of twentieth century British housing design, Scoffham (1984, p. 23) notes how density zoning, road widths, sight lines, the space required for underground services, street by-laws and daylighting angles were all to blame for pushing buildings further and further apart.

While higher densities are sometimes equated with poor quality environments, high quality urban design is – in principle – achievable at all densities. At higher density levels, however, good design becomes essential to protect amenity (particularly privacy standards) and to provide liveable environments. Preconceptions of high density development can elicit concerns: however, studies by Elizabeth Denby (1956) showed that the densities of highly desirable Georgian and early Victorian terraces were often much higher than those achieved by high-rise, supposedly high density, housing developments. Studies by Martin and March (1972) and March (1967) also dispelled some of the preconceptions about density (see Chapter 4). These stud-

ies showed that density must be considered in terms of the configuration of urban form – that is, as a product rather than a determinant of design. Box 8.2 shows three configurations of urban forms: a single point block; a traditional street layout and a perimeter block enclosing an open space. Each has the same density (75 dwellings per hectare) but a different arrangement of public and private space.

Despite an overarching preference for higher densities, Jacobs (1961, p. 221) concluded that 'proper' city densities were a 'matter of performance' and could not be based on abstractions about the quantity of land needed for X number of people. Similarly, Llewelyn-Davies (2000, p. 46) suggests the aim should be to generate a critical mass of people able to support urban services such as local shops, schools and public transport. Research by Owens (from P. Hall, 1998, p. 972) also suggests that there is no need for very high densities. Twenty-five dwellings per hectare, for example, would allow facilities with a catchment area of 8000 people to be within 600 metres of all homes, while a pedestrian scale cluster of 20 000–30 000 people would provide a sufficient threshold for many facilities without resort to high densities.

Considerations of density – and particularly of the density required to make public transit schemes viable – have often formed the basis of neighbourhoods designed for sustainability; for example, Calthorpe's (1993) idea of transit-oriented development (TOD) (Figure 8.20). Research in the UK suggests that net densities of 100 persons per

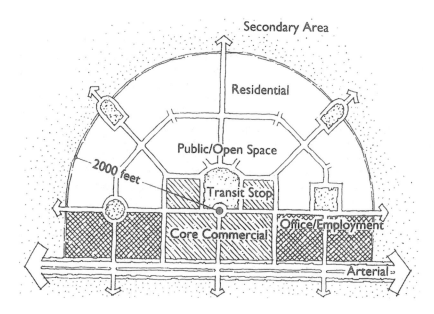

FIGURE 8.20
Transit-Oriented
Development (TOD)
(source: Calthorpe,
1993)

hectare (approximately 45 units/ha) are necessary to sustain a good bus service, while, in more central locations, a net density of 240 persons/ha (or 60 units/ha) will sustain a tram service (Llewe-lyn-Davies, 2000, p. 47). The argument is that if neighbourhoods are built at low densities, it is unlikely that public transit systems will ever become viable. This reflects Lang's pragmatic principle of urban design: if travel options are considered in terms of providing choice, then flexibility should be built in for the possibility of relative travel costs changing in the future.

ENVIRONMENTAL DESIGN

An essential part of urban design is the need to provide comfortable conditions within public spaces: if spaces are not comfortable, they are unlikely to be used. Levels of sunlight, shade, temperature, humidity, rain, snow, wind and noise have an impact upon our experience and use of urban environments. A number of design actions can help to make conditions more acceptable, including the configuring of space, and use of buildings, walls, trees, canopies and arcades for shade and shelter. Desirable conditions vary by season, and by the activities taking place.

The following sections concern environmental conditions in public spaces and around buildings, in terms of microclimate, sunlight and shelter, air movement about buildings, and lighting.

The microclimate

Microclimate is often neglected in urban design. Designers can have little influence on the overall macroclimatic situation and, except on very large sites or in designing new settlements, they often have only a limited effect on features affecting the climate at the meso-scale. Such features include the nature of the surroundings and topographical elements such as hills and valleys which affect exposure to wind. Design decisions have, however, an important influence in modifying the impact of the microclimate to make spaces more comfortable. Relevant factors at this scale include:

- The configuration of the proposed development, and its effect on and relationship to buildings and other influences at the site boundary.

- The positioning of access roads and pedestrian paths, trees and other vegetation, walls, fences and other obstructions.
- The orientation of internal and external spaces and façades with respect to the direction of sunlight and shade.
- The massing, grouping, and space between buildings.
- The wind environment.
- The positioning of main entrances and other openings acting as transitions between inside and outside conditions.
- Landscape, planting and pools/fountains to enhance natural cooling.
- Environmental noise and pollution. (Pitts, 1999)

Responding to both the local and global contexts, the need is for 'climate sensitive design'. While traditional designs were necessarily well suited to the local climate, in many countries this close association between climate and design has been severed by the use of rapid construction techniques, and the availability of fuels and building services systems to overcome any detrimental effects. The vogue for an architectural International Style also resulted in the inappropriate translation of building designs from one region to another, without regard to the local climate.

Designing for sun and shade

Sunlight penetration into urban places and into buildings helps to make them more pleasant places. It also encourages outdoor activities; reduces mould growth; improves health by providing the body with vitamin E; encourages plant growth; and provides a cheap, readily available source of energy for passive and active collection. The value of sunlight penetration varies over the seasons and, while places in the sun are desirable at some times of year, at other times shade is preferred.

Two major issues are of concern: orientation – in northern latitudes, for example, south-facing elevations receive the maximum sunlight and north-facing elevations the least – and overshadowing and shading. In terms of the latter, the following should be considered:

- The sun's position (altitude and azimuth) relative to public spaces and to the principal façades of buildings.

TABLE 8.1
Windspeed and effects

SITUATION	WINDSPEED (M/S)	EFFECT
Calm, light air	0–1.5	• Calm • No noticeable wind effect
Light breeze	1.6–3.3	• Wind felt on face
Gentle breeze	3.4–5.4	• Wind extends light flag • Hair is disturbed • Clothing flaps
Moderate breeze	5.5–7.9	• Raises dust, dry soil, loose paper • Hair disarranged
Fresh breeze	8.0–10.7	• Force of wind felt on body • Drifting snow becomes airborne • Limits of agreeable wind on land
Strong breeze	10.8–13.8	• Umbrella used with difficulty • Hair blown straight • Difficult to walk • Wind noise on ears unpleasant • Wind-borne snow above head height (blizzard)
Near gale	13.9–17.1	• Inconvenience felt when walking
Gale	17.2–20.7	• Generally impedes progress • Great difficulty with balance in gusts
Strong gale	20.8–24.4	• People blown over by gusts

(from Penwarden & Wise (1975), from Bentley *et al.*, 1985, p. 75)

- Site orientation and slope.
- Existing obstructions on the site.
- The potential for overshadowing from obstructions beyond the site boundary.
- The potential to overshadow nearby buildings and spaces. (Pitts, 1999)

Solar access can be evaluated by the use of charts such as a stereographic sun chart. As well as graphical and computer prediction techniques, physical models can be tested using a heliodon. If overshadowing is to be avoided during winter months (when solar gain is most advantageous), the spacing between buildings is very significant. Trees will also provide obstructions to solar access. If deciduous, they will perform the dual function of permitting solar penetration during the winter and a degree of shading in the summer. The spacing between tree and building is again critical.

The wind environment

Wind flow has a substantial effect on the comfort of pedestrians, the environmental conditions within public spaces and around building entrances and the activities that might occur there (Table 8.1). If the wind effect is to be minimised (as is usually the case), the following factors should be considered:

- Building dimensions should be kept to a minimum to reduce wind pressures.
- The larger building dimension should not face into the predominating wind (i.e. the long axis should be parallel to it).
- Building layouts should avoid creating tunnel effects (e.g. long parallel rows of relatively smooth-faced buildings should be avoided).
- As sheer vertical faces to tall buildings can generate substantial down draughts, the façades of tall buildings should be staggered and stepped back with increasing height away from the prevailing wind (i.e. tending towards a ziggurat form).
- Protection of pedestrians by the use of canopies and podiums, which reduce down draught at ground level.
- Buildings should be grouped in irregular arrays, but within each group, the heights should be

similar and the spacing between them kept to a minimum.

- Shelter belts (trees, hedges, walls, fences, etc.) can provide a degree of protection for buildings and pedestrians. They are most effective when correctly oriented and with a permeability to airflow of about 40 per cent, allowing wind to be diffused rather than forced over the obstruction which causes increased turbulence. (BRE, 1990; Pitts, 1999)

In very humid climates, external spaces may need to be designed to encourage a greater through-flow of cooling air. In more arid climates, fountains and water features in public spaces help cooling through the evaporation of water vapour.

Air quality is an increasingly important consideration in urban areas. Trees and other vegetation tend to filter air, while rainfall scrubs it. In high concentrations, pollution will tend to kill natural vegetation. To dissipate air pollution, good air circulation about buildings and within urban spaces is required – which may conflict with aesthetic desires for a sense of enclosure in urban spaces (see Chapter 7) (Figure 8.21).

Airflow inside buildings can be created by natural ventilation or by artificial mechanical ventilation or air conditioning. In general, designers should seek to minimise the need for artificial systems. If airflow is to provide natural ventilation and cooling, the plan form needs to be relatively shallow. For successful cross-ventilation, the cross-sectional depth should be a maximum of five times the floor-to-window head height (see Chapter 9).

Lighting

Natural lighting makes an important contribution to the character and utility of public space, and the play of light in urban spaces also has aesthetic dimensions. Louis Kahn wrote that: 'The sunlight did not know what it was before it hit a wall' (in von Meiss, 1990, p. 121). The amount of visible sky – particularly overhead, where it is brighter than at the horizon – is crucial to the quality of daylighting. Except where particularly tall or large buildings surround the space, adequate daylighting – as distinct from direct sunlight – of an urban space is rarely a problem. A basic rule of thumb, used in the UK, is that obstructions which subtend an angle of less than 25 degrees to the horizontal will not usually interfere with good daylighting, while greater obstructions need not interfere provided they are relatively narrow (Littlefair, 1991). The rule will change with relative latitude.

In general, buildings should make as much beneficial use of natural light as possible. The quality of the daylighting in a room depends on the design and position of fenestration relative to the depth and shape of the room, and on whether surrounding buildings obstruct light penetration. Shallower plans will be better lit than deeper ones (see Chapter 9).

Although artificial lighting can make a positive contribution to the character and utility of urban spaces, it is often designed with only vehicular traffic in mind and tends to be inefficient in energy use, resulting in light pollution. It has two key functions:

1. 'Statutory lighting' – provides basic lighting levels, to aid pedestrian way-finding and the secure use of the public realm at night, and the safe passage of vehicles.

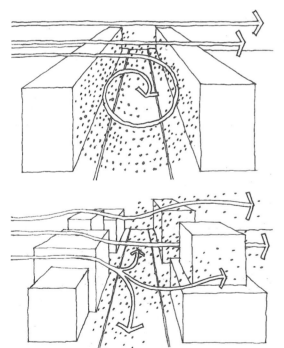

FIGURE 8.21
Air quality at street level. Street canyons lined with buildings of similar height, oriented perpendicular to the wind direction (upper diagram) tend to have poorer air circulation than street canyons lined with buildings of different heights and interspersed with open areas (lower diagram) (source: Spirn (1987, pp. 311–12) from Vernez-Moudon, 1987, p. 311)

2. 'Amenity lighting' – which enhances the streetscene through flood, feature and low-level lighting; and gives night-time colour and vitality through signs, shop-lighting and seasonal lighting.

In practice, the lighting of streets at night derives from a wide range of sources – street lamps, borrowed light from buildings, shop signs, etc. – and the ensemble needs careful consideration to meet both statutory and amenity needs. To achieve this and to enhance the night-time economy, a number of towns and cities, such as Croydon (London) and Edinburgh (Scotland), have adopted comprehensive lighting strategies. Well-lit streets and spaces are particularly important in making users feel safe and secure (see Chapter 6).

THE CAPITAL WEB

As discussed in Chapter 4, the capital web is made up of the above and below ground elements of the city's infrastructure. The major capital web considerations in urban design are: the provision of public open space; road and footpath design; parking and servicing; and other infrastructure. While these apply in most developments, this list is neither exclusive nor comprehensive.

Public open space

Public open space offers recreational opportunities, wildlife habitats, venues for special events, and the opportunity for the city to breathe. At the larger scale, areas of public open space should link into a network giving opportunities for the movement of people and wildlife between them. At a smaller scale, standards are often set by public authorities to ensure minimum provision: in the UK, the National Playing Fields Association requires 2.4 hectares (6 acres) per thousand population (1.6–1.8 hectares for outdoor sport, plus 0.6–0.8 hectares for children's playing space). Such provision should be locally accessible, within easy walking distance of all homes. The NPFA (1992) also suggest Local Areas of Play (LAPs) within 100 m of homes, and larger Locally Equipped Areas for Play (LEAPs) within 400 m.

The provision of open space is particularly important in higher density environments. Appropriate standards should be established in all new developments, with aspirational targets in areas with little existing provision. Rather than being an afterthought – as a use for Space Left Over After Planning (SLOAP) – open space should be an integrated and important part of the urban design vision for a place, often as a key focus for public life. A number of towns and cities, including the British New Towns, have developed sophisticated open space frameworks creating 'green' corridors through urban areas for recreational purposes and for wildlife. Integration of natural and built environments is a key objective of sustainable development.

Road and footpath design

The requirements of cars rather than people often dominate the design of urban environments. If vehicular speeds can be lowered – by controls and regulations, by speed bumps or other obstacles, or, more subtly, by manipulating and configuring sight lines – then car-oriented standards can be lowered as well. As discussed in Chapter 4, post-war concern for segregation of pedestrian and vehicular traffic, initially on the grounds of personal safety, often meant pedestrians could only cross busy roads by underground subways or overground foot bridges. Car-free pedestrian precincts have been used, with mixed success: some are almost deserted outside office hours, while others are very successful. Detailed analysis is necessary to determine why some are successful and others are not, but the mix of uses and the opportunity they provide for activity at different times of the day is likely to play a major part.

In general, the contemporary ethos is to design pedestrian-dominant rather than car-dominant environments: without banishing the car, such approaches give priority to pedestrians. This has seen extensive pedestrianisation of city centres; pavement widening/road-narrowing schemes; and the closing of subways and reintroduction of surface level crossings. Many residential streets have been traffic-calmed: the Dutch, for example, have employed the concept of the *woonerf* (home-zones in the UK). At a larger scale, there have been schemes to introduce road pricing, and – typically, in historic European cities – the banning of all cars from city centres.

Road and footpath design has a set of basic requirements:

- maintain safety and personal security through reducing vehicle speeds, discouraging road and footpath separation and increasing passive surveillance;
- increase permeability and access by all modes of travel but particularly by foot;
- encourage directness by acknowledging and emphasising 'desire lines' in development (i.e. the most convenient route to where people wish to go) and roads that are well connected to their surroundings;
- design in sympathy with the local context, to ensure an attractive development in which clearly defined spaces, landscaping and buildings dominate, rather than roads or cars;
- increase legibility through the design of layouts in which the overall structure and local visual references are clear.

These requirements must be reconciled with the needs and efficiency of the road network. The interests of the highways engineer in attaining road safety and efficiency may, however, conflict with the broader aim of overall environmental quality. Frequently, local authorities have adopted a hierarchy of highway standards which have led to over-engineering of many (particularly residential) environments, and over-reliance on simple standards to design new road systems. Increasingly, traffic-calming methods are being used, and more sophisticated design guidance from local authorities is abandoning hierarchical approaches to designing road layouts which now appear oversimplistic and encouraging car-dominance. The new design guidance proposes that highway considerations should move beyond matters of safety and vehicle flow efficiency, to encompass concern for environmental quality, pedestrian permeability and three-dimensional space design (Carmona, 2001, p. 283). Advice in the 1997 'Essex Design Guide' (Essex Planning Officers Association, 1997), for example, suggested:

- spaces should come first, with buildings arranged to fit the context and roads 'plumbed' in later (see Figures 8.22 and 8.23);
- designating 20 mph zones in residential areas;
- adopting a network of spaces rather than a hierarchy of roads;
- adopting a sustainable movement framework well related to public transport and an integrated mix of uses; and
- using 'connected' rather than cul-de-sac road layouts (Carmona, 2001, p. 306).

The overall need is to create pedestrian-dominant environments that offer a choice of modes of travel. There will inevitably be areas where cars dominate, and areas where pedestrians dominate. In resolving competing claims for space, the aim must be to avoid car-dependent environments, because that dependency reduces the potential to be sustainable. Cars can be reconciled to systems designed to give pedestrians, cycling and public transport priority, but it is difficult for other modes of travel to fit into systems designed for cars. The priorities for movement should therefore be: first by foot and cycle, then public transport and, finally, by car. This

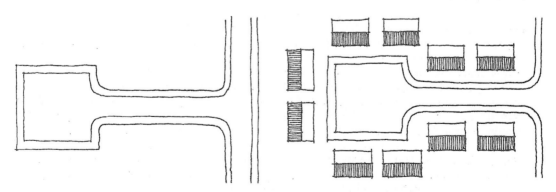

FIGURE 8.22
Many housing developments are laid out around roads without consideration of the spaces that are created between the individual (usually standard) housing units. This can be characterised as a 'roads first, houses later approach' – a form of road-dominated design that neglects other important elements of the residential environment (source: DETR, 1998, p. 23)

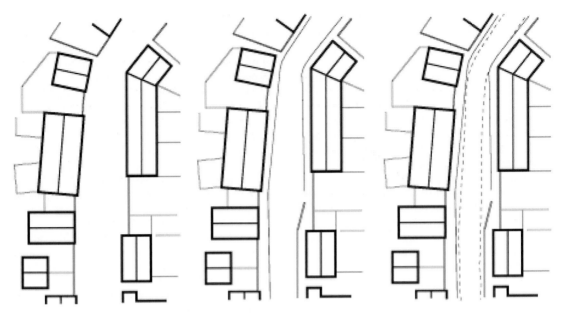

FIGURE 8.23
'Tracking' is the provision of the required carriageway width for vehicle movement within the overall width of the
street. The idea is an attempt to suggest alternatives to the 'roads first, houses later' approach to residential design.
Instead of taking the highway engineering requirements as the starting point for design (i.e. a 'roads first'
approach), the arrangement of buildings and enclosure is considered first and the roads are plumbed in later (i.e. a
'spaces first' approach). In the first diagram, buildings are arranged to form street enclosure. In the second,
footways are laid out in front of buildings to reinforce the space and enclosure. In the third, the carriageway width
is checked by plotting vehicle-tracking paths (source: DETR, 1998, p. 55)

requires routes for pedestrians or cyclists being built
into the plan from the outset, because fitting them
in later will be difficult, if not impossible.

Parking and servicing

Despite well-aired arguments for reducing reliance
on private cars, parking is a requirement of
contemporary living that is likely to remain for the
foreseeable future. Indeed, space for parking is
required within all environments, urban, suburban
or rural. A particular problem, however, is that of
integrating parking successfully into the streetscene
and nearby developments. Parking needs to be:

- sufficient to cater for contemporary needs;
- convenient (i.e. located close to destinations)
  for all users, including those with disabilities;
- attractive by limiting its visual intrusion (use of
  landscaping and quality materials can successfully integrate on- and off-street parking); and
- safe and secure.

Where locations are well served by public transport, the required parking standard may be
reduced. Establishing maximum rather than minimum parking standards can discourage car use –
although problems of overspill onto adjacent
streets must be considered. Car-free housing,
where residents contract not to own cars, has been
developed in a few locations that are well
connected with public transport, while some other
developments require purchasers to make additional payments for a parking space. Some cities
and developments have car club and car pool
schemes, where a range of cars – from people
carriers and four-wheel drive vehicles to small city
'run-arounds' – is owned and used collectively by
members. Car clubs are well established in several
northern European countries. In Germany, for
example, a club called *StattAuto* has 20 000
members and serves 18 cities with 1000 cars of
varying sizes (Richards, 2001, pp. 122–3). In the
US, some mortgage companies have experimented
with location specific mortgages. Where a property
is being bought in a location well served by public

transit, the mortgage loan may be higher than normal on the basis that the buyer does not have the expense of owning and running a car.

Contemporary developments also require space for servicing, including business deliveries; waste disposal, storage and collection; recycling points; emergency access; removals; cleaning and maintenance; and utilities access. However, many of these elements can be very disruptive in the streetscene. Due to their scale, service vehicles, for example, require wider streets, larger setbacks, open service yards and gaping service bays. In residential areas, in particular, intimacy and variety in the streetscene can be disrupted by the requirements of service vehicles including the statutory requirement for adequate access provision to be made for emergency vehicles. But servicing arrangements can be integrated with care and should not dictate the overall layout or character of an area.

Infrastructure

An area's infrastructure – above and below ground – has usually been built up over many centuries. With each urban intervention, it is adapted or extended. Above ground, the capital web incorporates the public space network and landscaping framework; any public transport network and infrastructure; public facilities (e.g. shops) and services (e.g. schools). Below ground it incorporates water supply networks; sewage disposal systems; electric grids; the gas supply networks; telephone networks; cable networks; combined heat and light systems; and underground transit systems.

Infrastructure networks are becoming increasingly important in, and as a key generative element of, the development of urban areas (Mitchell, 1994, 1999; Horan, 2000; Graham and Marvin, 2001). Unless there is ubiquitous provision, the network inevitably advantages one location over another, and the pattern of infrastructure is a significant factor in determining where development occurs. Graham and Marvin (2001, p. 18), however, note how architects, planners and urban designers have 'tended to neglect networked infrastructures and the flows and mobilities that they support . . . the networked infrastructures that knit buildings together, binding and configuring the broader spaces of metropolitan life'.

Until relatively recently, traditional street systems have adapted well to the requirements for below ground infrastructure. However, incremental and *ad hoc* provision has overloaded many streets, and causes conflicts – as shown by the poor state of many street trees whose root systems have been

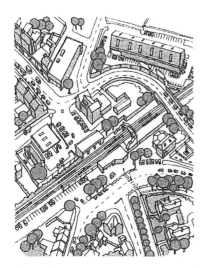
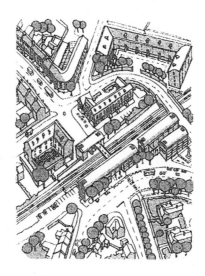

FIGURE 8.24
Intensification around suburban railway stations can introduce new residential and commercial uses on previously underused sites, thereby increasing an area's vitality and allowing residents on the surrounding (unchanged) suburban streets to meet more of their everyday needs locally (source: CPRE, 2001)

damaged. In general, there is a need to consider the seen and unseen capital web in the design process; to plan for flexibility and future changes/additions; and to integrate development in a sustainable manner, minimising the need for new infrastructure and reducing disruption to that which exists (see Graham and Marvin, 1996, 2001). New elements, especially public transport, are also a means to improve the public realm (see Richards, 2001) (Figure 8.24).

CONCLUSION

This chapter has discussed the functional dimension of urban design, reinforcing the notion of it as a design process. As discussed in Chapter 3, the criteria of good design – 'firmness', 'commodity', 'delight' and 'economy' – must be satisfied simultaneously. In any design process, there is a danger of narrowly prioritising a particular dimension – aesthetic, functional, technical or economic – and

of isolating it from its context and from its contribution to the greater whole. Discussing the design of speed humps from the perspective of engineers and of urban designers, for example, Appleyard (1991, pp. 7–8) argued that:

> The engineer will tend to design a speed hump solely for the purpose of slowing the traffic in a safe and cheap way. These humps can be quite ugly – lumps of asphalt that convey a negative controlling impression to the drivers. The urban designer favours more pleasant humps, perhaps made of bricks, that can also serve as raised crosswalks for pedestrians.

The latter is a multi-dimensional rather than a uni-dimensional solution. Appleyard (1991, p. 8), therefore, argues that while the economist may see the resolution of differences in terms of 'compromise' and 'trade-offs', the urban designer offers creative ingenuity and adds value through the resolution of the differences – in the example, combining functionality with visual and social objectives.

9

The temporal dimension

INTRODUCTION

This chapter concerns the temporal or 'time' dimension of urban design. Although sometimes considered to be a matter of working in three dimensions, urban design is four-dimensional: the fourth dimension being time. As time passes, spaces become lived-in places, made more meaningful by their time-thickened qualities. As Kevin Lynch (1972, p. 65) observes, we experience the passage of time in the urban environment in two ways: through 'rhythmic repetition': 'the heartbeat, breathing, sleeping and waking, hunger, the cycles of sun and moon, the seasons, waves, tides, clocks'; and through 'progressive and irreversible change': 'growth and decay, not recurrence but alteration'. Time and space are intimately related. In his excellent overview of the relationship between time and the built environment, *What Time Is This Place?*, Kevin Lynch (1972b, p. 241) argued that space and time 'are the great framework within which we order our experience. We live in time-places.' For Patrick Geddes, a city 'is more than a place in space, it is a drama in time' (from Cowan, 1995, p. 1).

In this chapter, three key aspects of the temporal dimension of urban design are discussed. First, as activities are fluid in space and time, environments are used differently at different times. Urban designers need to understand time cycles and the time management of activities in space. Second, although environments relentlessly change over time, a high value is often placed on some degree of continuity and stability. Urban designers need to understand how environments change, what stays the same and what changes over time. They also need to be able to design and manage environ-

ments that can accommodate the inevitability of time's passage. Third, urban environments change over time, and urban design projects, policies, etc., are implemented over time.

TIME CYCLES

The first way in which we know that time has passed is through rhythmic repetition. The main time cycles are based on natural cycles, the dominant one being the 24-hour circadian cycle that results from the Earth's rotation, and affects sleeping and waking and other bodily cycles. Working and leisure time, mealtimes, and so on, are overlain on this basic cycle. The cycle of the year and the changing seasons are also rooted in the period of the Earth's rotation around the sun. The tilt in the Earth's axis changes the angle of the sun relative to the Earth's surface, thereby varying the length of sunlit daytime through the year and creating the cycle of the seasons. Moving away from the equator, the effect of the different seasons becomes increasingly pronounced: in more northerly (or southerly) latitudes, winter days are much shorter and summer days much longer.

Facilitating and encouraging the use of urban spaces requires an understanding of the effects of the cycles of day and night, the seasons, and related cycles of activity. At different times of the day and night, the urban environment is perceived and used differently. It can be a rewarding and enlightening experience for urban designers to observe a 'life in a day' of a public space, or the same space over the course of the seasons: that is, to study its social anthropology and notice, for example, its changing rhythms and pulses – now busy, now quiet – and the different people using the space – more women at some times, more men at others.

Cycles of activity are also grounded in the changing seasons. During the winter in northern temperate climates, for example, even at noon, the sun is low in the sky. Days are typically grey, wet, windy and cold. People may use external spaces only when necessary. In the spring, leaves start to appear on trees, and people begin to linger in urban spaces, enjoying the warmth of the sun. In summer, the trees are in full leaf, the sun is high in the sky, days are long and light, and people opt to stay longer in urban spaces. In the autumn, the leaves turn rich reds and browns and eventually fall from the trees. People may linger in urban spaces to enjoy the last warmth of the sun before the onset of winter.

Urban designers may deliberately exploit the changing day and the changing seasons to bring greater variety and interest to urban spaces. Environments designed to reflect and enhance the changing day and season add to the richness of the urban experience. In addition to light and ventilation, windows allow occupants to maintain contact with the world outside, to be aware of weather and of the time of the day through the movements of the sun – an awareness that is both highly valued and psychologically necessary. Features highlighting the passing of the seasons add to the temporal legibility of urban spaces.

In many places it is particularly important to exploit the period when outdoor life and activity are possible. Discussing how 'winter Copenhagen' and 'summer Copenhagen' are very different cities, Gehl and Gemzoe (1996, p. 48) observe how, in winter, people's stride is generally brisk and purposeful; their stops few, brief and of necessity. During the summer, more people walk, and strides are slower and more leisurely. More strikingly, people stop more frequently, sit down, and generally spend time in the city. Twice as many people walk in the city centre in the summer as in the winter, and each spends – on average – four times as much time there: the people density is therefore eight times that of the winter, which explains why the quiet winter streets and squares swarm with people in summer (Gehl and Gemzoe, 1996, p. 48).

Some of the time cycles by which we structure our lives have less relation to natural cycles. Zerubavel (1981, from Jackson, 1994, p. 160) argues that much of our daily lives is structured according to 'mechanical time'. We no longer, for example, rise with the dawn and retire to bed at sunset. Zerubavel suggests that we are 'increasingly detaching ourselves from "organic and functional periodicity" which is dictated by nature and are replacing it by "mechanical periodicity" which is dictated by the schedule, the calendar and the clock'. Despite its historical – and decreasingly relevant religious and economic – basis, the rhythm of the week is highly artificial.

Krietzman (1999, p. 2) argues that the grip of the old discipline of time and time constraints is weakening. While this has been a historical process – for example, candles, gas lamps, and then electric light, all extended the useful hours of the day – the pace of change is accelerating. Krietzman (1999, p. 2) argues that although an exaggeration, the term '24-hour society' is a useful shorthand for the changes under way and serves as a metaphor for a 'different type of world'. This trend is more pronounced in certain cities in certain countries: for example, Krietzman (p. 10) shows how the UK is becoming a 24-hour society by noting how, since the late 1980s, the National Grid has recorded an increase in electricity usage between 1800 and 2200 hours, attributed to shops staying open later and staying lit, while telephone companies have noted an increase in night-time telephone traffic.

The 24-hour society is emerging from the weakening and breakdown of time structures which, in the modern period at least, constrained and regimented our lives. As a consequence, the use of time, and the pattern of activities, is being variously stretched and squeezed. Krietzman (p. 2) argues that: 'By colonising the night through the 24 Hour Society we cannot create time but we can provide the means to use the available time more effectively so that we can free ourselves from the coiled grip of the time squeeze.' While this offers new freedoms and opportunities, the costs and benefits fall differentially: those at the top have more freedom and flexibility; those at the bottom increasingly work longer shifts, often at unsocial hours.

In the same way that electronic communication has freed us from the constraints of space, there is also greater freedom from the constraints of time. If the distinctions between night/day and weekend/weekday are increasingly being eroded, what does this mean for the ways in which people use their time? In the short-term at least, it results in greater freedom and diversity and, at least initially, greater uncertainty. In a 24-hour society, patterns of use and activity are less regimented, more responsive to individual needs and preferences, and less predictable. Among other effects, it allows individuals to avoid peak times, thereby reducing congestion.

THE TIME MANAGEMENT OF PUBLIC SPACE

Mixed uses have generally been advocated on the basis that they create more life and activity in a location. While a key element of this is the spatial concentration of different land uses (see Chapters 6 and 8), activity must also be considered in temporal terms. Mono-functional areas tend to be narrowly time specialised. While housing is often thought of as a land use providing 24-hour activity, this is – more precisely – a function of occupancy. A high proportion of retired people and families, for example, may generate good day-time levels of activity, while occupancy mainly by working people may result in lower levels during the working day, but more in the evening and at night.

A downside of the 24-hour society is that it reduces the likelihood of the coincidence of people in time and space. This raises the spectre of the increasing atomisation of society, with a loss of the social bonding that occurs through shared events that bring people together and give them something in common. Jackson (1994, p. 161), for example, refers to the 'periodicity' provided by the arrival of trains in the towns of the great plains of North America, which represented 'a decisive influence in the patterns of social and working contacts in the small railroad towns'. Similarly, Zerubavel (1981, from Jackson, 1994, pp. 161–2) describes the social consequences of the sharing of schedules, calendars and routines: 'A temporal order that is commonly shared by a social group and is unique to it [as, for example, in a religious calendar] . . . contributes to the establishment of inter-group boundaries and constitutes a powerful basis of solidarity within a group.' Efficiencies and economies in the supply of services will, however, qualify and constrain the new freedoms: because shops, cafes, etc., can open 24 hours per day, it does not follow that they will.

Urban designers need to understand activity patterns, how to encourage activities through different time periods, and how to achieve synergies from activities happening in the same space and time. Lynch (1981, p. 452) argues that although 'activity timing' is as important as 'activity spacing', it is less often 'consciously manipulated': 'We have tended towards a greater precision of activity timing, and greater time specialisation: weekends, office hours, peak travel, and the like. Many spaces are used intensively for certain periods, and then stand empty for longer times.'

One of Jacobs' conditions for the generation of 'exuberant diversity' was that 'On successful streets, people must appear at different times' (Jacobs, 1961, p. 162). However, the timing of activities needs to be managed. Lynch (1981, p. 452), for example, recognised that activities may be prohibited at certain times to prevent conflicts; be separated in time to alleviate congestion; or be brought together in time to allow connections and a sufficient density of use (e.g. on market days). Urban places that are well peopled enable complementary activities to overlap in space and complexly interrelate, resisting the narrow time specialisation that fragments and compartmentalises activities.

Describing single-use buildings and single-purpose spaces occupied between certain hours and empty the remainder of the time as 'mono-chronic', Krietzman (1999, p. 146) argued that in a 24-hour society buildings and spaces need to be 'poly-chronic'. While public space is often naturally animated by the ebb and flow of people going about their everyday business, Montgomery (1995, p. 104) argued that this can also be stimulated through planned programmes of 'cultural animation' across a range of times and venues, encouraging people to visit, use and linger in urban spaces. Programmes usually involve a varied diet of events and activity. Therefore, as people visit an area to see what is going on, urban vitality is further stimulated and the public realm becomes animated by having more people on the streets and in cafes, etc. Montgomery stresses that attention to the 'soft' infrastructure of events, programmes and activities is as important for successful urban animation as the 'hard' infrastructure of buildings, spaces, street design, etc.

For people to choose to use the public realm, it must not only offer what they want but also do so in an attractive and safe fashion. As discussed in Chapter 6, safety is a prerequisite of a successful urban place. Peopled places are often safer places, while the areas that people are most concerned about are those that are deserted or crowded with the 'wrong kind' of people.

A widespread problem is lack of activity in the public realm during the evening and at night, with few uses and activities to attract a broad range of social groups. A particular issue is the 'dead' period in city centres between the end of the typical working day and the start of the night-time economy when people return to the centre in search of recreation and entertainment. The '24-hour city' and promotion and development of the 'evening economy' are relatively new approaches to revitalising city centres (Bianchini, 1994; Montgomery, 1994). They also form responses to the functional zoning policies and the 'hollowing out' of city centres that have occurred since the late 1960s.

The evening economy and 24-hour city concepts are influenced by cities in continental Europe that are inherently 24 hour, and those that since the 1970s have developed cultural policies to revitalise their urban night-life. The 24-hour concept has also been adopted as a means of regenerating and creating safer city centres (Heath and Stickland, 1997, p. 170). Unless evening economy and 24-hour city strategies are broadly based, they are susceptible to criticism of being male-oriented and alcohol-fixated with 'nothing to offer those workers with "carer" responsibilities who have no time to stay on in the town centre drinking the night away, as they have to get back home and start on the "second-shift" of cooking, housework and childcare' (Greed, 1999, p. 203). The need is for evening economies based on encouraging 'entertainment' (rather than 'alcohol') and activities for a wide range of social and age groups. There are also micro-management issues relating to conflicts between, for example, noise-generating activities (e.g. cafes, bars and music venues) and noise-sensitive activities (e.g. city centre residential uses).

The march of time

As well as through the repetitive rhythms of time, we also know that time has passed through evidence of progressive and irreversible change. In a very real sense, the past is fixed and the future open. While we may yearn to return to the city we knew as a child, or relive a wonderful moment, we are unable to do so. This is the relentless 'march of time'. The immediate kinaesthetic experience of urban space was discussed in Chapter 7. The long-term experience and passage of time within places will be discussed here.

Urban environments are continuously and inexorably changing. From the first design drawing to the final demolition, environments and buildings are shaped and reshaped by technological, economic, social and cultural change. Any intervention into the physical fabric of a place irreversibly changes its history for all time, becoming part of that history. All urban design actions are therefore contributions both to broader, open and evolving systems and to a greater whole. Knox and Ozolins (2000, p. 3), for example, argue that 'a building or other element of the built environment of a given period and type tends to be a carrier of the *zeitgeist* or "spirit" of its time. Every city can therefore be "read" as a multi-layered "text", a narrative of signs and symbols . . . the built environment becomes a biography of urban change' (Figure 9.1).

Until the Industrial Revolution, and except when natural forces or war wreaked wholesale destruction, change in the urban fabric was both gradual and relatively small scale. Cities evolved 'organically' over time, through seemingly 'natural' processes. Successive generations derived a sense of continuity and stability from their physical surroundings. Since the Industrial Revolution, the pace and scale of change have increased as both the processes of change, and the impact of those processes, have radically altered. City growth has become mechanical and artificial. Modernists argued that the means of controlling and directing processes of change needed to be radically rethought: societies needed large-scale social and economic organisation, harnessing the benefits of science, technology and rationalism.

One consequence of Modernism's enthusiasm for the zeitgeist was emphasis on the differences from, rather than the continuities with, the past. The legacy from the past was seen as merely a hindrance to the future. The pioneer Modernists visualised sweeping away the cramped and unhealthy cities of their time, and replacing them with a radically different environment of high-rise buildings standing among trees and vegetation. The clean sweep mentality led to a preference for comprehensive redevelopment schemes rather than more incremental – and arguably more sensitive – ones. It was also confidently argued that comprehensive redevelopment would provide significant physical improvements and was further justified by claims and desires for progress and modernity. The opportunity to develop such ideas came after 1945 in the reconstruction of war-damaged cities in Europe, and subsequently through slum clearance programmes and road-

FIGURE 9.1
Sacramento Old Town, Sacramento, California, USA. Except as museums – and increasingly as simulacra – of themselves, what is the future of such places?

building schemes. The post-war period therefore saw a dramatic acceleration in the pace and physical scale of the cycle of demolition and renewal in most cities in the developed world. Ashworth and Tunbridge (1990, p. 1) note how this period 'led to an abrupt break in the centuries-long evolution of the physical fabric of cities. The past and its values were rejected in favour of a "brave new world" whose creation threatened to destroy all trace of preceding architectural achievement.'

Although for most of the post-war period, destruction of much of the physical, social and cultural fabric of central and inner city areas was accepted without serious question, by the mid-1960s the social effects of this were becoming evident. Frequent and increasingly widespread public protest ushered in increased public consensus in favour of conservation and a desire to retain existing and familiar environments. Policies protecting historic areas were introduced all over the developed world during the 1960s and early

1970s, and conservation became an integral – rather than peripheral – part of planning and development, provoking a fundamental re-evaluation of ideas in architecture, planning and urban development.

Conservation

Lynch (1972, pp. 35–6) outlined a series of questions that encapsulate various debates about the purpose and practice of conservation:

Are we looking for evidence of climactic moments or for any manifestation of tradition we can find, or are we judging and evaluating the past, choosing the more significant over the less, retaining what we think of as best?

Should things be saved because they were associated with important persons or events? Because they are unique or nearly so or quite the contrary, because they were most typical of their time? Because of their importance as a group symbol? Because of their intrinsic qualities in the present? Because of their special usefulness as sources of intellectual information about the past?

Or should we simply (as we most often do) let chance select for us and preserve for a second century everything that has happened to survive the first?

Accepting that the reasons for conservation of historic buildings and environments are many, and often context and building specific, Tiesdell *et al.* (1996, pp. 11–17) list the more common justifications:

- *Aesthetic value*: historic buildings and environments are valued because they are intrinsically beautiful or have scarcity value.
- *Value for architectural diversity and contrast*: urban environments are valued for the architectural diversity that results from the combination or juxtaposition of many buildings of many different ages.
- *Value for environmental diversity and contrast*: within many cities, there is often a stimulating contrast between the human scale environment of their historic areas and the monumental scale of their CBDs.
- *Value for functional diversity*: a diverse range of different types of space in buildings of varying ages enables a mix of uses. Older buildings and areas may offer lower rents that allow economically marginal but socially important activities to have a place in the city.
- *Resource value*: as buildings are committed expenditure, their reuse constitutes the conservation of scarce resources, a reduction in the consumption of energy and materials in construction and good resource management.
- *Value for continuity of cultural memory and heritage*: visible evidence of the past can contribute educationally to the cultural identity and memory of a particular people or place, giving meaning to the present by interpreting the past.
- *Economic and commercial value*: older environments provide a distinctive sense of place that offers opportunities for economic development and tourism.

In most countries, preservation and conservation as a widespread and coherent practice is relatively recent. Lefebvre (1991, p. 360) describes how attitudes to conservation have typically changed over time:

countries in the throes of rapid development blithely destroy historic spaces – houses, palaces, military or civil structures. If advantage or profit is to be found in it, then the old is swept away. Later, however ... these same countries are liable to discover how such spaces may be pressed into the service of cultural consumption, of 'culture itself', and of the tourism and the leisure industries with their almost limitless prospects. When this happens, everything that they had so merrily demolished during the bellé époque is reconstituted at great expense. Where destruction has not been complete, 'renovation' becomes the order of the day, or imitation, or replication, or neo-this or neo-that.

Conservation policies and strategies came in three waves. The first involved protection of individual buildings and historic/ancient monuments. Although this started in many countries during the nineteenth century, more consistent and comprehensive practice developed in the period after 1945. Arising from the realisation that the settings of historic buildings also needed protection, a second wave of policies emerged during the 1960s and 1970s. These area-based policies were concerned with groups of historic buildings, townscape, and the spaces between buildings, and formed a reaction to the evident social, cultural and physical disruption caused by clearance and comprehensive redevelopment and by road building. Rather than being 'preservation' policies concerned with stopping or limiting change, these were 'conservation' policies about the inevitability and the management of change. Lynch (1972, p. 233), for example, argued that the key to conservation was to 'disentangle it from the idea of preserving the past'.

In most countries, the change from the protection of individual buildings to conservation areas rapidly developed from a restrictive concern with preservation to the management of change and revitalisation. The third, more fragmentary, wave, therefore, was the development of local revitalisation policies, stemming from realisation that once historic buildings and areas were protected, they needed to be in active and viable use. While the initial preservation policies had largely been concerned with the 'pastness' of the past, the later conservation and revitalisation policies were increasingly about a 'future for the past' (Fawcett, 1976). Having been saved *from* destruction, the next issue was what had buildings and spaces been saved *for*? There was also a simultaneous broadening of the locus of professional concern, from architects and art historians to planners, urban designers, economic development specialists and others.

The continuity of place

Conservation – and the concomitant concern for the uniqueness of places and their history – was instrumental in the evolution of the contemporary concept of urban design. Many current approaches to urban design attempt to respond to the existing sense of place, stressing 'continuity with', rather than a 'break from', the past. In a world of rapid change, visual and tangible evidence of the past is valued for the sense of place and continuity it conveys. Particular value is placed on the sense of place and the relative permanence of its character and identity. Despite constant change, because the elements of the city change at different rates, some essence of its identity is retained. In many cities, for example, street and plot patterns have accommodated incremental change. As discussed in Chapter 4, Buchanan (1988, p. 32) argued that the movement network, and the monuments and civic buildings within and adjacent to it are the relatively permanent parts of the city. Within this more permanent framework, individual buildings come and go. It is the parts that endure over time that contribute to the sense of continuity and progression of time within that place. 'Robust' patterns of development, therefore, provide stability and continuity of place.

The relative permanence of an urban space helps establish its qualities as a meaningful place, while its physicality provides a tangible record of the passage of time and embodies 'social memory'. Focusing on the effect of time on the changing fabric of a city, Aldo Rossi (1966, 1982) discussed the idea of a city's 'collective memory', where urban form was a repository of culture from the past and for the future. Rossi argued that the fabric of the city consists of two elements: the general urban 'texture' of buildings lining streets and squares, which changes over time; and 'monuments', and large-scale buildings whose presence gives each city its particular character and embod-

ies the 'memory' of the city (see also Boyer, 1994).

There are, however, alternative attitudes to the physical continuity of places. Lynch (1984, p. 451), for example, notes the imperative that joins change with progress:

The failure to respond to change not only makes it impossible to respond to the inevitable flux of events but it is also a failure to improve. Old buildings are generally obsolete buildings: old habits are constrictive. The initial costs and recurring maintenance cost of permanent things far outweigh the resources needed to replace them periodically with new materials. Cities should be built of light, temporary structures, so that people can easily change them as their lives change.

As well as a disdain for much of the built legacy of the past, Modernists embraced ideas about the 'impermanence' of buildings – ideas based on the potential of industrial production. Buildings, like cars, could be mass-produced, and designed to be discarded once their immediate utility was exhausted (see MacCormac, 1983, p. 741). Such attitudes are antithetical both to architecture's traditional place-making and place-defining qualities, and to considerations of environmental sustainability.

Taken to extremes, however, preservation and conservation can obstruct and even halt a city's evolution and development. Emphasising the necessity of adaptability, Lynch (1972, p. 39) argued that environments that could not be changed 'invited their own destruction':

We prefer a world that can be modified progressively against a background of valued remains, a world in which one can leave a personal mark alongside the marks of history ... The management of change and the active use of remains for present and future purposes are preferable to an inflexible reverence for a sacrosanct past.

To preserve the capacity for change, the need is for environments capable of evolution: those that can welcome the future and accommodate the present without severing the thread of continuity with the past. (Burtenshaw et al., 1991, p. 159) (Figure 9.2)

The issues are not black and white, however. Total preservation is rarely completely right or total redevelopment completely wrong. Instead, it is usually a matter of balance. Lynch (1972, p. 236),

FIGURE 9.2
Older buildings give both material and symbolic stability to an area, together with a sense of history and permanence. New interventions generally reflect progress and advancement. The protected views of St Paul's Cathedral in London are designed to maintain the city's sense of history with Sir Christopher Wren's dome symbolising the city. This can be contrasted with the demand for new high-rise office development in the Square Mile that reflects the City's contemporary role as a world financial centre

for example, advocated exposing 'successive eras of history' and inserting new material that enhances the past by 'allusion and contrast', with the aim of producing 'a setting more and more densely packed with references to the stream of time rather than a setting that never changed'. Such approaches emphasise the necessity for new development to express its own zeitgeist.

To work within established contexts, urban designers need to understand how environments adapt to change and, more importantly, why some adapt better than others. It is also important to distinguish what is fundamental to the sense of place, and should remain, from what is less important and can change. The visual and physical continuity of valued places relates to issues of the 'obsolescence' of buildings and environments, the time frames of change, and the 'robustness' and 'resilience' of the built fabric and other physical attributes of that place. Going beyond narrower conceptions of 'conservation', these interrelated concepts are all aspects of the effects of time and change on buildings and environments.

Obsolescence

Obsolescence is the reduction in the useful life of a capital good. Buildings become obsolescent largely due to the inability of 'fixed' urban structures and locations to adapt to technological, economic, social and cultural change. The typical building, when commissioned, will be constructed to contemporary standards and will usually be 'state of the art' with regard to its function, and appropriately located for that function. As the building ages, and the world around it and factors relating to its profitability all change, the building becomes increasingly obsolescent relative to newer buildings. Eventually it falls out of use and is abandoned and/or demolished and the site redeveloped.

There are several interrelated dimensions of obsolescence, some are attributes of buildings and/or their functions, while others relate to the area as a whole:

- *Physical/structural obsolescence*: the building's fabric and/or structure deteriorates through the effects of time, weather, earth movement, traffic vibration, poor maintenance.

- *Functional obsolescence*: with regard to contemporary standards, the building's fabric is no longer suited for its current use. This can also arise from external factors on which the use of the building depends (e.g. difficulties of access in narrow streets or traffic congestion).
- *Locational obsolescence*: primarily an attribute of the land use rather than the building, this is due to its fixed location relative to changes in wider patterns of accessibility, labour costs, etc.
- *Legal obsolescence*: for example, when a public agency determines certain minimum standards of functionality that the building does not, or cannot, achieve. The introduction of new standards of, for example, fire safety, can also render a building obsolete.
- *Image/style obsolescence*: a product of changing perceptions of the building. In the immediate post-war period, for example, older buildings were demolished to build newer ones whose style or image expressed their modernity. As values have changed, older buildings have become more desirable (Lichfield, 1988; Tiesdell *et al.*, 1996).

Obsolescence is rarely absolute. A further dimension is *economic or relative obsolescence* – the obsolescence with regard to the cost of alternative opportunities, which includes the competition from other buildings/areas; the cost of alternative development on the site; and/or the cost of development on an alternative site.

When buildings are regarded as obsolescent, a distinction should be made between obsolescence in their *current use* and that for *any use*. A warehouse in a city centre might be obsolete in its current use, but convertible to residential use (i.e. the obsolescence is cured by the change of use). A further distinction should also be made between 'curable' obsolescence (which is cost-efficient to cure) and non-curable obsolescence (which is not cost-efficient to cure – at least, at the present time).

Larkham (1996, p. 79) notes that conservation controls afford historic buildings an 'administrative layer of protection' – effectively creating a form of non-physical resilience (see below) – which prolongs their normal life cycle but increases the likelihood of obsolescence. While conservation controls may constrain, inhibit or deter rehabilitation and new development, they do so to ensure the survival – conservation – of the particular building or environment. Conservation of historic areas and buildings frequently entails keeping them in active use, thereby providing the necessary finance to maintain the historic fabric. Typically this involves reconciling a mismatch between the (historic) 'fabric' and the economic activities to be undertaken there. Remedy can arise from changes in occupation with new uses or activities replacing the former ones. Alternatively, the fabric itself may be adapted to contemporary requirements through various modes of renewal, such as refurbishment, rehabilitation, conversion, or demolition and redevelopment.

Fitch (1990, pp. 46–7) identifies a series of levels of intervention (types of change) to historic buildings:

- *Preservation*: maintenance of the artefact in its current physical condition.
- *Restoration*: returning the artefact to the physical condition it had at some previous stage of its life.
- *Refurbishment (conservation and consolidation)*: physical intervention in the fabric of the building to ensure its continued performance.
- *Reconstitution*: piece-by-piece reassembly of a building, either in-situ or on a new site.
- *Conversion (adaptive reuse)*: adaptation of a building to accommodate a new use.
- *Reconstruction*: recreation of vanished buildings on their original site.
- *Replication*: construction of an exact copy of an existing building.
- *Façadism*: preservation of the façade of an historic building, with a new building behind it.
- *Demolition and redevelopment*: demolition and clearance, with new development on the site.

While this illustrates the range of options, what is desirable or possible in any particular situation varies. Nevertheless, as Lowenthal (1981, p. 14) observes, 'there is little point in "saving" the past if what is saved is debased or altered beyond recognition'. Dealing with existing or historic buildings and environments is no longer a case of new being better than old, or vice versa, but about the nature of the relationship between the two (Powell, 1999). In considering the character of existing buildings and environments, there are more permutations than a fawning, restrictive reverence or contemptuous dismissal. Furthermore, as discussed in Chapter 5, there are also issues concerning authenticity and 'reinvented places'.

Time frames of change

An essential element of urban design's time dimension is the need for designers to understand what stays the same and what changes over time: that is, the time frames of change. As discussed in Chapter 4, Conzen (1960) emphasised the difference in stability of the major morphological elements. While street and plot patterns survive a long time, buildings and, in particular, land uses, are less resilient. In many places, however, buildings have lasted for hundreds of years, helping to sustain a sense of time within that place – although the uses within them have often changed, their exterior appearance and form remain. Such buildings have qualities of robustness (see below). The survival of what are now seen as historic buildings and environments largely happened prior to the widespread practice of state intervention into the property market to protect them. Buildings from the past 'survived fortuitously largely on their own merits, and chiefly because they continued to serve useful purposes' (Burke, 1976, p. 117). While this may have been through simple economic necessity, it also expressed certain aesthetic and cultural values: the urban scene was considered sufficiently desirable – culturally, economically, or both – to be retained rather than demolished.

For Duffy (1990), a building can be seen as a series of layers of longevities: the 'shell' or structure lasts the lifetime of the building; the 'services' (cabling, plumbing, air conditioning, elevators, etc.) are replaced every fifteen years or so; the 'scenery' (the layout of partitions, dropped ceilings, etc.) changes every five to seven years; while 'sets' (the layout of furniture) change over weeks and months. Brand (1994, pp. 13–15) extends and develops this idea to create a series of six systems:

- *Site*: the legally defined lot, whose boundaries and context outlast generations of buildings.
- *Structure*: the foundation and load-bearing elements, whose life ranges from thirty to three hundred years and more.
- *Skin*: the exterior surfaces, which – keeping up with fashion or technology, or for wholesale repair – may change every 20 years or so. (Note that with load-bearing masonry, the skin is also the structure, while with cladding systems the skin can be unclipped and changed relatively easily.)
- *Services*: the communications wiring, electrical wiring, plumbing, sprinkler system, heating, ventilating, and air conditioning, and moving parts such as lifts and escalators, which are replaced every seven to fifteen years.
- *Space plan*: the interior layout (i.e. where walls, ceiling, floors and doors go) changes according to the land use: commercial space changes more frequently than that of a family house.
- *Stuff*: chairs, desks, phones, pictures, etc. (i.e. things that move around daily or weekly).

The systems are differently paced: 'site' and 'structure' are the slowest; 'stuff' and 'space plan' the quickest. The key to robust buildings – those able to accommodate change – is to allow the faster-paced systems to change without the need for change in the slower-paced systems (i.e. changing the services should not require change to the structure). More particularly, the key issue is that in robust buildings, the structure should not impose and restrict the freedom of the more rapidly changing systems. Equally, it may be that the building's character is embedded in the slower moving systems.

Resilience and robustness

The overlapping concepts of 'resilience' and 'robustness' are sometimes used interchangeably. There are important differences, however. Resilience is the ability to *resist* change without undue deformation: that is, it resists physical and structural obsolescence. Robustness is the ability to *accommodate* change without significant change in physical form: that is, it resists functional obsolescence. Robustness is not just about form and function, however, as there is usually some additional significance deriving from the values, meanings and symbols associated with and embodied by the form. Robust buildings also need 'charm'. While minor – and sometimes major – inconveniences may be indulged in buildings with charm, in buildings lacking charm they can often prove fatal (Figure 9.3).

An early discussion of robustness was by Stanford Anderson in his book *On Streets* (1978). Anderson drew on Gans' argument that physical settings can be interpreted both as 'potential' environments providing a range of environmental possibilities and opportunities and that, at any moment in time, what is achieved is the 'resultant' or 'effective' environment (see Chapter 6). For Anderson, the 'latent' environment consisted of the

FIGURE 9.3
New Concordia Wharf, London, UK. As industrial lofts and warehouses converted to residential apartments connote 'artistic' and 'bohemian' qualities, the desire to convert such buildings is not just a consequence of the building's functionality but also its character

FIGURE 9.4
Bankside power station converted to the Tate Modern, London, UK

environmental possibilities (whether recognised or not) not currently being exploited. For example, when industrial lofts were constructed, their later residential use was not anticipated. Robustness is therefore a function of the relationship between a building's form and the uses it accommodates. Many land uses are relatively adaptable and can be accommodated within a variety of forms. Buildings, by contrast, are less flexible and overspecialisation reduces their potential to accommodate changing uses.

Despite Modernist functionalist doctrines that 'form follows function', the relationship between activities/land uses and spaces/forms is complex. Lynch (1972, p. 72), for example, observed that 'Activities shift cyclically and progressively within their relatively unchanging spatial containers. The form of these containers cannot therefore "follow function" unless the use of a space is reduced to some single, invariant type of behaviour.' Tschumi (1983, p. 31) identifies three types of relationship between form and function:

- *indifference*, where 'space' and 'event' are functionally independent of one another;
- *reciprocity*, where spaces and events are interdependent, fully conditioning each other's existence; and
- *conflict*, where space designed for one function subsequently accommodates a completely different one.

There is usually some additional meaning derived from the latter: a riverside power station converted to an art gallery can add new meaning to the artwork displayed (Figure 9.4).

Although robustness is the quality of averting, avoiding or delaying, the loss of vitality occasioned by the onset of functional obsolescence, functional obsolescence is not solely an attribute of the building: it also relates to external factors, which can both create obsolescence and restore the utility of buildings without changing them. The office stock of the City of London provides an interesting example. By the early 1980s, office buildings needed to handle the additional heat load resulting from increased use of personal computers, and the cabling required for increased electronic and electrical servicing of workstations. While new buildings could be designed with larger floor to floor heights to allow for additional cooling equipment and raised floors, the existing stock faced the prospect of obsolescence. However, a new generation of personal computers with internal fans, together with the introduction of fibre-optic cables, extended the useful life of much of the City's office stock, and the anticipated functional obsolescence did not materialise. Brand (1994, p. 192) makes the general point that, because technology changes faster than buildings and is usually more flexible, it is better to let the technology adapt to the building rather than vice versa.

Robustness embodies the concept of 'long life/loose fit', the designing-in of buildings' capacity for change and adaptation. The capacity for change is a function of a building or environment's adaptivity. Lynch (1972, pp. 108–9) argues that 'environmental adaptivity' can be achieved by:

- providing *excess capacity* at the outset;
- providing *generous communication facilities*;
- separating those elements likely, from those unlikely, to change; and
- allowing *space for growth* at the ends, sides or within sectors.

Brand (1994, p. 174) argues that, as the evolution of organisations and buildings is 'always and necessarily surprising', adaptivity cannot be predicted or controlled and that, in practice, 'All you can do is make room for it – room at the bottom.'

As the future is unknowable, the lifetime of buildings is also unknowable: those intended only for the short-term often survive into what becomes the long-term; buildings intended for the long-term sometimes only survive a short time. The choices are to design environments and buildings for the short term – either through what Lawson (2001, pp. 194, 195) terms 'non-committal' design which tends to produce bland, neutral results, or 'throwaway design' meant for the present only, with obsolescence built in and the designed object intended to be thrown away and replaced with a more up-to-date version – or to design for the long-term. The former suggests a fundamental lack of commitment to place – the light (and fleeting) touchdown of global capital as it arrives in a locality, while constantly looking for a better opportu-

nity elsewhere. The sustainable option is to design robust buildings with charm and character, built for the long-term.

The spiral of decline caused by a spatial concentration of buildings falling out of use and being abandoned is often precipitous. Rybczynski (1995, p. 42) cites a survey of housing abandonment in the US, which found that the 'tipping point' in a neighbourhood occurred when just 3–6 per cent of the structures were abandoned. Abandonment can have economic and/or physical causes. The best strategies in terms of the physical fabric are 'preventive maintenance' (routinely servicing materials and systems in the building, to prevent failure); and/or designing and constructing the building so as to reduce the need for maintenance (Brand, 1994, p. 112). The longer buildings and environments are expected to last, the more the maintenance and other running costs will overwhelm the initial capital costs of construction; hence the greater the incentive for owners to invest in better construction to reduce future maintenance costs. This, however, relates to the distribution of costs between the developer and initial funders and subsequent owners, occupants, tenants and users (see Chapter 10).

Given the difficulty of predicting changes that might occur during a building's expected life, there is value in learning from buildings that have successfully coped with change. Studies by Duffy (1990), Bentley *et al.* (1985), Moudon (1987) and Brand (1994) identify three key factors that influence the long-term robustness of buildings – cross-sectional depth, access, and room shape. In Brand's hierarchy, these are all essentially aspects of 'structure'.

(i) Cross-sectional depth

This has a critical impact on the need for artificial lighting and ventilation, which in turn affects the variety of uses that can be accommodated. As most uses require natural light and ventilation, buildings that are too deep cannot easily change use. Llewelyn-Davies (2000, p. 94) outlines the implications of different depths:

- depths of less than 9 m provide the potential for good daylighting and ventilation, but are usually too shallow for a central corridor and have limited flexibility in internal planning;
- depths of between 9 and 13 m provide naturally lit and ventilated space and the opportunity for a central corridor (and, therefore, optimum robustness);

- depths of between 14 and 15 m allow for subdivision, but some artificial ventilation and lighting is usually required;
- depths greater than about 16 m are more energy intensive, requiring increasing amounts of artificial ventilation and lighting.

(ii) Access

As all buildings need some links to the outside world, the number of access points – and egress points, in case of fire – governs how readily a building can adapt to a variety of uses. Building height is a particular constraint in this respect. In a tall building, the upper floors have restricted links to the outside, making them less suitable for a wide range of uses.

(iii) Room shape and size

For robustness, room sizes need to accommodate a broad range of activities and be capable of subdivision (which may relate to window positions) or connection to create larger spaces. In domestic buildings, for example, rooms that are 10–13 square metres in area can serve as bedrooms, kitchens, living rooms or dining rooms. Dwellings with rooms of this size prove relatively robust in changing from, for example, family houses to a number of smaller flats (Moudon, 1987). Brand (1994, p. 192) also contends that the rectangle is the only configuration of space that grows well, subdivides well and is efficient to use.

Building configurations that support robustness thus tend to be shallow in plan, relatively low-rise, with many points of access, and regularly shaped rooms or spaces. While not all buildings can take this form, much of the building stock in a locality can. Few land uses have highly specialised requirements, and even those that do, usually have less specialised parts.

Urban space should also be robust and resilient. A set of key properties can be identified:

- *Open* – not filled with 'paraphernalia', immovable landscaping, or needless subdivision into small single-use areas.
- *Flexible* – capable of subdivision, or use as a large space for a variety of uses/events.
- *Varied* – not dominated by one mode of travel (e.g. roads), by infrastructure requirements, or by a single use. Many market squares, for example, cater for a market one day, a special

event the next, and quiet contemplation or car parking thereafter.
- *Comfortable* – responsive to differing microclimatic and weather needs – offering shelter, but also access to the sun when required (see Chapter 8).
- *Sociable* – supporting the different types and patterns of social activity.

Not only must sustainable environments be designed for robustness, they must also facilitate maintenance. While high quality materials help, their detailing and maintenance regimes are also important. Francis Tibbalds (1992, p. 72), for example, warned that: 'unlike a landscape that will mature over time, a building, unless well cared for, will do the exact opposite – it will deteriorate'. In this respect, urban designers can learn from landscape designers, who are necessarily acutely conscious that design is a matter of directing a process of continuous change, where success depends on carefully managing what has been created.

THE MANAGEMENT OF CHANGE

Involving interventions into existing places, the creation of new places, and management and stewardship, urban design operates across a number of time frames – almost all of which necessitate a long-term perspective. While designers may have a relatively short-term involvement in particular development projects, the created environments tend to be used over the long-term. Decisions have potentially long-lasting implications and effects. Furthermore, given the short-termism of markets and market behaviour, urban designers must consider long-term issues relating to, for example, environmental sustainability.

Rather than change itself – which people expect, anticipate and often welcome – it is its pace and scale, and the sense that it is not amenable to local control, that may present problems. Control requires the involvement of key stakeholders, and the development of processes of involvement and consultation (see Chapter 12). As personal associations with our immediate environment are valued and we draw comfort from its stability, the loss of familiar surroundings can be distressing, particularly when experienced over a short period and on a large scale. The comprehensive redevelopment that was common practice from the late 1940s to the mid-1970s wreaked havoc in many cities, alienating many people from their communities and destroying cherished places and environments. Although that era has passed, the continuing trend towards large-scale rather than incremental growth has led, in some places, to the development of an increasingly controlled and monotonous urban fabric – lacking the diversity and character of places that have developed incrementally. Alexander's starting point in his essay 'A City is Not A Tree' (1965), for example, was that 'artificial' cities (i.e. those with tree-like structures), do not have the complexity, life and vitality of 'natural' cities (i.e. those with semi-lattice structures).

In small-scale, incremental change, 'mistakes' are small and can be corrected relatively easily. In essence, this is how older urban environments have developed. Joel Garreau (1999, p. 239) noted how, throughout the 8000 years that humans have been building cities, development has followed the same basic pattern:

First there's a wild, enthusiastic wave of growth. Then there's a bank collapse. During the collapse, people figure out which were the horrible mistakes they made and promise to fix them if the banks ever open again. Sooner or later the gods relent and the banks reopen, and there's a second wave of growth that heads off in the newly enlightened mode. That is followed by another bank collapse, during which new wisdom is concocted. Seven or so cycles and several centuries into this process and you end up with Paris or Manhattan. The reason old cities look so good is that you see few of the preceding mistakes. They've been torn down or covered by ivy or marble.

By contrast, in large-scale development, every effort must be made to eliminate 'mistakes' because they are much more difficult to correct. Mistakes are inevitable, however, and often have to be lived with. In *The Oregon Experiment*, Christopher Alexander (1975, p. 77) argued that 'large-lump' development was based on the idea of *replacement*, while piecemeal growth was based on *repair*. As replacement meant consumption of resources, he argued that repair was better ecologically. There were, however, more practical differences:

Large-lump development is based on the fallacy that it is possible to build perfect buildings. Piecemeal growth is based on the healthier and

more realistic view that mistakes are inevitable . . . Piecemeal growth is based on the assumption that adaptation between buildings and their users is necessarily a slow and continuous business which cannot, under any circumstances, be achieved in a single leap. (Alexander, 1975, pp. 77–9)

It is clear that many of the most successful developments of the 1990s represent reactions to the well-documented mistakes of the 1960s. Furthermore, although cycles of growth and decline still mark eras of investment and stagnation, the pace of change has quickened to such a degree that much of what was built in the 1960s and 1970s has already been redeveloped.

Many urban design commentators have asserted the value of incremental and small-scale change. Kevin Lynch (1972), for example, argued that: 'If change is inevitable, then it should be moderated and controlled so as to prevent violent dislocation and preserve a maximum of continuity with the past.' Distinguishing between 'cataclysmic money' and 'gradual money', Jane Jacobs (1961, p. 307) noted that cataclysmic money was destructive and 'behaved like manifestations of malevolent climates beyond the control of man – affording either searing droughts or torrential, eroding floods'. By contrast, gradual money behaved like 'irrigation systems, bringing life-giving streams to feed steady continual growth'. Similarly, Tibbalds (1992, p. 77) argued that if contemporary development occurs incrementally – 'healing or mending the edges as it goes' – then it is likely to be found to be more acceptable.

When changes take place over a longer period of time and in an incremental manner, mixing the new and unfamiliar with the old and familiar, they are often seen as exciting, but also comfortable and acceptable. Lowenthal (1981, p. 16), for example, argued against 'over-abrupt change' in the physical environment and in favour of 'anchoring' the 'excitement of the future' in the 'security of the past'. Such processes replicate the historic development of older towns and cities that have grown slowly and organically. Tibbalds (1992, p. 78) recommended incremental development as a way of ameliorating the 'pain of change':

Blood transfusions, rather than organ transplants, are required . . . an approach characterised by a more contextual organic, incremental and sensitive way of thinking and designing. We need, then, to encourage the development of smaller sites, set limits on the extent of site assembly and break up the larger sites into more manageable components.

In *A New Theory of Urban Design*, Alexander *et al.* (1987) attempted to theorise and systematise processes of urban development with a focus on incremental change. They argued that the organic quality of older towns and cities does not and cannot exist in those being built today and that what is required, therefore, is a process that creates 'wholeness in urban development': 'it is the *process* above all which is responsible for wholeness . . . not merely the form. If we create a suitable *process* there is some hope that the city might become whole again. If we do not change the process, there is no hope at all' (p. 3). They argued that there are fundamental rules in any process of growth that achieves organic development:

- the whole grows piecemeal, bit by bit;
- the whole is unpredictable: when it starts coming into being, it is not clear how it will develop or where it will end;
- the whole and its parts are coherent and truly whole, not fragmented;
- the whole inspires feeling: it has the power to move us. (p. 14)

They argued that contemporary towns and cities follow a completely different development pattern to that of organic development, where, while growth might be piecemeal, the different elements remain fragmented and unrelated to a growing whole. A single overriding rule was, therefore, formulated: 'Every increment of construction must be made in such as way as to heal the city' (p. 22). Seven intermediate principles were developed for implementing this rule (see Box 9.1).

While the thrust of Alexander's rules is wholly laudable, whether regulatory and development interests could be persuaded to follow them is highly debatable. Despite the above views and opinions, economic and political realities make large-scale developments inevitable. Dovey (1990, p. 8) argues that the economic context often favours 'mega-projects' bringing massive one-off investments, jobs and political kudos. The flexibility of capital investment by multinational corporations enables them to play cities off against each other. Governments are induced to compete for projects on an 'all-or-nothing' basis, often overruling – and undermining – regulatory and design processes in

---

BOX 9.1 – ALEXANDER'S SEVEN RULES OF ORGANIC GROWTH

(source: adapted from Alexander *et al.*, 1987)

Rule I: Piecemeal growth guarantees that no project is too large. There should be a mixed flow of small, medium and large projects in about equal quantities, and a mix of uses.

Rule II: The growth of larger wholes should be a slow incremental process in which every building increment helps to form at least one larger whole in the city that is both larger and more significant than itself. Individual increments should initially hint at the creation of a larger whole; subsequent increments will then define and complete this whole.

Rule III: Visions should be the source of all increments, so that every project is first experienced, and then expressed as a vision.

Rule IV: Every building should create coherent and well-shaped positive urban space in such a way that the space, rather than the building, becomes the main focus of attention. To help achieve this aim, there should be a hierarchy of urban elements with pedestrian space prioritised, followed by buildings, then roads and finally parking.

Rule V: The layout of large buildings should be arranged so that the entrances, main circulation, main divisions, interior open space, daylight and movement within the building are all coherent and consistent with the position of the building in the street and in the neighbourhood.

Rule VI: The construction should be such that the structure of every building generates wholes in the physical fabric through the appearance of their structural bays, columns, walls, windows, building base, etc.

Rule VII: The formation of centres is the end result of making things 'whole'. Thus, every whole must be a centre in itself and must also produce a system of centres around it. In this context, a centre may be a building, a space, a garden, a wall, a road, a window, or a complex of several of these at the same time.

---

order to secure the investment. Furthermore, despite the emphasis in the urban design literature on small-scale incremental change, there are occasional needs for 'big bang' developments with sufficient size and scale to change fundamentally

FIGURE 9.5
Brindleyplace, Birmingham, UK, is a 'big bang' development – a project with sufficient critical mass to fundamentally change the nature and economy of an area in ways that would not happen incrementally. Through the use of a detailed master plan, issues of place-making were addressed in a coherent and joined-up manner. The resulting development is more than the sum of its individual parts

the nature and economy of a place in ways that could never happen incrementally. Such developments also have the potential to address issues of place-making in a coherent and joined-up manner, and to fund the provision of major new elements of the capital web, including new urban spaces (see Chapter 10) (Figure 9.5).

A public authority providing – or developers agreeing on – a master plan, urban design framework or urban design code, can provide a way of relating individual developments and decisions (see Chapters 10 and 11). Nevertheless, such developments need to be designed and managed to allow for subsequent incremental change. Large developments often need the landownership to be consolidated into a single body, but, to allow for the subsequent incremental change, for that landownership to be broken down. Jacobs (1961, p. 307), for example, warned that: 'All city building that retains staying power after its novelty has gone . . . requires that its locality be able to adapt, keep up to date, keep interesting, keep convenient, and this in turn requires a myriad of gradual constant, close-grained changes.' The ongoing single control regime of large lump developments may be stultifying, and – because it lacks the internal capacity and stimulus for creativity, innovation and development – may only result in a slow managed decline.

From her studies of change and stability in San Francisco neighbourhoods, Anne Vernez Moudon

(1987, p. 188) emphasised the importance of the pattern of landownership in enabling incremental change. Small lots enabled constant fine-grain adaptation instead of the sudden and potentially devastating changes that come with large parcels. Smaller lots also gave greater individual control and greater variety – the more owners, the more gradual and adaptive the ongoing change: 'the place looks a little different every year, but the overall feel is the same from century to century' (Brand, 1994, p. 75). It can also be argued that sustainability requires a capacity for organic development, rendering clean-sweep redevelopment unnecessary.

Given the dangers of disjointed incrementalism, it is important that some overall vision or set of rules is available to guide developments towards agreed objectives – however broadly defined – giving the confidence necessary to attract investment and ensuring that the individual increments will result in a coherent whole. In effect, this is what Alexander's seven rules sought to achieve. A key skill of urban designers is the creation of a vision exploiting the opportunities presented by a site or context, and the development of plans and strategies capable of being implemented successfully. The activity of urban design is always open-ended and evolving, which makes interventions in and contributions to other dynamic systems. It is therefore naive to consider any design proposal, intervention or action as producing an end state or finite solution.

BOX 9.2 – GROWTH OF CAR-FREE STREETS AND SQUARES IN COPENHAGEN

(source: adapted from Gehl and Gemzoe, 2000)

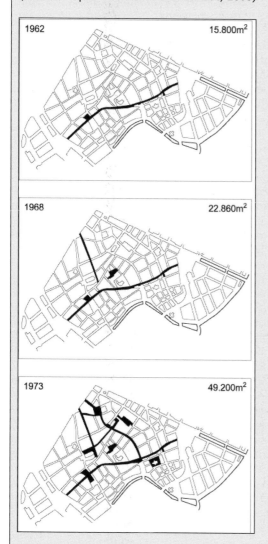

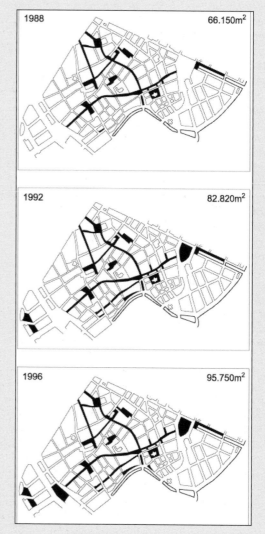

The area of car-free streets and squares in Copenhagen has grown significantly in the last forty years, increasing from 15 800 square metres in 1962 to nearly 100 000 squares metres in 1996. Major studies of the use of public space in the city were undertaken in 1968, 1986 and 1995. While the 1968 studies showed that the newly pedestrianised streets were popular as walking and shopping streets, the 1986 study showed the growth of a new and more active urban culture and informal public life. The 1995 study showed that this development had continued. An important contributory factor in the growth of an informal public life was the development of a cafe culture – largely unknown when the first streets were pedestrianised. The city now offers more than 5000 outdoor cafe chairs. Furthermore, although it had been expected that the climate would severely limit the potential to develop public life in Denmark, the season for outdoor seating at cafes has greatly been extended. From a summer season lasting three or four months, it now stretches over seven months from April to November (Gehl and Gemzoe, 2000, p. 57).

Given commitment to its aims and objectives, an urban design framework or master plan provides certainty in the longer-term, thereby reducing development risk. It should also retain sufficient flexibility to adapt to underlying and evolving processes of change. Visions and implementation strategies typically form a series of projects, over different time frames, with short-term, medium-term and long-term actions and objectives. If the short- and medium-term actions do not work, however, the long-term position will not be achieved.

An overarching lesson seems to be that, while radical change can still happen, it should – where possible – happen incrementally and at a pace that allows people to adapt and respond. The well-documented experience of pedestrianisation in Copenhagen is instructive (Gehl and Gemzoe, 1996, 2001). The programme began in 1962 with the pedestrianisation of the city's main street, Stroget – a pioneering experiment that aroused much public debate. By 1973, pedestrianisation had been completed, and subsequent efforts concentrated on reclaiming and improving city squares (Box 9.2). For Gehl and Gemzoe (2001, pp. 55–9), the gradual expansion of the city's system of car-free and almost car-free spaces had three main advantages:

- City residents had time to develop a new city culture and to discover and exploit the opportunities.
- People had time to change their travel practices. Parking in the city centre was reduced by 2–3 per cent per year, and car owners gradually became accustomed to the idea that driving and parking in the city centre were more difficult, while cycling and using public transport became much easier.

- Due to the success of previous measures, it became easier for the city's politicians to take further incremental decisions about pedestrianisation schemes.

Gehl and Gemzoe concluded that the city centre's gradual transformation from 'car culture' to 'pedestrian culture' had made possible an equally gradual development of city life and city culture: radical change had happened gradually and with public consent and approval.

CONCLUSION

When considering the temporal dimension of urban design, the overarching need is for urban designers to understand the implications and impact of time on places. Time involves both change that happens in cycles and change that occurs in progressive, unfolding and irreversible ways. Change itself both responds to and shapes further change. Urban designers need an awareness of potential change and of opportunities and constraints that may arise; of how change can be managed; how places change over time; how to anticipate the impacts of actions; how and why development will occur; and even how materials will weather. Kevin Lynch (1972, p. 240), for example, argued that 'effective action' and 'inner well-being' depend on 'a strong image of time: a vivid sense of the present, well connected to future and past, perceptive of change, [and] able to manage and enjoy it'. The final part of this chapter has already anticipated the discussion in the third part of this book, which concerns the key processes of urban design – development, control and communication.

PART III

IMPLEMENTING URBAN DESIGN

10
The development process

INTRODUCTION

Awareness of the development process, particularly of the balance between risk and reward that drives it, helps urban designers gain a deeper understanding of both the context in which they operate and the forces acting upon the process by which their design policies, proposals and projects originate and are implemented. Urban designers lacking such an awareness and understanding are at the development industry's mercy. Furthermore, as they frequently need to argue the case for urban design and, more particularly, the case for *better quality* urban design, their arguments can be more persuasive if informed by this awareness.

Focusing on the role of urban design and the urban designer in the development process, this chapter is in four main sections. The first outlines the principles of property development and the development process. The second concerns the 'pipeline' model of the development process. The third concerns roles and relationships in the development process and the fourth issues of urban design quality. Although discussion focuses on urban design practice in terms of urban development design, this necessarily includes the interface with design policies, guidance and control, which are the specific focus of Chapter 11.

LAND AND PROPERTY DEVELOPMENT

The land and property development process involves the combination of various inputs – land, labour, materials and/or finance (capital) – in order to achieve an output or product. Classically it is the 'entrepreneur' who brings these together and adds

value to them. In property development, entrepreneurs are usually known as developers, and the product is a change of land use and/or a new or altered building, intended to have a higher value than the cost of the transformation. Ambrose (1986) sees the process as a series of transformations: capital is converted into raw materials and labour bought as commodities in the market place; these are converted into another saleable commodity (i.e. a building); which is then converted back into money (i.e. capital) by selling the commodity in the market place. For the process to be profitable, the amount received from sales must be greater than the cost of production. A calculus of reward, mediated by the risk of achieving that reward, therefore, drives the process.

Rather than a one-off sequence of transformations, for most developers the process is one of a recurring cycle. There is also an important time dimension: rapid turnover of capital in development projects allows it to be recycled more quickly, generating profits more rapidly and reducing risk.

The process of designing and producing the built environment involves a variety of 'actors' or decision-makers, each with their own objectives, motivations, resources and constraints, and connected in various ways. As Michael Ball (1998, Ball *et al.*, 1998) has argued, the development process is a function of social relations specific to time and place, involving a variety of key actors (e.g. landowners, investors, financiers, developers, builders, various professionals, politicians, consumers, etc.). The state – local and national – is also an important actor, both in its own right and as a regulator of the other actors. These sets of relations represent what Ball terms the 'structures of building provision'. Ball argued that these need to be seen in terms of their specific linkages – functional, historical, political, social and cultural – with the broader structural elements – economic and institutional – of the political economy.

To facilitate understanding of the development process, several models have been devised. These have been grouped as follows:

• *Equilibrium models* – derived from neo-classical economics, these assume that development activity is structured by economic signals about effective demand, as reflected in rents, yields, etc.

• *Event-sequence models* – derived from estate management, these focus on the management of stages in the development process.
• *Agency models* – derived from behavioural or institutional explanations, these focus on the actors and their relationships in the development process.
• *Structure models* – grounded in political economy, these focus on the way markets are structured, the role of capital, labour and land in the development process, and the forces that organise the relationships and drive the dynamics of the process.

BOX 10.1 – THE PIPELINE MODEL OF THE DEVELOPMENT PROCESS

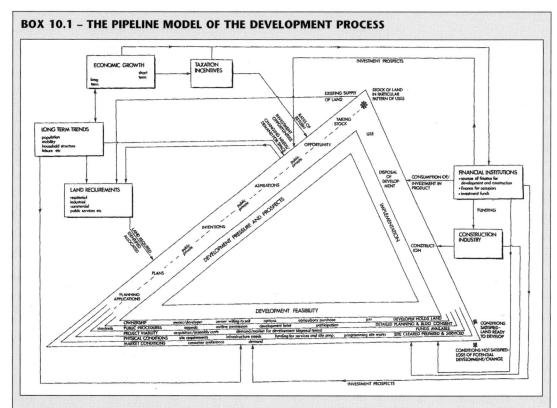

The development pipeline model (source: Barrett *et al.*, 1978)

Barrett *et al.*'s model divides the development process into three broad sets of events – development pressure and prospects, development feasibility, and implementation – each of which forms one side of a triangular 'pipeline'. External factors shown in black boxes generate development pressure and prospects along the first side, culminating in the identification of specific sites at the lower left-hand angle. Development feasibility is tested along the second side.

Implementation – the third side – includes both the process of construction and the transfer of the completed development into its new use and occupation. Sites move around the pipeline at varying speeds and, at any particular point in time, sites with development potential will be at different points. Operating as a spiral, producing a fresh pattern of land use at the end of each cycle, the model shows that the development process is dynamic and cyclical (Adams, 1994).

- *Institutional models* – these describe events and agencies, and explain how they relate to broader structural forces (Healey, 1991).

The following outline of the development process is based on an event-sequence model. While such models provide a good introduction to the development process, they tend to understate aspects that other models emphasise, such as the differential power of the various actors and institutions involved. Furthermore, they do not explain why urban development takes the form it does.

THE DEVELOPMENT PIPELINE MODEL

Barrett, Stewart and Underwood's 'development pipeline' model – an event-sequence model – is shown in Box 10.1 and discussed below (adapted from Adams, 1994). Although the discussion focuses principally on private sector development, the stages and principles are broadly similar regardless of whether the developer is the public sector or a non-profit organisation. Table 10.1 summarises urban designers' roles at each stage.

Development pressure and prospects

External influences – economic growth, fiscal policies, the impact of long-term social and demographic trends, technological developments, market restructuring, etc. – create development pressure and prospects, which trigger activity within the pipeline. When development opportunities arise, appropriate sites are sought, with activity really beginning when a development proposal finds an appropriate site, or a development site finds a suitable proposal.

Initiation of development may come from a developer or third party (including the public

TABLE 10.1
Development process and urban designers

| STAGE | URBAN DESIGNER'S ACTIVITIES | |
	ACTING FOR DEVELOPER	ACTING FOR PUBLIC SECTOR
DEVELOPMENT PRESSURE AND PROSPECTS	• Spots 'opportunity' • Identifies suitable sites • Provides 'vision' • Prepares brief/master plan for site	• Anticipates development pressure/opportunities • Spots and promotes development opportunities • Prepares planning policy framework • Provides 'vision' • Prepares development framework/development code • Prepares development brief for site/master plan for area • Directs/attracts development to suitable sites • Influences developer's brief for the site
DEVELOPMENT FEASIBILITY	• Carries out feasibility study • Provides advice • Prepares design proposals • Negotiates with planning authority • Prepares and submits planning application	• Negotiates with developer • Provides advice • Comments on design proposals • Makes decision/recommendation on planning application
IMPLEMENTATION	• Quality of scheme may seal commitment with funders • Ensures quality of development • Influences management of development	• Ensures quality of development • Influences management of development

sector) anticipating demand for a certain type of development and seeking an appropriate site. It may also come from the site owner (or third party) who envisages a higher value use for an existing site. In both cases, urban designers may be involved in demonstrating the site's potential. To direct or attract development to particular sites or areas (or direct it away from others), a planning authority might establish a planning policy framework, and/or prepare a development brief, master plan or development framework (see Chapter 11). Development frameworks or briefs might be produced either *proactively* to encourage interest in a development site or *reactively* following a developer's interest in it. To expedite the process, they may be produced by developers.

As well as identifying a site and a development proposal, this stage is also likely to include initial ideas about the form the development might take and an outline financial appraisal. In essence, this is a 'back of an envelope'-type analysis, combining a broad assessment of the likely costs and subsequent value, with a more subjective judgement based upon experience and feel for the market. If the proposed development is worth pursuing further, the feasibility stage – the second part of the pipeline – develops this initial assessment in more detail.

Development feasibility

In the pipeline model, feasibility is tested in five ways, each relating to a particular set of influences or constraints. For development to occur, all five streams must be successfully negotiated. If the development is not feasible, it will be changed or abandoned. Successful developers are, nonetheless, skilled in confronting and overcoming constraints.

(i) Ownership constraints
Prior to development, developers need to know whether they will be able to acquire the site, or rights over it. Land availability is often restricted by planning, physical, valuation or ownership constraints (Adams *et al.*, 1999). Multiple ownership, for example, may require land assembly or the development of a partnership to carry out the project. In some cases, public sector compulsory purchase or acquisition powers can be used to facilitate land assembly.

(ii) Physical conditions
To determine whether the site can accommodate the proposed development, its physical conditions

are assessed (e.g. ground levels, soil structure, levels of contamination). As physical constraints can normally be expressed in terms of extra costs (i.e. additional preparation, design, or construction costs), they do not necessarily prevent development. As well as the site's physical conditions, its physical capacity (subject to criteria of 'good' urban form) to accommodate satisfactorily the intended volume of development will also be assessed. This is intrinsically a design issue. Design proposals start as a concept sketch, getting progressively more detailed as the development proposal increases in certainty, and ultimately having sufficient detail for the development to be built. Considerations of good urban form might be internal and might limit or determine density, massing and/or height, guided by, for example, the developer's concern to build a certain quality of development. Most schemes have a client or project brief, prepared by the developer for the architect and other designers, setting out the design parameters, the GFA (gross floor area) of different uses, and the indicative budget. Alternatively, considerations of site capacity may be external and may, for example, be imposed through planning policies, a zoning ordinance, a development brief, an urban design framework or a master plan.

(iii) Public procedures
All legal and other public procedure issues relating to the site and/or the proposed development must be assessed, including the likelihood of obtaining planning/development consent. While not always affecting the principle of development, legal and/or planning constraints usually affect its design, layout and cost. In countries with zoning systems (e.g. the US and many parts of Europe), provided the proposed development accords with the zoning ordinance, there is automatic planning consent – a 'development permit' may also be required. Zoning systems may be supplemented by a design review panel focusing on the design proposals. In the discretionary planning system in the UK, acts of 'development', including material changes of use, require the planning authority's formal consent. A separate building regulation consent is also required. Consents may also be required for a range of issues pertaining to land and property ownership; conservation and/or historic preservation; diversion or closure of rights of way, light, and support; actions necessary to connect with main services and infrastructure; etc.

– all of which may incur cost or delay to the development process (see Chapter 11).

(iv) Market conditions

Appraisal of market conditions assesses whether there is demand both now and in the future for the proposed development. Forecasting future demand involves considerations of risk and uncertainty. As market conditions may change during the development process, it is a matter of risk whether demand at the time of completion will be strong enough to make the development viable. To reduce exposure to risk, developers often arrange a pre-let or pre-sale, tying in a future occupier or purchaser at an early stage. In a fragile market, development is unlikely to commence without this, since it may be necessary to secure funding for development. In markets with strong demand, developers may be less concerned with securing a pre-let because it could reduce their return. They, therefore, trade off between risk and reward. Market conditions are monitored throughout development, so that, where possible, changes can be made in order to maximise the return on the finished product. In a difficult economic climate, while design quality is often a first casualty as developers try to cut costs, some developers deliberately invest more in design in order to differentiate their product. Conversely, in a developers' – rather than buyers' – market, tenants and purchasers (investors) often have to take what is available and design issues may become less important in their decision-making.

(v) Project viability

Project viability assesses whether demand can be met at the desired rate of profit. For private sector development, this assessment includes analysis of the market (i.e. the likely demand) for the proposed development and the potential returns in relation to the costs and the risk to be borne. In the public sector, it assesses whether appropriate forms of cost recovery are available, whether the development constitutes an appropriate use for public money (relative to other purposes for which the money could be used), whether it provides value for money, and accords with any cost yardsticks or benchmark costs for similar developments.

In simple terms, appraisals consider four related factors: the end or expected value of the development; land acquisition costs; development costs; and the developer's profit or required level of profit. The latter is important because, if the developer cannot achieve the desired level of profit, other sites and developments may be more attractive. For a development to be viable, its expected value must be greater (at least to the extent of the required profit), than the costs of development and land acquisition.

A common method of appraisal is the 'residual method'. At it simplest, this involves subtracting the total projected development costs (e.g. building costs, legal and agents' fees, professional fees, costs of borrowing, developer's profit, etc.) from the estimated capital value of the completed development to establish the residual value of the land (i.e. what the developer can afford to pay for the land to enable a reasonable return). Alternatively, if the land price is held constant, the method can be used to determine whether a target rate of profit can be achieved. Other than by shaving profit margins, developers cannot absorb additional or unexpected costs. If they create additional value, additional costs can be passed onto the purchaser or occupier; if they do not create additional value, the developer reduces the price offered to the landowner. As landowners often refuse to sell their land at a lower price, developers usually have to find development proposals offering a higher end value. If they are unable to do so, the project becomes unviable.

The residual method has two basic weaknesses. First, by assuming that costs will be spread evenly over the development period, it is not sensitive to the timing of expenditure and revenues. Cash flow appraisals can overcome this. Second, by relying on single figure 'best estimates', it hides uncertainty and risk. Sensitivity analysis, which looks at a range of possible outcomes and then narrows them down to probable outcomes, can remedy this.

Design and costing of development proposals occur in parallel, and in increasing detail as the scheme progresses. Viability studies may, for example, highlight the need for design modification, to increase the land uses likely to produce most revenue. To be financially viable, a site may require a greater volume or intensity of development than it appears able to accommodate. Urban design skills may be needed to put the volume of development required for financial viability onto the site, while retaining the development's quality. Design is, however, intrinsically limited and cannot totally overcome disadvantages of a poor location or lack of (economic) demand (Cadman and Austin-Crowe, 1991, p. 19).

If development appears to be viable, funding must be sought. Project viability therefore also assesses whether the developer can obtain the necessary finance and on what terms. The terms involve certain risks for the developer: when funds are borrowed and interest charged, steep rises in interest rates, for example, may cause development projects to be postponed or abandoned. Developers normally arrange two types of finance: short-term finance – *development funding* – to cover costs during the development period, and longer-term finance – *investment finance* – to cover the cost of holding the completed development as an investment (whereby, the developer becomes an investor) or, alternatively, to find a buyer (or investor) for the completed scheme. These are discussed later in the chapter.

To reduce exposure, help cash flow, and/or acquire greater operational flexibility, developers – where possible – phase development so that some parts are finished and earning income before the whole is complete. Developments may also be designed so that non-revenue-generating elements occupy the later phases. In a residential development, for example, the developer might build the houses first, leaving the community centre and open space until later. This logic can also be reversed: if the non-revenue generating elements help sell or let the revenue-generating elements, they may be built at the same time, or even before the other elements. At Brindleyplace in Birmingham (UK), for example, the central public space

was completed before the surrounding office blocks (Figures 10.1 and 10.2). If the initial phases of a development prove to be unsuccessful, the decision may be taken not to complete the development or to change the design of later phases. Equally, if the initial phases are successful, subsequent phases may be changed in order to maximise more successful, and minimise less successful, elements. Phasing considerations also affect design: if the development is to be let or sold in phases, each one must be designed to appear complete, and tolerably self-sufficient.

Implementation

The developer's ultimate aim is to produce a marketable development: that is, one for which occupiers and/or purchasers (investors) are willing and able to pay a rent and/or purchase at a price that at least covers development and site acquisition costs. The final, implementation, stage includes both construction and sale or letting. If the developer retains the project for letting, then his/her role changes to that of an investor (see below). Once implementation starts, developers lose their flexibility of action. The main task is to ensure that work is carried out at the appropriate speed, cost and quality. Developers are particularly reliant on their builders, and expect their profes-

FIGURE 10.1
If non-revenue generating elements enable early sales or lets of revenue-generating elements, they may be built at the same time or even in advance of other elements. At Brindleyplace (Birmingham, UK), the central public space was completed before the surrounding office blocks

FIGURE 10.2
A development's design, or particular aspects of it, facilitate its marketing. At Bindleyplace (Birmingham, UK), the design included a tower that does not provide usable office space, but which enabled the development to be seen from the city centre

sional team to monitor the builder's performance, and be concerned simultaneously about time, cost, and quality. In the short-term, time and cost can crowd out concerns for quality, but in the long-term they recede in importance relative to quality.

DEVELOPMENT ROLES AND ACTORS

To more fully understand the development process, it is necessary to identify the key actors, their motivations and objectives, their relationships relative to each other, their motivation for involvement in the development process and, more generally, why they might pursue – or be persuaded to provide – higher 'quality'. In this and the following section, the event-sequence model is extended by considerations of 'agency' and 'structure' (adapted and extended from Henneberry, 1998). Agency is the term for the way in which development actors define and pursue their strategies, interests and actions (Adams, 1994, p. 65). It is set within a broader context, or 'structure', consisting of the economic and political activity, and prevailing values, that frame individual decision-making (e.g. market and regulatory frameworks).

Different actors perform different roles in the development process. Although, for the purpose of analysis, roles are considered individually, in practice a single actor often performs several roles. Volume housing developers, for example, typically combine the roles of developer, funder and builder. As well as identifying actors and the roles they perform, it is also necessary to understand the reason for their involvement (i.e. their motivation). Each development role can be considered in terms of five generalised criteria:

- *Financial objectives* – whether the actor's primary concern is for cost minimisation or for profit maximisation.
- *Time-span* – whether the actor's involvement and interest in the development is primarily short- or long-term.
- *Design: functionality* – whether an actor has a *specific* concern for the development's ability to serve its functional purpose (i.e. to be used as an office).
- *Design: external appearance* – whether an actor is *primarily* concerned with the development's external appearance.
- *Design: relation to context* – whether a development's relation to its context is a primary concern to the development actor.

These are summarised in Table 10.2 and 10.3.

While each actor internally trades off between criteria, the interactions and differential power of actors also mean that criteria are traded off between actors. Achieving high quality urban design may not be a criterion shared by all participants in the process, while 'quality' may mean different things to different actors. The objective can be constrained by a wide variety of factors, many of which lie outside the designer's or developer's sphere of influence. These factors might include.

- the requirements and preferences of clients/customers, which may conflict with those of the wider community;
- market conditions;
- limitations and costs imposed by the site;
- the need for various consents (legal, planning, development, highways adoption, etc.), and public sector regulatory and statutory requirements;

- limits on the rents that can be achieved in particular locations;
- the short-termism often inherent in investment decisions (longer-term exposure increases the risk involved).

Successful developers and urban designers are, however, skilled in confronting and overcoming constraints and obstacles.

Developers

The term 'developer' embraces a wide range of agencies, from, for example, volume house builders to small local house builders and self-builders, and with levels of profit motivation ranging from the most profit-driven private sector developers, through central and local government, to non-profit organisations, such as housing associations. Some developers specialise in particular market sectors such as retail, office, industrial or residential, while others operate across a range of markets. Some establish a niche market, such as the conversion of historic buildings. Some concentrate upon projects in or around a particular town or city, while others operate regionally, nationally and internationally.

Based on how they operate, Logan and Molotch (1987, from Knox and Ozolins, 2000, pp. 5–6) identified three types of developers:

- 'Serendipitous entrepreneurs' who acquire land and property in various ways (perhaps through inheritance or as a sideline to their regular business) and then find that it would be more valuable sold or rented for some other use.
- 'Active entrepreneurs' who anticipate changing patterns of land use and land values, and buy and sell land accordingly.
- 'Structural speculators' operate strategically, anticipating changing patterns and seeking to influence or engineer change for their own benefit (e.g. by influencing the route of a road, changing the zoning ordinance or development plan, or encouraging public expenditure in certain locations).

All developers are motivated by the opportunity to appropriate the development value of sites. Development value is a function of the gap between the value of the property and/or land in its existing use, and its value in a 'higher and better' use, less the costs of acquiring the land and producing the higher

TABLE 10.2
Motivation of 'demand side' development actors (i.e. those who, in some way, 'consume' the development)

DEVELOPMENT ROLE	Time scale	PRICE — Financial strategy	FACTORS OF MOTIVATION — Functionality	DESIGN ISSUES — External appearance	Relation to context
INVESTORS (Investment funding)	Long-term	Profit maximisation	**Yes** But primarily as means to financial end.	**Yes** But primarily as means to financial end.	**Yes** To extent that there are benefits to making positive connections.
OCCUPIERS	Long-term	Cost minimisation	**Yes**	**Yes** But only to extent that external appearance symbolises/represents them and their business.	**Yes** To extent that there are benefits to making positive connections.
PUBLIC SECTOR (Regulation)	Long-term	Neutral (in principle).	**Yes**	**Yes** To extent that it forms part of a greater whole.	**Yes** To extent that it forms part of a greater whole.
ADJACENT LANDOWNERS	Long-term	Protect property values	No	**Yes** To extent that new development has positive or negative externalities.	**Yes** To extent that new development has positive or negative externalities.
GENERAL PUBLIC	Long-term	Neutral	**Yes** To extent that buildings are used by general public.	**Yes** To extent that it defines and forms part of public realm.	**Yes**

(Source: adapted and extended from Henneberry, 1998)

TABLE 10.3
Motivation of 'supply side' development actors (i.e., those who, in some, way, 'produce' the development or contribute to its production)

DEVELOPMENT ROLE	Time scale	PRICE Financial strategy	FACTORS OF MOTIVATION	DESIGN ISSUES	
			Functionality	External appearance	Relation to context
LANDOWNER	Short-term	Profit maximisation	No	No	No
DEVELOPERS	Short-term	Profit maximisation	Yes But only to financial end.	Yes But only to financial end.	Yes To extent that there are positive or negative externalities.
FUNDERS (devt finance)	Short-term	Profit maximisation	No	No	No
BUILDER	Short-term	Profit maximisation	No	Yes	No
ADVISER I EG Man Agent	Long-term	Profit maximisation/seeking	Yes	Yes But primarily to financial end.	No
ADVISER II EG Architect	Short-term	Profit maximisation/seeking	Yes	Yes But indirectly, to extent that external appearance reflects on them and their future business.	No

(Source: adapted and extended from Henneberry, 1998)

value use. Rather than being fixed to a particular site or piece of land, development value often 'floats' over a wider area and may 'shift' from one site to another. As Reade (1987, p. 16, from Adams, 1994, p. 35) notes, if a steadily expanding city is surrounded on all sides by agricultural land, all owners may hope to sell land at a price higher than its value in agriculture (i.e. there is a 'hope value'). In practice, only a few owners can (at this moment in time) sell their land for development. Development value, therefore, 'floats' over an extensive area, but settles on only a small part of it. Similarly, while there might, for example, be several possible sites for a multi-screen cinema complex within a city centre, the development value may largely be appropriated by the first one to be completed: any subsequent developments must compete with it. Provision of new infrastructure or development will also 'shift' the development value from one site to another. Planning controls shift value by giving land a particular designation (e.g. housing or agricultural) and, in discretionary planning systems, by granting – or refusing – planning consent.

In general, the developer aims to appropriate the development value by meeting an unmet demand for development. Developers therefore orchestrate the assembly of inputs (sites, finance, professional advice, construction, etc.) and seek to make a profit by selling the completed development at a price greater than the cost of producing it. A calculus of reward mediated by the risk of achieving that reward therefore drives the process. In the main, developers' objectives are short-term and financial – they are interested in design to the extent that it serves financial ends.

In the private sector, as their primary concern is a marketable product, developers (the supply side) must anticipate the needs and preferences of investors and occupiers (the demand side). In principle, occupiers make demands of building owners (i.e. investors), who make demands of developers, who set the brief for building designers. The possible occurrence of producer–consumer gaps is discussed below. In responding to, and balancing the needs of, investors and occupiers, developers tend to see 'design' as essentially a means to a financial end rather than as an end in itself. Their general design concerns include:

- investor and occupier requirements, preferences and tastes, and, in particular, the 'price' to be achieved for a product responding to these;

- flexibility of building and site layout to meet changing circumstances;
- buildability;
- cost efficiency and value for money; visual impact (including the image of the development as an aid to sale or letting);
- and management implications (including the development's 'running costs') (Rowley, 1998, p. 163).

While there is often demonisation and stereotyping of developers, their thinking is often broader than the stereotype suggests. Individual developers are often very concerned with the quality of the development and strongly support urban design guidelines where their value in maintaining environmental quality – and thereby property values – is clear. Some developers look beyond immediate market pressures and consider broader civic responsibilities and obligations. Many derive psychic benefits through their close association with certain buildings and developments. Furthermore, due to the discipline of operating in a market economy, developers may often have a greater awareness of consumers' needs and preferences than many designers.

Landowners

Landowners own land prior to the commencement of development. With the exception of those holding land in expectation of developing it, such as builders or developers with land banks, landowners do not normally take an active role in the development process, and simply release land for development when offered a sufficient price (Adams, 1994). Their objectives are therefore usually short-term and financial.

Every parcel of land is unique – at least by dint of its location. As location is fixed, ownership is a source of power, particularly where spatial monopolies can be created. Housing developers, for example, compete for land in particular locations. Where readily developable land is in short supply, once a developer has acquired the land or purchased an 'option' – an agreement to buy the land at a specified price before a specified date or upon some specified event occurring – and has gained consent for development, s/he effectively has a local monopoly, providing greater freedom to set quality levels and prices in their own interest.

Landowners influence the outcome of the development process in four main ways.

1. *By releasing or not releasing land*: Adams (1994) distinguishes between 'active' and 'passive' landowners. Active landowners develop their own land (i.e. become developers), enter into joint venture developments, or make their land available for others to develop. They may try to overcome site constraints to make their land more marketable or suitable for development. Passive landowners, by contrast, take no particular steps to market or develop their land, rarely attempt to overcome site constraints and may – or may not – respond to offers from potential developers. There may often be sound reasons for this passivity: they may, for example, wish to prevent development, or to retain the land for later use. If owners of land with development potential are unwilling to sell, passive ownership may become a major constraint to development. Where public authorities are involved in or support the principle of development, powers of compulsory purchase or 'vesting' can be used – although this is typically time-consuming and costly. If land is not freely available, development may take the form of 'scattered' growth, where, rather than growing incrementally outward from a centre, it leapfrogs land that is not available.
2. *Through the size and pattern of the land parcels released, which have a major impact on the subsequent pattern of development*: Knox and Ozolins (2000, p. 5), for example, contrast the large ranchos and mission lands around Los Angeles that formed the basis of extensive tracts of uniform suburban development, with East Coast cities where the early pattern of land holdings was fragmented and subsequent development more piecemeal.
3. *Through any conditions imposed on the subsequent nature of development*: Landowners may release parcels of land with contractual provisions or restrictive covenants limiting the nature of development (Knox and Ozolins, 2000, p. 5). They may set down a site plan (in two dimensions) or an urban design framework (in three dimensions) that influences or controls development. Urban morphologists have shown that platting or subdivision of land for the purpose of sale or development has a major influence on its development (see Chapter 4).
4. *Through leasing rather than selling land*: Due to their long-term interest in the land, freeholders granting leases are often concerned with the quality of what is built there. As Sudjic (1992, pp. 34–5) observes, in this sense development is closer to farming than to trade. Aiming to produce a regular income rather than accumulate capital by selling assets entails taking a longer-term view on the economic health of the properties, and the careful management of tenants and the uses to which they put their premises. The intention is to build a continuing relationship rather than a one-off transaction. Contractual provisions in leaseholds, for example, were responsible for the form of much of Georgian London.

Adjacent landowners

Owners of land, sites or buildings adjoining or close to a development site seek to ensure that any development of that site does not reduce – and preferably increases – their property values. A building's relation to its context – and, indeed, its external appearance – can be considered as spillover effects. Buildings are interdependent assets: their value is in part a function of the value of the neighbourhood, which in turn derives – again, in part – from the value of each building. All developments contribute to a neighbourhood's composite value. There can be positive neighbourhood effects, where the value of the neighbouring buildings increases the value of a development, and negative neighbourhood effects. New developments, therefore, either enhance or detract from the neighbourhood's composite value. Adjacent owners' objectives are therefore long-term, financial and design-related in terms of external appearance and relation to context.

Funders and investors

Unless developers use their own capital, they must arrange finance on the most favourable terms available, with regard to cost and flexibility. When borrowing money, they must take lenders' concerns into consideration. Those investing resources in urban development do so for their own purposes, which are usually concerned with making profits. If acceptable profits are not achieved, they will invest elsewhere.

Developers normally arrange two types of finance: short-term development funding, and longer-term investment finance.

Funders

Short-term finance – development funding – is needed to cover costs during the development period (i.e. costs associated with land acquisition, construction and professional services). The principal short-term funders are clearing and merchant banks. On completion, when long-term finance is raised, the development finance is repaid. Funding for a development is typically raised through a combination of equity and debt finance. Lenders of debt finance will, however, be repaid with interest, but do not normally have a legal interest in the project (except as security in the event of default) or an entitlement to share in profits. Lenders of equity finance participate in the risks and rewards of development, are entitled to share in profits, and have a legal interest in the project.

To assist their funding package, developers sometimes seek government or other subsidy schemes, which often take the form of low interest loans, grants, subsidies, or – less commonly – joint ventures. As grants and subsidies are typically used to make socially desirable but economically marginal projects viable, eligibility for support is usually couched in terms of 'social' rather than 'economic' objectives. Although developers are often astute in arguing that their projects are socially desirable and non-viable without gap funding, the intention is not to subsidise developers' profit.

The objectives of development funders are typically short-term and financial. Their interest in design is primarily as a means towards a financial end. Lenders of equity finance have more interest in the totality of the development, including its design.

Investors

The second type of finance is longer-term, covering the cost of holding the completed development as an investment. Investors are the purchasers (and subsequently sellers) of completed schemes. As investment essentially requires foregoing the current use of resources for enhanced benefit at a later date, investors in property are primarily interested in the (potential) income flow from user rents, which is capitalised into the property's exchange or investment value. For commercial and industrial development, the principal investors are

insurance companies and pension funds. For residential development they are owner–occupiers.

Investors generally look for investment opportunities that satisfy the following criteria:

- *Security of capital and income* (i.e. low risk) – in general, the more secure an investment, the lower the risk that capital invested will be lost, or that expected income will not arise. Investors may diversify their investment through the development of portfolios that balance risk.
- *Potential growth of income and capital* (i.e. high returns) – although high returns may be achieved through income growth, capital growth, or both combined, capital growth and high overall returns ultimately depend on the prospects for income growth (i.e. from user rents).
- *Flexibility* (i.e. high liquidity) – investors look for the ability to change their investments to produce the best returns. Liquidity depends on such factors as the existence of potential purchasers, transfer costs, the investment's overall size and its capacity for subdivision; in general, the more liquid an investment, the easier it is to sell, in whole or in part. (Adams, 1994)

In practice, no investment offers complete security, perfect liquidity and guaranteed profitability. As each investment represents a different combination of these attributes, investors trade off among them. Higher expected returns are required from higher-risk investments (i.e. the investor sacrifices security in pursuit of greater return). Institutions have tradiationally adopted a risk-averse approach to property investment, concentrating funds on what appears to be the most secure, liquid and profitable 'prime property' (i.e. property in the best locations, let on long leases to tenants of 'unquestionable' covenant).

As a type of investment opportunity, property has characteristics that distinguish it from other forms of investment such as stocks, shares and government bonds. Property investments are, for example, fixed in their location, heterogeneous, generally indivisible and entail responsibilities for management (e.g. collecting rents, dealing with repairs and renewals and lease negotiations). It also takes a large amount of capital to buy a small amount of property, and there tend to be high costs involved in the transfer of property holdings. Property investments are, nevertheless, generally durable and typically provide a source of income. The total supply of land (and property) is also fixed; the supply in a particular land use can change, but is relatively fixed in the short term.

Investors often use yield as a means of gauging the performance of investments and to balance risk with return. In markets that exhibit significant uncertainties, investors generally seek developments that deliver a high yield and a quicker turnaround on their investments. In buoyant markets, with significant competition between investors for investment opportunities, yields will generally fall. A low yield therefore indicates a healthy investment market and high capital values. Such circumstances will generally promise that profits will increase in the near future as rents rise to reflect new capital valuations.

As their return takes the form of present and future rental income and capital appreciation, the objectives of investors are typically long-term, financial and design-related to the extent that this achieves financial ends (see below). Acquisition policies of large, property investment companies, for example, tend to be risk-averse: that is, they seek properties that will minimise their risks (e.g. of being unable to dispose of a property at a target price or unable to let it at a target rental level). The properties they seek therefore need to produce an increasing rental income over a long period of time; be flexible and easily adapted to alternative occupiers; be acceptable to tenants with sound credit ratings; and be acceptable to other investing institutions (Rowley, 1998, p. 164). The acquisition policies of smaller property companies may, however, differ from this; such companies often play an important role in urban regeneration (see Guy et al., 2002).

Development advisers

Advisers provide professional advice and services to developers and other development agents. They include marketing consultants, estate agents, solicitors, planners, architects, engineers, facility managers, site agents, quantity surveyors, cost consultants, etc. As most advisers earn one-off profits in the form of fees, their objectives are typically short-term and financial. Some advisers – such as management agents of investment properties – earn fees for continuing involvement: their objectives are typically long-term, financial and functional. Some – such as architects and urban design practitioners – earn one-off profits in the form of fees, and may also use the completed project as an advertisement for their services. They may also derive significant psychic benefits from their involvement in the project. Their objectives are therefore typically long-term, financial and design-related.

Builders

Builders – or contractors (and subcontractors) – seek to make a profit by constructing the development at a cost lower than the price paid by the client for the work and materials involved. Their objectives are primarily short-term and financial. As builders may also use the development as an advertisement for their services, they have an interest in its design. Many builders also engage in development, operating as developers.

Occupiers

Occupiers – those who rent or buy space – derive direct use and benefit from completed development. They are primarily interested in its use value, especially in matters affecting business productivity and operating costs, such as appearance, comfort, convenience and efficiency. Their objectives are typically long-term, financial and design-related with respect to functionality and perhaps also to external appearance (see below).

As the utilisation of property depends on both its price and its physical qualities, occupiers trade off between financial (e.g. rent levels) and physical (e.g. quality, character, neighbourhood) attributes. Although occupiers normally treat the space they rent as one of the factors necessary for the production or delivery of their goods or services and assess its contribution to this aim, they may also be concerned with what the building represents or symbolises (e.g. status, solidity, quality). To communicate certain messages, companies may commission 'trophy' buildings, or seek out existing buildings and/or locations based on the image of their firm and the self-images of their staff and potential staff. External appearance or image may be important to an occupier or investor, but its value – or, more precisely, its 'worth' to a particular owner or occupier – is relatively 'intangible' and hard to price. Furthermore, although a company's buildings might once have been an element of its marketing strategy, as the scale of markets increases that element becomes decreasingly important.

Although a company's buildings might now be considered less important than its website, major firms continue to invest in high quality buildings, often by commissioning their own, giving them a more commanding role in the development process (see example one in Box 10.2). While in part this is a strategy to reinforce brand identity, it is increasingly an attempt to attract and retain key workers by providing working environments that inspire creativity and reduce absenteeism. This suggests recognition of and concern for buildings' functionality and their contribution to employee satisfaction. The concern may extend to spaces surrounding the building. Research by Carmona *et al.* (2001), for example, identified a strong occupier-driven demand for better quality environments.

The public sector

The public sector (government bodies, regulatory agencies and planning authorities) seeks to regulate the development and use of land through the planning system, other means of regulation, provision of infrastructure and services, and involvement in land assembly and development. In general, it does not act directly on private sector actors (developers, landowners, etc.), but by establishing the public policy and regulatory framework, it provides the context for private sector investment decision-making, it influences the incentives and sanctions available, thus making some actions more likely than others.

Public sector bodies generally negotiate with developers over the principle and detail of development proposals. As well as meeting the planning authority's basic requirements (those that are non-negotiable), there will often be scope for negotiation and bargaining. The planning authority might require certain 'planning gains' (e.g. public open space, or contributions to infrastructure), while the developer might offer certain gains to make the scheme more acceptable to the authority and/or the local community. In some countries planning gains are a legal requirement (e.g. through exaction fees), compensating the local community for the development's negative spillover effects. Negotiation provides opportunities for urban designers on both sides of the

BOX 10.2 – CONSUMER–PRODUCER GAPS IN THE DEVELOPMENT PROCESS

(source: adapted from Henneberry, 1998)

Example One

A company builds an office building from its own resources for its own occupation, performing the roles of developer, funder, owner and occupier, and carrying the costs and benefits of higher quality features/higher quality design. As a single actor combines several development roles, the conflict between different objectives and motivations is *internalised* and traded off to produce the optimal outcome (subject to budget constraints).

Example Two

A developer builds an office which is funded by, and pre-sold to, an investor (i.e. funder and investor) who intends to rent it to tenants (i.e. occupiers). The funding/sale arrangement reduces the developer's risk, while the funder's long-term outlook/preferences will have an influence on the building's design. The costs and benefits are distributed among developer, investor, and the future occupier, who is as yet unknown and has no direct influence on building design and specification. While the developer and the investor/owner must anticipate and provide for the occupiers' needs, the likelihood of more costly features beneficial to the occupier being included within a scheme is reduced. Thus, while a single actor combines the roles of funder and owner/investor, there are gaps between this actor, the developer and the occupiers, and another gap between the developer and the occupiers. Development quality frequently falls through these gaps.

process to influence the design and quality of a proposed development (e.g. by encouraging and/or requiring the developer to invest more time or money in improving quality). In the UK, design is a material consideration in development control decisions: a planning authority can – in principle – reject a proposal solely on design grounds. As refusal of planning consent, and the probable need to go to appeal, costs the developer both time and money, it is extremely undesirable. Developers therefore generally negotiate with planning authorities to ensure that consent for the development is likely to be forthcoming, while planning authorities can encourage developers to make changes at the risk of not receiving consent. This empowers the planning authority's urban designers in their negotiations with developers.

Although planning controls are often seen as constraints on development, this is a narrow view. While they may reduce the reward for the development of a particular site, they protect the context and composite property values of the area or neighbourhood, and provide a more secure investment environment (i.e. by limiting what can be done to adjacent sites). Typically, developers favour planning controls but – to reduce their development risk – want greater certainty and clarity in their operation. Environmental improvements also create a more secure investment environment.

In principle, the public sector acts in the collective or public interest. In practice, however, it may be difficult to discern what this is, while the various levels of government and other public agencies may frequently act in their own, narrower self-interest. The role of the public sector is discussed more fully in Chapter 11. In relation to any particular scheme, the public sector's objectives are typically long-term, functional and design-related.

The community (general public)

The community at large – residents, businesses and general public – consume the products of the development process directly and indirectly (i.e. to the extent that the development is visible from or is part of the public realm). They therefore represent a further part of the demand side of the development process. As they consume developments in aggregate (i.e. across property lines), concern is for each development's contribution to the greater whole. The community's objectives are typically long-term and design-related in terms of external appearance and contribution to context.

As well as being (passive) recipients of the products of the development process, the community and individuals thereof may actively affect the development process through, for example, protests over specific development projects, participation or consultation on particular projects, and/or involvement in interest groups and organisations. Through the democratic process, they – indirectly, and perhaps in principle only – control the public sector side of the development process.

DEVELOPMENT QUALITY

In considering issues of development quality, we must consider the relationships between different actors. In most economies they are related through market processes and market structures. Given the discipline of a market economy, actors only become involved in the development process to the extent that it contributes to achievement of their objectives. Two issues follow from this: the characteristics of a proposed development will be assessed according to the degree to which they contribute to each actor's objectives; and, as actors may have different objectives for the same development, there may be conflict and negotiation between them (Henneberry, 1998). Three key issues arise: the possibility of a gap, or gaps, between the producer and consumer sides of the development process; the role of the urban designer within the producer side of the development process; and considerations of urban design quality over and above those of development quality.

The producer–consumer gap

The costs and benefits of any particular element of a development project are not neutral in their (perceived) impact on the development actors (Henneberry, 1998). For example, high quality, low maintenance materials increase initial development costs, reduce long-term occupation costs and enhance long-term functionality: the costs are borne by the developers, but the benefits accrue to the occupier. To the extent that increased costs are passed on in the purchase price, investors bear higher costs, recouped from occupiers through higher rental levels: to the extent that lower occupation costs and greater functionality increase rental and capital value, higher returns are achieved. What is significant in Tables 10.2 and 10.3 is that supply-side actors tend to have short-term and financial objectives (i.e. the development is a financial commodity), while demand-side actors tend to have long-term and design objectives (i.e. the development is an environment to be used).

Where differing objectives and motivations must be traded off between roles played by one actor or organisation (as developer, funder, investor and occupier), conflict is internalised and can be traded off to produce the most satisfactory outcome, subject to budget constraints. Where differing objectives and motivations must be reconciled externally (through market transactions), there is scope for mismatches or gaps between supply and demand (i.e. a producer–consumer gap) (see Box 10.2). Because user/owners are unknown and unable to directly inform the design and development process, producer–consumer/user gaps are features of all speculative developments. The lack of direct consumer input, combined with consumers having to buy what is offered for sale, means that developers can produce 'poorer quality' developments/environments which serve narrow financial purposes only. Thus, although the supply side (the developer) has to anticipate the demand side's needs and requirements, it tends to produce, if possible, a product that suits its own objectives. In general, better quality development is more likely when development roles are combined in ways that bridge the producer–consumer gap. Although professionals, such as real estate agents, often act as proxies for the occupiers, this may present other problems because the interests of the proxy can never correlate exactly with those of the actual occupants.

Where producer–consumer gaps occur, the achievement of a balance of costs and benefits among all actors is critically dependent on supply-side actors being convinced that providing benefits will result in higher prices/values or, at least, enable cost recovery (Henneberry, 1998). If occupiers do not recognise or appreciate the benefits of particular design elements by being prepared to pay the higher prices/rents for them, then developers (especially) and funders/investors (generally) are unlikely to provide or fund them.

This issue can be considered in terms of 'appropriate quality' and 'sustainable quality'. While, in theory, 'good' (urban) design should add value to property development, Rowley (1998, p. 172) suggests that, in the UK at least, the notion that 'better buildings mean better business' is both new and debatable:

> The dominant attitude in private-property decision making is still the 'appropriate' quality view: this holds that high-quality development, however defined, is unnecessary so long as there is some sort of market for the development at a lower standard; which may be easier to maintain, at least in the short-term; which may demand less skill and care to produce; and which, it is assumed, can be delivered at a lower initial cost . . . The opposing attitude is

> that high quality helps generate long-term commercial success: this is termed the 'sustainable' quality view.

If a higher quality building is produced than occupiers and investors are prepared to pay for, the extra costs incurred must be met by the developer. In short, there is over-specification. Prudent and profit-maximising developers therefore attempt to match closely the quality sought by the consumer, with the quality of the product supplied: in other words, developers build developments at sufficient or appropriate levels of quality where 'sufficient' and 'appropriate' are judged against short-term criteria. In principle, the higher the specifications, the greater the risk that buyers cannot be found at the price required to cover the additional costs (Rowley et al., 1996).

This argument, however, assumes that there is a cost involved in producing higher quality developments. While this may be true where better 'design' is seen primarily as a function of higher specification or better quality materials, it is less true where it is seen in terms of, for example, better layouts and configurations of buildings and spaces (i.e. those that have better links and connections with the surrounding context). In this respect, better urban design may involve no additional costs and may add value (Carmona et al., 2001).

The urban designer's role

Given the prevalence of producer–consumer gaps and the structural estrangement of developers (producers) and users (consumers) in the development process, it is necessary to look more closely at the producer side, and in particular at the urban designer's role within it. In practice, there is usually no single producer: the 'producer' side typically consists of a number of actors with differing objectives. While Tables 10.2 and 10.3 summarise how development actor's motivations vary, McGlynn's (1993) powergram illustrates the powers of the various actors (see Figure 10.3). She draws basic distinctions between actors who can exercise *power* to initiate or control development; those with a legal or contractual *responsibility* towards some aspect of development, and those with an interest or *influence* in the process.

Although broad brush, the powergram graphically illustrates how power is concentrated among those actors (i.e. developers and funders) able to

| Actors | Suppliers | | Producers | | | | | Consumers |
| Elements of the built environment | Land owner | Funder | Developer | Local authority | | Architects | Urban designers | Everyday users |
				Planners	Highway engineers			
Street pattern	−	−	○	○	●	−	○	○
Blocks	−	−	−	−	−	−	○	−
Plots - subdivision & amalgamation	●	●	●	○ (in U.K.)	−	−	○	−
Land/building use	●	●	●	●	⊕	○	○	○
Building form - height/mass	−	●	●	●	−	⊕	○	○
- orientation to public space	−	−	○	⊕	−	−	○	○
- elevations	−	○	○	●	−	⊕	○	○
- elements of construction (details/materials)	−	○	●	⊕	−	⊕	○	○

KEY: ● Power — either to initiate or control
⊕ Responsibility — legislative or contractual
○ Interest/influence — by argument or participation only
− No obvious interest

FIGURE 10.3
McGlynn's powergram (source: McGlynn and Murrain, 1994)

initiate and control development directly. It also shows the wide-ranging interest of designers (but also their lack of any real power to initiate or control development), and the lack of power wielded by the users of development, including the local community. Actors on the right-hand side of the powergram (designers and users) therefore rely primarily on argumentation, alliances and participation to influence the process.

The powergram also shows the apparent correspondence between the objectives of the designer and those of users and the general public. Urban designers are therefore indirectly charged with representing users' and the general public's views within the producer side of the development process. In looking more closely at the designer's role, Bentley (1999) suggests a series of metaphors – 'heroic form-giver', 'master and servant', 'market signals', and 'battlefield' – to describe the relationship between actors.

(i) Heroic form-giver
This suggests that the form of a development is generated through the creative efforts of particular actors (e.g. architects) and that built environment professionals are the main agents in shaping urban space. Bentley (p. 30) argues that this is a 'powerful myth', which overstates the role of designers, exposing them to criticism for developments (or aspects of development) that are beyond their

control. The overstating of the role played by architects and other professionals has been termed a 'fetishising' of design (Dickens, 1980), whereby the focus on 'buildings' and 'architects' radically understates the broader context of social and economic processes surrounding the urban environment's production.

(ii) Master and servant
This suggests that development form is determined by power plays between the various actors in which those with the most power can issue orders to those with less: that is, developers make the main decisions, for which designers merely provide 'packaging'. It nevertheless understates the role of designers and other built environment professions. Bentley (p. 32) suggests the prevalence of this idea may be because it enables less powerful actors to adopt positions of resignation or compliance, simply doing the developer's bidding rather than struggling to achieve better outcomes.

(iii) Market signals
This suggests that, rather than being forced into line, resource-poor actors passively respond to market signals: while they have the scope to disagree, they appreciate who is paying their salaries/fees, and do their bidding without question. For Bentley, this understates or ignores the practical difficulties of controlling the development 'team'

and the inherent uncertainty in the development process. Where complex knowledge is used, detailed control of experts requires equally well-qualified controllers. As the transaction costs of such controls and supervision are frequently prohibitive, professional autonomy is unavoidable and is not necessarily checked by actors knowing 'on which side their bread is buttered'. Bentley (p. 35) also alludes to problems arising from members of the development/design team having incentives to emphasise and differentiate their contributions, working according to their own value-systems – architects stressing the 'art' dimension, surveyors the 'financial' dimension – and having objectives that may conflict with those of their clients. In the latter case, it is even more difficult for the developer to exercise close control. Designers can act not only against the interest of their client, but also against the interests of society at large. Concluding that this situation seems fraught with potential disaster for all concerned – clients/developers do not have the knowledge to design buildings themselves, while their professional advisers are difficult to control – Bentley (p. 36) suggests the situation is better conceived as a 'battlefield' than as a 'friendly and bustling' market place.

(iv) The battlefield

This suggests that actors negotiate, plot and scheme to achieve the development form they want. For Bentley, this is the most convincing metaphor. The opportunity space for negotiation is set by internal and external constraints – or 'rules' – on the development actors. For private sector developers, the 'rules' relate to budget constraints, appropriate rewards and the amount of risk to be incurred: externally enforced through sanctions such as bankruptcy, such rules are not optional and cannot simply be ignored. The various webs of rules create 'fields of opportunity' within which all actors operate. In negotiating effectively, the difficulty lies in knowing the limits of other actors' opportunity fields. A key question for the designer, for example, is how far developers can be pushed. Bentley (p. 39) argues that the more actors understand other actors' opportunity fields (e.g. if designers understand financial feasibility calculations), the more effectively they can target their own resources.

Through the need for planning/development consent, both the designer's and the developer's opportunity space will be externally constrained by public sector requirements. Some designers working for developers acknowledge support from planning and public authorities in terms of changing developer's attitudes and expanding the field for design. It has also been argued that, without the constraints provided by the context, budget, policy framework, etc., there is little for designers to respond to in generating design ideas. Kevin Lynch (1972, p. 38) argued that: 'Designers are aware that it is easier to plan where there are some commitments than it is when the situation is completely open . . . The fixed characteristics restrict the range of possible solutions and therefore ease the agony of the design search.'

Internally, the client's (developer's) brief sets the initial agenda and broad parameters for design. Providing the starting point for discussion and negotiation, it contains some elements that are negotiable and others that are not. Designers may have a great deal of freedom to interpret the brief or, alternatively, may be asked merely for 'packaging' or 'styling' (i.e. because all the fundamental design decisions have been made according to a preset formula or design brief or because the design exercise consists of laying out standard units. Discussing the phenomenon of 'developers' vernacular', Rabinowitz (1996, pp. 34–6) observed how significant design decisions were often made before projects reached the designer, and that because they had been shown to 'work' and were based on the 'needs of the market place', the more prescriptive parameters in the client's brief were neither 'arbitrary nor capricious'. Such approaches constrain the ability of designers to respond to the local context, and frequently result in formulaic and standardised designs unrelated to the locale. In considering fields of opportunity, there is value in designers attempting to extend the accepted field for design. It is by extending the field of opportunity that innovation occurs. If successful, it is incorporated into, and extends, mainstream practice.

In discussing how architects negotiate with clients/developers about design – and implicitly, therefore, about design quality – Bentley (p. 37) identifies three types of power that designers deploy:

* through knowledge and expertise, which is a product of their learning, research, professional experience, and awareness of precedents;
* through their reputation, which is why they have been hired, and which endows them with 'cultural capital';

- through initiative, because it is usually only 'designers' who make proposals for physical designs.

Each type involves power to influence, rather than compel, outcomes. In essence, designers need to argue that good design is in developers' self-interest: providing a higher quality product should have financial benefits for the developer and, indeed, benefits to other actors (see Carmona et al., 2001, p. 29) (Table 10.4). It may, for example, enable higher returns (i.e. the design of a higher quality housing development without incurring extra cost improves the cost/value balance, allowing units to be sold for a higher price and/or more quickly). Good design exploits a site's positive features, or minimises the effect of negative ones. It may also convince the planning authority of the acceptability of a greater volume of development on the site than had originally been envisaged (Table 10.4).

Urban design quality

Improvements in the quality of individual developments are a necessary but not sufficient condition for 'good' urban design. Developers responding to the needs of occupiers and investors can still exclude the needs of the general public and of society at large. Segregated housing estates – in extreme form, gated communities – and inward-focused developments provide what purchasers and occupiers purportedly want, but contribute little to the public realm. Such developments lack connections to and integration with the local context.

From an urban design perspective, it can be argued that the process and product of development is often flawed because it is essentially concerned with individual developments rather than the creation of places. Sudjic (1992, pp. 44–5), for example, observes how developers are considered to have no interests in the public realm and, instead, concentrate on 'creating manageable chunks of development' – an office building, shopping centre, or industrial park. In Christopher Alexander's terms, these developments are 'objects' rather than 'relationships'. This can be seen as an inevitable outcome of market-driven development and reiterates the role of urban design as a means of joining up otherwise fragmented environments. As discussed in Chapter 1, for example, Sternberg (2000, p. 275) argues that: 'Operating according to an impersonal and autonomous logic, real estate markets slice up and sub-divide the urban environment into self-contained compartments, generating cities that are incoherent and fragmented.'

The Project for Public Space (www.pps.org, accessed December 2001) argues that the typical development process is flawed because it focuses on 'projects' and 'disciplines'. As a result:

- Its goals are narrowly defined.
- It is only capable of addressing superficial design and superficial political issues.
- Its scope and assessment are defined by the boundaries of disciplines.
- It imposes an external value system.
- It relies on professionals and 'experts'.
- It is expensive and is funded by government, developers, corporations, etc.
- It sets up the community to resist changes.
- Its solutions are centred around static design and are unresponsive to usage.
- It results in a limited experience of place, and limited civic engagement in the public realm.

The essential need is for ways of encouraging – or compelling – developers to see their development in the wider context, to look across site boundaries, and to contribute to the making of places. The Project for Public Space (2001), for example, suggests recasting the development process to focus on 'places' and 'communities'. It claims that such a development process would:

- Grow out of a place and its potential for civic engagement.
- Allow communities to articulate their aspirations, needs and priorities.
- Provide a compelling shared vision that would attract partners, money and creative solutions.
- Encourage communities to work collaboratively and effectively with professionals.
- Design would become a secondary tool to support the desired uses.
- Solutions would be flexible and build on existing successes.
- Commitment would grow as citizens are empowered to actively shape their public realm.

Managing, guiding or controlling the development process can be done in ways that both recognise the collective interest and exploit the self-interest of developers. Buildings are interdependent assets, and developers typically attempt to benefit from a

TABLE 10.4
Beneficiaries of value in urban design

STAKEHOLDERS	SHORT-TERM VALUE	LONG-TERM VALUE
Landowners	• Potential for increased land values	
Funders (short-term)	• Potential for greater security of investment depending on market	
Developers	• Quicker permissions • Increased public support • Higher sales values • Distinctiveness • Increased funding potential • Allows difficult sites to be tackled	• Better reputation • Future collaborations more likely
Design professionals	• Increased workload and repeat commissions for high quality, stable clients	• Enhanced professional reputation
Investors (long-term)	• Higher rental returns • Increased asset value • Reduced running costs • Competitive investment edge	• Maintenance of value/income • Reduced maintenance costs • Better resale values • Higher quality, longer-term tenants
Managing agents		• Easier maintenance if high quality materials
Occupiers		• Happier workforce • Better productivity • Increased business confidence • Fewer disruptive moves • Greater accessibility to other uses/facilities • Reduced security expenditure • Increased occupier prestige • Reduced running costs
Public interests	• Regenerative potential • Reduced public/private discord	• Reduced public expenditure • More time for positive planning • Increased economic viability for neighbouring uses/development opportunities • Increased local tax revenue • More sustainable environment
Community interests		• Better security and less crime • Increased cultural vitality • Less pollution • Less stress • Better quality of life • More equitable/accessible environment • Greater civic pride • Reinforced sense of place • Higher property prices

(Source: adapted from Carmona et al., 2001, p. 29).

neighbourhood's positive externalities (e.g. pedestrian flows or particular views) and avoid negative ones (e.g. poor views, noise). In practice, however, they have often been more concerned about the negative externalities, and have created inward-focused developments where the milieu is amenable to control. Such developments detract from their context, and reduce its value – providing a justification for further inward-focused developments and engendering a vicious spiral where each succeeding increment of development further reduces the incentive for successive developments to contribute to that context. If urban design is to be a process of making better places, this spiral must be arrested and reversed. If there is to be a virtuous circle, then every increment of development must contribute to a greater whole. For this to come about, developers have to respect and have confidence in the context, and in the rules that control development in that area, or in some kind of self-binding set of 'rules'. This happened to a degree in the past through the limitations of available building materials and construction techniques and the limited power to initiate development. This is also what, in effect, Alexander *et al.* proposed in their *A New Theory of Urban Design* (1987) (see Chapter 9).

While there may be collective benefits in creating a positive context and outward-oriented developments that benefit from and enhance their context, individual developers may not be willing to do this. The neighbourhood effect works in both directions: it does not, for example, benefit any individual property owner to improve their property (and, thereby, the context) unless all other property owners do the same. In essence, there is a collective action problem, whereby individuals acting in what they perceive to be their own self-interest produce an outcome that is worse for everyone.

Collective action problems can be resolved through the coercive powers of a higher authority (the state or, in some circumstances, the landowner) or through co-operative action. There are at least three ways to achieve the necessary co-ordination and to ensure that – in principle – all increments of development contribute to a larger whole:

1. Where there is a single overarching landownership, the landowner can create and impose a master plan, development framework, or development code (see Chapter 11) to be followed by the landowner undertaking development, or by developers purchasing interests in the land (i.e. through restrictive covenants attached to the sale of the land). This would typically deal with issues of place making, overall coherence and the relation between the parts and the whole, and with problems at the transition between the area of development and the wider local context.

2. A public authority can perform the same role in terms of establishing a master plan, development framework, or development code, which would – by private agreement or through statutory powers – be binding on all developers operating in the locality. In this instance, the public authority has a leading and co-ordinating role and, in principle, acts in the collective interest. It may also develop the master plan in consultation or collaboration with local stakeholders.

3. Rather than 'command and control' models, the third model is more collaborative and voluntary. Various developers, landowners, community groups and other stakeholders come together and agree a 'vision', a master plan, development framework, development code, etc., and the method of realising it, which would be binding on all.

These are ideal situations, however – not least because it is rarely possible to get all (potential) developers and (potential) stakeholders together at the same time, or to achieve a mutually beneficial consensus. In each case, the plan or vision is not intended to be immutable. Inevitably it is made at one point in time, and reviewed/revised later. The advantages of master plans, development frameworks or development codes are to ensure and enhance the composite value of all investments in the area and to reduce development risk. These also provide incentives for developers to accept the necessary constraints on their freedom of operation. To be effective, urban design frameworks also need some degree of consensus about what constitutes a 'good' place, and a commitment to achieving it. Achieving quality in these respects is probably more difficult than implementing the organisational mechanisms. This also provides a justification for public intervention into the private development process (see Chapter 11).

Public authorities can undertake other actions to help develop a sense of confidence and certainty in a locality. These include:

- *Investing in flagship projects and/or subsidising development*: Flagship projects are usually large-scale development schemes, and generally have three overlapping purposes: to act as demonstration projects showing, for example, the commercial success of that use in that location or, more generally, of the location itself; to act as exemplar projects setting standards for subsequent developments; and/or by their scale, to create a critical mass of development, or a particular type of development, within the area.

- *Investing in area-based improvements*: Although key initial and demonstration projects are necessary, revitalisation frequently needs to be encouraged on a wider basis, with measures to improve the area on a comprehensive rather than piecemeal basis – the intention being to create a widespread positive neighbourhood effect. Environmental improvements might be crucially important in changing the image of an area. These measures indicate a commitment to the area and usually form the basis for 'place marketing' and other promotional campaigns.
- *Investing in infrastructure improvements*: The provision, pattern and design of new infrastructure can often establish design intentions, principles and standards (Figure 10.4). This was the essence of David Gosling's unrealised

proposals for the Isle of Dogs, in London's Docklands, which were intended to exploit the potential of the Greenwich Axis as an organising device for new infrastructure and, thereafter, new development (see Gosling and Maitland, 1984, pp. 147–51).

CONCLUSION

Discussion in this chapter has included the land and property development process; development roles and actors and their interrelation; and the issue of development quality. In the absence of mechanisms that compel better quality urban design, developers (and, more generally, the producer side of the development process) will only be convinced to act where it can be demonstrated that investment in quality will be compensated by additional value. As argued above, in contrast to higher architectural quality and better quality materials, better urban design may involve no additional costs. Research in the UK has shown – albeit tentatively – the link between better urban design and higher value and investment returns (Carmona *et al.*, 2001). Research in the USA (Vandell and Lane, 1989; Eppli and Tu, 1999), Europe (Garcia Almerall *et al.*, 1999) and

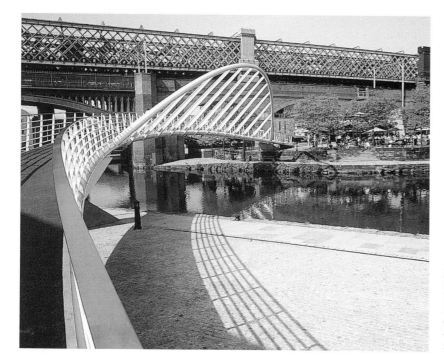

FIGURE 10.4
Castlefields, Manchester, UK. The provision of new infrastructure elements can enhance character and set design standards

Australia (Property Council of Australia, 1999) supports this finding. The UK research indicated ten key ways in which better quality design could add value to development:

- In higher returns on investments (good rental returns and enhanced capital values).
- In establishing new markets that may not have previously existed (i.e. for city centre living) and opening up new areas by differentiating products and raising their prestige.
- By responding to a clear occupier demand that also helps to attract investment.
- By helping to deliver more lettable area (higher densities) on sites.
- By reducing management, maintenance, energy and security costs.

- In more productive and contented workforces.
- By supporting the 'life-giving' mixed-use elements in developments.
- By opening up new investment opportunities, raising confidence in development opportunities, and attracting public sector grant funding.
- By creating an economic regeneration and place-marketing dividend.
- By delivering viable planning gain, and reducing the burden on the public purse of improving poor quality urban design. (Carmona *et al.*, 2001)

Complementing the discussion in this chapter, the next chapter discusses the public sector role in securing and maintaining high quality environments.

11

The control process

INTRODUCTION

This chapter concerns the public sector's role in securing and maintaining high quality environments. It examines how public agencies use a range of statutory powers not only to provide a quality threshold over which development proposals must pass, but also to guide, encourage and enable appropriate development, and to work towards the enhancement of the public realm. In reviewing the range of mechanisms available to public authorities, particular reference is made to a major source of urban design action, that of public sector design control/review. The public sector's role is much more than that of 'controlling' or 'guiding' design and development. In its various forms, it has the potential to influence urban quality through a wide range of statutory and non-statutory functions (see Box 11.1). These enable the public sector to be an important contributor to the quality of the built environment both in its own right and by influencing,

and requiring high quality development from the private sector. A study of London's urban environment expressed these public sector activities as 'policies and processes', 'maintaining influences' and 'enabling factors' (Figure 11.1).

Kevin Lynch (1976, pp. 41–55) identified four modes of action for public authorities: 'diagnosis' (appraisal); 'policy'; 'design'; and 'regulation'. Two further modes can be added – 'education and participation'; and 'management' (Rowley, 1994, p. 189). These six modes are used to organise this chapter. Although relating particularly well to public sector actions in urban design, most of these modes of action also relate directly to private sector activity. Most of the following discussion on appraisal, design and participation, for example, is relevant to urban design throughout the public and private sectors. Before discussing the detail of the public sector's role, it is necessary briefly to address the broader question of the public sector's legitimacy in seeking to intervene.

BOX 11.1 – ACTIONS PERFORMED BY PUBLIC SECTOR

- Urban management and maintenance.
- Town centre management.
- Conservation activity.
- Land use allocation (zoning).
- Design control/review.
- Design guidance, policy and briefing.
- Advertisement control.
- Urban regeneration and grant making.
- Transport management, investment and planning.
- Parking control.
- Public education.

- Image-building and promotion.
- Local environmental action such as Local Agenda 21.
- Land reclamation.
- Public involvement and participation.
- Open space and recreational resources.
- Social housing funding and/or provision.
- Public order management and crime control.
- Partnership and joint venture schemes.
- Public building and demonstration projects.
- Building/development permits/control.
- Cultural events and public art.

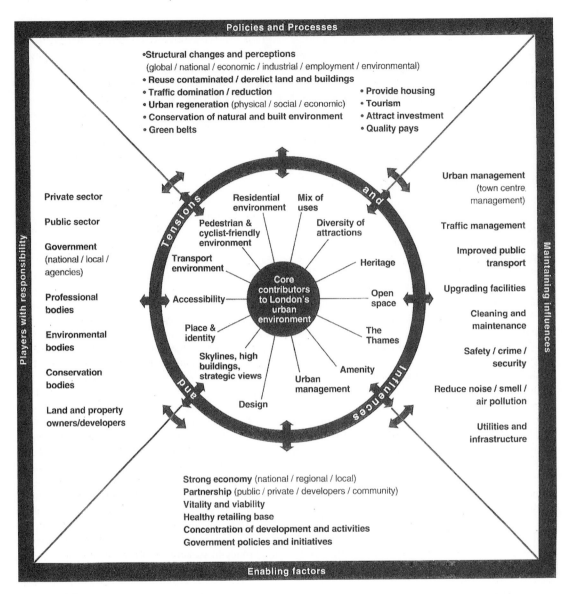

FIGURE 11.1
Core contributors to the quality of London's urban environment. The diagram highlights the relationships between public agencies and the private sector, as well as the core qualities each aims to influence (source: Government Office for London, 1996)

PUBLIC SECTOR INTERVENTION

Although public intervention and regulation of development might seem an appropriate response to the dysfunction of (land and property) markets that results in poor quality design and development, this is to assume that the solution to imperfect markets is (perfect) government. However, just as markets fail, so do governments. The presumption that 'good' design guidance and control automatically provides 'good' design must therefore be treated with caution and scepticism. The situation is complex and raises fundamental questions about the state's role in a market economy. As some forms of public sector intervention and regulation are inevitable – there is no such thing as a 'free' market – debate is about what *type* of intervention, and *how* intervention occurs. It is crucially important, for example, for urban designers to understand where public sector interventions into the private sector development process can be most effective (i.e. typically before or during the design stage rather than after it). Rather than controls for the sake of controls, the need is for 'smart' controls. John Punter (1998, p. 138), for example, highlights how public sector control in the UK has changed from an inherently negative concern with *design control* to a more positive concern for *design quality*. He argues that the traditional view of design has been of a static 'end product' (a piece of built form) rather than a dynamic process (creative problem-solving) through which the built form is produced. When considered as a process, Punter argues that notions of design 'control' by a planning authority are 'clearly problematic'. In the UK, government advice has consistently stressed that the chief responsibility for design quality rests with the client and the designer, and the notion of design 'control' is giving way to that of a collective pursuit of quality. The need, therefore, is for controls and interventions that demonstrate understanding and appreciation of development and design as processes (see Chapter 3).

Those proposing and implementing urban design controls or guidelines need a clear idea of the intended outcomes, otherwise the policies and guidelines will operate in a vacuum. This requires either a *vision* of what good urban form/urban design is or the *means* (i.e. the cognitive skills/principles) to recognise it when it is presented. In noting how practice has changed in the US, Duany *et al.* (2000, p. 177) note how 'some cities are emerging from a prolonged crisis of confidence in which they abdicated initiative to market forces rather than providing a predictable environment for the market to thrive in'.

Before there can be urban design controls or guidelines, urban design practitioners – and perhaps some politicians – operating inside and around the public sector, must win the political arguments and persuade politicians and other decision-makers that concern for design quality is beneficial and worthwhile. If they are to have any impact at all, those with the power to make a difference – the developers, investors and occupiers – must also be persuaded of the benefits of investing in good design (see Chapter 10). Given their role in influencing urban quality, practitioners working in the public sector, and politicians, need

both a better-developed understanding of urban design and to move from being unknowing to become knowing urban designers. Urban design practitioners therefore have an important role not just as advocates but also as educators.

Carmona (2001, p. 132) argues that the priority given to design by public authorities is evident in four key ways: through the development of design criteria considered relevant to the public interest and appropriate for guidance and control; through responses to, and concern for, local context; through the value placed on the different mechanisms used to control design; and through the resources devoted to design and to the process of securing better quality environments. Taken together, these factors largely define an authority's approach to design. The more sophisticated authorities will typically have:

- *A broad conception of design*, extending beyond 'aesthetics' and basic 'amenity' considerations, to include a concern for environmental quality that encompasses urban design and sustainability – economic, social and environmental.
- *An approach to design informed by context*, based on appraisal of areas and sites and on public consultation and/or participation.
- *An integrated hierarchy of design guidance* extending from the strategic city/district scale (or beyond), to area-specific guidance for large-scale regeneration, conservation or development projects, to design guidance for particular sites and development opportunities.
- *An urban design team* with the means and capabilities to engage in the design process by preparing proactive policy/guidance frameworks and design briefs to identify and guide development opportunities, and to respond positively to development proposals (Carmona, 2001, pp. 132–66).

A number of cities – Birmingham, Portland, Barcelona, Amsterdam – already have such approaches, and others are beginning to develop them. A range of factors can, however, undermine local initiative. These include lack of political will to engage in design concerns (nationally and locally); the state of local investment and property markets; innate 'conservatism' and anti-development attitudes of local communities; incapacity of the historic fabric to accommodate change; lack of skilled designers (particularly those with urban design expertise); and unwillingness on the part of developers and investors to consider issues of, and invest in, design quality.

DIAGNOSIS AND APPRAISAL

In Chapter 3, the nature of urban design as a process was discussed and related to the key stages of an integrated model of design process: setting goals; analysis; visioning; synthesis and prediction; decision-making; and evaluation. Appraisal can be considered as both the start (i.e. analysis) and the end (i.e. evaluation) of the design process. It sets the initial parameters from which design proposals or policies are developed and feeds back into the process as outcomes are evaluated.

Universal or meta-principles of urban design provide a framework for action, with each site or locality possessing its own unique set of qualities, opportunities and threats. Private sector developments and public sector interventions begin with appraisal as the starting point for the generation of design proposals. For the public sector, a systematic analysis of context has an extra dimension because the wide range of scales at which public authorities operate – district/region-wide, area-wide and site-specific – necessitates differing types of analysis. For all but the largest private sector developments, analysis generally remains at the site-specific scale.

In most countries, public authorities emphasise the importance of respecting the local context. In the UK, for example, central government design advice has consistently emphasised the need to evaluate development proposals by reference to their surroundings. The intangible as well as the more tangible qualities of place should – where possible – be the subject of appraisal at the district/region-wide, area-wide, and site-specific scales. Punter and Carmona (1997, pp. 117–19) identify the appraisal methods most frequently used by planning authorities:

- Townscape analysis and notations, such as those developed by Gordon Cullen to highlight the visual and perceptual character of place.
- Pedestrian behaviour, accessibility and traffic movement studies.
- Surveys of public perceptions and the meanings attached to places, including Lynch-style legibility analysis.
- Historical and morphological analysis of settlements, including figure-ground studies.

- Environmental audits and ecological and environmental inventories, combining visual analysis with quantitative and qualitative environmental measures.
- SWOT analyses of an area, focusing on prescription rather than simply description.

Appraisal at the district/region-wide scale

Appraisal at this scale ranges from evaluating the broad character of the underlying natural landscape, through identifying distinctive areas of towns and cities (e.g. neighbourhoods or quarters), to understanding the complex capital web and movement patterns of urban areas. These provide means to understand urban growth patterns, and to relate new development to existing urban areas in a sustainable fashion (Figure 11.2).

Such large-scale spatial analysis happens most frequently and with greatest sophistication with regard to natural (rural) landscapes. One of the largest identified 181 landscape character zones in England, each with its own detailed nature conservation, landscape character and ecological character descriptions (Countryside Commission & English Nature, 1997). On a smaller, but still regional, scale, such analysis has been advocated by a number of influential urban design researchers (e.g. Lynch, 1976; Hough, 1984).

In many parts of Europe – Germany in particular – landscape/ ecological analysis now forms the basis for strategic design and planning decision-making. This is often directed towards identifying the area's 'landscape capacity' (i.e. the degree of modification before it is unacceptably damaged), its sensitivity and the potential for new development to strengthen positive attributes and ameliorate negative ones. The capacity of settlements to accommodate development in a manner that enhances the established character and ensures that growth occurs in a sustainable fashion, should also be a fundamental part of strategic design decision-making.

As tensions between the need for new development and the preservation of established character occur most acutely in historic urban contexts, it is here that work on urban capacity points out a possible new direction for large-scale spatial analysis. In Chester (UK), for example, much of the city and its surrounding landscape are of significant conservation importance, making new development extremely challenging, and necessitating a

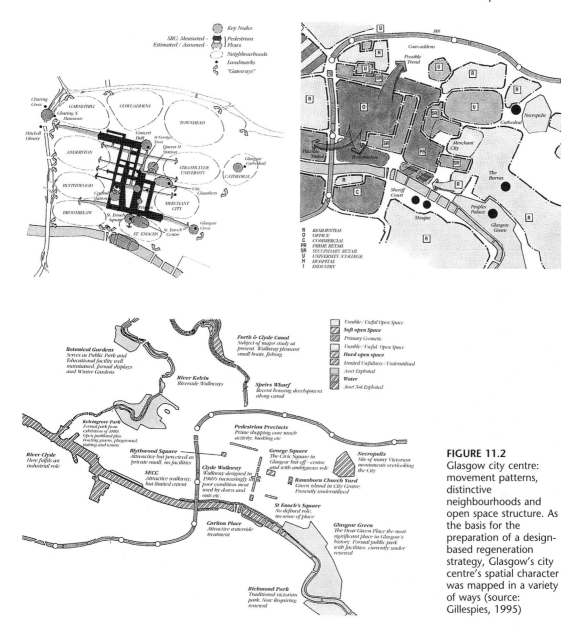

FIGURE 11.2
Glasgow city centre: movement patterns, distinctive neighbourhoods and open space structure. As the basis for the preparation of a design-based regeneration strategy, Glasgow's city centre's spatial character was mapped in a variety of ways (source: Gillespies, 1995)

strategic conservation-led approach to growth. Linking such a strategy to broader sustainable objectives indicated the necessity of examining the city's carrying capacity and led to a city-wide assessment encompassing analysis of physical, ecological and perceptual capacity (Arup Economics and Planning, 1995, pp. 14–18) (Figure 11.3). The analysis formed part of a broader drive to develop strategic guidelines for development.

Area-wide appraisal

At this scale, appraisal often precedes the formulation of design policies and guidance. It is, however, frequently expensive, time-consuming, dependent on skilled manpower (often in short supply in the public sector), and remains generalised in nature. It is also most comprehensively undertaken in historic (designated) areas.

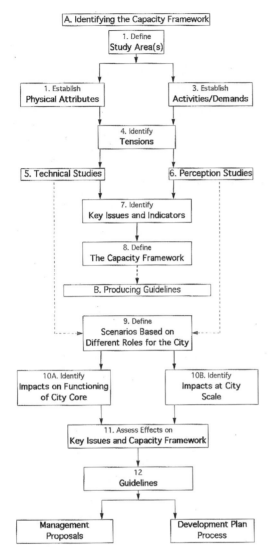

FIGURE 11.3
Methodology for the Chester Environmental Capacity Study (source: Arup Economics and Planning, 1995)

While, in part, this reflects the increased scope for public sector intervention in such areas, it also reflects the more comprehensive guidance available to practitioners. English Heritage (1997), for example, the body charged with guiding and administering much of the conservation legislation in England – regards appraisal as the basis for conservation and planning action and offers a checklist to guide such analysis (Box 11.2). Despite approaching appraisal from a historic and predominantly visual perspective, the checklist provides a clear and concise articulation of character. The objective for urban designers is to develop their own conception based on their knowledge of the relevant issues in an area and the skills and resources available to undertake analysis. The approach might, for example, include analysis of the morphological, visual, perceptual, social, functional, political and economic contexts.

In the UK, to provide a systematic approach to area appraisal, the Urban Design Alliance created 'Placecheck' (www.placecheck.com), a method of assessing the qualities of a place, showing what improvements are needed, and focusing on people working together to achieve them. It encourages local groups (including local authorities) to come together to ask a series of questions about their city, neighbourhood or street, and to record the answers by a variety of methods including photographs, maps, plans, diagrams, notes, sketches and video. The aim is to develop a better understanding and appreciation of places and to provide a prompt for the production of positive forms of guidance such as urban design frameworks, codes, briefs, etc.

Initially, three key questions are asked: What do you like about this place?; What do you dislike about it?; What needs to be improved? Fifteen more specific questions then focus on who needs to be involved in improving the place, and how it is used and experienced:

The people
- Who needs to be involved in improving the place?
- What resources are available locally to help get involved?
- What other methods might we use to develop our ideas about improvement?
- How can we make the most of other programmes and resources?
- How can we raise our sights?
- What other initiatives could improve the place?

The place
- How can we make this a special place?
- How can we make this a greener place?
- How can the streets and public spaces be made safer and more pleasant for people on foot?
- How else can public spaces be improved?
- How can the place be made more welcoming and easier for people to find their way around?
- How can the place be made adaptable to change in the future?

BOX 11.2 – CHECKLIST FOR ASSESSING CHARACTER

(source: adapted from English Heritage, 1997)

Location and population	Set the area within the context of the wider settlement, and understand how the area's social profile informs its character.
Origins and development of area	Establish how the area has grown and evolved, particularly by tracing its morphological lineage.
Prevailing and former uses within area	Understand how uses have moulded the character of an area, with regard to form and layout of the buildings and spaces, and to the public realm's social characteristics.
Area's archaeological significance	Expert assessment may be desirable to ensure proper regard is paid to underlying archaeology.
Architectural and historic qualities of buildings	Refer to dominant architectural styles or building traditions, and to groups of buildings making a special contribution to character or roofscape.
Contribution of unlisted buildings	Ensure that buildings without statutory protection in their own right are still recognised for the contribution (or detraction) they make to the area's character.
Character and relationship of spaces within area	Ensure that regard is given to the relationship between public and private space, seen as a means of defining townscape; visual characteristics (particularly means of enclosure); and the ways in which spaces function and are used.
Prevalent and traditional building materials, textures, colours and details	Detail on buildings, floorscape street furniture, etc., often provides much of the visual interest in an area and makes a major contribution to establishing local distinctiveness.
Contribution of green spaces, trees and other natural landscape features	Recognise the vital part the natural and man-made green environment makes to the character of urban areas.
Area's setting and relation to its surroundings	Have regard to the landscape/townscape context, particularly the topography, views, and vistas to countryside or landmarks.
Extent of loss, intrusion or damage to area	Negative features or significant threats often have as great an impact on character as positive ones.
Existence of any neutral areas	Ensure that all opportunities for enhancement are recognised, including ones for contemporary design.

- How can better use be made of resources?
- What can be done to make the most of public transport?
- How can routes be better connected? (Cowan, 2001b, p. 11)

These questions are broken down into over one hundred further questions to provide additional prompts to thinking. Intended to be used in a variety of ways, the approach has been widely tested through a series of pilot projects. A less sophisticated form of analysis – the SWOT analysis – can also be used to similar effect. SWOTs involve brainstorming and recording a place's strengths and weaknesses, the opportunities that could be exploited, and the likely threats. The value of Placecheck and SWOT techniques is that they move beyond analysis to identify potential courses of actions. Both techniques are also appropriate at the site-specific scale.

Site-specific appraisal

In the private and public sectors, site-specific appraisal is a prerequisite for design and development. Lynch and Hack (1984) argued that each context and study inevitably requires the adoption of its own approach to appraisal in order to

BOX 11.3 – CHECKLIST FOR SITE-SPECIFIC APPRAISAL

(source: adapted from Chapman and Larkham, 1994, p. 44)

- *Record general impressions of the site*: e.g. existing sense of place; use notes, sketches, plans, photographs to record information including legibility.
- *Record site's physical characteristics*: e.g. site dimensions/area, features, boundaries, slopes, ground conditions, drainage and water resources, trees and vegetation, ecology, buildings and other features.
- *Examine relationships between site* and *surroundings*: e.g. land uses, roads and footpaths, public transport nodes and routes, local facilities and services and other infrastructure.
- *Consider environmental factors affecting the site*: e.g.,orientation, sunlight/daylight, climate, microclimate, prevailing winds, shade/shelter, exposure, pollution, noise, fumes, smells.
- *Assess visual* and *spatial characteristics*: e.g. views, vistas, panoramas, attractive features or buildings, eyesores, quality of townscapes and surrounding spaces, landmarks, edges, nodes, gateways, spatial sequences.
- *Note any danger signals*: e.g. subsidence, land-slips, poorly drained or marshy ground, fly-tipping, vandalism, incompatible activities or adjacent uses, sense of security.
- *Observe human behaviour*: e.g. desire lines, behaviour settings, general atmosphere, gathering places and activity centres.
- *Consider area's background* and *history*: e.g. local and regional materials, traditions, styles, details, prevailing architectural and urban design context, urban grain and archaeological significance.
- *Assess existing mix of uses*: e.g. variety, on site, around site, contribution to vitality.
- *Research statutory* and *legal constraints*: e.g. ownership, rights of way, planning status (policies and guidelines), planning conditions, covenants, statuary undertaker's services.
- *Use a SWOT analysis*: can provide the starting point for design appraisal and brief writing, focusing attention on prescription as well as description.

site-specific appraisal should be to identify both those features worthy of protection, and the potential for improvement, and, as a result, to define principles and proposals that respect or ameliorate these qualities. Chapman and Larkham (1994, p. 44) provide a useful appraisal checklist (Box 11.3). Further techniques for site/area appraisal through graphic representations are discussed in Chapter 12. More extensive discussions of appraisal can be found in the *Urban Design Compendium* (Llewelyn-Davies, 2000, pp. 18–30) and *By Design* (DETR/CABE, 2000, pp. 36–40).

POLICY, REGULATION AND DESIGN

Reflecting their joint emphasis (in the public sector context) on guiding and controlling the design of development, these three modes of action can be combined. As direct public sector investment in the creation of new environments is increasingly uncommon, the public sector's role in securing high quality development is often restricted to these functions. Nevertheless, most systems of local governance include extensive urban design powers, usually through interrelated processes of planning, conservation and building control, to ensure that private sector design proposals serve the 'public interest'.

Usually based on restrictions of private property rights, controls on design and development invariably arouse great passions and sometimes controversy. Those who perceive themselves to be most directly affected – designers and developers – often make the most strident case against such forms of control or, somewhat paradoxically, manage to hold the inherently contradictory attitude that design controls should apply to everyone other than themselves. Writing in a US context, Brenda Case Scheer (1994, pp. 3–9) articulated many of the perceived problems with public sector design control/review. She suggests that it is:

- Potentially time-consuming and expensive.
- Easy to manipulate through persuasion, pretty pictures and politics.
- Performed by overworked and inexperienced staff.
- Inefficient at improving the quality of the built environment.
- The only field where lay people are allowed to rule over professionals directly in their area of expertise.

develop concepts based on an understanding of a place's distinctive characteristics, coherent patterns and equilibrium. These may include negative as well as positive characteristics. The aim of

- Grounded in issues of personal rather than public interest, particularly in maintaining property values.
- Violating rights to free speech.
- Rewarding ordinary performance and discouraging extraordinary performance.
- Arbitrary and vague.
- Encouraging judgements that go beyond issues outlined in adopted guidelines.
- Lacking due process (because of the sheer variety of issues and processes of control).
- Failing to acknowledge that there are no rules to create beauty.
- Promoting principles that are abstract and universal, not specific, site-related or meaningful at the community scale.
- Encouraging mimicry and the dilution of the 'authenticity' of place.
- The 'poor cousin' of urban design because of the focus on individual projects at the expense of a broader vision.
- A superficial process.

In another contribution to the same book, Rybczynski (1994, pp. 210–11) outlined why, despite their perceived faults, processes of design control/review continue to command significant commitment in public authorities. Given the frequency and ferocity of debates on the issue, he argued that such processes are 'extremely effective', reflecting both public dissatisfaction with the idea of professional expertise and an apparent lack of consensus in the architectural profession about what constitutes good design. He suggested that review processes should be used to guarantee at least a minimum compatibility between 'new' and 'old', and are of particular value because they reflect and promote deeply held public values. Noting that such values have recently had a 'nostalgic' rather than 'visionary' flavour, he considers this understandable in an era when new building techniques and materials have unleashed a multiplicity of design styles and possibilities, many of which contrast unhappily with established contexts. He concludes that:

Historic experiences of design review in cities as disparate as Sienna, Jerusalem, Berlin, and Washington D.C., suggest that public discipline of building design does not necessarily inhibit the creativity of architects – far from it. What it does have the potential to achieve . . . is a greater quality in the urban environment as a whole. Less emphasis on the soloist and more on ensemble playing will not be a bad thing. (p. 211)

Although the debates will undoubtedly continue, the processes increasingly carry political commitment and, at least in the West, widespread public endorsement.

Policy

Perhaps the most persistent critique of public sector attempts to influence design through statutory processes has been the charge that, as design is essentially a subjective discipline, such attempts are inevitably highly value-laden and prejudiced – or, in Case Sheer's analysis, 'arbitrary, vague and superficial'. In the UK, such charges have long been the focus of debate on the validity of policy-based attempts to influence design quality. Government guidance nevertheless shows the emphasis changing; such that by 1997 the reference to subjectivity had disappeared.

- 1980: 'Planning authorities should recognise that aesthetics is an extremely subjective matter. They should not therefore impose their tastes on developers simply because they believe them to be superior.' (Circular 22/80, para. 19)
- 1992: 'Planning authorities should reject obviously poor designs which are out of scale or character with their surroundings. But aesthetic judgements are to some extent subjective and authorities should not impose their taste on applicants simply because they believe it to be superior.' (PPG1, para. A3)
- 1997: 'Local planning authorities should reject poor design, particularly where their decisions are supported by clear plan policies or supplementary design guidance which has been subjected to public consultation and adopted by the local planning authority.' (PPG1, para. 17)

The change epitomises the evolution of government thinking on design – which has also had the development industry's tentative support (Carmona, 2001, pp. 176–99). The evolution is premised on an acknowledgement that design issues can be addressed objectively only on the basis of preconceived policy and guidance, preferably based on a systematic assessment of character. It demonstrates a move away from a primary emphasis on detailed architectural design (i.e. aesthetics) and towards urban design as the focus for guiding design.

The gradual move towards more 'certain', policy-based approaches to design control coincided with the change to a so-called 'plan-led' planning system in the UK in 1991. This modified the discretionary system of development control, which had offered great flexibility to planning authorities (because they were not bound by the plans they produced), but also greater uncertainty for developers. The plan-led system nevertheless still features a large degree of discretion because the plan is not legally binding and is only one (albeit the most important) of a range of 'material considerations'. The system attempts to balance certainty with flexibility. Unfortunately, however, because of the general lack of sophisticated policy tools and appropriately skilled planning officers (particularly in design), frustration continues because the system often achieves neither (Carmona *et al.*, 2001, p. 75).

The UK government's attempt to treat design on a more objective basis lags behind practice in other parts of Europe and the US. Systems employed in Germany, France, and some American cities, for example, are based on a mixture of legally binding zoning provisions, and design guidance through development plans or design codes. In the US, for example, zoning controls carry the status of police powers. As well as entitlement rights to those wishing to develop, such powers confer on local authorities legally guaranteed means to control development. In the US, zoning controls have significant impact on the urban and architectural design of areas – albeit primarily through controlling the mix of uses, morphological characteristics (e.g. building line, plot depth and width, etc.) and the three-dimensional form of development (e.g. height, setbacks, density, etc.). More fundamental urban design criteria and detailed architectural controls are rarely the subject of zoning.

Zoning can nevertheless prove a somewhat blunt instrument for influencing the quality of urban design. Additional guidance is provided by many municipalities – a well-known and sophisticated example of which is Portland, a city with a reputation as one of America's best planned and designed cities (Punter, 1999). In part, this reputation is derived from a clear (and effective) policy framework combining a spatial design strategy for the city with a set of Central City Fundamental Design Guidelines (see Figure 11.4), which are condensed into a design checklist for assessing all projects designed for the city centre (Portland Bureau of Planning, 1992). The aims of the checklist are to:

Project: ______
Case File No: ______
Date: ______

Applicable	Does Comply	Does not Comply	
			A. PORTLAND PERSONALITY
☐	☐	☐	A1 Integrate the River
☐	☐	☐	A2 Emphasize Portland Themes
☐	☐	☐	A3 Respect the Portland Block Structures
☐	☐	☐	A4 Use Unifying Elements
☐	☐	☐	A5 Enhance, Embelish, and Identify Areas
☐	☐	☐	A6 Re-use/Rehabilitate/Restore Buildings
☐	☐	☐	A7 Establish & Maintain a Sense of Urban Enclosure
☐	☐	☐	A8 Contribute to the Cityscape, The Stage, & the Action
☐	☐	☐	A9 Strengthen Gateways
			B. PEDESTRIAN EMPHASIS
☐	☐	☐	B1 Reinforce & Enhance the Pedestrian System
☐	☐	☐	B2 Protect the Pedestrian
☐	☐	☐	B3 Bridge Pedestrian Obstacles
☐	☐	☐	B4 Provide Shopping & Viewing Places
☐	☐	☐	B5 Make Plazas, Parks, & Open Space Successful
☐	☐	☐	B6 Consider Sunlight, Shadow, Glare, Reflection, Wind & Rain
☐	☐	☐	B7 Integrate Barrier-Free Design
			C. PROJECT DESIGN
☐	☐	☐	C1 Respect Architectural Integrity
☐	☐	☐	C2 Consider View Opportunities
☐	☐	☐	C3 Design for Compatibility
☐	☐	☐	C4 Establish a Graceful Transition between Buildings & Public Spaces
☐	☐	☐	C5 Design Corners that Build Active Intersections
☐	☐	☐	C6 Differentiate the Sidewalk Level of Buildings
☐	☐	☐	C7 Create Flexible Sidewalk Level Spaces
☐	☐	☐	C8 Give Special Attention to Encroachments
☐	☐	☐	C9 Integrate Roofs & Use Rooftops
☐	☐	☐	C10 Promote Permanence & Quality in Development

FIGURE 11.4
Central city fundamental design checklist, Portland, Oregon

- encourage urban design excellence;
- integrate urban design and preservation of heritage into the development process;
- enhance the character of Portland's central districts;
- promote the development of diversity and areas of special character;
- establish an urban design relationship between the central city districts and the centre as a whole;

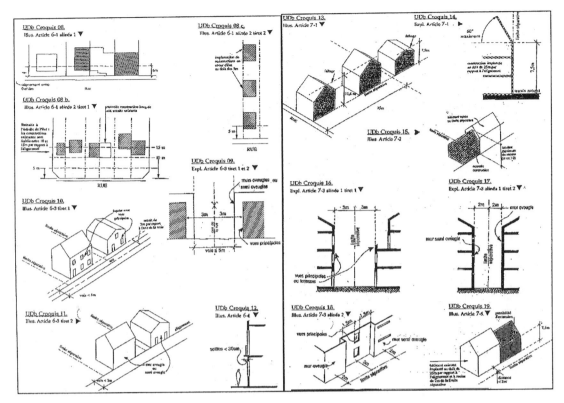

FIGURE 11.5
Ville de Montreuil, Plan d'Occupation des Sols, extract showing three-dimensional siting and height prescriptions
(source: Tranche, 2001)

- provide for a pleasant, rich and diverse pedestrian experience;
- provide for humanisation through promotion of the arts;
- assist in creating a 24-hour central city that is safe, humane and prosperous; and
- assure that new development is at a human scale and relates to the character and scale of areas and of the central city as a whole.

Systems of incentive zoning are widespread in the US, whereby, in exchange for extra floor space, developers provide public amenities such as better design features, landscaping or public spaces. Although such bonus systems are effective at delivering public amenities, their limitations and abuses have discredited them as a means to achieve better design (Cullingworth, 1997, pp. 94–9). Problems include the tendency of developers to see bonuses as 'as-of-right' entitlements; to increase building floorspace, height and volume;

and to fail to deliver amenities after taking the bonuses – together with the inherently inequitable and time-consuming nature of a system that lacks clear ground rules, and often delivers poor quality public amenities (Loukaitou-Sideris and Banerjee, 1998).

The German and French planning systems provide for a strategic plan – *Flächennutzungsplan* in Germany and *Schéma Directeur* in France – to guide large-scale spatial planning and design decisions, including those relating to key open space, landscape, conservation and infrastructure provision. This is often supplemented at the local scale by more detailed plans – *Bebauungsplan* in Germany and *Plan d'Occupation des Sols* in France. These are akin to zoning ordinances, in which detailed codes covering layout, height, density, landscaping, parking, building line and external appearance can be laid out for each zone or plot. Detailed design guidance is also now common in both countries (Figure 11.5).

Experience in Europe and parts of the US helps to demonstrate the value and utility of well-conceived policy and guidance mechanisms in providing the basis for objective public sector intervention in design (see Hillman, 1990). In England, where central government largely establishes the planning agenda for interpretation by local planning authorities, the government's recent conversion to the cause of urban design quality has been epitomised by the publication of *By Design: Urban Design in the Planning System: Towards Better Practice* (DETR/CABE, 2000). The guidance argues that, while the planning system holds the key to delivering good urban design, this can best be achieved through the provision of a policy framework based on a clear set of objectives. Seven general principles are identified (see Chapter 1) which, the guide argues, should be interpreted through design policy. In the UK context, the most important tool for this is currently the development plan, which – in principle – should clearly set out the design principles against which development proposals will be assessed.

Reflecting research on design policies in England (Punter and Carmona, 1997), *By Design* recognised that policies are often vague and ill conceived, and suggested that adopted design principles should be based on clear understanding and appreciation of the local context. In the UK, this has usually been demonstrated in documents outside the statutory planning process. Local design guides, for example, often address particular contexts (e.g. town centres, conservation areas, residential areas, rural areas) or particular types or aspects of development (e.g. shop fronts, landscape design, housing, materials). Such guides are usually far more detailed than the policies in the development plan. They expand and explain policy for their target audience, relating general policies to particular areas or developments. Two of the best and most sophisticated examples of local design guides are *A Design Guide for Residential and Mixed Use Areas* (Essex Planning Officers Association, 1997) and the *City Centre Design Strategy* for Birmingham (Tibbalds *et al.*, 1990).

To overcome problems of vagueness, *By Design* relates policy objectives to the physical form of development. The guide's authors argue that this approach ensures that policy moves beyond generalised aspirations and explains how the principles can be interpreted in the light of particular circumstances. They boldly claim that: 'Any policy, guidance or design that cannot be seen clearly as a

	OBJECTIVES							
FORM	Character	Continuity and Enclosure	Environmental Quality	Accessibility	Legibility	Adaptability	Diversity	Efficiency
Layout: Structure								
Layout: Urban Grain								
Density								
Scale: Height								
Scale: Massing								
Appearance: Details								
Appearance: Materials								
Landscape								

FIGURE 11.6
Although not included in the final version of *By Design*, this 'thinking machine' (or matrix) was developed to relate policy objectives to the physical form of development (source: Campbell and Cowan, 1999)

response to one or more of the urban design objectives will contribute nothing to good urban design. Equally, any policy, guidance or design that is not expressed clearly in terms of one or more aspects of development form will be too vague to have any effect' (Campbell and Cowan, 1999). Although not included in the final guidance, the authors developed a 'thinking machine' (or matrix) as a means to link objectives explicitly to form (Figure 11.6).

Although well-conceived and articulated policies should provide a key means for the public sector to influence and direct urban design policy, the extent of this influence is limited. It will never, for example, substitute for willingness to invest in design quality by the development industry and by government (local and/or national). Arguments for high – and higher – quality urban design must be won in all arenas.

Design and regulation

As different means to implement broad policy objectives, 'design' and 'regulation' are considered together. Design is taken first because, in the public sector context, it offers a refinement of policy mechanisms as well as being the first stage of implementation.

The process of policy writing for development plans, zoning ordinances or design guides is part of the wider design process and is a creative problem-solving process in itself. As they relate to future development proposals, which at the time of writing are usually unknown, most design policies are abstract in nature. Those in British local plans, for example, are intended to guide development over a projected ten-year period. Thus, beyond broad spatial design strategies indicating how an authority's plan area will develop over the long-term, development plans have not tended to indicate design proposals. To ensure that design principles are considered at the site-specific level, many public authorities provide design guidance for particular sites through the use of design briefs, frameworks and codes. These are the next stage in a hierarchy of design guidance, and relate the broad design policies and guidance in development plans, zoning ordinances and design guides, to site-specific development. Although resource intensive to prepare, such guidance is widely regarded as effective both in making public design aspirations explicit, and in securing better design (Carmona, 2001, pp. 284–8). Indeed, the whole of the English planning system is to be recast to reflect these more local and physical approaches, once more linking planning with the articulation and promotion of a clear vision for locations (Department for Transport, Local Government and the Regions, 2001). Existing development plans will be replaced with shorter-term Action Plans for localities, co-ordinated at the strategic level by constantly updated Local Development Strategies. Design briefs, master plans and urban design frameworks all provide models for the new Action Plans (Carmona *et al.*, 2002).

Design (development) briefs

In the UK, design briefs are the usual means of providing site-specific design guidance. Depending on local circumstances, briefs may emphasise design concerns, broad planning issues, or development/management issues. Hence, 'development brief' is the generic term for 'design', 'planning' and 'development' briefs (Figure 11.7). Design briefs are of particular value in a variety of ways, including:

- Providing a positive and proactive approach to planning and design.

- Ensuring that important design issues are considered.
- Offering a basis from which to promote sites and negotiate on development proposals; encouraging collaborative approaches to design.
- Ensuring that the public interest is considered alongside private interests (particularly the levering of public amenities from developments).
- Offering a quick and straightforward means of providing greater certainty and transparency in the design decision-making process.

As design briefs bring public design guidance to its most prescriptive level, authorities have to be aware that – to avoid stifling innovation or creativity – guidance should be market aware and flexible. Formats vary widely, depending on a site's nature and sensitivity, the range of issues to be addressed, political considerations, and the past practice of authorities. Depending on the resources available for their preparation, some use flexible site-specific formats, while others use similar checklists for all sites.

Briefs generally include a mix of 'descriptive' elements (i.e. information on site characteristics and context), 'procedural' elements (i.e. outlining the application procedures) and 'prescriptive'

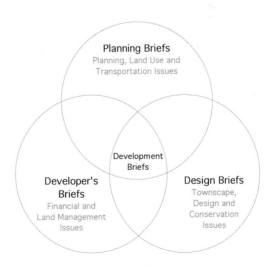

FIGURE 11.7
Types of development briefs (source: Chapman and Larkham, 1994, p. 63)

elements (i.e. spelling out the authority's intentions). They also generally cover the following areas:

- *Background and statement of purpose*: e.g. the circumstances under which the guidance is prepared, and its relation to wider design policy, spatial strategies, and planning gain requirements.
- *Survey and analysis*: e.g. of the built and natural environment, including identification of any specific constraints or opportunities for development.
- *Planning and design requirements*: e.g. spelling out in policy form the key criteria against which any proposals will be assessed.
- *Engineering* and *construction requirements*: e.g. highways and other infrastructure specifications.

- *Procedures for application*: e.g. outlining how the guidance is to be used to evaluate schemes and any procedures or additional presentational and survey requirements.
- *Indicative design proposals*: e.g. outlining development possibilities for the site, including phasing requirements, but without providing unnecessary detail or stifling innovation.

Design frameworks and design codes

Design frameworks and design codes provide similarly positive planning tools, although neither these nor design briefs necessarily have to be produced by the public sector. Design frameworks can be used to guide major development by co-ordinating its key design features and by setting out a spatial framework for infrastructure, landscape and the distribution of land uses (Figure 11.8). They are

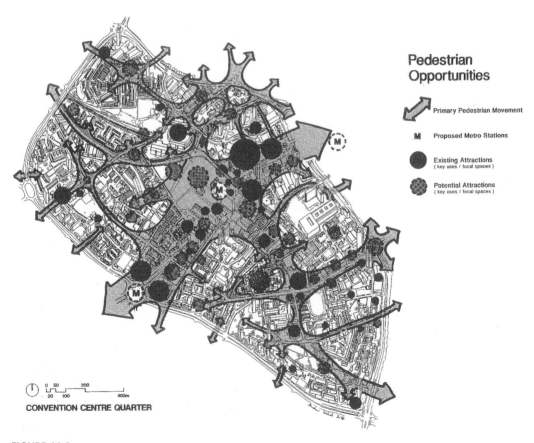

FIGURE 11.8
Good examples of design frameworks have been developed from the *Birmingham Urban Design Studies* as a means to relate the general design principles in the *City Centre Design Strategy* to the level of individual city quarters, such as the *Convention Centre Quarter, Planning and Urban Design Framework* (source: Birmingham City Council, 1994)

frequently described as master plans, when a clear three-dimensional vision of future development form is required as well as two-dimensional plans and diagrams (see below).

Design codes tend to be used for larger developments. They establish a set of principles which guide development, enabling the detail to be developed later. Often used alongside a master plan, they have reached their greatest degree of sophistication and simplicity in the planning of New Urbanist developments in the US, where the design code typically consists of one or two diagrams and charts (Figure 11.9). These (usually private) endeavours – the best known of which is the new settlement of Seaside in Florida – offer valuable lessons for the public sector. Established prior to development, the codes are analogous to other site constraints (i.e. they are one of the factors that need to be taken into account by the designer). Elizabeth Plater-

Zyberk, one of the designers of the Seaside code, argues that

> *control and freedom can co-exist most effectively when incorporated in regulations that precede the act of design, framing parameters of a given programme, rather than conflicting in judgement exerted on the completed design. Review without regulations, or some clearly articulated intention, is nonsensical, painful at least, and often resulting in banal compromise as holistic conceptions submit to fragmented adjustments.* (From Case Sheer and Preiser, 1994, p. vii)

New Urbanists have developed these policy tools to include:

- A site layout or plan – usually termed a *master plan* – based on compact, mixed-use neighbourhood principles, and allocating particular building types to particular sites.

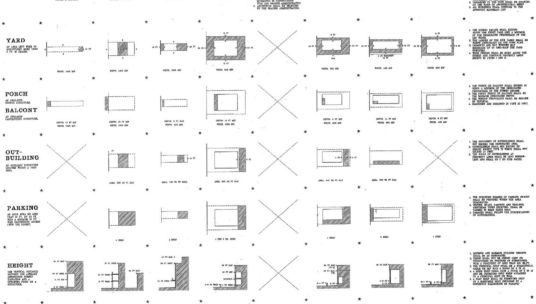

FIGURE 11.9
The Seaside urban code. Design codes tend to be used for larger developments and establish a set of principles to guide development, enabling the detail of projects to be developed at a later date. Often used alongside a master plan, they have reached their greatest degree of sophistication – as well as simplicity – in the planning of New Urbanist developments. The Seaside code was originally designed with the expectation that most building design would be by plan-smiths rather than by architects (source: DPZ Architects in Duany *et al.*, 1989)

- An *urban code* that establishes specific street and space sections to encourage pedestrian movement, and specific building types and their relation to the public spaces – including building lines, heights, parking, outbuildings, porches and fences.
- An *architectural code* to direct imagery and character in line with a sense of place.
- A *landscape code* to enhance public spaces and the compatibility of new landscape elements with the natural ecosystem.

New Urbanist codes are not conventional 'words-and-numbers codes' focusing on land uses, road layouts, highways standards, etc., while containing no vision or expectation about the desired urban form. Instead, they illustrate graphically and pictorially the key principles such as street profiles, building volume, and, in particular, the relationship of buildings to streets (i.e. how private property defines public space). As Duany *et al.* (2000, p. 177) argue, rather than 'specifying what it does not want, this code specifies what it does want'.

Typically regulating elements such as roof pitch and use of materials, the architectural code is the most controversial. Duany *et al.* (p. 211) highlight contradictions in the criticism of such codes:

> Colleagues who complain to us about Seaside usually have two criticisms. The first is the restrictiveness of the architectural code, and the second is the significant number of over-decorated 'gingerbread' cottages there. They are usually surprised to learn that the gingerbread houses at Seaside demonstrate not the requirements of the (largely style-neutral) code but the code's inability to overcome the traditional tastes of the American housing consumer. The only way to have wiped out the hated architecture would have been to tighten the hated code.

Depending on what level of control is desired, the architectural codes can be made more or less prescriptive. Some architectural codes have exemptions for designs of intrinsic merit or for certain building types (such as public buildings). Some developments have an urban code but not an architectural code. One criticism of the use of New Urbanist codes is that they are treated as 'formulae' and are thereby considered either to constrain the designer unduly or, conversely, to make the need for a designer redundant. Intended as guides rather than as prescriptions, the codes need to be interpreted by designers.

In common with all design policy instruments, the most effective briefs, frameworks and codes are promotional and comprehensive; encourage innovative design and presented in easily understandable and usable formats for applicants, professionals and public alike; and combine policy-based information with indicative design ideas. Good practice guidance on their preparation is available from the Urban Design Group (2002).

Design review and evaluation

Briefs, frameworks and codes provide means of moving broad policy objectives closer to realisation. They – and the policies on which they build – fulfil essentially the same function: offering a basis against which to evaluate development proposals. Their preparation can be characterised in the form of a simple equation:

$$\begin{array}{c} \text{Central government/state and regional/} \\ \text{strategic policy} \\ + \\ \text{Local vision (based on design} \\ \text{conception/objectives adopted)} \\ + \\ \text{Appraisal of locality} \\ = \\ \text{A policy base as a means to objectively} \\ \text{review and control design (design policies,} \\ \text{ordinances, briefs, frameworks, codes)} \end{array}$$

Once prepared, they provide the means to operate regulatory processes – design review/control – on the basis of clearly identified and publicly available policy objectives. In the US, regulation of this nature began with a perceived need to regulate the aesthetic impact of billboard advertising in the public realm. The aim was to control the potential for offence to the visual sensibilities of the average person – 'safety, morality and decency' were controllable within the constitution, while aesthetics were not (Cullingworth, 1997, p. 103). In Europe, powers to control design typically developed from the need to improve basic health and amenity standards in urban housing, usually as the forerunner to comprehensive planning systems.

In most countries, design review and control are tied to the broader planning process, successful negotiation of which is needed in order to secure planning consent or a permit to build. Design review is typically dealt with either as an integral part of planning (i.e. as one part of the wider

BOX 11.4 – INTEGRATED AND SEPARATED DESIGN REVIEW PROCESSES

(source: adapted from Blaesser in Case Scheer and Preiser, 1994)

INTEGRATED DESIGN CONTROL/REVIEW PROCESS

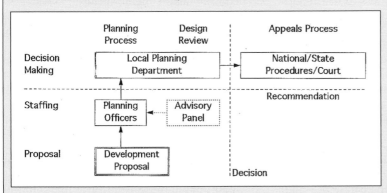

In this model, design is treated as an integral part of wider planning processes. Connections between design and other planning issues – economic development, land uses, social infrastructure, etc. – can be made, understood and weighed one against the other, and informed and balanced judgements made. However, design objectives can be, and often are, sacrificed in the pursuit of short-term

economic and social objectives. The UK's process of design control provides an integrated approach. Some authorities convene non-statutory design panels to advise the planning committee on matters of design. In England, an independent design review is also available from the Commission for Architecture and the Built Environment (CABE).

SEPARATED DESIGN CONTROL/REVIEW PROCESS

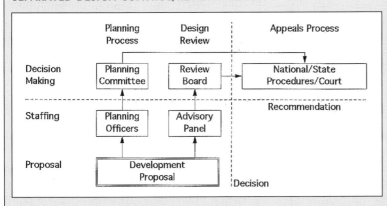

In this model, decisions on design are isolated from other planning concerns, with a separate body responsible for reviewing and controlling design. Design issues receive an appropriate weighting before development consents are granted or refused, usually by staff with well-developed design awareness: this is frequently not the case in the integrated model. A shortcoming of this model is the difficulty of making the necessary connections between design and other planning issues, some of

which – such as decisions on land-use zoning, density, and transport/infrastructure provision – have a major impact on design outcomes. In these circumstances, design is often reduced to a matter of 'mere' aesthetics. Many municipalities in the US have separated models, with the review boards frequently having only an advisory role to the planning commission. In some instances, the review board has delegated powers to make final decisions on matters of design.

regulation process) or separately but clearly linked. These can be considered as 'integrated' and 'separated' models of design review (see Box 11.4).

In some systems, processes of development and/or design control are tied to a further regulatory function of the public sector; that of building control. This usually deals with detailed health and safety aspects of construction standards and design realisation of the private realm (e.g. space standards, ventilation requirements, structural stability). In the UK, these aspects are separated from broader urban design and planning processes, and handled through different statutory instruments and procedures. In Germany, although legislation distinguishes between planning and building law, the latter is open to local amendment and can have a much greater impact on architectural design through, for example, control of building form and materials. Whatever the relationship, the interface between such micro-design regulation and the macro-design typically dealt with through planning processes requires careful co-ordination, particularly for issues crossing the administrative divide (e.g. disabled access and energy use/conservation).

Whatever administrative procedures are adopted to review the design of development, proposals go through similar processes of design evaluation. These include not only formal procedures of application presentation and public consultation, but also more informal procedures of appraisal, consultation with specialists, and negotiation with controllers (Punter and Carmona, 1997, p. 303). As such procedures rely on a coherent and comprehensive policy and guidance base already being in place, those charged with making decisions about a proposed development (i.e. planning officers) should:

Before an application is received:
- enable potential developers to consult the authority about design proposals;
- if necessary, instigate design briefing procedures;
- if appropriate, initiate collaborative and/or participative arrangements.

After an application has been received:
- appraise the site and its surroundings to establish the design context;
- review established design policies for the site;
- review the application to ensure design aspects are clearly and appropriately presented;
- instigate public consultation procedures;

- obtain skilled/specialist advice (e.g. design panel procedures, historic building specialist, landscape specialists);
- on the basis of information gathered/received, negotiate design improvements;
- consider and negotiate implementation requirements (e.g. phasing, planning gain, reserved matters, etc.);
- finally, make a reasoned recommendation or decision to grant, grant with conditions, or refuse permission.

After a negative decision has been made:
- where necessary, use the information gathered/received to fight any appeal;
- use the appeal decision to monitor evaluation procedures, where necessary revising design policy and guidance.

After a positive decision has been made (or an appeal successfully made):
- carefully monitor design implementation (if necessary, enforcing decisions/conditions);
- evaluate design outcomes;
- use the information collected to monitor wider evaluation procedures, where necessary revising design policy and guidance (from Carmona, 2001, p. 159).

In a less structured way, project teams (public or private sector) evaluate their own projects following a similar process. Such evaluations include:

- an ongoing process of gathering information to inform designing and decision-making;
- seeking additional specialist expertise as and when required;
- evaluation of design proposals against the original objectives/brief and any new information;
- making a decision to: proceed with the scheme to presentation/implementation; retain certain aspects of the design for refinement and reject others for redesign; reject the scheme in its entirety and redesign;
- the ongoing learning process as schemes are finished and implemented and new ones begun, drawing from: experience of the design process itself; reactions of others (including the client) to the proposals; and, if implemented, feedback on the scheme's performance.

In addition to the standard public sector project evaluations (e.g. assessing schemes against site appraisals, established policy and guidance, skilled advice and the results of any consultation activity), other techniques are used for the economic and socio-environmental impact of schemes. Various cost–benefit analysis and environmental impact assessment techniques are the most frequently used (Moughtin *et al.*, 1999, pp. 139–49). However, by seeking to measure those aspects that are readily quantifiable, particularly in monetary terms (e.g. employment, traffic impacts, levels of pollution), such assessments may oversimplify less tangible impacts such as the loss of culturally important buildings or the positive impact of a well-designed public realm; the value of which can be underestimated or ignored. Because of the resources they employ, these methods tend to be used only on larger schemes – particularly those associated with major infrastructure projects.

In *By Design* (DETR/CABE, 2000), it is argued that the 'art of urban design' lies in applying good practice principles to the particular conditions of an area or site. It argues that such principles should be capable of being expressed as performance criteria, permitting assessment of the extent to which they

FIGURE 11.10
The policy 'toolkit': Advocated in *By Design* (DETR/CABE, 2000), the policy toolkit is in two parts: (i) the 'hardware' or the means to control and guide design utilising policy instruments (e.g. design policies in development plans, supplementary design guides, design frameworks, briefs and codes) and (ii) the 'software' or the encouragement of high design standards through proactive management of the planning system. The latter involves encouraging the use of skilled designers (in authorities and by developers), encouraging effective collaboration between stakeholders, and monitoring outcomes through regular audits (appraisals) of the built environment (source: Campbell and Cowan, 1999)

have been achieved (Figure 11.10). While strongly supporting the need for collaborative approaches to urban design, it also notes that these are not a substitute for good designers, but are essentially 'a way of making space for them to design creatively, and helping them avoid later finding themselves tripped up by matters of public policy, economics or local context which they failed to take into account' (Campbell and Cowan, 1999). Those charged with writing and implementing design policy must recognise that regulation will never be a substitute for good design proposals in the first place.

Monitoring and review

The final stage in the design process is the feedback loop that involves learning from past experience and using the lessons to inform future practice. Arguing that growth and learning are essential parts of design, Zeisel (1981, p. 16) suggested it is 'a process that, once started, feeds itself both by drawing on outside information and by generating additional insight and information from within'. The more urban designers learn from past experiences, the more likely they are to repeat their successes and avoid mistakes. This also applies at the organisational level, emphasising the importance of public authorities and consultancies systematically monitoring their work and using the results to review both their design/management processes and the design outcomes.

All design policy and guidance should be regularly monitored to assess how effectively it meets its objectives, with the resulting information used to improve the effectiveness of policy and guidance frameworks (Punter and Carmona, 1997, pp. 311–14). For urban design schemes, monitoring should include assessments of completed projects against the original brief and/or policy objectives and post-occupancy evaluations. In the public sector, assessments of the results of planning appeals (i.e. how many are won and lost and why) and the quality of planning applications received can also be monitored. Monitoring activity should involve all the actors involved in making decisions – council officers and elected planning committee members – as well as the users of the service and final scheme – architects, developers, civic and amenity societies and the wider community.

As an optional post-implementation activity – and because staff, resources and energies are usually redirected to new projects – systematic monitoring is rarely undertaken. Nevertheless, in the public sector, increasingly sophisticated methods are employed to monitor public services in order to audit service quality. In the UK, the development of performance indicators across local government services enables comparison of levels of performance (DETR, 2000). In the US, performance indicators are a well-established part of the zoning process (Porter *et al.*, 1988). Performance indicators often rely, however, on quantitative measures of performance (e.g. the speed of processing planning applications) that only indirectly measure the qualitative dimensions of urban design through, for example, measuring the number of applications submitted by architects, or the number of design-related planning appeals won.

By focusing only on aspects amenable to quantitative measurement, decision-making processes can become distorted. More fundamental approaches to monitoring include quality audit processes (DETR/CABE, 2000, p. 81). These involve systematic review of the practices and policies – preferably also the outcomes – of public sector services, in order to evaluate their success in meeting clearly defined objectives. Audits of this nature, however, tend to focus on processes rather than processes *and* outcomes.

Other approaches to monitoring urban design quality include:

- establishment of design awards schemes, which also provide an incentive to strive for better design;
- use of design advisory panels, which can reflect on completed schemes as well as on schemes seeking planning consent; and
- elected councillors and officers touring completed projects, to consider design issues, and to show decision-makers the impact of their decisions.

As well as formal approaches to monitoring, it is also important to establish informal practices that include monitoring and review processes as an everyday component of working arrangements. Such practices can be as simple as making time before beginning a project to research what has worked elsewhere; recording personal impressions; or holding informal discussions with colleagues in order to feed views back into formal policy review procedures or ongoing design and decision-making processes.

EDUCATION, PARTICIPATION AND MANAGEMENT

The time scale over which such concerns necessarily operate connects the final two modes of action – 'education and participation' and 'management'. Over the long-term, education and participation provide the means to inspire greater commitment to environmental quality among the population at large, while management represents ongoing stewardship of the urban environment, which may help stimulate feelings of identification with place.

Long-term commitment to the quality of the urban environment by the public sector and the local community is essential because – despite having moved up the political agenda – issues of environmental quality are often sacrificed when perceived to be in conflict with economic and social goals. However, as awareness of the link between environmental quality and economic prosperity and social well-being grows, so does the demand for a better quality environment. This demand, from across the range of stakeholders, stems from a variety of factors, including:

- Companies and individuals having a direct financial stake in the environment or property they own (for many householders their primary financial asset is their house).
- More people being better travelled, and more aware of high quality environments to compare with their own.
- The link between environment, health and contemporary lifestyles being clearly accepted and regularly debated.
- Built environment issues being newsworthy, nationally and locally.

The final factor is particularly important in keeping issues of quality high on the political agenda, ensuring commitment to public involvement and investment in the processes of urban management and change.

Education and participation

For most lay participants, awareness of environmental quality derives from personal experience and the media rather than from formal education. For professionals operating within the urban environment, it is particularly important to develop a broad knowledge base covering their own, and other, perspectives on securing environmental quality. In the UK, demand for greater environmental awareness and training was a key outcome of the 'Quality in Town and Country' initiative (DoE, 1996), a national cross-profession consultation exercise. Perception that the general public lack taste and visual literacy has long been considered an important barrier to achieving a better designed environment by the architectural profession, as is the dearth of design skills in planning, and of enlightened patronage in the development industry (Punter and Carmona, 1997, pp. 338–40) (Figure 11.11).

The Urban Task Force (1999, pp. 157–68) also identified low levels of urban design skills as a key barrier to delivering an Urban Renaissance in England. Subsequent Government research (Arup Economics and Planning, 2000) found two types of urban design skills base in local government. A small group of (mainly large) urban authorities employing urban design staff who perform both a proactive role in area redevelopment and a reactive role through the development control process; and a much larger group of (mainly smaller) often rural/suburban authorities largely reliant on non-specialist planning staff to deliver a purely reactive service. Concurrent work revealed a dearth of urban design education for students in professional planning, architecture, surveying, engineering and landscape design courses, resulting in the continuing delivery of young professionals to the job market without a grounding in cross-professional urban design (University of Reading, 2001).

Research in both the UK and the US has consistently shown that lay and professional tastes on design can be very different (see Nasar, 1998). In any one place, architects' tastes often differ from those of planners, which differ from those of local politicians and the general public. As the design disasters of the post-war period remind us, professionals should be extremely wary of dismissing lay taste. Taking local public opinion on board in design projects helps to ensure that proposals are supported by those most affected by their impact.

Involving end users and local populations in the design process also offers an effective means for pursuing wider design awareness and educational goals. The cross-disciplinary 'Quality in Town and

FIGURE 11.11
Contemporary patterns of patronage (source: Louis Hellman)

Country' consultation exercise clearly indicated a development industry-wide commitment – at least in principle – to involving local communities in the design decision-making processes (DoE, 1996, pp. 8–10). This commitment is, however, rarely translated into practice beyond token efforts or minimum statutory requirements.

In the UK, planning authorities are statutorily required to consult local residents and interest groups when preparing development plans (including design policies) and considering planning applications. They are also encouraged to consult the same groups when preparing supplementary forms of design guidance. As more fundamental forms of participation are not required, efforts remain at the level of tokenism (see Chapter 12), with, for example, consultation on design policies rarely producing anything beyond broad expressions of support by amenity and resident groups and complaints of overprescription and inflexibility from designers and developers. As a result, despite consultation on development plans usually being undertaken with considerable rigour, public concerns are rarely mentioned as either explicit or implicit sources of design policy or guidance (Punter and Carmona, 1997, p. 136). Where it does occur, greater public involvement in the development of policy can help to:

- develop and refine policies;
- ensure that the gap between professional and lay tastes is minimised;
- build consensus about appropriate levels of intervention and prescription;
- give extra weight to policies and guidance in an area which is frequently challenged;
- ensure that amenity interests and design professionals are working towards mutually agreed goals; and
- develop a sense of local ownership for policy and guidance.

For a discussion of more fundamental forms of participation, see Chapter 12.

MANAGEMENT

The final element to be dealt with in this chapter concerns the everyday management of the urban environment. As discussed in Chapter 1, the process of urban design has been defined as the design and management of the public realm.

Management processes are central to urban design and particularly to public sector regulatory functions. In a more circumscribed role, they involve day-to-day management of established environments, helping to maintain and enhance urban quality. The public sector has a key part to play here, particularly through its management of transport, urban regeneration, conservation, and maintenance and cleansing processes – all major contributors to urban quality.

(i) Transport
Issues of transportation dominate debates about the sustainability of urban living patterns. While easily thought of – at least at the macro scale – as someone else's problem, for urban design practitioners they are fundamental to decisions about (at one end of the urban design remit) the spatial design of settlements and (at the other end) the comfort and liveability of urban space. At the macro scale, much debate focuses on political issues of private versus public transport provision, on means to move people efficiently around urban areas, and on policy-based means to restrict car use. Decisions at the macro scale and within the political arena will, however, eventually feed through to the micro scale.

Urban design practitioners have an important role to play when designing new environments, in ensuring that vehicular needs are balanced with those of other users of space (e.g. pedestrians, cyclists and public transport) (see Chapter 4). Most day-to-day decisions concerning transport provision, however, involve the management of existing environments – a role central to securing and maintaining a high quality public realm. In the public sector, the aim should be to encourage equitable access for all sections of society, for example by:

- taming the use of private cars;
- freeing space for pedestrians and cyclists;
- reducing auto-dependency, and, where possible, providing a choice of travel modes;
- integrating public transport at local, and wider, scales.

(ii) Regeneration
Urban design has the potential to make an important contribution to urban regeneration. The ongoing processes of adaptation and change

presuppose both development and decline – with the former often dependent on the latter happening before reinvestment and renewal can occur. The public sector has a key role to play in managing these processes, through planning activity and urban regeneration policy, including land reclamation, place promotion, direct investment (i.e. in infrastructure) and provision of subsidies or starting capital for revolving funds. In order to manage and guide the regeneration and revitalisation of particular areas (e.g. historic urban quarters, city centres, inner city areas, peripheral estates, or whole cities or regions), *ad hoc* agencies or partnerships are often created. These may take many forms, and are often termed 'growth coalitions', 'growth machines' or public–private partnerships (Logan and Molotch, 1987). Many are three-way partnerships including private, public and voluntary/community sectors.

Partners usually contribute differing resources, powers and abilities, such as finance (public subsidies and development finance), planning and legal powers (in particular, the ability to acquire development land) and what might be regarded as community 'consent' or 'approval'. Some partnerships/agencies are (more) executive, and carry out development, while others are (more) facilitative, enabling development by others (usually private developers or non-profit organisations). Whatever the mechanisms used to deliver regeneration activity – local government, public/private partnerships, voluntary agencies, or government quangos such as urban development corporations – it is increasingly accepted that effective regeneration requires the creation of sustainable social and economic structures, alongside investment in urban design (Urban Task Force, 1999).

Positive actions on the supply side by local authorities, revitalisation agencies and partnerships, or others committed to an area, can also be used to stimulate demand. The methods employed include: encouraging or subsidising flagship projects; subsidising development; area-based improvements; provision of infrastructure; restricting opportunities for a competitive supply; and/or the development of urban design master plans or frameworks.

An urban design 'master plan' or a 'development framework' can guide new development on a green field or brown field site or the revitalisation of a historic area. While green field sites have little or no existing infrastructure, brown field sites are likely to have an established pattern of infrastructure and usually a number of existing buildings, providing character but also limiting the possible options. As the terms 'master plan' and urban design or development 'framework' are often used in a loose and interchangeable fashion, it is necessary to define them more precisely. Both are area-based design guidance: a master plan is the more prescriptive and detailed document, explaining how a site or series of sites will be developed, describing and illustrating the proposed urban form in three dimensions, describing how the proposal will be implemented, and setting out the costs, phasing and timing of development. Master plans have been criticised for inflexibility, and for proposing a greater degree of control than is actually necessary or possible. Garreau (1991, p. 453, from Brand, 1994, p. 78), for example, defines master planning as 'that attribute of a development in which so many rigid controls are put in place, to defeat every imaginable future problem, that any possibility of life, spontaneity, or flexible response to unanticipated events is eliminated'. As a less rigid alternative to the master plan, a design framework can be used. Design or development frameworks generally set out broad urban design policies and principles rather than more detailed intentions, providing scope for interpretation and development within the framework's parameters.

Urban design master plans or frameworks might:

- provide an overall 'vision' or concept to guide development;
- set standards and expectations of quality;
- ensure minimum levels of quality (i.e. prevent a reduction in potential value by prohibiting poor quality development);
- provide degrees of certainty for all parties (investors, developers, occupiers, and the local community); and
- provide co-ordination, and ensure that the component parts contribute to a greater whole (e.g. avoid 'bad neighbour' developments that reduce amenity) (see Chapter 10).

As development involves a calculation of reward and risk, these actions are intended to reduce risk, and provide a more secure investment environment. Better quality urban design helps ensure that regeneration is sustainable, while poor quality urban design might reduce the speed at which regeneration propagates through local economies (Carmona *et al.*, 2001, pp. 76–7).

(iii) Conservation

Cities such as Boston in the US, and Barcelona, Birmingham and Glasgow in Europe, have used high quality design to establish a new image for, and confidence in, their central areas, which has helped to sustain wider regeneration activity. Each city's built heritage and existing character was used as a starting point for regeneration activity. Therefore, used positively, conservation can offer a powerful tool to deliver urban regeneration objectives (see English Heritage, 2000, pp. 8–10).

Although inextricably linked to wider planning and regeneration activity, and largely reliant on private sector investment, conservation represents a further area of public sector activity. It is a key means of delivering contextually respectful urban design that builds on established patterns of development and associations with place. In most regulatory and planning systems, conservation mechanisms:

- operate through a separate legislative base;
- look to the past for reference points to anchor and inform the present;
- look to the future, accepting the inevitability and desirability of change; and
- link these by 'capturing' and developing what is locally distinctive in the environment to inform contemporary development.

Conservation activity can thus reflect the widespread public support for preserving the familiar and cherished local scene. By such means, it can also avoid the criticism that such activity merely panders to an unhealthy obsession with the past (particularly in the English-speaking world) and to a desire to 'theme park' heritage, preserving physical artefacts as traces of bygone patterns of life without the activities that gave rise to them in the first place.

Interpreted broadly, conservation encompasses a wide and forward-looking agenda encapsulating concepts such as diversity, identity, place, community, distinctiveness and sustainability (Figure 11.12). This notion of conservation can be seen as a more forceful application of urban design principles: one which could be incorporated under most of Lynch's modes of action. It is included here because conservation controls represent an overarching management regime applicable to certain environments, which – based on assessment of their value – benefit from additional policy and regulatory mechanisms. English Heritage's checklist

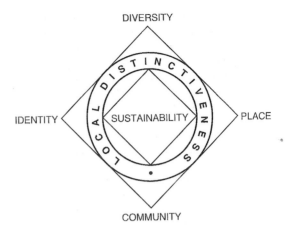

FIGURE 11.12
Conserving local distinctiveness: the agenda

for assessing character (see Box 11.2) illustrates the scope of the conservation concern.

The tensions between economic forces for redevelopment and a widespread desire to maintain established social and physical structures are at their greatest in sensitive historic contexts, as are tensions between desires for innovation and continuity in design (see Chapter 9). To control these tensions effectively, most conservation controls create a two-tier system, with designated buildings and areas subject to a regime of quality control, operating in addition to the statutory planning processes operating elsewhere – for example: 'listed buildings' and 'conservation areas' in the UK; the 'National Register of Historic Places' and historic preservation districts in the US; *'buildings inscrit'* or *'classés'* and *'Zones de Protection du Patrimonies Architectural et Urbain'* in France.

(iv) Maintenance

In a Royal Fine Art Commission study of London, Judy Hillman (1988, p. viii) complained that:

> *Too much of London has become dirty, degrading and depressing. Under foot litter abounds, scattered by people and the wind from pavements to streets and forecourts, often dumped hours in advance of collection or simply left in plastic parcels at the foot of almost any vertical object. Meanwhile the men, women and children, for whom the city exists, are squashed onto pavements narrowed by guard rails, bollards, grey poles, lampposts, telephone, letter, litter and traffic light control boxes, salt*

and grit containers, bus stops and shelters, public conveniences, trees, sometimes in tubs, and a few plants. Visually streets have become a nightmare, a situation which is compounded by a proliferation of yellow lines, yellow flashings, signs, usually dirty, estate agency boards, graffiti and fly-posting.

Towns and cities across the world display the problems Hillman describes. In 1980s London, they were compounded by lack of resources and absence of effective urban governance. A lack of proper maintenance can easily precipitate a spiral of decline. Wilson and Kelling's (1982) 'broken windows' theory of crime prevention, for example, argues that if a window in a building is broken and left unrepaired, the rest of the windows will soon be broken. They explain that: 'Window-breaking does not necessarily occur on a large scale because some areas are inhabited by determined window-breakers, whereas others are populated by window-lovers. Rather, one unrepaired window is a signal that no one cares, and so breaking more windows costs nothing.' Wilson and Kelling also argued that the failure to deal promptly with minor signs of decay in a community, such as graffiti or soliciting by prostitutes, could result in a rapidly deteriorating situation as hardened offenders move into the area to exploit the breakdown in control.

Effective maintenance of the public realm requires the creation and preservation of a clean, healthy and safe environment. While the public sector often takes the ultimate responsibility, contributions – either positive or negative – are likely to come from a range of public and private sources – refuse and environmental health services, transport authorities, planning authorities, parks and recreation departments, police authorities, statutory undertakers, private businesses, community organisations and the public. Indeed, it is this diversity of interests, and the incremental changes for which they are responsible, which makes the process of urban management difficult.

The sense of a deterioration in the public realm to which Hillman refers explains – in part – the popularity of out-of-town shopping malls, where the retail environment is maintained, designed, policed and regulated by a single, clearly identifiable private interest. In the UK, recognition of the competitive threat of out-of-town retail developments and their effect on the 'vitality and viability' of traditional town and city centres during the 1980s and (particularly) 1990s, led to a rethinking of urban management and the emergence of integrated Town Centre Management. In places as diverse as the centres of major urban conurbations and small country market towns, town centre managers have been employed to co-ordinate actions, monitor changes, act as town centre janitors, promote and market town centres, and advocate and enable programmes of improvement. A Royal Fine Art Commission report produced almost ten years after Hillman's proposed a programme of action to enhance character and improve convenience and, thereby, to breathe new life into urban centres (Davis, 1997). The checklist produced not only illustrates the diversity of public sector action required, but also the extent of co-ordination required between public sector agencies and between public and private sector interests, in order to procure and maintain high quality urban design (Table 11.1).

CONCLUSION

In this chapter, the public sector contribution to encouraging, securing and maintaining high quality urban and environmental design has been presented and discussed. Diverse, all-pervasive and potentially highly positive, this role can be encompassed in the six modes of action:

- *Appraisal/diagnosis* – analysis of context, to understand the qualities and meanings of place.
- *Policy* – provision of policy instruments to guide, encourage and control appropriate design.
- *Regulation* – the means of implementing policy objectives through negotiation, review and statutory processes.
- *Design* – development and promotion of specific design and development solutions, from large-scale infrastructure to site-specific solutions.
- *Education* and *participation* – 'spreading the word' and involving potential users in the process.
- *Management* – the ongoing management and maintenance of the urban fabric.

As the public sector – like the private sector – rarely operates in isolation, it is the successful partnership between public and private that, over time, offers the greatest potential for successful, sustainable urban design.

TABLE 11.1
Improving the high street environment

QUALITIES OF CONVENIENCE	ACTIONS TO IMPROVE CHARACTER	QUALITIES OF CHARACTER	ACTIONS TO ENHANCE CHARACTER
Welcome	• Tidy up car park entrances • Make car park interiors welcoming • Integrate paths to the high street • Clarify pedestrian direction signs	**Pavements**	• Specify quality pavements • Reduce street furniture clutter • Rationalise traffic street furniture
		Shops	• Improve shop fronts • Reduce impact of vacant shop fronts • Relate shop signs
A cared for place	• Eliminate flyposters and graffiti • Clear litter and rubbish • Position waste recycling bins	**Urban space**	• Design infill development • Create incidental urban space • Plant street trees • Introduce seasonal colour
Comfort and safety	• Calm traffic	**Street life**	• Encourage market stalls and kiosks • Vary activities in urban spaces • Establish special events
		Local landmarks	• Accentuate landmarks • Design paving for special places • Install public lighting • Place art in public places

(Source: adapted from Davis, 1997).

12

The communication process

INTRODUCTION

This chapter concerns the communication process in urban design. As the fate of urban design ideas and projects is often significantly affected by designers' abilities to convey ideas effectively, urban designers need to represent and communicate ideas – both visually and verbally – clearly and logically, to a variety of audiences. The best ideas and principles may be of little value if they are not communicated effectively. Furthermore, as design is a process of exploration and discovery, drawing and other forms of representation and communication are an integral part of that process. The chapter focuses on three main issues. The first is the act of communication. The second is participation as a form of communication. The third is the means and methods of presentation.

COMMUNICATION, PERSUASION AND MANIPULATION

When urban designers seek to secure a commission, gain support for a project, obtain funding, or secure permission for a development proposal, processes and issues of communication come to the fore. Designers need to be able to promote their services to potential clients, whether private individuals, companies, government organisations or politicians. Every project must be presented to a variety of audiences, the nature and type of which will vary from 'client' representatives, to other professionals, representatives from the public sector, funding institutions, the local community, the media, etc. Communication requires oral and graphic presentation skills tailored to the particular

audience, with presentations regarded as a means to an end, rather than as an end in themselves; the end being to achieve something worthwhile on the ground.

Communication is not a straightforward process. Significant issues of power, manipulation, seduction and misinformation are involved. In his book, *Representation of Places: Reality and Realism in City Design*, Peter Bosselmann (1998, p. 202) notes how proponents will show a proposal to its best advantage, with negative impacts played down or omitted, while opponents will be just as selective in highlighting the negative and acknowledging few, if any, benefits.

In principle, there are two fundamental types of communication: *informative communication* where the main objective is to furnish information to enable a better understanding of a project; and *persuasive communication* aimed at securing acceptance, approval, consent, or funding for it. The distinction is somewhat academic – in practice, all forms of communication are both persuasive and informative. A more important distinction is made between communications that are intentionally persuasive, accidentally or unconsciously persuasive, or deliberately manipulative. While various techniques can be used to represent the 'reality' of schemes, because images can be manipulated, it is the communicators' choice whether – or to what extent – to manipulate 'reality'.

While persuasion and manipulation are closely related, manipulation operates primarily by keeping the audience ignorant. Dovey (1999, p. 11) suggests that a common practice is where the representation of design projects is distorted to produce a form of 'manipulated consent' from ignorant participants. 'Seduction' is another form of manipulation. As Dovey (1999, p. 11) explains, it is a highly sophisticated practice that manipulates the interest and desires of the subject and entails 'the constructions of desire and self-identity . . . with significant implications for the built environment'. While seduction is usually positive and manipulation negative, both involve the exercise, and perhaps abuse, of power. The potential for manipulation is ever present. In commenting on the 'sometimes miraculous images' used to illustrate development proposals, Biddulph (1999, p. 126) notes the difficulty of differentiating between the 'future environment' and 'advertisement'.

Rather than confusing, seducing or manipulating an audience, communications might be used to challenge it, and to expose and reveal new insights. Designers frequently want to show an audience something they had not previously considered. To communicate schemes and ideas, designers may employ metaphors, analogies and/or evoke precedents. Trancik (1986, p. 60), for example, notes that precedents can be an effective tool for communication: 'By demonstrating the intention of a design through example, a designer can provide an immediately recognisable image, a familiar ambience that explains the goal of the proposal.' Precedents and metaphors should be used with caution, however: images of Italian hill towns were used, for example, to sell the concept of Cumbernauld new town, sited on an exposed and windswept hill top north of Glasgow.

Issues of power are an inevitable part of communication – for example, the first speaker has the power of initiation and agenda-setting, which subsequent speakers must challenge. To be effective, communicators need credibility based on criteria such as 'trust' and 'respect'. An audience may not be deceived by seduction or manipulation, but obviously manipulative communicators will lose credibility, and what they are communicating will be treated with suspicion. John Forester (1989) discussed the concept of communication in planning. Transposing 'urban design' for planning, his arguments remain appropriate. Urban designers must:

routinely argue practically and politically, about desirable and possible futures. If they fail to recognise how their ordinary actions have subtle communicative effects, they will be counterproductive, even though they may mean well. They may be sincere but mistrusted, rigor-

ous but unappreciated, reassuring but resented. Where they intend to help, [urban designers] may instead create dependency and where they intend to express good faith, they may raise expectations unrealistically with disastrous consequences. But these problems are hardly inevitable. When [urban designers] recognise the practical and communicative nature of their actions, they can devise strategies to avoid these problems and to improve their practice as well. (Forester, 1989, pp. 138–9)

In discussing his concept of the 'ideal speech situation', Jurgen Habermas (1979) argued that we expect speech to be comprehensible, sincere, legitimate and truthful. Interpreting Habermas' ideas, Forester (1989, p. 144) argued that mutual understanding depends on the satisfaction of four criteria:

Without comprehensibility in interaction, we have not meaning but confusion. Without a measure of sincerity, we have manipulation or deceit rather than trust. When a speaker's claims are illegitimately made, we have the abuse rather than the exercise of authority. And when we cannot gauge the truth of what is claimed, we will be unable to tell the difference between reality and propaganda and fact.

These are 'ideal' conditions. In practice, their value may be as a measure of how far real speech falls short of them.

Communication gaps

Effective communication is a two-way process of 'speaking' and 'hearing', involving connection between a communicator and an audience. Although a means of empowering people so that they can contribute constructively, communication may be adversely affected by 'gaps' in the connection. It is important for urban designers to appreciate where such communication gaps may arise and to be aware of how to overcome them. There is, for example, typically a gap between the producers and consumers of the urban environment (see Chapter 10). There are also communication and social gaps between designer and user, and between professional and layperson. If their desire is to make places for people, urban designers need to narrow rather than exacerbate these gaps.

(i) The professional–layperson gap

Through their training and education, urban design practitioners acquire the skills necessary to represent both what exists and what might become 'reality'. This is simultaneously a strength and a weakness: Lang (1987), for example, argues that environmental design professionals remain overwhelmingly locked into a 'pictorial' mode that treats the city as a work of art rather than a setting for everyday life. Similarly, Hubbard (1994, p. 271) argues that

> design training and socialisation inculcates a professional perspective which emphasises the objective, physical qualities of the environment and discourages a more personal, subjective response . . . one can comfortably assume that such disparities reflect fundamental differences in the ways in which designers and non-designers think about their surroundings, not simply differences in the way they express themselves.

This problem is not simply a matter of professional perspective, but is inherent in any act of representation. As Bosselmann (1998, p. xiii) recognises, because the real world's 'richness and complexity' cannot be completely represented, designers inevitably select from reality an 'abstraction of actual conditions': 'For them the process of representation is a complex form of reasoning. What they choose to represent influences their view of reality and very significantly defines the outcome of designs and plans, and thus the future form of cities.'

This raises issues regarding the nature of professional expertise, and potential gaps between the professional and the layperson. Rather than considerations of 'experts' and 'non-experts', it is better to conceptualise this in terms of different types of expertise. This is of particular note in situations where urban design practitioners are dealing with communities and users. Bentley (1999) suggests distinguishing between 'local' and 'global' expertise. He argues that professionals have 'global' expertise, while local people have 'local' expertise. Each needs to be respected in the design process and in the making of places that are responsive, meaningful and valued by their users.

As well as through pictures and images, the professional–layperson gap may be exacerbated through the use of words and language. Urban design practitioners need both to think spatially and to express spatial concepts, ideas and princi-

ples in words. In securing permissions and consents and in supporting graphic submissions, for example, they may need to write design statements. However, language, words, phrases, slang and shorthand versions of common concepts can create communication gaps. Duany *et al.* (2000, p. 213) observed how some architects try to regain a 'sense of power' through what they describe as 'mysticism': 'by developing illegible techniques of representation, and by shrouding their work in inscrutable jargon, designers are creating increasingly smaller realms of communication'. They cite an example from the *Harvard Graduate School of Design News* (Winter/Spring 1993, p. 13) describing the plan for a single-family house:

> These distortions elicit decipherment in terms of several constructs that allow the house to analogise discourse and call for further elucidation. These constructs are continually motivated and frustrated by conflicts in their underlying schemata and the concrete form in which they are inscribed. They refer to the ideal or real objects, organisations, processes and histories which the house approximately analogises or opposes.

A more positive example of the use of language in urban design concerns the improvements in Birmingham (UK) during the 1990s (Wright, 1999, p. 298). Prior to the late 1980s, there had been very little concept of a physical vision for the city and it was considered important to communicate urban design ideas and principles so that people could understand what was intended. The key phrases used – 'mending our city'; 'breaking the concrete collar'; 'a good environment is good business'; 'streets and squares'; 'city living'; and 'giving the streets back to the people' – captured the essence of important urban design principles without unnecessary jargon.

(ii) The designer–non-designer gap

There is a gap between designers and non-designers. Those with little design appreciation may tend to see shapes and lines on a piece of paper as just that (i.e. in two dimensions). By contrast, designers read drawings spatially, as representing three-dimensional objects that define and are defined by space. The act of drawing – and of design – involves an important nexus between hand, eye, and brain. Mechanical and computer-aided forms of drawing reduce the fluency of this connection.

While it may simply be different, designers need to appreciate how they are different. Some volume house builders, for example, employ 'technicians' (rather than 'designers') to 'design' housing layouts using standardised layouts and house types and a two-dimensional site plan. This may happen without the technician ever having visited the site and appreciated the qualities and potential of the local context.

(iii) The reality–representation gap

In general, greater realism in the representation of a scheme increases the likelihood of viewers understanding the project as they would in the real world. A common problem, however, is that perception cannot be fully represented graphically. Many representations present an individual and primarily visual experience that fails to portray wider perceptual and social elements – for example, as we move through space, our view and sensual perception of the environment changes. As techniques for representation increase in sophistication and realism, we increasingly confront problems arising from the confusion of realism in representations (i.e. a realism–reality gap). The crux of the problem is not that forms of presentation can be realistic, distorting, misleading, or not, but the need to recognise the potential for this and, where possible, to correct for it. Representations must not be confused with reality; audiences may need to be educated to appreciate the limitations, strengths and weaknesses of representation techniques. As is discussed later, scale models can be particularly misleading.

(iv) The powerful–powerless gap

Although the gap between the powerful and the less powerful in urban design manifests itself in many ways, it is often a function of gaps between 'paying' and 'non-paying' clients (see Chapters 1 and 3) and between producers and consumers (see Chapter 10). In economic theory, where markets work, the consumer has sovereignty and the producer provides what s/he wants. In practice, that situation rarely prevails and imbalances in economic power are sometimes corrected through the use of governmental and regulatory power. In 1969, Sherry Arnstein developed her ladder of participation illustrating eight levels of citizen involvement (Figure 12.1). While the lower levels are generally tokenistic, processes further up the ladder involve greater transfers of power to citizens. Arnstein (1969, p. 216) argued that 'partici-

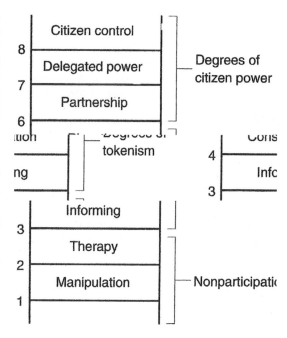

FIGURE 12.1
Arnstein's ladder of participation

pation of the governed in their government' is – in principle – 'the cornerstone of democracy'. A 'revered idea', 'vigorously applauded by virtually everyone', she noted that this applause is 'reduced to polite handclaps . . . when this principle is advocated by the have-not[s] . . . And when the have-nots define participation as redistribution of power.'

In this respect, design is no different to any other area of public policy. Assuming a zero-sum game, the more power that is transferred to local populations, the less resides with those financing, developing, designing and politically sanctioning the project. More generally, this may also mean empowering those on the right-hand side of the McGlynn's powergram (see Chapter 10). Power is a complex phenomenon and is best considered to be multi- rather than uni-dimensional: that is, rather than some actors having power and other actors having none (which is how it is conceived in Arnstein's model), all have some power and they interact in complex ways (see Lukes, 1975).

Partnerships are a form of power-broking in which conflicts of interest are resolved internally. Revised power relationships may be justified by the increased potential for early resolution of conflicts, with collaborative and supportive arrangements leading to more sustainable outcomes, added value through more considered design policies and proposals, and greater commitment to development/design proposals through broader ownership of the processes that led to them. As well as executive agencies and support coalitions, partnerships in urban design may also operate as pressure/lobby groups, usually to defend the amenity of an area.

The sense of ownership of the environment by local populations can easily be undermined, along with the willingness of economic interests to invest in an area. In such circumstances, the public sector is frequently left to cope with the social, economic and environmental fallout.

(v) The designer–user gap

A perennial problem in design is that designers' priorities and aspirations may not be congruent with those of users. During the 1960s and 1970s, designers looked to the social sciences for information and guidance about human behaviour and needs. Social research offered the specious ability to make predictions about human behaviour, derived from environmental settings. Designers often treated these as scientific data, although theirs was a 'misplaced certainty'. It is questionable who, if anyone, was to blame for this – researchers who were extravagant in their claims and did not adequately qualify their research, or the designers who ignored the qualifications. Heavily qualified information, however, is unlikely to be welcome to practitioners. Jenks (1988, p. 54) notes how:

> tentative guidelines may be edited and summarised, and recommendations made upon which action can be taken. In turn, recommendations may be translated into guidelines, design principles or standards to facilitate the designer's task. There is nothing inherently wrong with this, and it is undeniably useful. However, once turned into that epitome of certainty, a standard or guideline, the rationale, the reasoning and the careful qualifications tend to get lost. At that stage it may not even be clear whether the standard or recommendation is authoritative, or whether it is based on research or supposition.

More fundamentally, Vischer (1985) suggested the need to change from what she termed a 'needs and preferences' model of user research, to an 'adaptation and control' model, concerned with developing users' abilities to adapt and control their environment. The conceptual shift is from users as passive expressers of needs and preferences, to users as active agents of change. 'Adaptation' refers to users' ability to change themselves and their behaviour in response to different environmental contexts. 'Control' refers to users' ability to change the physical dimensions of an environment they are not motivated to adapt.

Research into users' needs and preferences is usually based on the assumption that if people cannot make their voice heard, project sponsors should advocate users' perspective to designers. Implied here is the idea that more of users' needs could be met if more information about them was available during the design process (Vischer, 1985, p. 289). The model is based on at least three (questionable) assumptions:

- That questioning can identify users' needs and preferences. As users are often unable to formulate exhaustive lists in rank order of need and preference, researchers have to make assumptions, introducing their own values into the needs assessment process.
- That appropriate design of the physical environment can result in users' needs being met.
- That users have a relatively passive role. As Vischer (p. 291) notes, identifying and responding to users' needs places the users' in a passive, recipient role in terms of their behavioural relationship to the environment and also places the researcher (who identifies needs) and the designer (who responds to needs) in key roles of responsibility regarding the ultimate fit between users and environments'. She therefore argues that the model fails to recognise users' active role as both agent in the operation of the environment and as instigator of environmental change.

Vischer (pp. 293–4) concludes that giving users some control over their environment may be more effective than trying to design a direct response to their needs as they express them: 'Users are not passive and inert entities . . . they take an active role in their environments, interacting with it and adjusting it to suit changing situations.'

PARTICIPATION AND INVOLVEMENT

Community involvement in the process of urban design is increasingly promoted as a means of overcoming – or at least reducing – the professional–layperson, powerful–powerless and designer–user gaps. Participation takes many different forms, broadly conceptualised as top-down or bottom-up approaches.

Top-down approaches tend to be instigated by public authorities and/or developers, usually to gauge public opinion and gain public support for proposals. Development options or policy proposals are prepared as the focus for a participation exercise. The danger is that the agenda may already be largely set, leading to manipulation of local opinion rather than to genuine participation. More positively, such approaches may offer an effective use of resources by using professional expertise to mobilise, co-ordinate and interpret community opinions.

Bottom-up approaches are instigated and led from grass roots level, usually in response to some perceived opportunity or threat. While these exercises offer highly effective means to influence political decision-making processes, they suffer from their time-consuming nature, the time and commitment required to develop expertise, and frequent failure to connect aspirations with the resources needed to put them into effect. Ideally, whatever approach is adopted, the aim – short- or long-term – should be to develop a mutually advantageous dialogue and perhaps partnership between public, private and voluntary stakeholders.

Rudlin and Falk (1999, p. 213) discuss the need to create and maintain a support coalition for design ideas, principles and proposals, in the context of Manchester City Council's design guide for the city's Hulme area (Hulme Regeneration Ltd, 1994). The design guide initially met with a lot of opposition from private and social housing developers, police, traffic engineers and institutional investors and it was a struggle to maintain the principles and ideas contained within it. What helped in Hulme was the strong coalition established between the consultant professionals and the local politicians.

An essential part of a support coalition comes from the local community and those directly affected by proposals. Public involvement and consultation can be an important means of building support for urban design principles and proposals. Research by the Urban Design Group (1998, p. 17) identified a high level of demand by local communities for involvement in the planning and management of their local environment. Moreover, by involving communities, a sense of ownership of the resulting decision may be engendered, the eventual urban design quality of the scheme may be improved, and the benefits more equitably distributed.

In any consultation/participation exercise, three distinct activities should be recognised: dispersing information; gathering information; and promoting a dialogue. In direct contrast to the third, the first two are essentially one-way (monological) forms of communication. Although communities have frequently been involved as part of a consultation exercise on development proposals, such approaches have often tended merely to inform rather than to solicit views for use in the design process. They have also been indirect rather than hands-on and have taken place after-the-fact rather than during the design process. Consequently the community's engagement has been slight, and the benefits of their involvement minimal. Such approaches feature towards the lower end of Arnstein's ladder.

In an attempt to bring communities more fully into the design process, a range of more active participatory mechanisms have been developed that seek to promote dialogue and two-way interaction. These work most effectively when they are initiated from the bottom up and less effectively if imposed from above – although some initial encouragement and support may be required. The more common methods are:

- *'Planning for Real'* exercises, utilising large-scale models to encourage non-confrontational community involvement in identifying and addressing problems. Participants are encouraged to make suggestions by filling out suggestion cards and attaching these to the model, to be pursued in detail at follow-up group meetings. The process relies on members of the community trying out different ideas, with the professionals recording the results, arbitrating and acting as enablers and facilitators.
- *Action planning events/community charettes*, collaborative events enabling sections of local communities to work with independent specialists from a variety of disciplines to produce proposals for action. Events, usually staged over several days, involve briefing from key

stakeholders, analysis of the physical context, workshops and brainstorming sessions, synthesis and presentation of proposals, reporting back, and dissemination of results.

- *Urban design assistance teams (UDATs)* are a variation on action planning where multi-disciplinary teams from outside the area 'parachute in' to facilitate an event and, with the local community, 'brainstorm' an approach to a problem and thereby help the local community devise recommendations for action. UDATs should be community inspired and led (Figure 12.2).

A number of publications now categorise the wide array of participation approaches. Recent examples include the New Economics Foundation's *Participation Works! 21 Techniques of Community Participation for the 21st Century* (1998) and the Urban Design Group's *Involving Local Communities in Urban Design* (UDG, 1998). Together these reports identified seventy-eight separate techniques (Box 12.1). The UDG (1998, pp. 18–19) report also identifies twenty-two general prompts that apply to community planning and design situations:

1. Involve all those affected.
2. Encourage local ownership of the process.
3. Plan your own process carefully.
4. Agree rules and boundaries.
5. Quality not quantity.
6. Involve all sections of the community.
7. Spend money.
8. Get value for money.
9. Accept different agendas.
10. Accept varied commitment.
11. Be honest.
12. Be transparent.
13. Learn from others.
14. Accept limitations.
15. Use experts.
16. Use outsiders carefully.
17. Use facilitators.
18. Be visual.
19. Follow up.
20. Maintain continuity.
21. Have fun.
22. Go for it!

Personal computers provide opportunities for greater public participation in the design and development process. Information such as text, illustrations, video, audio, and computer files can be readily communicated to any number of different sources, and as a result, virtual design studios and digital design on the Internet will inevitably increase (see Graham and Marvin, 1996). As collaborative design projects become increasingly prominent, the World Wide Web provides a medium for the communication and storage of design information, and for integrated working, with real-time discussion groups. In time, people will be able to experience virtual representations of urban design projects. Access to the Internet should also enable greater community participation in urban design at the local level.

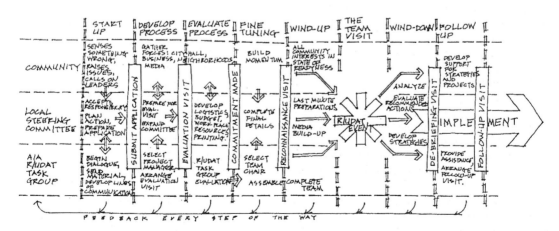

FIGURE 12.2
The Urban Design Assistance Team Process

BOX 12.1 – APPROACHES TO PARTICIPATION

(source: UDG, 1998 and New Economics Foundation, 1998)

Action planning	Design game	Participatory strategic
Activity mapping	Design workshop	Participatory theatre
Act create experience (ACE)	Development trust	Planning aid
Adaptable model	Elevation montage	Planning day
Appreciative inquiry	Enspirited envisioning	Planning for real
Architecture centre	Environment shop	Planning weekend
Architecture week	Finding home – visualising our	Process planning session
Awareness raising day	future by making maps	Real time strategic change
Beo	Fish bowl	Resource centre
Best fit slide rule	Forum	Roadshow
Briefing workshop	From vision to action	Round Table workshops
Broad-based organisation	Future search conference	Social audit
Capacity building workshop	Guided visualisation	Street stall
Choices method	Imagine!	Table scheme display
Citizen advocacy	Interactive display	TalkWorks
Citizens juries	Issues, aims, expectations,	Task force
Community appraisals	challenges and dialogues in a	Team syntegrity
Community design centre	day	Time dollars
Community indicators	Local sustainability model	Topic workshop
Community plan	Mobile planning unit	Trail
Community planning forum	Mock-up	Urban design game
Community projects fund	Neighbourhood planning office	Urban design soapbox
Community site management	Open design competition	Urban design studio
plans	Open house event	Urban studies centre
Community strategic planning	Open space workshop	Visual simulation
Consensus building	Parish maps	Web site
Design assistance team	Participatory appraisal	
Design day	Participatory building appraisal	

Although much more needs to be achieved in providing information and resources to involve and empower local communities, existing good practice can be drawn upon. In choosing the correct approach, urban designers should address the following key questions:

- What are the main aims?
- What commitment exists among the organisers?
- What are their values, and how can these be reflected in the adopted approach?
- What resources exist and what is the time scale?
- What level of participation is required?
- How can local ownership of the process be encouraged?
- How can quality of participation be balanced with quantity?
- How can disenfranchised groups be involved?
- What role (if any) should experts play?
- How can momentum be maintained?

The various approaches available indicate the effort required to move beyond tokenistic consultation procedures. Given differing publics (societal groups) and forms or techniques of public participation and information exchange (e.g. public meetings, exhibitions, focus groups, technical reports), a matrix of possibilities can be created, helping urban designers to devise programmes of participation and consultation tailored to local needs and circumstances.

REPRESENTATION

Urban designers typically develop and present ideas, concepts and proposals through sketches, diagrams and other forms of graphic representation. Baker (1996, p. 66) emphasises that diagrams are the 'essential tool' of analyst and designer, and that their use stimulates 'thought patterns capable of considerable dexterity. This dexterity – the ability to grasp the essence of a concept – and through this understanding to fully develop an idea, is central to the act of design.' Bosselmann (1998, p. xiii), however, offers a cautionary reminder that, while urban design practitioners usually know the power and limitations of representation, 'they may take for granted how representation influences design thinking'. Thus, as well as communicating the qualities of a design to others, modes of representation employed in designing inevitably direct our thinking.

Techniques of representation range from elementary two-dimensional maps and diagrams to highly sophisticated interactive visualisations representing all four dimensions – three spatial and one temporal. In essence, all representations are abstractions of reality. Peter Bosselmann (1998, p. 3) argues that 'pictures do not mimic what we see': while we might assume that photography truthfully records the world around us, 'no optical system exists to mimic the task performed by our eyes'.

The conventional methods of graphic representation are the perspective and the plan view (Bosselmann, 1988, pp. 3–18). These are so commonplace that it is difficult to conceive of a time when they did not exist. Filippo Brunelleschi (1377–1466) is usually credited with the discovery – or rediscovery – of linear perspective. Thirty years after Brunelleschi's death, Leonardo da Vinci drew the first known example of a plan view, based on an actual survey for the small town of Imola in Italy's Emilia Romana. Bosselmann (p. 18) argues that these two methods – 'map' and 'perspective' – represent two ways of looking at and understanding the world: Brunelleschi's represents the earlier view, an understanding of the world based on the evidence of visual experience; while Leonardo's map 'symbolises our need to go beyond direct experience, to explain the structure of things, the theory behind the phenomena we can see'. Bosselmann argues that these two methods of representation introduced a division in professional thinking between the 'clarity of abstractions' (the view from above) and 'befuddling richness and confusion' (the ground-level view). Although the former could be considered to be the 'architect's view' and the latter the 'planner's view', to adequately represent a place both methods are required. While the map and the perspective are both abstractions, the latter is more closely related to our actual experience.

In general, representations of three and four dimensions, such as animations, photomontage, computer-generated models and artists' impressions, are more easily understood by laypeople than plans and conceptual diagrams. As such, urban designers need to represent both that which exists and, more importantly, what might become 'reality'. Due to the inherent richness and complexity of 'real' environments, this can only be done by abstraction, aiming to create visual representations that can be readily understood as substitutes for reality.

The method by which urban design proposals are presented is of considerable importance. Urban designers need to be aware of the most appropriate method(s) of communicating an urban design project. The graphic techniques available for representing urban design ideas, proposals, projects or analysis can be divided into four categories:

1. Analytical and conceptual.
2. Representations of two dimensions.
3. Representations of three dimensions.
4. Representations of four dimensions.

The remainder of this chapter outlines the implications of these techniques, and the increasingly important role of modern technological development.

Analytical and conceptual representations

Analytical and conceptual diagrams of the urban context are essential tools of the urban designer. They include site analyses, townscape notations and pedestrian activity maps. In discussing the role they play in design analysis and in communicating the act of design, Baker (1996, p. 66) observes that diagrams:

- are selective;
- are about clarity and communication;
- reveal the essence;
- are often simple;
- separate out issues, so as to better comprehend the complex;
- allow a degree of artistic licence;
- can have a vitality of their own; and
- can explain form and space better than words or photographs.

Analytical diagrams are important in enabling the identification and understanding of constraints that could influence a design. They are usually carried out at the initial stage of a project, as part of a site survey and analysis. They consist of representations of a site, together with contextual information that aids understanding of opportunities and potential problems. Other graphic methods of analysing a site and its environment include sun path, daylight and shadow diagrams, and wind-flow assessments.

Conceptual diagrams representing initial or embryonic ideas in an abstract form are often used to explain the key principles of a project and how it functions. As discussed in Chapter 11, the site survey and analysis form an important resource for the design process.

Analytical and conceptual diagrams are often highly abstract, using symbols, annotations, images and words to convey ideas and principles, rather than the intended 'reality' of the scheme or site (Figure 12.3). They often aid understanding of the context and/or design proposal, and can

enable designers to keep sight of their original intent – the 'vision' – during the design development stages of a project and in decision-making processes. Schematic, functional and flow diagrams are similar to concept drawings in that they are part of the thought process in the initial design stages. They can emphasise relationships between different parts of a project and/or add the fourth dimension of time by identifying movement, direction, intensity, and potential conflicts.

Urban designers often use Kevin Lynch's elements of imageability – paths, nodes, edges, districts and landmarks – in analysing areas and sites, usually by recording the incidence of Lynch's elements on a plan view. While a common and useful technique, it can, as Lynch (1984, p. 251) warned, misunderstand the purpose of his original study, which was to remind designers of the necessity of consulting those who live in a place. Lynch lamented that, while plans had been 'fashionably

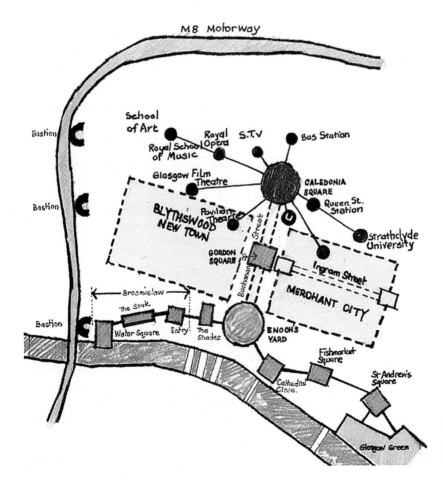

FIGURE 12.3
Concept diagram for central Glasgow (source: Mackinsey Cullen in Gillespies, 1995, p. 6)

decked out' with nodes, etc., there had been few attempts to reach out to the actual inhabitants. Instead of his 'new jargon' 'opening a channel by which citizens might influence design, the new words became another means of distancing them from it'. A more meaningful record of imageability can be obtained by returning to Lynch's own methods of undertaking mental mapping exercises with users of the environment (see Chapter 5).

Some urban designers have developed notational systems to represent urban design qualities or features. Lynch's elements, for example, are often used to communicate ideas about built form and spaces without having to deal with the specificities of buildings. Notations can be an important and effective means of communication between urban designers and the communities with which they are working. Various forms of notation are now used as methods for appraising and conveying the character of context. An early example was Gordon Cullen's 'notation' to represent townscape (Cullen, 1967), which included denotations for the broad types and perceptions of environment encountered. Four primary divisions were defined:

- humanity (i.e. the study of people);
- artefacts (i.e. buildings and objects);
- mood (i.e. the character of place); and
- space (i.e. the physical space).

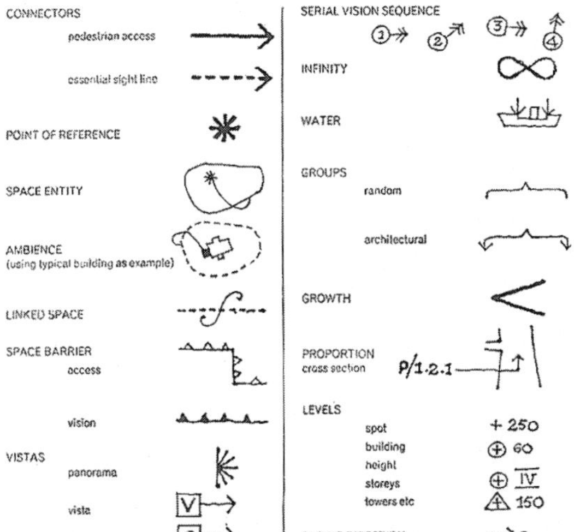

And secondary parameters categorise the primary divisions:

- the range of the category;
- its usefulness;
- its behaviour; and
- its relationships.

'Indicators', the most frequently emulated (and useful) part of the system, denoted isolated qualities that exist in their own right, such as levels and heights; boundaries; spatial types; connections; views and vistas; etc. (see Figure 12.4).

While a number of other systems have been developed since Cullen's, no definitive system exists. Systems are always likely to vary from project to project, but they should all be capable of easy interpretation, adaptation and addition. In Portland, Oregon, for example, city planners developed a coherent notation for conveying urban design ideas in order to express the design frameworks established in *The 1988 Central City Plan* (Figure 12.5).

A further graphic means of analysing urban design is through the use of pedestrian activity maps (Figure 12.6). These diagrams record observations about where people gather, sit, stand, or hurry through spaces. Recording the times of day and climatic conditions, they enable analysis of how people use urban spaces. They can also be used to plot and analyse movement patterns, as in Appleyard's (1981) famous study of how traffic volumes affect pedestrian movement patterns in residential streets (see Chapter 4). Alternatively, the Project for Public Space (2001) has utilised time-lapse photography and video techniques to compress periods of street activity into a few minutes of screen action, giving a stronger impression of movement and activity patterns.

Figure-ground studies, space syntax analysis (see Chapter 8), and analysis of the cross-sections of spaces, provide means to undertake and communicate morphological analyses. Figure-ground techniques derive from Giambattista Nolli's survey of Rome (1736–48), in which he used white to represent publicly accessible space and black to represent the coverage of buildings (see Figure 4.6 – note that the interiors of churches and other public buildings are also white). These drawings highlight the relationships between solids or mass, and voids. They can reveal the urban grain of an area and highlight aspects of the relationship of new development with its surrounding context. Such drawings enable

FIGURE 12.4
Cullen's notation (source: Cullen, 1967)

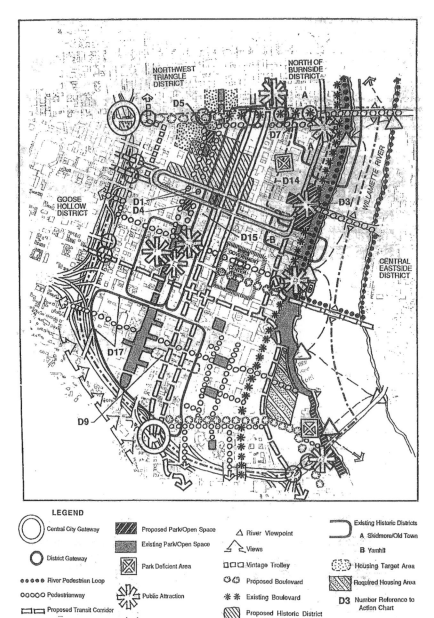

LEGEND

○ Central City Gateway

○ District Gateway

●●●●● River Pedestrian Loop

○○○○○ Pedestrianway

▭◁▷ Proposed Transit Corridor

▭▭ Existing Transit Corridor

▨ Proposed Park/Open Space

▨ Existing Park/Open Space

⊠ Park Deficient Area

✳ Public Attraction

△ Water Taxi

△ River Viewpoint

△ Views

▭▭▭ Vintage Trolley

◐◑ Proposed Boulevard

✳ ✳ Existing Boulevard

▨ Proposed Historic District

⊐ Existing Historic Districts

A Skidmore/Old Town

B Yamhill

⊞ Housing Target Area

▨ Required Housing Area

D3 Number Reference to Action Chart

▬▬ District Boundary

FIGURE 12.5
Portland: central city plan (source: Punter, 1999, p. 82)

a better understanding of relationships and patterns, revealing what is not immediately apparent and perhaps changing how an area or project is perceived.

'Tissue' studies are used to evaluate urban form and the size and scale of spaces, against well-known and/or successful precedents (Hayward, in Hayward and McGlynn, 1993, pp. 24–9). The tech-nique involves overlaying one site plan with another (at the same scale), enabling an appreciation of the size and scale of different urban areas.

Sieve maps can also be used to overlay different layers of spatial information. In their simplest form, tracing paper overlays are used, on an ordinance survey base, each drawn to map different constraints. This can help identify parts of an area

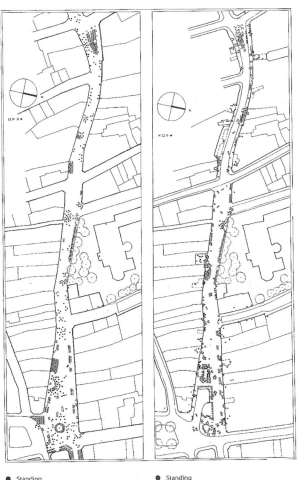

● Standing
✕ Sitting
△ Musicians, Performers
☐ Vendors and Waiters

Wednesday, 19 July, 1995

Time:	13.30 p.m.
Weather:	Fine, 23° C.
Standing:	340 persons
Sitting:	389 persons
Total:	753 persons

● Standing
○ Standing and talking
☐ Standing and waiting
✕ Sitting

Monday, 23 July, 1968

Time:	12:00 noon
Weather:	Fine, 20° C.
Standing:	429 persons
Sitting:	324 persons
Total:	729 persons

FIGURE 12.6
Pedestrian activity map for the same street in Copenhagen on Wednesday 19 July 1995 and Monday 23 July 1968 (source: Bosselmann, 1998, p. 44)

or site that present difficulties for development because of one, or a combination of, constraints (Moughtin *et al.*, 1999, p. 70). When undertaken using Geographic Information Systems (GIS), many layers of socio-economic and physical data can be combined and compared. Public authorities often collect and maintain extensive GIS-based data on issues as diverse as population statistics, social deprivation patterns, traffic levels, pollution levels, environmental resources, and existing land uses (a particularly important component of urban design analysis). Combined with site studies, such data can provide a powerful analytical tool for urban design.

Representations of two dimensions

This section concerns two means of representing urban design in a two-dimensional form: orthographic projections, and Geographic Information Systems (GIS).

(i) Orthographic projections

Orthographic projections represent three dimensions in two-dimensional drawings, by means of plans, sections and elevations. A series of vantage points is usually required to illustrate a scheme. Plans and elevations are abstracted views, plans from above, and elevations facing straight on, with no distortions due to perspective (being drawn as if seen from infinity). Sections complement plans and elevations – which on their own rarely provide sufficient information – by showing the vertical dimension relative to the horizontal one (Figure 12.7). They can also show and enable exploration of the relationship between inside and outside spaces and between different levels. Orthographic projections are an important means of communicating design projects, particularly as part of a package of working or construction drawings displaying the scheme at a true scale.

(ii) Geographic information systems

More recent additions to the range of tools available to urban designers are Geographic Information Systems (GIS), computer-based systems for the handling of geographically referenced information. They contain information on utilities and services, schedules of spaces and accommodation, and transportation routes, and can store, display and manipulate visual and audio information – such as photographic and video images – in association with more traditional forms of data. This multi-layered approach takes GIS beyond the realms of two-dimensional representation. A considerable amount of information related to an area can be stored within the system, including data related to both buildings and spaces, and the way they are used. Traditionally the domain of geographers and urban planners, GIS systems are increasingly used in urban design analysis and in the design process.

The main disadvantage of two-dimensional representations is that the layperson may have difficulty in interpreting such drawings, which often bear little resemblance to real views of spaces or townscapes. They are, however, a key means of communicating design information between professionals, and are relatively quick and cheap to produce when compared to more sophisticated graphic and visual representations.

Representations of three dimensions

Three-dimensional representations communicate in a more widely understandable form. However, their production usually requires more skill, is time consuming, and is more costly than two-dimensional graphics. Despite their additional realism, these diagrams – with the exception of physical models – are still communicated through a 2D medium such

FIGURE 12.7
Sections are particularly useful in communicating the relationship between internal and external spaces (source: Papadakis, 1993, p. 102)

as paper or a computer screen. The most commonly used means of representing urban design are perspective drawings, sketches, paraline drawings, computer-aided design, and physical models.

(i) Perspective drawings

Brunelleschi's experiments with linear perspective as a technique for representing realism and defining the location of objects in space marked a turning point in visual representation (Figure 12.8). Perspectives represent the optical effect where the eye perceives parallel lines as converging with distance. Perspective drawings are useful both to convey finalised design proposals and as quick sketch aids at a project's concept stage. They can convey abstract qualities, such as mood, character and atmosphere, much better than orthogonal drawings, and are therefore valuable in enabling non-professionals to understand a design. They are, however, only useful when they represent views as they are seen – artistic licence is often used on perspectives so that the view illustrated may not be experienced in reality. Another potential pitfall is that rendering a new development in the same technique as the existing context on an illustration can help it appear to 'fit in', when in reality this may not be the case. Equally, without full rendering, a perspective gives little sense of materials, texture or colour.

(ii) Sketches and photomontages

By helping to portray an idea quickly while aiding observation and analysis of the environment, sketches are important communication devices, useful in investigating an early design idea, to test visual effects, or to set a design in context. Rather than as ends in themselves, they should be considered as part of the process of understanding. By superimposing an illustration of a design onto a photographic image, photomontage can also provide a realistic impression, giving a good idea of whether it integrates with the existing context (although, for a realistic effect, attention needs to be paid to details such as shadows). Such presentations are popular with clients, local planning authorities and the general public who can quickly understand and react to proposals.

(iii) Paraline drawings

Based upon orthographic projections, paraline drawings convey a third dimension through the representation of length, breadth and height in one drawing, using axonometric or isometric projections (Figure 12.9). They enable space to be organised by volume rather than by area as with orthographic views. They aid visual perception, but only to a limited degree because perspective effects are ignored.

FIGURE 12.8
Vriedman de Vries *On Perspective* 1599 (source: Porter, 1997, p. 16)

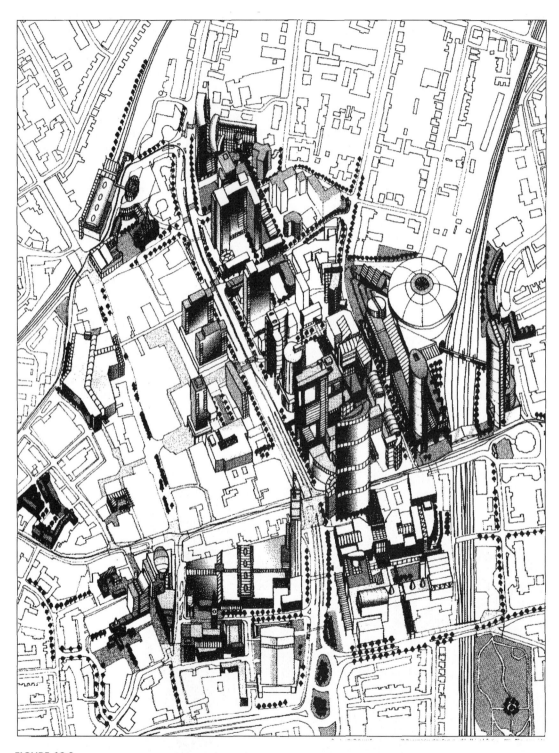

FIGURE 12.9
Isometric and axonometric projections are useful in communicating three-dimensional form. This axonometric of central Croydon, London, UK, shows development possibilities (source: EDAW, 1998)

(iv) Computer-aided design

The use of computer-aided design (CAD) enables ideas to be resolved quickly and alternatives to be generated (Figure 12.10). The designer is encouraged to think in three dimensions from the initial stages of a project. Software can calculate and simulate artificial and daylight conditions, materials, etc., through the application of textures and colours, and computer models can take on an extra dimension of realism with animation, through the addition of people, vehicles, landscaping, street furniture, and other objects.

Computer-generated three-dimensional models of urban areas help in assessing the impact of new buildings and alterations to existing townscape, allowing development/design proposals to be 'slotted' into an existing computer model and viewed from any angle (see Bosselmann, 1998, pp. 100–19). Options such as colour schemes, materials, roof pitches, heights, and fenestration can be tested and amended far more accurately and in less time than with traditional media. Design issues can therefore be resolved quickly and efficiently, with almost instant revisions. Computer technology can also be used to supplement freehand techniques by scanning in images and enhancing them with computer techniques

(daylighting, shadows, etc.). The possibility of the technology's presentational 'gloss' overshadowing a scheme's attributes, however, must be guarded against, as well as any tendency for the technology to unduly dictate the design.

(v) Models

To enable better understanding and communication of a project, physical models can complement or replace drawings (Figure 12.11). Depending upon its application and the stage of the project at which it is constructed, the role of a model varies:

- *Conceptual models* used in the initial design stages are essentially three-dimensional diagrams, expressing and exploring the designer's initial ideas.
- *Working models* used during design development enhance understanding of spatial and sequential relationships, and may be used for simulating lighting and climatic conditions.
- *Presentation models* represent the final design solution. Suitably embellished with 'entourage' (e.g. people, landscape, vehicles, etc.), they usually form important aids to the project's communication and marketing rather than to decision-making.

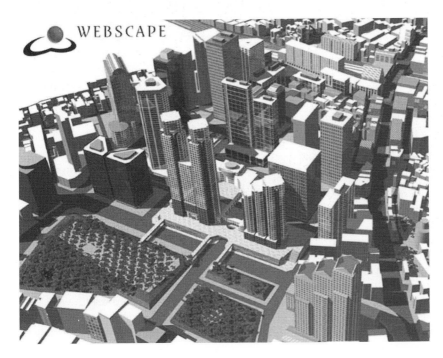

FIGURE 12.10
Computer-aided urban townscape model of central Tokyo (source: Webscape.com)

FIGURE 12.11
Urban model (photograph: Glynn Halls). Credit:
Matthew Byron, Alisdair Russell and Peter Wraight

While models are a long-established method of representing architectural and urban form, they raise particular issues concerning the realism–reality gap. By presenting a three-dimensional version of a proposed development, models may seem more 'truthful' than drawings, but problems arise in trying to understand what the full-sized building and its environment will be like. This is a means–ends confusion: the observer is seduced into seeing the model as an end rather than as a means to another end. Conway and Roenisch (1994, p. 200), for example, note how models can be seductive:

> Beautifully made . . . they remind us of the doll's houses, model frames and railways that we played with as children. The seductiveness . . . is not only to do with their size and the materials used, it is also to do with their clarity and cleanliness of the forms, the way they are lit and the way shadows fall. They represent pure, ideal buildings that are removed from their context and are not subject to the wear and tear of weather and time.

Models may also appear to represent an ideal world: 'Even if these models are finely detailed and fully coloured, and include people, trees and cars in scale with the buildings, the world that they inhabit has no litter, no graffiti, no poor or elderly, and we have no clue about where the sun might shine' (Conway and Roenisch, 1994, p. 200).

A certain idealisation – or abstraction – of models is often deliberate: it helps to highlight certain features, while emphasising that it is only a model (a representation of reality). Grey and white models tend to show form better because the shadows are sharper. Such models also allow designers and clients to keep their options open regarding materials, finish and colour. Equally, however, such models abstract buildings from their surroundings. Some urban designers suggest that the most appropriate scale for models is 1:300, their function being to explore and communicate the intended massing of the development and spaces created, rather than to show buildings in detail. Larger-scale models usually require architectural detail which distracts from the urban space design issues being discussed.

Representations of four dimensions

As experiencing an urban environment is a dynamic activity involving movement and time (see Chapter 9), the addition of a time dimension to graphic representations can enhance understanding and communication. For centuries, designers and artists have tried to capture such experiences in graphic and visual terms – the Cubists, for example, attempted it with work such as Duchamp's *Lady Descending the Stair*. Several techniques of spatial representation have been developed to record and communicate the experience of complex interacting three-dimensional events through the sequential description of space and time.

Three types of four-dimensional representation are considered here: serial vision; video animations; and computer-aided animations and virtual reality.

(i) Serial vision

Serial vision is a method of communicating the experience of townscape by introducing movement through a series of sequential illustrations. Gordon Cullen's sketches in *The Concise Townscape* (1971), and Edmund Bacon's diagrams in *Design of Cities* (1974) embody the concept that movement can be read and understood as a pictorial sequence. As discussed in Chapter 7, Cullen advocated the idea of serial vision as a tool of both visual analysis and creative design. Whereas traditional static images illustrate space at a certain moment in time, serial vision attempts to show the temporal unfolding of movement as a dynamic activity: its images can be thought of as resembling the pages of an old-fashioned flicker book (see Figure 7.4). However, as Bosselmann (1998) observes, serial vision graphics do not provide a sense of how we actually experience and interpret places, nor how we generate a sense of structure and location in space.

(ii) Video animations

Accustomed to television and video technology, people can easily understand projects presented through video images. Computer-generated video presentations are used to communicate projects to clients, planning authorities, funding institutions and members of the community. Video technology engages viewers through visual, aural, kinaesthetic, spatial and temporal senses, allowing them to make more accurate judgements regarding dimensions and proportions than from still pictures. However, viewers are restricted to a predetermined and scripted route, which restricts perception of the environment and thus to an extent predetermines feedback. As in serial vision, the field of vision is too narrow to truly represent and capture what human eyes can see and other senses perceive. Representations inevitably eliminate some information, available to peripheral vision, that might attract attention.

(ii) Computer imaging and animation

Whereas traditional representations are static (i.e. fixed viewpoints in space), computers can show movement through space, although presentation is still confined to the two-dimensional abstraction of the computer screen. A range of new technologies – such as virtual reality – emerged during the 1990s, which could have a significant impact upon urban design. Indeed, few new computer technologies have captured the imagination in the way that virtual reality has. Previously, the only way to enable walking through a project in real time was to construct a full-scale mock-up. Now, sophisticated, high-speed computer power combined with images, sound and other effects can create an interactive system so fast and intuitive that the computer disappears from the user's mind, leaving the computer-generated environment as the reality. Viewers can perceive and understand an environment in their own way, enabling better-informed feedback and participation.

Representations of urban environments and design proposals in four dimensions are likely to be increasingly important in the communication, promotion and selling of projects. However, this evolving technology must be harnessed to enhancing the understanding of proposals by both designer and layperson. New techniques offer a highly realistic and interactive environment, with choice of movement giving freedom to viewers to choose their own routes, as opposed to the pre-programmed walk-through of traditional manual and computer presentations. Despite its obvious potential designers need to be aware of dangers in the persuasiveness of virtual reality. The technology also needs to be simplified and made less expensive to gain widespread professional adoption. Virtual reality nevertheless offers the opportunity to bridge the gap between what you see and what you get in urban design. As part of the creative process, and as a decision-making and presentational tool to aid understanding and evaluation, its importance will increase.

Many visual and graphic techniques exist to communicate the experience of places. As communication technology becomes increasingly familiar to both professionals and the public, this should open up opportunities for it to be used to its full potential. The previous sections have shown the increasingly important role that technology is playing in the representation and communication of urban design. Since the 1970s, film, television and computers have also been increasingly exploited as design media. As a means of representation, computer-aided design has superseded all previous methods. Indeed, using a computer – in some form – is now standard practice in nearly all design offices.

Although new technology offers the opportunity to make information more accessible and comprehensible, designers need to appreciate the many roles that a computer can play in the design process, as well as its advantages and disadvantages for each task. The ability to communicate design more persuasively raises important issues regarding the ethics of communication. State-of-the-art visualisations of projects often mean that few people understand precisely how the data is manipulated or can access the information to verify a simulation's accuracy. It is important therefore that technological developments are harnessed to enable better understanding and involvement of the public in decisions affecting their environment. The use of technology could help to create an increased awareness of urban design, and facilitate the ability for everyone to react to, and interact with, proposals for the built environment.

CONCLUSION

Communication in urban design covers all aspects of verbal and non-verbal presentation, as well as the ability to listen to, and appreciate and respect the views, values and aspirations of, others. In the communication of any urban design project it is important to give as true a representation of the project as possible to all interested parties. Communication is an important tool that can influence decision-making (Figure 12.12).

There are a number of implications of the media chosen, including the appropriateness, cost, time, and designers' skill. It is important, though, to design the project rather than the presentation. Given the influence of presentational techniques on the way in which designers perceive their creations, the mode of representation can have a strong influence on the scheme's design – designers need to be wary of designing for the representational media rather than for the real world. There is also an increasing trend for designers to use presentation methods that are so abstract and complex that only other designers can understand them. This form of professional elitism – usually from the 'architecture as fine art' school – may do little to persuade an audience of the merits of high quality urban design and undermines effective communication of design ideas.

Everyone perceives the urban environment in a different way, as we each respond to the particular phenomena that attract us. The way the environment is seen is conditioned by our background, familiarity with the place, purpose within it, and/or mode of travel (see Chapter 5). In communicating urban design projects, the aim should be to enable viewers to perceive a scheme in similar ways to reality. Good visual images should provide legible and understandable information for a wide and varied audience, enabling evaluation by those affected by the design. Presenters need to understand the context of the communication process, and thus understand the audience and adapt a presentation as appropriate. Presenters should also be aware of potential barriers to communication, including social, psychological or technical factors, and the use of language and non-verbal communication such as body language.

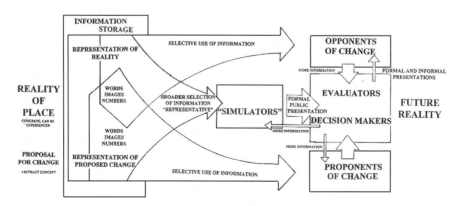

FIGURE 12.12
Design communication model (source: Bosselmann, 1998, p. 202)

13

Holistic urban design

INTRODUCTION

In general terms, this book has moved from theory through to practice. Part I began with general discussion about the nature of urban design and the role of the urban designer. Discussion moved on to review the evolution of urban design and its impact on urban form and a number of overarching contexts – local, global, market and regulatory. In Part II, key areas of urban design thought were reviewed in the form of six dimensions – morphological, perceptual, social, visual, functional, and temporal. In Part III, the nature and roles of the public and private sectors in delivering and sustaining high quality urban design were explored. The overarching definition used throughout has been that urban design is about making places for people. This definition asserts the importance of four themes:

- urban design being concerned with people;
- urban design valuing 'place';
- urban design operating in the 'real' world, with the designer's field of opportunity typically constrained by market and regulatory forces; and
- urban design as a design process.

In this final chapter, we stress and reiterate the fourth and final point in this overarching definition – urban design as a design process.

'QUESTIONING' URBAN DESIGN

In essence, this book should be understood as a discussion of how to make 'places' out of 'spaces'

– although, as has been noted previously, this is done not so much by urban designers as by the people who inhabit space with their activities and, thus, turn them into places. To focus and structure this discussion, a loose structure of key areas of urban design action has been used, which can accommodate and relate most of the key contributions to urban design thought. It, nevertheless, remains open to debate where to place individual contributions (particularly since, due to the integrative nature of urban design, most writers and commentators range across the different dimensions). The book's structure also emphasises urban design's multi-dimensional and multi-layered nature. While it is structured for convenience, our experience is not. Our experience of urban environments is an integrative one, but, to understand it better, it is necessary to dissect it and analyse the constituent parts. Conversely, to design – to create new places and to make positive contributions and interventions into existing places – those constituent parts need to be drawn together and considered as a whole.

In making the case for urban design, this book has not sought to produce a 'new' theory in a prescriptive fashion, nor to offer a new definition of the subject, or a formulaic 'solution' to urban design. The discussion in Chapter 1, for example, showed that while many definitions of urban design are appropriate and valuable, they are also limiting and contestable. Although some useful frameworks from distinguished urban designers were presented, they were accompanied by the caveat that they should not be treated as inflexible dogma, nor reduced to mechanical formulae. Application of a formula negates the active process of design, and downgrades the role of the designer. No single set of rules or objectives can capture the scope and complexity of urban design, nor offer a step-by-step formula for a successful outcome. Design is an exploratory, intuitive and deductive process, involving research into the problem posed, and into the variable and specific conditions of time and place. This is not to say that the complex interactions between the processes and elements in any one place cannot be examined, nor that these cannot give generic clues as to why some places succeed while others fail.

It is also necessary to have a continually questioning and inquisitive approach to urban design. As in any design process, there are no 'right' or 'wrong' answers, only 'better' and 'worse' ones,

the quality of which may only be known in time. Bryan Lawson (2001, p. 247) argues that design typically 'requires action in the form of decisions, even in the face of inadequate time and knowledge. For these reasons sometimes it is useful to oversimplify in order to structure thought enough to make design decisions slightly less arbitrary. We cannot hope to make them perfect.' The necessary attitude is encapsulated in Frank Lloyd Wright's response to a question asked near the end of his career regarding what he thought was his best building. Wright replied: 'The next one.'

A number of recent publications (e.g. Tibbalds *et al.*, 1990; DETR, 1998; Cowan, 2001) take the helpful approach of setting out a series of prompts

---

BOX 13.1 – QUESTIONING 'URBAN DESIGN'

Defining urban design
- Will the project have an impact – no matter how small – on the public realm?
- Will the project contribute to the creation or enhancement of a meaningful place?

The contexts
- Does the project respect, understand, learn from and integrate with the existing context?
- Are the proposals environmentally supportive or, at least, environmentally benign?
- Are the proposals economically viable and designed to provide sustainable quality?
- Has the proposal involved and garnered the support of stakeholders?

Morphological
- Have morphological patterns been understood and positively extended to create distinct urban blocks and coherent networks of well-connected, fine-grained, streets and spaces?

Perceptual
- Will the project contribute to the creation of an established or new sense of place?
- Will the project create a legible and meaningful public realm?

Social
- Will the development encourage an accessible and safe use of the public realm?
- Will the development provide opportunities for social interaction, social mix and diversity?

Visual
- Have buildings, streets and spaces, hard and soft landscaping and street furniture been considered together to create drama and visual interest and to reinforce or enhance the sense of place?

Functional
- Will the mix and distribution of uses animate the public realm and support necessary, optional and social activities?
- Does the planned infrastructure integrate with and, where necessary, extend the established capital web?

Temporal
- Have the proposals been considered across different time horizons – day and night, summer and winter, long and short term?
- Will the project enable an incremental mix of old with new, avoid comprehensive redevelopment as far as appropriate, and be 'whole' at each stage, repairing its edges as it goes?

Developing urban design
- Is the scheme financially feasible and able to offer security to developers, investors and occupiers over short-, medium- and long-term horizons?

Controlling urban design
- How have public aspirations been expressed and reflected in the proposed development?
- Have long-term management and maintenance issues been considered?

Communicating urban design
- Are the vision and/or the proposals clearly communicated to, understandable by and owned by stakeholders – including the community?

and/or posing a set of questions to establish an agenda of issues for both 'knowing' and 'unknowing' urban designers. As an attempt to bring together some of the various contributions and dimensions discussed in this book, Box 13.1 offers a series of questions. Rather than a complete conceptualisation of or prescriptive agenda for urban design, the intention is to provide a modest reminder of key issues. The questions can be used to evaluate proposed schemes, but more appropriately might be used to ask why some places succeed while others fail.

THE CHALLENGE

The day-to-day problems of achieving high quality urban design are real, and are illustrated by the difficulty of finding high quality examples of contemporary urban design. A wide range of barriers can be highlighted that militate against the delivery of better quality urban design (Carmona *et al.*, 2001, pp. 32–3). Many of these have been discussed or alluded to in earlier chapters, but include:

- *Low awareness*: There is variable awareness of urban design issues among investors and occupiers concerning the value given to environmental quality (in its broadest sense) in the success of their operations. Research suggests that different submarkets have different levels of concern and sophistication as regards design: retailers, for example, tend to be more aware of the contribution of design than are office occupiers.
- *Poor information*: The scarcity of reliable information about the preferences of prospective occupiers and investors adds to the risk of departing from conventional and 'safe' standards of design quality.
- *Unpredictable markets*: The timing of a development in relation to the fluctuations of the property and investment market often dictates attitudes towards investing in urban design quality, as perceived risk changes. The cyclical behaviour of property markets can, therefore, be a barrier to good urban design.
- *High land costs*: High land costs can reduce profit margins and leave little room for extra investment in quality, especially since, in property markets, prices adjust only slowly and imperfectly.
- *Fragmented land ownership*: Fragmented patterns of land ownership can increase the

time and uncertainty of the development process, leading to fragmented and unco-ordinated developments.
- *Unco-ordinated development*: Individual acts of development are often unco-ordinated, and do not aggregate into a greater whole. In general, larger sites (once assembled into single landownership) are more likely to address issues of 'place-making', making it easier for investors to capture beneficial 'externalities' in the form of rents and capital values. Equally, small-scale incremental development, particularly when co-ordinated in some (perhaps unconscious) way, will often produce 'better' places.
- *Combative relationships*: Confrontational relationships between developers and the public sector increase the time taken to develop, thus increasing uncertainty and risk.
- *Economic conditions*: Uncertainty and instability in the general economy can often lead to shorter-term investment decisions and less investment in design.
- *Lack of choice*: Constraints in the supply of the right quality of property in a desired location reduce the contribution of design considerations in occupier decision-making – occupiers may often trade poorer development for an alternative location.
- *Short-termism*: The structure of capital markets, with planning horizons of three to five years, makes it difficult for many businesses to engage in the long-term planning necessary for investment in better design. This is also shown by the preference for short-term and one-off transactions rather than a long-term relationship involving repeat custom.
- *Perceptions of cost*: The perception among occupiers that, while many benefits of good design accrue to the wider community (i.e. they are social benefits), it is the occupiers who pay for it, in higher rents, running costs and commercial rates (i.e. they involve private costs).
- *Decision-making patterns*: Many of the most important urban design decisions are taken not by planners, developers or designers, but by people who may not think of themselves as being involved in urban design (i.e. unknowing urban designers). Such actors often lack appreciation of the wider consequences of the decisions they make, particularly their impact on the urban environment.

- *Negative planning*: Largely reactionary, as opposed to 'positive' and proactive, approaches to urban design across many local authorities, and a general failure to link concerns for urban regeneration with those for better urban design.
- *Skills deficit*: The low levels of urban design skills on both sides of the development process represent a significant and consistent impediment to the effective delivery of better design.

Such constraints should be seen as challenges for urban designers. Successful designers are skilled in confronting and overcoming constraints. Urban design is not simply a passive reaction to change, but also a positive attempt to shape change and make better places. As discussed in a more specific sense in Chapter 10, urban designers can deploy three particular types of power and influence: through the knowledge and expertise produced by their learning, research and professional experience, and, more generally, by their awareness of precedents; through their reputation, which is why they are hired and which endows them with 'cultural capital'; and through initiative and being proactive. To succeed, however, urban designers also need political and operational skills. Tibbalds (1988a, pp. 12–13), for example, identified a set of personal skills required by successful urban designers, which includes the following:

- Being able to operate at a high level (i.e. being a force to be reckoned with, and appreciated by politicians, administrators, industrialists, developers, etc.).
- Being passionately concerned with achievability (i.e. putting all manner of design ideas to practical effect).
- Being outward looking and able to show due deference and humility to other professions and to the community.
- Being able to argue cogently and convincingly for the necessary resources of finance, land and manpower to see their ideas through.
- Possessing astute financial awareness.
- Being idealistic but realistic (i.e. able to recognise why things go wrong).
- Having an unfettered imagination, and commitment to quality and to finishing the job.

As Tibbalds (1988a, p. 13) correctly noted, these skills are only a means to an end: the real end is to achieve something worthwhile on the ground. Equally, without the means, there is no end.

The barriers listed above highlight the importance of the public sector in establishing a political and regulatory climate within which good design can flourish. In cities demonstrating the best examples of urban design – Barcelona, Copenhagen, Birmingham, Portland, San Francisco, Sydney – the barriers have been overcome. In such places, as well as the positive role played by public authorities in ensuring the right climate for design, the positive role played by private sector developers and investors working to ensure a shared commitment to quality across different stakeholder groups has often been equally significant. If commitment from all sectors is there, then there is the potential to create contemporary public places and urban space to rival the best in any century. Figures 13.1–13.3 illustrate three examples where this has been the case.

If many of the barriers to delivering better quality urban design relate to the processes of design, development and public regulation, then (as with sustainable development) so do many of the solutions. Certain process-related barriers – local market conditions, the macro-economy, etc. – are almost impossible for urban designers (or, indeed, any built environment professionals) to influence. Other factors are only amenable to influence over extended periods of time and with national/state or regional action. They include awareness of urban design among key actors; established patterns of decision-making; the cost of land; the nature of the planning system and other regulatory mechanisms. These were discussed in Chapter 3 as the market and regulatory contexts for urban design, which, for practical purposes, urban designers often have to accept as givens.

There are, nevertheless, a series of constraints that urban designers, their clients and local communities can influence: the availability of information on demand and on public preferences; the consolidation of land and development opportunities; the operation of the planning process as a positive force for change; education about the value of better design; the availability of appropriately skilled individuals in both public and private sectors; and the formulation and adoption of a coherent local vision. Most of all, urban design practitioners can move beyond short-sighted, hard-edged professional approaches, and adopt collaborative working relationships.

FIGURE 13.1
Aker Brygge, Oslo, Norway. Effectively producing a new city centre quarter for Oslo, the Aker Brygge is a successful piece of urban design. Attracting six million people annually, its success as urban design is built on its:

- diverse range of uses – cafes, restaurants, retail, festival shopping, offices, two theatres, theatrical academy, residential, cinemas, health centre, kindergarten;
- morphological form – positive relationship to its waterside setting, sequence of spaces lined with active uses, pedestrian-friendly car-free status, good pubic transport connections, and high permeability (visually and physically) without compromising the intimacy of the key space;

- architectural mix – a rich mix of bold contemporary architecture with revitalised historic buildings;
- response to climate – with protected pockets, interior walkways and spaces for the winter and uses that spill out into the external spaces in good weather; and
- size and density – 64 hectares of high density but with relatively small buildings and with a good resident and working population.

A HOLISTIC APPROACH

To conclude this book, it is worth re-stressing the holistic nature of urban design. In any design process, there is a danger of narrowly prioritising a particular dimension – aesthetic, functional, technical or economic – thus isolating it from its context and from its contribution to the greater whole. Much of the so-called 'functionalism' of Modernist architecture suffered from this problem. According to that approach, functional requirements were primary and would generate building layout, form and visual expression. Reacting to the overcrowded and unhealthy conditions of the industrial cities, Modernists argued that people needed more light, fresh air, sun and greenery. New housing, for example, could be designed by rigidly following key criteria such as daylighting standards which lead to the spreading out of buildings. Such an approach may appropriately emphasise one aspect of design to the probable detriment of others such as integration of the development into its local context (e.g. by connection into existing movement patterns) and

FIGURE 13.2

Bankside, London, UK. Bankside is a major success story of urban design in London. The diversity of its attractions and dramatic nature of its context with views across the Thames to the Cities of London and Westminster make the experience a major draw for tourists and Londoners. It is not, however, a conventional piece of urban design in the form of a new development. Instead, it is a rejuvenated – and still evolving – riverside walk stretching from east of Tower Bridge to Westminster Bridge and taking in London's Design Museum, Southwark Cathedral, historic Borough Market, the Globe Theatre, Tate Modern (art gallery), and the National Theatre, along with a host of other entertainment, arts, residential, commercial, retail and restaurant/cafe uses. Dominated by the pedestrian route, along which most of the attractions are arranged, the urban form is a mix of high-density traditional space and contemporary commercial developments. The historic public realm has been the subject of considerable public sector investment, and includes high quality public art and landscaping. It also includes a number of successful contemporary interventions such as Tower Bridge Piazza and the Coin Street social housing development. Architecturally, a number of iconic set pieces add to the area's appeal – Tower Bridge, the London Assembly Building, the converted Bankside power station, the Millennium Bridge (shown above), the London Eye and the Royal Festival Hall. The quantity and quality of visual and social stimuli make Bankside a memorable place. Its success is all the more significant because of the diversity of players responsible for its creation, including a proactive local authority regeneration team and a host of voluntary, community and commercial interests. In large part, the area has been revitalised through managed incremental development (rather than through any grand master plan), and through a concern for quality around the unifying theme of the Thames Path.

the preferences and choices of those likely to live there.

In Chapter 3, a fourth criterion – economy – was added to the well-established trinity of 'firmness, commodity and delight', and it was argued that each must be satisfied simultaneously. 'Economy' is interpreted not only in the narrower financial sense of respecting budget constraints, but also (and more importantly) in its widest sense – reflecting the imperative of minimising environmental costs. The need to address complex sustainability issues represents perhaps the greatest challenge of the

FIGURE 13.3
Pioneer Courthouse Square, Portland, Oregon, USA. Located in the centre of Portland's downtown, Pioneer Courthouse Square is a successful piece of urban design. The square's long gestation period contributed both to its character and to the sense of ownership felt for it by the city's citizens. In 1952, the former grand Portland Hotel was demolished and a two-storey garage structure constructed. In the early 1960s, there was a proposal to replace the garage with a public square, but it was not until 1972 that the Downtown Plan for Portland designated the block for future use as a public square. The city eventually purchased the land in 1979 and, in 1980, an international competition was held to select a design for the square. Although a citizen jury chose a scheme by a local firm of architects, a change of mayor and the formation of the Downtown Business Association for Portland Process halted plans. A grass roots action group – Friends of Pioneer Square – fought to retain the project, raising US$1.6 million by selling sponsorship of the square's benches, trees and lights, plus more than 60,000 paving bricks. Opened in 1984, the square offers a variety of spaces providing varying degrees of refuge and exposure, opportunities for people-watching and a variety of sitting locations. Its centre is palpably pregnant with opportunity and hosts three hundred events annually. The square has also played a significant role in restoring Portland's downtown as the region's social and economic centre, while an enlightened transport policy has made it the main terminal of a regional light-rail

twenty-first century. Those engaged in the design and management of urban areas have the potential to play an important role in addressing this challenge. In different ways, sustainability impacts on each of the dimensions of urban design:

- *Morphological* – resource consumption and pollution (particularly through movement) is strongly influenced by the configuration of the urban pattern.

- *Perceptual* – the psychological welfare of people is intimately related to the social stability of places, and how they are valued and looked after.
- *Social* – patterns of living can both reinforce and undermine environmental well-being.
- *Functional* – mixing uses, building at higher densities and coping with the local environment all impact on energy usage.
- *Visual* – diversity in the built and natural environment is a key sustainable principle, while

concern for aesthetic fulfilment indicates a willingness to invest in sustainable quality.

- *Temporal* – the pursuit of sustainable development is a long-term goal accomplished through many small-scale interventions.

Achieving sustainable development is also a political challenge. Hildebrand Frey (1999, p. 144) argues that:

> to achieve sustainable city regions requires the rethinking not only of the city and city region but also of current policies, approaches and professional responsibilities as well as education. What is needed is a strong political will to act upon this commitment by implementing strong, co-ordinated policies, approaches and strategies; and this equates with a kind of gentle and friendly revolution. Half-heartedness will not achieve sustainable city regions.

Despite its role in delivering environmental quality – and unlike, for example, the field of architecture – there are very few 'big names' in urban design. In part, this is because good urban design is often unobtrusive. It blends in and 'disappears' – we do not notice that it is there. Conversely, poor urban design often stands out. Indeed, it may only be noticed when it does not work. Good urban design may often be like the referee in a football (soccer) match who has a 'good' game by not being noticed. Furthermore, in delivering good urban design, the contribution of the individual is almost always eclipsed by that of the team. This, in turn, reflects the nature of urban design as a process of joining-up – both joining-up environments and places, and joining-up professionals and other actors with each other, with communities, and with those who wish to invest. In the contemporary context, good urban design is almost always achieved through collaborative design and working processes.

To achieve its full potential, urban design considerations need to figure more centrally in the decision-making processes of public and private actors and in the programmes of educators in built environment and related fields. There also needs to be a general cultural shift towards perspectives that are more appreciative and mindful of urban design. It is hoped that this book will make a contribution on these fronts. If urban design is about making public places for people, the challenge is to design urban spaces that people will want to use.

Bibliography

Abbott, C. (1997), *Portland: Gateway to the North-West*, American Historical Press, Washington.

Adams, D. (1994), *Urban Planning and the Development Process*, UCL Press, London.

Adams, D., Disberry, A., Hutchison, N. and Munjoma, T. (1999), *Do Landowners Constrain Urban Redevelopment?* RICS Research Findings 34.

Aldous, T. (1992), *Urban Villages: A concept for creating mixed-use developments on a sustainable scale*, Urban Villages Group, London.

Alexander, C. (1965), A City is Not a Tree, *Architectural Forum*, 122 (1 and 2), April/May, also in Bell, G. and Tyrwhitt, R. (1992) (eds), *Human Identity in the Urban Environment*, Penguin, London.

Alexander, C. (1975), *The Oregon Experiment*, Oxford University Press, Oxford.

Alexander, C. (1979), *The Timeless Way of Building*, Oxford University Press, Oxford.

Alexander, C., Ishikawa, S. and Silverstein, M. (1977), *A Pattern Language: Towns, Buildings, Construction*, Oxford University Press, Oxford.

Alexander, C., Neis, H., Anninou, A. and King, I. (1987), *A New Theory of Urban Design*, Oxford University Press, New York.

Ambrose, P. (1986), *Whatever Happened to Planning*, Methuen, London.

Anderson, S. (1978) (ed.), *On Streets*, MIT Press, Cambridge, Mass.

Appignanesi, R. and Garratt, C. (1999), *Introducing Postmodernism*, Icon Books, London.

Appleyard, D. (1976), *Planning a Pluralist City: Conflicting realities in Ciudad Guyana*, MIT Press, Cambridge, Mass.

Appleyard, D. (1980), Why buildings are known: A predictive tool for architects and planners, in Broadbent, G., Bunt, R. and Llorens, T. (1980) (eds), *Meaning and Behaviour in the Built Environment*, John Wiley & Sons, Chichester.

Appleyard, D. (1981), *Liveable Streets*, University of California Press, Berkeley.

Appleyard, D. (1982), Three kinds of urban design practice, in Ferebee, A. (1982) (ed.), *Education for Urban Design*, Institute for Urban Design, New York.

Appleyard, D. (1991), Foreword, from Moudon, A.V. (1991), *Public Streets for Public Use*, Columbia University Press, New York, pp. 5–8.

Appleyard, D. and Lintell, M. (1972), The environmental quality of city streets: The residents' viewpoint, *Journal of the American Institute of Planners*, **38**, 84–101.

Appleyard, D., Lynch, K. and Myer, J. (1964), *The View from the Road*, MIT Press, Cambridge, Mass.

Ardrey, R. (1967), *The Territorial Imperative: A Personal Inquiry into the Animal Origins of Property and Nations*, Collins, London.

Arefi, M. (1999), Non-place and placelessness as narratives of loss: Rethinking the notion of place, *Journal of Urban Design*, **4**, 179–93.

Arendt, H. (1958), *The Human Condition*, University of Chicago Press, Chicago.

Arnheim, R. (1977), *The Dynamics of Architectural Form*, University of California Press, Berkeley.

Arnstein, S. (1969), A Ladder of Citizen Participation, *American Institute of Planners Journal*, July, pp. 216–24.

Arup Economics and Planning (1995), *Environmental Capacity, A Methodology for Historic Cities*, Cheshire County Council, Chester.

Arup Economics and Planning (2000), *Survey of Urban Design Skills in Local Government*, DETR, London.

Ashworth, G.J. and Tunbridge, J.E. (1990), *The Touristic-Historic City*, Belhaven Press, London.

Attoe, W. and Logan, D. (1989), *American Urban Architecture: Catalysts in the Design of Cities*, University of California Press, Berkeley.

Auge, M. (1995), *Non-places: An Introduction to an Anthropology of Supermodernity*, Verso, London.

Bacon, E. (1974, 1992), *Design of Cities*, London, Thames & Hudson (first published in 1967).

Baker, G. (1996), *Design Strategies in Architecture: An approach to the analysis of form*, second edition, London: E & FN Spon.

Ball, M. (1986), The built environment and the urban question, *Environment & Planning D: Society & Space*, **4**, 447–64.

Ball, M. (1998), Institutions in British Property Research: A Review, *Urban Studies*, **35**, 1501–17.

Ball, M., Lizieri, C. and MacGregor, B.D. (1998), *The Economics of Commercial Property Markets*, London, Routledge.

Banham, R. (1976), *Megastructures: Urban Features of the Recent Past*, London, Thames and Hudson.

Banerjee, T. (2001), The Future of Public Space: Beyond

Invented Streets and Reinvented Places, *APA Journal*, **67**, 9–24.

Banerjee, T. and Baer, W.C. (1984), *Beyond the Neighbourhood Unit*, Plenum Press, New York.

Banerjee, T. and Southworth, M. (1991) (eds), *City Sense and City Design: Writings and Projects of Kevin Lynch*, MIT Press, Cambridge, Mass.

Barnett, J. (1974), *Urban Design as Public Policy*, Harper & Row, New York.

Barnett, J. (1982), *An Introduction to Urban Design*, Harper & Row, New York.

Barr, R. and Pease, K. (1992), A place for every crime and every crime in its place: an alternative perspective on crime displacement, in *Crime, Policing and Place: Essays in Environmental Criminology*, Evans, D.J., Fyfe, N.F. and Herbert, D.T. (eds), London, Routledge.

Barrett, S., Stewart, M. and Underwood, J. (1978), *The Land Market and the Development Process*, occasional paper 2, SAUS, University of Bristol, Bristol.

Barthes, R. (1967), *Elements of Semiology*, Hill & Wang, New York.

Barthes, R. (1968), The death of the author, in Barthes, R. (1977), *Image–Music–Text*, Flamingo, London, pp. 2–8.

Barton, H. (1995), Going Green by Design, *Urban Design Quarterly*, Issue 57, January, pp. 13–18.

Barton, H., Davis, G. and Guise, R. (1995), *Sustainable Settlements: A Guide for Planners, Designers, and Developers*, Local Government Management Board, Luton.

Baudrillard, J. (1983; in French, 1981), *Simulations*, Semiotext, New York.

Baudrillard, J. (1994; in French, 1981), *Simulacra and Simulation*, University of Michigan, Ann Arbor.

Bell, P.A., Fisher, J.D., Baum, A. and Greene, T.C. (1990), *Environmental Psychology* (third edition), Holt, Rinehart & Winston, Inc., London.

Ben-Joseph, E. (1995), Changing the Residential Street Scene: Adopting the Shared Street (Woonerf) Concept to the Suburban Environment, *Journal of the American Planning Association*, **61**, 504–15.

Bentley, I. (1976), What is Urban Design? Towards a Definition, *Urban Design Forum*, No. 1.

Bentley, I. (1990), Ecological Urban Design, *Architects Journal*, **192**, 69–71.

Bentley, I. (1998), Urban design as an anti-profession, *Urban Design Quarterly*, Issue 65, p. 15.

Bentley, I. (1999), *Urban Transformations: Power, people and urban design*, Routledge, London.

Bentley, I., Alcock, A., Murrain, P., McGlynn, S. and Smith, G. (1985), *Responsive Environments: A Manual for Designers*, Architectural Press, London.

Bianchini, F. (1994), Night cultures, night economies, *Town & Country Planning*, **63**, 308–10.

Biddulph, M. (1995), The value of manipulated meanings in urban design and architecture, *Environment & Planning B: Planning & Design*, **22**, 739–62.

Biddulph, M. (1999), Book review of Bosselmann, P. (1998), Representation of Place: Reality and Realism in City Design, *Journal of Urban Design*, **4**, 125–7.

Biddulph, M. (2000), Villages don't make a city, *Journal of Urban Design*, **5**, 65–82.

Birmingham City Council (1994), *Convention Centre Quarter, Planning & Urban Design Framework*, Birmingham City Council, Birmingham.

Blake, P. (1974), *Form Follows Fiasco*, Little & Brown, Boston.

Blakely, E.J. and Snyder, M.G. (1997), *Fortress America: Gated Communities in the United States*, Brookings Institution Press, Washington DC and Lincoln Institute of Land Policy, Cambridge, Mass.

Blowers, A. (1973), *The City as a Social System: Unit 7: The Neighbourhood: Exploration of a Concept*, Open University, Milton Keynes.

Blowers, A. (1993), *Planning for a Sustainable Environment*, Earthscan Publications Ltd, London.

Boddy, T. (1992), Underground and overhead: Building the analogous city, in Sorkin, M. (1992) (ed.), *Variations on a Theme Park*, Noonday Press, New York, pp. 123–53.

Booth, N.K. (1983), *Basic Elements of Landscape Architectural Design*, Elsevier, Oxford.

Borchert, J. (1991), Future of American cities, in Hart, J.F. (ed.) (1991), *Our Changing Cities*, John Hopkins Press, Baltimore.

Bosselmann, P. (1998), *Representation of Places: Reality and Realism in City Design*, University of California Press, Berkeley.

Bottoms, A.E. (1990), Crime prevention in the 1990s, *Policing and Society*, **1**, 3–22.

Boudon, P. (1969), *Lived-in Architecture: Le Corbusiers Pessac Revisited*, MIT Press, Cambridge, Mass.

Boyer, M.C. (1992), Cities for Sale: Merchandising History at South Street Seaport, in *Variations on a Theme Park: The New American City and the End of Public Space*, Sorkin, M. (ed.), New York, Hill & Wang, pp. 3–30.

Boyer, M.C. (1993), The city of illusion: New York's public places, in Knox, P. (1993) (ed.), *The Restless Urban Landscape*, Prentice Hall, Eaglewood, California, pp. 111–26.

Boyer, M.C. (1994), *The City of Collective Memory*, MIT Press, Cambridge, Mass.

Boyer, M.C. (1996), *Cybercities*, MIT Press, Cambridge, Mass.

Brand, S. (1994), *How Buildings Age: What happens after they are built*, Penguin Books, Harmondsworth.

Braunfels, W. (1988), *Urban Design in Western Europe: Regime and Architecture 900–1900*, University of Chicago Press, Chicago.

Breheny, M. (1992a) (ed.), *Sustainable Urban Development and Urban Form*, Pion, London.

Breheny, M. (1992b), The Contradictions of the Compact City: A Review, in Breheny, M. (1992) (ed.), *Sustainable Urban Development and Urban Form*, Pion, London.

Breheny, M. (1995), The Compact City and Transport Energy Consumption, *Transactions of the Institute of British Geographers*, **20**, 81–101.

Breheny, M. (1997), Centrists, Decentrists and Compromisers: Views on the Future of Urban Form, in Jenks, M., Burton, E. and Williams, K. (1997) (eds), *Compact Cities and Sustainability*, E & FN Spon, London, pp. 13–35.

Brill, M. (1989), Transformation, nostalgia and illusion in public life and public place. In *Public Places and Spaces*, Altman, I. and Zube, E. (eds), New York, Plenum Press.

Broadbent, G. (1990), *Emerging Concepts of Urban Space Design*, Van Nostrand Reinhold, New York.

Brolin, B.C. (1980), *Architecture in Context: Fitting New Buildings With Old*, Van Nostrand Reinhold, New York.

Buchanan, P. (1988a), What city? A plea for place in the public realm, *Architectural Review*, No. 1101, pp. 31–41.

Buchanan, P. (1988b), Facing up to façades, *Architects Journal*, **188**, 21–56.

Building Research Establishment (BRE) (1990), *BRE Digest 350: Climate and Site Development*, BRE, Watford.

Building Research Establishment (BRE) (1999), *An Assessment of the Police's Secured by Design Project*, BRE, Watford.

Burke, G. (1976), *Townscapes*, Harmondsworth, Penguin.

Burtenshaw, D., Bateman, M. and Ashworth, G.J. (1991), *The European City: A Western Perspective*, London, David Fulton Publishers.

Cadman, D. and Austin-Crowe, L. (1991, Cadman and Tapping, 1995), *Property Development* (third edition edited by Topping, R. and Avis, M.), Chapman & Hall, London.

CAG Consultants (1997), *Sustainability in Development Control, A Research Report*, Local Government Association, London.

Calhoun, C. (1992) (ed.), *Habermas and the Public Sphere*, Mit Press, Cambridge, Mass.

Calthorpe, P. (1989), Pedestrian Pockets: New strategies for suburban growth, in Kelbaugh, D. (1989) (ed.), *The Pedestrian Pocket Book: A New Suburban Design Strategy*, Princeton University Press, Princeton, pp. 7–20.

Calthorpe, P. (1993), *The Next American Metropolis: Ecology, community and the American Dream*, Princeton Architectural Press, New York.

Campbell, K. and Cowan, R. (1999), Finding the Tools for Better Design, *Planning*, No. 1305, 12 February, pp. 16–17.

Caniggia, G. and Maffel, G.L. (1979), *Composizione Architettonica e Tipologia Edilizia: 1, Lettura dellEdilizia di Base*, Marsilio Editori, Venice.

Caniggia, G. and Maffel, G.L. (1984), *Composizione Architettonica e Tipologia Edilizia: 2, Il Oprogettonell Edilizia di Basi*, Marsilio Editori, Venice.

Cantacuzino, S. (1994), *What makes a good building? An inquiry by the Royal Fine Arts Commission*, RFAC, London.

Canter, D. (1977), *The Psychology of Place*, Architectural Press, London.

Carmona, M. (1996), Sustainable Urban Design: The Local Plan Agenda, *Urban Design Quarterly*, Issue 57, pp. 18–22.

Carmona M. (1998a), Design Control – Bridging the Professional Divide, Part 2: A New Consensus, *Journal of Urban Design*, **3**, 331–58.

Carmona, M. (1998b), Urban design and planning practice, from Greed, C. and Roberts, M. (1998), *Introducing urban design: Interventions and responses*, Longman, Harlow.

Carmona, M. (2001), Housing Design Quality: through policy, guidance and review, Spon Press, London.

Carmona, M., Carmona, S. and Gallent, N. (2001), *Working Together: A Guide for Planners and Housing Providers*, Thomas Telford, London.

Carmona, M., de Magalhaes, C. and Edwards, M. (2001), *The Value of Urban Design*, CABE, London.

Carmona, M., Punter, J. and Chapman, D. (2002), *From Design Policy to Design Quality: the Treatment of Design in Community Strtegies, Local Development Frameworks and Action Plans*, London, Thomas Telford Publishing.

Carr, S., Francis, M., Rivlin, L.G. and Stone, A.M. (1992), *Public Space*, Cambridge University Press, Cambridge.

Carter, S.L. (1998), *Civility: Manners, Morals and the Etiquette of Democracy*, Harper Perennial, London.

Case Scheer, B. and Preiser, W. (eds) (1994), *Design Review: Challenging Urban Aesthetic Control*, Chapman & Hall, New York.

Case Scheer, B. (1994), Introduction: The debate on design review, in Case Scheer, B. and Preiser W. (eds), *Design Review: Challenging Urban Aesthetic Control*, Chapman & Hall, New York, pp. 3–9.

Castells, M. (1989), *The Informational City*, Blackwells, Oxford.

Chapman, D. and Larkham, P. (1994), *Understanding Urban Design, An Introduction to the Process of Urban Change*, University of Central England, Birmingham.

Chermayeff, S. and Alexander, C. (1963), *Community and Privacy*, Pelican, Harmondsworth.

Chih-Feng Shu, S. (2000), Housing layout and crime vulnerability, *Urban Design International*, **5**, 177–88.

Clarke, R.V.G. (ed.) (1992), *Situational Crime Prevention: Successful Case Studies*, Harrow & Heston, New York.

Clarke, R.V.G. (ed.) (1997), *Situational Crime Prevention: Successful Case Studies*, 2nd edition, Harrow & Heston, New York.

Clifford, S. and King, A. (1993), *Local Distinctiveness: Place, Particularity and Identity*, Common Ground, London.

Cold, B. (2000), Aesthetics and the built environment, in *Design Professionals and the Built Environment: An Introduction*, Knox, P. and Ozolins, P. (eds), London, Wiley.

Coleman, A. (1985), *Utopia on Trial: Vision and Reality in Planned Housing*, Shipman, London.

Collins, G.R. and Collins, C.C. (1965), Translators Preface, in Sitte, C. (1889), *City Planning According to Artistic Principles* (translated by Collins, G.R. and Collins, C.C., 1965), Phaidon Press, London, pp. ix–xiv.

Commission of the European Communities (CEC) (1990), *Green Paper on the Urban Environment, EUR 12902*, CEC, Brussels.

Congress for the New Urbanism (1999), *Charter for the New Urbanism* (http://www.cnu.org/charter.html).

Conrads, U. (1964), *Programmes and Manifestos of Twentieth Century Architecture*, Lund Humphries, London.

Conway, H. and Roenisch, R. (1994), *Understanding Architecture: An introduction to architecture and architectural history*, Routledge, London.

Conzen, M.P. (1960), Alnwick: a study in town plan analysis, *Transactions, Institute of British Geographers*, **27**, 1–122.

Cook, R. (1980), *Zoning for Downtown Urban Design*, Lexington Books, New York.

Council for the Protection of Rural England (CPRE) (2001), *Compact Sustainable Communities*, CPRE, London.

Countryside Commission & English Nature (1997), *The Character of England: Landscape, Wildlife & Natural Features*, English Nature, Peterborough.

Cowan, R. (1995), *The Cities Design Forgot*, Urban Initiatives, London.

Cowan, R. (1997), *The Connected City*, Urban Initiatives, London.

Cowan, R. (2000), Beyond the myths on urban design, *The Planner*, 17 November, p. 24.

Cowan, R. (2001a), Responding to the Challenge, *Planning*, Issue 1413, 6 April, p. 9.

Cowan, R. (2001b), *Arm Yourself With a Placecheck: A Users Guide*, Urban Design Alliance, London.

Crang, M. (1998), *Cultural Geography*, Routledge, London.

Crawford, M. (1992), The world in a Shopping Mall, in *Variations on a Theme Park: the New American City and the End of Public Space*, Sorkin, M. (ed.), New York, Hill & Wang, pp. 3–30.

Crowe, T. (1991), *Crime Prevention through Environmental Design*, Oxford, Butterworth-Heinemann.

Cullen, G. (1961), *Townscape*, Architectural Press, London.

Cullen, G. (1967), *Notation*, Alcan, London.

Cullen, G. (1971), *The Concise Townscape*, Architectural Press, London.

Cullingworth, B. (1997), *Planning in the USA: Policies, Issues and Processes*, Routledge, London.

Curdes, G. (1993), Spatial organisation of towns at the level of the smallest urban unit: plots and buildings, in Montanari, A., Curdes, G. and Forsyth, L. (eds) (1993), *Urban Landscape Dynamics: A multi-level innovation process*, Avebury, Aldershot, pp. 281–94.

Dagenhart, R. and Sawicki, D. (1992), Architecture and planning: the divergence of two fields, *Journal of Planning Education & Research*, **21**, 1–16.

Dagenhart, R. and Sawicki, D. (1994), If urban design is everything, maybe its nothing, *Journal of Planning Education & Research*, **13**, 143–6.

Davis, D. (1987), Late Postmodern: the end of style, *Art in America*, June, pp. 5–23.

Davis, C. (1997), *Improving Design in the High Street*, Architectural Press, Oxford.

Davis, M. (1990), *City of Quartz: Excavating the future in Los Angeles*, Verso, London.

Davis, M. (1998), *Ecology of Fear: Los Angeles and the imagination of disaster*, Picador, London.

Davison, I. (1995), Viewpoint: Do We Need Cities Any More? *Town Planning Review*, **66**, iii–vi.

Dear, M. (1995), Prolegomena to a postmodern urbanism, in Healey, P., Cameron, S., Davoudi, S., Graham, S. and Mandanipour, A. (1995) (eds), *Managing Cities: The New Urban Context*, John Wiley, Chichester, pp. 27–44.

Dear, M. and Flusty, S. (1999), The postmodern urban condition, in Featherstone, M. and Lash, S. (1999) (eds), *Spaces of Culture: City-Nation-World*, Sage Publications, London, pp. 64–85.

Dear, M. and Wolch, J. (1989), How territory shapes social life, in Wolch, J. and Dear, M. (eds) (1989), *The Power of Geography: How territory shapes social life*, Unwin Hyman, Boston.

De Jonge, D. (1962), Images of urban areas: Their structure and psychological foundations, *Journal of the American Institute of Planners*, **28**, 266–76.

Denby, E. (1956), Oversprawl, *Architectural Review*, December, pp. 424–30.

Department of Environment, Transport and Regions (DETR) (1998), *Places, Streets and Movement: A Companion Guide to Design Bulletin 32 Residential Roads and Footpaths*, DETR, London.

Department of Environment, Transport and Regions (DETR) (1999), *Good Practice Guidance on Design in the Planning System*, DETR, London.

Department of Environment, Transport and Regions (DETR) (2000a), *Best Value Performance Indicators 2001/2002*, DETR, London.

Department of Environment, Transport and Regions (DETR) (2000b), *Survey of Urban Design Skills in Local Government*, DETR, London.

Department of Environment, Transport and Regions/Commission for Architecture and the Built Environment (DETR/CABE) (2000), *By Design: Urban Design in the Planning System: Towards Better Practice*, DETR, London.

Department of Environment (DoE) (1992), *Planning Policy Guidance Note 12: Development Plans and Regional Planning Guidance*, HMSO, London.

Department of Environment (DoE) (1994), *Quality in Town and Country: A Discussion Document*, DoE, London.

Department of Environment (DoE) (1996), *Analysis of Responses to the Discussion Document Quality in Town and Country*, HMSO, London.

Department of Environment (DoE) (1997), *Planning Policy Guidance: General Policy and Principles (PPG1)*, The Stationery Office, London.

Department for Transport, Local Government and the Regions (DTLR) (2001), *Green Paper: Planning: Delivering a Fundamental Change*, London.

Dickens, P.G. (1980), Social sciences and design theory, *Environment & Planning B: Planning & Design*, **7**, 353–60.

Downs, A. (2001), What does "Smart Growth" really mean? *Planning* (American Planning Association), April.

Dovey, K. (1990), The Pattern Language and its enemies, *Design Studies*, **11**, 3–9.

Dovey, K. (1999), *Framing Places: Mediating power in built form*, Routledge, London.

Duany, A. and Plater-Zyberk, E. (1991), *Towns and Town-Making Principles*, Rizzoli, New York.

Duany, A., Plater-Zyberk, E. and Chellman, C. (1989), New Town Ordinances and Codes, *Architectural Design*, **59**, 71–5.

Duany, A. and Plater-Zyberk, E. with Speck, J. (2000), *Suburban Nation: The rise of sprawl and the decline of the American Dream*, North Point Press, New York.

Dubos, R. (1972), *A God Within*, New York, Charles Schribners Sons.

Duffy, F. (1990), Measuring Building Performance, *Facilities*, May.

Dyckman, J.W. (1962), The European motherland of American urban romanticism, *Journal of the American Institute of Planners*, **28**, 277–81.

Eco, U. (1968), Function and sign: semiotics in architecture, in *The City and the Sign: An Introduction to Urban Semiotics*, Gottdiener, M. and Lagopoulos, A. (eds), New York, Columbia University Press.

EDAW (1998), *Croydon 2020: The Thinking and the Vision Ideas Competition*, London Borough of Croydon, London.

Edwards, B. (1994), *Understanding Architecture through Drawing*, E & FN Spon, London.

Ekblom, P., Law, H. and Sutton, M. (1996), *Safer Cities and Domestic Burglary*, London, Research and Statistics Directorate, Home Office.

Elkin, T., McLaren, D. and Hillman, M. (1991), *Reviving the City: Towards Sustainable Urban Development*, Friends of the Earth, London.

Ellin, N. (1996), *Postmodern Urbanism*, Blackwells, Oxford.

Ellin, N. (1997) (ed.), *The Architecture of Fear*, Princeton Architectural Press, London.

Ellin, N. (1999), *Postmodern Urbanism* (revised edition), Blackwells, Oxford.

Ellin, N. (2000), The Postmodern Built Environment, in Knox, P. and Ozolins, P. (2000) (eds), *Design professionals and the built environment: An introduction*, Wiley, London, pp. 99–106.

English Heritage (1997), *Sustaining the Historic Environment: New Perspectives in the Future*, English Heritage, London.

English Heritage (1998), *Conservation-led Regeneration: The Work of English Heritage*, English Heritage, London.

English Heritage (2000a), *Streets for All: A Guide to the Management of Londons Streets*, English Heritage, London.

English Heritage (2000b), *Power of Place: The future of the historic environment*, English Heritage, London.

English Partnerships (1998), *Time for Design 2*, English Partnerships, London.

Engwicht, D. (1999), *Street Reclaiming, Creating Liveable Streets and Vibrant Communities*, New Society Publishers, British Columbia.

Entrikin, J.N. (1991), *The Betweenness of Place: Towards a Geography of Modernity*, John Hopkins University Press, Baltimore.

Environmental Protection Agency (EPA) (2001), What is Smart Growth? *EPA Fact Sheet*, Environmental Protection Agency (United States), April 2001.

Eppli, M. and Tu, C. (1999), *Valuing the New Urbanism: The Impact of New Urbanism on Prices of Single Family Houses*, Urban Land Institute, Washington DC.

Essex County Council (1973), *A Guide to Residential Design*, Essex County Council, Colchester.

Essex Planning Officers Association (EPOA) (1997), *A Design Guide for Residential and Mixed Use Areas*, EPOA, Essex.

Evans, G., Lercher, P., Meis, M., Ising, H. and Kofler, W. (2001), Community Noise Exposure and Stress in Children, *Journal of Acoustical Society of America*, **109**, 1023–27.

Fainstein, S. (1994), *The City Builders: Property, politics and planning in London and New York*, Blackwell, Oxford.

Fawcett, J. (1976) (ed.), *The Future of the Past: Attitudes to Conservation 1740–1974*, London, Thames & Hudson.

Featherstone, M. (1991), *Postmodernism and Consumer Culture*, Sage Publications, London.

Featherstone, M. (1995), *Undoing Culture: Globalisation, Postmodernism and Identity*, Sage Publications, London.

Featherstone, M. (2000), The Flaneur, the city and the virtual public realm, *Urban Studies*, **35**, 909–25.

Featherstone, M. and Lash, S. (1999) (eds), *Spaces of Culture: City-Nation-World*, Sage Publications, London.

Felson, M. and Clarke, R.V. (1998), *Opportunity Makes the Thief: Practical theory for crime prevention*, Police Research Series Paper 98, Home Office, London, p. 25.

Fishman, R. (1987), *Bourgeois Utopias: The rise and fall of suburbia*, Basic Books, New York.

Fitch, R. (1990), *Historic preservation: Curatorial Management of the Built Environment*, University Press of Virginia, Charlottesville.

Fitzpatrick, T. (1997), A tale of tall cities, *The Guardian On-Line*, 6 February, p. 9.

Flusty, S. (1994), *Building Paranoia: The proliferation of interdictory space and the erosion of spatial justice*, Los Angeles Forum for Architecture and Urban Design, West Hollywood, CA.

Flusty, S. (1997), Building Paranoia, in Ellin, N. (1997) (ed.), *Architecture of Fear*, Princeton Architectural Press, New York, pp. 47–59.

Flusty, S. (2000), Thrashing Downtown: Play as resistance to the spatial and representational regulation of Los Angeles, *Cities*, **17**, 149–58.

Ford, L. (2000), *The Spaces Between Buildings*, The John Hopkins University Press, London.

Forester, J. (1989), *Planning in the Face of Power*, University of California Press, Berkeley.

Francescato, D. and Mebane, W. (1973), How citizens view two great cities, in Downs, R. and Stea, D. (1973) (eds), *Image and Environment*, Aldine, Chicago.

Franck, K.A. (1984), Exorcising the ghost of physical determinism, *Environment & Behaviour*, **16**, 411–35.

Frey, H. (1999), *Designing the City, Towards a More Sustainable Urban Form*, E & FN Spon, London.

Frieden, B.J. and Sagalyn, L. (1989), *Downtown Inc.: How America rebuilds cities*, MIT Press, Cambridge, Mass.

Fyfe, N. (1998) (ed.), Images of the Street: Planning, identity and control in public space, Routledge, London.

Galbraith, J.K. (1992), *The Culture of Contentment*, Penguin Books, London.

Gans, H.J. (1961a), Planning and social life: friendship and neighbour relations in suburban communities, *Journal of the American Institute of Planners*, **27**, 134–40.

Gans, H.J. (1961b), The balanced community: homogeneity or heterogeneity in residential areas? *Journal of the American Institute of Planners*, **27**, 176–84.

Gans, H.J. (1962), *The Urban Villagers: Groups and Class in the Life of Italian-Americans*, New York, Free Press.

Gans, H.J. (1967), *The Levittowners: Ways of Life and Politics in a New Suburban Community*, Allen Lane & The Penguin Press, London.

Gans, H.J. (1968), *People and Planning: Essays on Urban Problems and Solutions*, Penguin, London.

Garcia Almerall, P., Burns, M.C. and Roca Cladera, J. (1999), An economics evolution model of the environmental quality of the city, paper presented at the *6th European Real Estate Society (ERES) Conference*, Athens, Greece, 23–25 June.

Garreau, J. (1991), *Edge City: Life on the new frontier*, Doubleday, London.

Garreau, J. (1999), Book review of Kay, J.H. (1997), *Asphalt Nation: How the Automobile Took Over America and How We Can Take it Back*, in *Journal of Urban Design*, **4**, 238–40.

Gehl, J. (1996, first published 1971), *Life Between Buildings: Using public space* (third edition), Arkitektens Forlag, Skive.

Gehl, J. and Gemzoe, L. (1996), *Public Spaces – Public Life*, The Danish Architectural Press, Copenhagen.

Gehl, J. and Gemzoe, L. (2000), *New City Spaces*, The Danish Architectural Press, Copenhagen.

Gibberd, F. (1953a, 1969), *Town Design*, Architectural Press, London.

Gibberd, F. (1953b), The Design of Residential Areas, in Ministry of Housing and Local Government (MHLG) (1953), *Design in Town & Village*, HMSO, London.

Giddens, A. (2001), *The Global Third Way Debate*, Polity Press, Bristol.

Giedion, S. (1971), *Space, Time and Architecture*, fifth edition, Harvard University Press, Cambridge, Mass.

Gillespies (1995), *Glasgow City Centre Public Realm, Strategy and Guidelines*, Strathclyde Regional Council, Glasgow.

Gleave, S. (1990). Urban Design, *Architects Journal*, 24th October, **192**, 63–64.

Gordon, P. and Richardson, H. (1991), The commuting paradox – Evidence from the top twenty, *Journal of the American Planning Association*, **57**, 416–20.

Gordon, P., Richardson, H. (1989), Gasoline Consumption and Cities – A Reply, *Journal of the American Planning Association*, **55**, 342–5.

Gore, T. and Nicholson, D. (1991), Models of the land development process: A critical review, *Environment & Planning A*, **23**, 705–30.

Gosling, D. (1996), *Gordon Cullen: Visions of Urban Design*, Academy Editions, London.

Gosling, D. and Maitland, B. (1984), *Concepts of Urban Design,* Academy, London.

Gottdiener, M. (1995), *Postmodern Semiotics: Material culture and forms of postmodern life*, Blackwell, Oxford.

Gottdiener, M. and Lagopoulos, A. (1986), *The City and the Sign: An Introduction to Urban Semiotics*, New York, Columbia University Press.

Government Office for London (1996), *London's Urban Environment, Planning for Quality*, HMSO, London.

Graham, S. (2001), The Spectre of the Splintering Metropolis, *Cities*, **18**, 365–8.

Graham, S. and Marvin, S. (1996), *Telecommunications and the City: Electronic spaces, urban places*, Routledge, London.

Graham, S. and Marvin, S. (1999), Planning cybercities? Integrating telecommunications into urban planning? *Town Planning Review*, **70**, 89–114.

Graham, S. and Marvin, S. (2001), Splintering Urbanism: Networked infrastructures, technological mobilities and the urban condition, Routledge, London.

Greed, C. (1999), Design and Designers Revisited, in *Introducing Urban Design: Interventions and Responses*, Greed, C. and Roberts, M. (eds), Harlow, Longman, pp. 197–9.

Greed, C. and Roberts, M. (eds) (1998), *Introducing Urban Design: Interventions and Responses*, Addison Wesley Longman, Harlow.

Gummer, J. (1994), More Quality in Town and Country, *Department of the Environment News Release 713*, DoE, London.

Guy, S., Henneberry, J. and Rowley, S. (2002), Development cultures and urban regeneration, *Urban Studies*, **39**, 1181–96.

Habermas, J. (1962), *The Structural Transformation of the Public Sphere* (translated by Burger, T. and Lawrence, F., MIT Press, Cambridge, Mass.

Habermas, J. (1979), *Communication and the Evolution of Society* (translated by McCarthy, T.), Beacon Press, Boston.

Hall, D. (1991), Altogether misguided and dangerous – A review of Newman and Kenworthy (1989), *Town & Country Planning*, **60**, 350–1.

Hall, P. (1995), Planning and Urban Design in the 1990s, *Urban Design Quarterly*, Issue 56, pp. 14–21.

Hall, P. (1998), *Cities in Civilisations: Culture, Innovation and Urban Order*, Weidenfeld & Nicolson, London.

Hall, P. and Imrie, R. (1999), Architectural practices and disabling design in the built environment, *Environment & Planning B: Planning & Design*, **26**, 409–25.

Hall, T. (1998), *Urban Geography*, Routledge, London.

Hannigan, J. (1998), *Fantasy City: Pleasure and profit in the postmodern metropolis*, Routledge, London.

Hart, S.I. and Spivak, A.L. (1993), *The Elephant in the Bedroom: Automobile dependence and denial: Impacts on the economy and environment*, New Paradigm Books, Pasadena.

Harvey, D. (1989a), *The Condition of Postmodernity: An enquiry into the origins of cultural change*, Basil Blackwell, Oxford.

Harvey, D. (1989b), *The Urban Experience*, Blackwell, Oxford.

Harvey, D. (1997), The New Urbanism and the Communitarian Trap, *Harvard Design Magazine* (Winter/ Spring), pp. 8–9.

Hass-Klau, C. (1990), *The Pedestrian and City Traffic*, Belhaven Press, London.

Hass-Klau, C., Crampton, G., Dowland, C. and Nold, I. (1999), *Streets as Living Space: Helping public spaces play their proper role*, Landor, London.

Haughton, G. and Hunter, C. (1994), *Sustainable Cities*, Jessica Kingsley Publishers, London.

Hayward, R. and McGlynn, S. (1993) (eds), *Making Better Places, Urban Design Now*, Butterworths Architectural Press, Oxford.

Healey, P. (1991), Models of the development process: A review, *Journal of Property Research*, **8**, 219–38.

Healey, P. (1992), An institutional model of the development process, *Journal of Property Research*, **9**, 33–44.

Healey, P. and Barrett, S. (1990), Structure and agency in land and property development processes: Some ideas for research, *Urban Studies*, **27**, 89–104.

Heath, T. (1997), The Twenty-Four Hour City Concept: A review of initiatives in British cities, *Journal of Urban Design*, **2**, 193–204.

Heath, T. and Stickland, R. (1997), Safer Cities: The Twenty-Four Hour Concept, in Oc, T. and Tiesdell, S., *Safer City Centres: Reviving the Public Realm*, Paul Chapman, London, pp. 170–83.

Henneberry, J. (1998), Development process, course taught at the Department of Town and Regional Planning, University of Sheffield.

Hiedegger, M. (1962), *Being and Time*, Harper & Row, New York.

Hiedegger, M. (1969), *Identity and Difference*, Harper & Row, New York.

Hildebrand, F. (1999), *Designing the City: Towards a More Sustainable Urban Form*, London, E & FN Spon.

Hillman, J. (1988), *A New Look for London*, HMSO, London.

Hillman, J. (1990), *Planning for Beauty*, RFAC, London.

Hillier, B. (1973), In defence of space, *RIBA Journal*, November, pp. 539–44.

Hillier, B. (1988), Against enclosure, in Teymur, N., Markus, T. and Wooley, T. (1988) (eds), *Rehumanising Housing*, Butterworths, London, pp. 63–88.

Hillier, B. (1996a), *Space is the Machine*, Cambridge University Press, Cambridge.

Hillier, B. (1996b), Cities as movement systems, *Urban Design International*, **1**, 47–60.

Hillier, B. and Hanson, J. (1984), *The Social Logic of Space*, Cambridge University Press, Cambridge.

Hillier, B., Leaman, A., Stansall, P. and Bedford, M. (1986), Space Syntax, *Environment & Planning B: Planning & Design*, **13**, 147–85.

Hillier, B., Penn, A., Hanson, J., Gajewski, T. and Xu, J. (1993), Natural Movement: or configuration and attraction in urban pedestrian movement, *Environment & Planning B: Planning & Design*, **20**, 29–66.

Hitchcock, H.R. and Johnson, P. (1922), *The International Style: Architecture since 1922*, W.W. Norton & Company, New York.

Hodgson, G.M. (1999), *Economics and Utopia: Why the Learning Economy is Not The End of History*, London, Routledge.

Holford, W.G. (1953), Design in Town Centres, in Ministry of Housing and Local Government (MHLG) (1953), *Design in Town & Village*, HMSO, London.

Hope, T. (1986), Crime, community and environment, *Journal of Environmental Psychology*, **6**, 65–78.

Horan, T.A. (2000), *Digital Places: Building Our City of Bits*, Urban Land Institute, Washington.

Hough, M. (1984), *City Form and Natural Process: Towards a new urban vernacular*, Routledge, London.

HRH, The Prince of Wales (1988), *A Vision of Britain: A Personal View of Architecture*, London, Doubleday.

Hubbard, P.J. (1992), Environment-behaviour studies and city design: A new agenda for research? *Journal of Environmental Psychology*, **12**, 269–77.

Hubbard, P.J. (1994), Professional versus lay tastes in design control – an empirical investigation, *Planning Practice and Research*, **9**, 271–87.

Hulme Regeneration Limited (1994), *Rebuilding the City: A Guide to Development*, Manchester City Council, Manchester.

Huo, N. (2001), *The Effectiveness of Design Control in China*, unpublished PhD thesis, Glasgow, University of Strathclyde.

Huxtable, A.L. (1997), *The Unreal America: Architecture and Illusion*, The New Press, New York.

Imrie, R. and Hall, P. (2001), *Inclusive Design: Designing and Developing Accessible Environments*, Spon Press, London.

Isaac, D. (1998), *Property Investment*, Macmillan, Basingstoke.

Isaacs, R. (2001), The Subjective Duration of Time, *Journal of Urban Design*, **6**, 109–27.

Ittelson, W.H. (1978), Environmental perception and urban experience, *Environment & Behaviour*, **10**, 193–213.

Jackson, J.B. (1994), *A Sense of Place, A Sense of Time*, Yale University Press, New Haven.

Jacobs, A.B. (1993), *Great Streets*, MIT Press, Cambridge, Mass.

Jacobs, A. and Appleyard, D. (1987), Towards an urban design manifesto: A prologue, *Journal of the American Planning Association*, **53**, 112–20.

Jacobs, J. (1961, 1984 edition), *The Death and Life of Great American Cities: The failure of modern town planning*, Peregrine Books, London.

Jameson, F. (1984), Postmodernism or the cultural logic of late capitalism, *New Left Review*, No. 146, pp. 53–92.

Jarvis, R. (1994), Townscape revisited, *Urban Design Quarterly*, No. 52, October, pp. 15–30.

Jarvis, R. (1980), Urban environments as visual art or social setting, *Town Planning Review*, **151**, 50–66.

Jencks, C. (1969) (ed.), *Meaning in Architecture*, The Cresset Press, London.

Jencks, C. (1977), *The Language of Post Modern Architecture*, Rizzoli, London.

Jencks, C. (1980), The Architectural Sign, in Broadbent, G., Bunt, R. and Jencks, C. (1983) (eds), *Signs, Symbols and Architecture*, John Wiley, Chichester, pp. 71–118.

Jencks, C. (1984), *Late Modern Architecture*, Rizzoli, London.

Jencks, C. (1986), *What is Postmodernism?* St Martins Press, London.

Jencks, C. (1987), *The Language of Post-Modern Architecture*, London, Academy Editions.

Jencks, C. (1990), *The New Moderns: From Late to Neo-Modernism*, Academy Editions, London.

Jenks, M. (1988), Housing problems and the dangers of certainty, in Teymur, N., Markus, T.A. and Woolley, T. (eds) (1988), *Rehumanising Housing*, Butterworth, London, pp. 53–60.

Jenks, M., Burton, E. and Williams, K. (1996) (eds), *The Compact City, A Sustainable Urban Form?* E & FN Spon, London.

Jenks, M., Burton, E. and Williams, K. (1997a) (eds), *Compact Cities and Sustainability*, E & FN Spon, London.

JMP Consultants (1995), *Travel to Food Superstores*, JMP Consultants, London.

Jupp, B. (1999), *Living Together: Community Life on Mixed Tenure Estates*, London, DEMOS.

Katz, P. (1994), *The New Urbanism: Towards an Architecture of Community*, McGraw-Hill, New York.

Kaplan, S. (1987), Aesthetics, affect and cognition: Environmental preferences from an evolutionary perspective, *Environment & Behaviour*, **191**, p. 12.

Kaplan, S. and Kaplan, R. (1982), *Cognition and Environment: Functioning in an uncertain world*, Praeger, New York.

Kay, J.H. (1997), *Asphalt Nation: How the automobile took over America and how we can take it back*, Crown, New York.

Kelbaugh, D. (1997), *Common Place: Toward Neighbourhood and Regional Design*, University of Washington, Seattle.

Kidder, R.M. (1995), *How Good People Make Tough Choices: Resolving the dilemmas of ethical living*, Simon & Schuster, New York.

Kindsvatter, D. and Van Grossman, G. (1994), What is Urban Design? *Urban Design Quarterly*, Spring/Autumn, pp. 9–12.

King, R. (2000), The built environment, in Knox, P. and Ozolins, P. (2000) (eds), *Design professionals and the built environment: An introduction*, Wiley, London.

Klosterman, R.E. (1985), Arguments for and against planning, *Town Planning Review*, **56**, 5–20.

Knox, P.L. (1984), Styles, symbolism and settings: the built environment and the imperatives of urbanised capitalism, *Architecture et Comportment*, **2**, 107–22.

Knox, P. (1987), The social production of the built environment: Architects, architecture and the post-Modern city, *Progress in Human Geography*, **11**, 354–78.

Knox, P. (1993), *The Restless Urban Landscape*, Prentice Hall, Englewood Cliffs, New Jersey.

Knox, P. (1994), *Urbanisation*, Prentice Hall, Englewood Cliffs, New Jersey.

Knox, P. and Marston, S.A. (1998), *Places and Regions in*

a Global Context: Human Geography, Upper Saddle River, Prentice Hall.

Knox, P. and Ozolins, P. (2000), The built environment, in Knox, P. and Ozolins, P. (2000) (eds), *Design professionals and the built environment: An introduction*, Wiley, London, pp. 3–10.

Knox, P. and Pinch, S. (2000), *Urban Social Geography: An Introduction*, Prentice Hall, Harlow.

Kostof, S. (1991), *The City Shaped: Urban patterns and meanings throughout history*, Thames & Hudson, London.

Kostof, S. (1992), *The City Assembled: The elements of urban form through history*, Thames & Hudson, London.

Kreitzman, L. (1999), *The 24 Hour Society*, Profile Books, London.

Krieger, A. (1995), Reinventing public space, *Architectural Record*, **183**(6): 76–77.

Krier, L. (1978a), The reconstruction of the city, in Deleroy, R.L. (1978), *Rational Architecture*, Archives d'Architecture Moderne, Brussels, pp. 38–44.

Krier, L. (1978b), Urban transformations, *Architectural Design*, **48**(4).

Krier, L. (1979), The cities within a city, *Architectural Design*, **49**, 19–32.

Krier, L. (1984), Houses, places, cities, *Architectural Design*, **54**(7/8).

Krier, L. (1987), Tradition – Modernity – Modernism: Some Necessary Explanations, *Architectural Design*, **57**(1/2).

Krier, L. (1990), Urban Components, in Papadakis, A. and Watson, H. (1990) (eds), *New Classicism: Omnibus Edition*, Academy Editions, London, pp. 96–211.

Krier, R. (1979; first published in German in 1975), *Urban Space*, Academy Editions, London.

Krier, R. (1990), Typological elements of the concept of urban space, in Papadakis, A. and Watson, H. (1990) (eds), *New Classicism: Omnibus Edition*, Academy Editions, London, pp. 212–19.

Kropf, K.S. (1996), An Alternative Approach to Zoning in France: Typology, Historical Character and Development Control, *European Planning Studies*, **4**, 717–37.

Krupat, E. (1985), *People in Cities: The Urban Environment and its Effects*, Cambridge, Cambridge University Press.

Kunstler, J.H. (1994), *The Geography of Nowhere: The rise and decline of America's man-made landscape*, Simon & Schuster, New York.

Kunstler, J.H. (1996), *Home from Nowhere: Remaking our everyday world for the 21st century*, Simon & Schuster, New York.

Lagopoulos, A.P. (1993), Postmodernism, geography and the social semiotics of space, *Environment & Planning D: Society & Space*, **11**, 255–78.

Lane, R.J. (2000), *Jean Baudrillard*, Routledge, London.

Lang, J. (1987), *Creating Architectural Theory: The Role of the Behavioural Sciences in Environmental Theory*, Van Nostrand Reinhold, New York.

Lang, J. (1989), Psychology and Architecture, *Penn in Ink* Newsletter of Graduate School of Fine Arts, University of Pennsylvania, Fall, pp. 10–11.

Lang, J. (1994), *Urban Design: The American Experience*, Van Nostrand Reinhold, New York.

Lang, J. (1996), Implementing Urban Design in America: Project types and methodological implications, *Journal of Urban Design*, **1**, 7–22.

Langdon, P. (1992), How Portland does it: A city that protects its thriving, civil core, *Atlantic Monthly*, **270**, 134–41.

Langdon, P. (1994), *A Better Place to Live: Reshaping the American Suburb*, The University of Massachusetts Press, Amherst.

Lange, B. (1997), *The Colours of Copenhagen*, Royal Danish Academy of Fine Arts, Copenhagen.

Larkham, P. (1996a), Settlements and growth, in Chapman, D. (1996) (ed.), *Neighbourhoods and Places*, E & FN Spon, London, pp. 30–59.

Larkham, P. (1996b), *Conservation and the City*, Routledge, London.

Lasch, C. (1995), *The Revolt of the Elites and the Betrayal of Democracy*, London, W.W. Norton.

Lash, S. and Urry, J. (1994), *Economies of Signs and Space*, Sage, London.

Laurie, M. (1986), *An Introduction to Landscape Architecture* (second edition), Elsevier, Oxford.

Lawrence, R.J. (1987), *Houses, Dwellings and Homes: Design, Theory, Research and Practice*, Wiley, New York.

Lawson, B. (1980, 1994), *How Designers Think: The design process demystified*, Butterworth Architecture, Oxford.

Lawson, B. (2001), *The Language of Space*, Architectural Press, London.

Layard, A., Davoudi, S. and Batty, S. (2001), *Planning for a Sustainable Future*, Spon Press, London.

Leccese, M. and McCormick, K. (eds) (2000), *Charter of the New Urbanism*, New York, McGraw-Hill.

Le Corbusier (1927), *Towards a New Architecture* (1970 edition), Architectural Press, London.

Le Corbusier (1929), *The City of Tomorrow and its Planning* (reprinted 1947), London, Architectural Press.

Ledrut, R. (1973), *Les images de la ville*, Anthropos, Paris.

Lee, T. (1965), Urban neighbourhood as a socio-spatial schema, from Proshansky, H.M., Ittleson, W.H. and Rivlin, L.G. (eds) (1970), *Environmental Psychology: Man and His Physical Setting*, Holt Rinehart & Winston, New York, pp. 349–70.

Lefebvre, H. (1991), *The Production of Space*, Basil Blackwell, London.

Lewis, R.K. (1998), *Architect? A candid guide to the profession* (revised edition), MIT Press, Cambridge, Mass.

Lichfield, N. (1988), *Economics in urban conservation*, Cambridge University Press, Cambridge.

Linden, A. and Billingham, J. (1998), History of the Urban Design Group, in Urban Design Group (1998), *Urban Design Source Book*, UDG, Oxford, pp. 40–3.

Littlefair, P.J. (1991), *Site Layout Planning for Daylight and Sunlight: A Guide to Good Practice*, Building Research Establishment, Watford.

Littlefair, P.J., Santamouris, M., Alvarez, S., Dupagne, A., Hall, D., Teller, J., Coronel, J.F. and Papanikolaou, N. (2000), *Environmental site layout planning: Solar access, microclimate and passive cooling in urban areas*, BRE/European Commission JOULE/DETR, London.

Llewelyn Davies (2000), *Urban Design Compendium*, English Partnerships/Housing Corporation, London.

Llewelyn Davies, Weekes, Forestier-Walker and Bor, W. (1976), *Design Guidance Survey: Report on a Survey of Local Authority Guidance for Private Residential Development*, DoE & Housing Research Federation, HMSO, London.

Lloyd-Jones, T. (1998), The scope of urban design, in

Greed, C. and Roberts, M. (1998), *Introducing Urban Design: Intervention and Responses*, Longman, Harlow.

Lofland, L. (1973), *A World of Strangers: Order and Action in Urban Public Space*, Basic Books, New York.

Logan, J.R. and Molotch, H.L. (1987), *Urban Fortunes: The Political Economy of Place*, Berkeley, California, University of California Press.

Lohan, M. and Wickham, J. (2001), *Literature Review: Car Systems in European Cities – Environment and Social Exclusion.* Report for the European Commission, SceneSusTech, available at www.tcd.ie/erc/cars/reports.html.

London Docklands Development Corporation (1982), *Isle of Dogs Development and Design Guide*, LDDC Publications, London.

Loukaitou-Sideris, A. and Banerjee, T (1998), *Urban Design Downtown: Poetics and Politics of Form,* University of California Press, Berkeley, CA.

Lovatt, A. and O'Connor, J. (1995), Cities and the night time economy, *Planning Practice & Research*, **10**, 127–34.

Lowenthal, D. (1981), Introduction, from Lowenthal, D. and Binney, M. (1981), *Our Past Before Us – Why do We Save It*, Temple Smith, London, pp. 9–16.

Loyer, F. (1988), *Paris Nineteenth Century: Architecture and Urbanism*, New York.

Lucan, J. (1990), *OMA – Rem Koolhaas: Architecture 1970–1990*, Princeton Architectural Press, New York.

Lukes, S. (1975), *Power: A Radical View*, Macmillan, Basingstoke.

Lynch, K. (1960), *The Image of the City*, MIT Press, Cambridge, Mass.

Lynch, K. (1972a), Openness of open space, in Banerjee, T. and Southworth, M. (1990) (eds), *City Sense and City Design: Writings and Projects of Kevin Lynch*, MIT Press, Cambridge, Mass, pp. 396–412.

Lynch, K. (1972b), *What Time Is This Place?* MIT Press, Cambridge, Mass.

Lynch, K. (1976), *Managing the Sense of a Region*, MIT Press, Cambridge, Mass.

Lynch, K. (1981), *A Theory of Good City Form*, MIT Press, Cambridge, Mass.

Lynch, K. (1984), Reconsidering *The Image of the City*, in Banjeree, T. and Southworth, M. (1991) (eds), *City Sense and City Design: Writings and Projects of Kevin Lynch*, MIT Press, Cambridge, Mass, pp. 247–56.

Lynch, K. and Carr, S. (1979), Open Space: Freedom and Control, in Banerjee, T. and Southworth, M. (1991) (eds), *City Sense and City Design: Writings and Projects of Kevin Lynch*, MIT Press, Cambridge, Mass, pp. 413–17.

Lynch, K. and Hack, G. (1994; first published 1984), *Site Planning*, MIT Press, Cambridge, Mass.

MacCormac, R. (1978), Housing and the Dilemma of Style, *Architectural Review*, **163**, 203–6.

MacCormac, R. (1983), Urban reform: MacCormac's manifesto, *Architects Journal*, June, pp. 59–72.

MacCormac, R. (1987), Fitting in Offices, *Architectural Review*, May, pp. 62–7.

McGlynn, S. (1993), Reviewing the Rhetoric, in *Making Better Places, Urban Design Now*, Hayward, R. and McGlynn, S. (eds). Architectural Press, Oxford, pp. 3–9.

McGlynn, S. and Murrain, P. (1994), The politics of urban design, *Planning Practice & Research*, **9**, 311–20.

McHarg, I. (1969), *Design with Nature*, Doubleday & Company, New York.

Madanipour, A. (1996), *Design of Urban Space: An inquiry into a socio-spatial process,* John Wiley & Sons, Chichester.

Malmburg, T. (1980), *Human Territoriality,* Mouton Publishers, New York.

Manchester City Council (1994), *Rebuilding the City: A Guide to Development in Hulme*, Manchester.

Mandix (1996), *Energy Planning: A Guide for Practitioners*, London, Royal Town Planning Institute.

March, L. (1967), Homes beyond the fringe, *Architects Journal*, July, pp. 25–9.

Marcus, C.C. and Sarkissian, W. (1986), *Housing as if People Mattered: Site design guidelines for medium-density family housing*, University of California Press, Berkeley.

Marsh, C. (1997), Mixed Use Development and the Property Market, in Coupland, A. (1997), *Reclaiming the City: Mixed use development*, London, E & FN Spon, pp. 117–48.

Martin, L. (1972), The Grid as Generator, in *Urban Space and Structures*, Martin L. & March, L. (eds), Cambridge University Press, Cambridge.

Martin, L. and March, L. (1972), *Urban Space and Structures*, Cambridge University Press, Cambridge.

Maslow, A. (1968), *Towards a Psychology of Being,* Van Nostrand, New York.

Maxwell, R. (1976), An Eye for an I: The failure of the townscape tradition, *Architectural Design*, September.

Mayo, J. (1979), Suburban Neighbouring and the Cul-de-Sac Street, *Journal of Architectural Research*, **7**(1).

Mazumdar, S. (2000), People and the built environment, in Knox, P. and Ozolins, P. (2000) (eds), *Design professionals and the built environment: An introduction*, Wiley, London, pp. 157–68.

Meyrowitz, J. (1985), *No Sense of Place*, Oxford University Press, Oxford.

Michell, G. (1986), *Design in the High Street*, Architectural Press, London.

Middleton, R. (1983), The architect and tradition: 1: The use and abuse of tradition in architecture, *Journal of the Royal Society of Arts*, November, pp. 729–39.

Milgram, S. (1977), *The Individual in a Social World: Essays and Experiments*, Addison Wesley, Reading, Mass.

Mitchell, D. (1995), The End of Public Space? People's Park, Definitions of the Public, and Democracy, *Annals of the Association of American Geographers*, **85**, 108–33.

Mitchell, W.J. (1994), *City of Bits: Space, Place and the Infobahn*, MIT Press, Cambridge, Mass.

Mitchell, W.J. (1999), *E-Topia: Urban Life, Jim – But Not As We Know It*, MIT Press, Cambridge, Mass.

Mitchell, W.J. (2002), City Past and Future, *Urban Design Quarterly*, Winter, Issue 81, pp. 18–21.

Mitchell, W.J. (2000), Foreword: The Electronic Agora, in Horan, T.A. (2000), *Digital Places: Building Our City of Bits, Urban Land Institute*, Washington, DC, ix–xii.

Mitchell, W.J. (2001), Rewiring the City, *Building Design*, 10 September, p. 10.

Mohney, D. and Easterling, K. (1991), *Seaside: Making a Town in America*, Princeton Architectural Press, New Haven.

Montgomery, J. (1994), The Evening Economy of Cities, *Town & Country Planning*, **63**, 302–7.

Montgomery, J. (1995), Animation: a plea for activity in urban places, *Urban Design Quarterly*, No. 53 (January), pp. 15–17.

Montgomery, J. (1998), Making a City: Urbanity, Vitality and Urban Design, *Journal of Urban Design*, **3**, 93–116.

Montgomery, R. (1989), Architecture invents new people, in Ellis, R. and Cuff, D. (eds) (1989), *Architects People*, Oxford University Press, Oxford, pp. 260–81.

Morris, A.E.G. (1994), *A History of Urban Form Before the Industrial Revolution*, Longman, Harlow (first published 1972).

Morris, E.W. (1996), Community in Theory and Practice: A framework for intellectual renewal, *Journal of Planning Literature*, **11**, 127–50.

Moudon, A.V. (1986), *Built for Change: Neighbourhood Architecture in San Francisco*, MIT Press, Cambridge, Mass.

Moudon, A.V. (1987), *Public Streets for Public Use*, Columbia University Press, New York.

Moudon, A.V. (1992), The evolution of twentieth-century residential forms: An American case study, in Whitehead, J.W.R. and Larkham, P.J. (1992) (eds), *Urban Landscapes: International Perspectives*, Routledge, London, pp. 170–206.

Moudon, A.V. (1994), Getting to know the built environment: typo-morphology in France, in Franck, K. and Scneekloth, L. (1994) (eds), *Ordering Space: Types in Architecture and Design*, Van Nostrand Reinhold, New York, pp. 289–311.

Moughtin, C. (1992), *Urban Design, Street and Square*, Butterworth Architecture, Oxford.

Moughtin, C., Cuesta, R., Sarris, C. and Signoretta, P. (1999), *Urban Design, Method and Techniques*, Architectural Press, Oxford.

Moughtin, J.C., Oc, T. and Tiesdell, S.A. (1995), *Urban Design: Ornament and Decoration*, Butterworth-Heinemann, Oxford.

Mulholland Research Associates Ltd (1995), *Towns or Leafier Environments? A Survey of Family Home Buying Choices*, House Builders Federation, London.

Mumford, L. (1938), *The Culture of Cities*, Harcourt Brace, New York.

Mumford, L. (1961), *The City in History: Its origins, its transformations and its prospects*, Harcourt Brace Jovanovich, New York.

Murphy, C. (2001), Customised Quarantine, *Atlantic Monthly*, July–August, pp. 22–4.

Nasar, J.L. (1998), *The Evaluative Image of the City*, Sage, London.

National Playing Fields Association (NPFA) (1992), *The Six Acre Standard: Minimum Standards for Outdoor Playing Space*, NPFA, London.

New Economics Foundation (1998), *Participation Works! 21 Techniques of Community Participation for the 21st Century*, New Economics Foundation, London.

Newman, O. (1973), *Defensible Space: People and Design in the Violent City*, Architectural Press, London.

Newman, O. (1995), Defensible Space – A New Physical Planning Tool for Urban Revitalisation, *Journal of the American Planning Association*, **61**, 149–55.

Newman, P. and Kenworthy, J. (1989), Gasoline Consumption and Cities: A comparison of US cities with a global survey, *Journal of the American Planning Association*, **55**, 24–37.

Newman, P. and Kenworthy, J. (2000), Sustainable Urban Form: The Big Picture, in Williams, K., Burton, E. and Jenks, M. (2000) (eds), *Achieving Sustainable Urban Form*, E & FN Spon, London, pp. 109–20.

Norberg-Schulz, C. (1965), *Intentions in Architecture*, MIT Press, Cambridge, Mass.

Norberg-Schulz, C. (1969), Meaning in Architecture, in Jencks, (1969) (ed.), *Meaning in Architecture*, The Cresset Press, London.

Norberg-Schulz, C. (1971), *Existence, Space and Architecture*, London, Studio Vista.

Norberg-Schulz, C. (1980), *Genius Loci: Towards a phenomenological approach to architecture*, Rizzoli, New York.

Oc, T. and Tiesdell, S. (1997), *Safer City Centres: Reviving the Public Realm*, Paul Chapman Publishing, London.

Oc, T. and Tiesdell, S. (1999), The fortress, the panoptic, the regulatory and the animated: Planning and urban design approaches to safer city centres, *Landscape Research*, **24**, 265–86.

Oc, T. and Tiesdell, S. (2000), Urban design approaches to safer city centres: The fortress, the panoptic, the regulatory and the animated, in Gold, J.R. and Revill, G. (2000) (ed.), *Landscapes of Defence*, Prentice Hall, Harlow, pp. 188–208.

Oldenburg, R. (1999), *The Great Good Place: Cafes, coffee shops, bookstores, bars, hair salons and the other hang-outs at the heart of a community* (second edition), Marlowe & Company, New York.

Osbourne, D. and Gaebler, T. (1992), *Reinventing Government*, New York: Plume Publishing.

Owens, S. (1992), Energy, environmental sustainability and land-use planning, in Breheny, M. (1992) (ed.), *Sustainable Urban Development and Urban Form*, Pion, London.

Papadakis, A. and Toy, M. (1990), *Deconstruction: A Pocket Guide*, Academy Editions, London.

Papadakis, A. (1990) (ed.), *Terry Farrell: Urban Design*, Academy Editions, London.

Papadakis, A. and Watson, H. (1990) (eds), *New Classicism*, Academy Editions, London.

Parfect, M. and Power, G. (1997), *Planning for Urban Quality, Urban Design in Towns and Cities*, Routledge, London.

Pearce, D. (1989), *Conservation Today*, London, Routledge.

Penwarden, A.D. and Wise, A.F.E. (1975), *Wind Environment Around Buildings: A Building Research Establishment Report*, London, HMSO.

Pepper, D. (1984), *The Roots of Modern Environmentalism*, London, Croom Helm.

Perry, C. (1929), The Neighbourhood Unit, in Lewis, H.M. (1929) (ed.), *Regional Plan for New York and its Environs, Volume 7, Neighbourhood and Community Planning*, New York.

Pisarski, A.E. (1987), *Commuting in America: A national report on commuting patterns and trends*, ENO Foundation for Transportation, Westport, Connecticut.

Pitts, A. (1999), Technologies and Techniques, presentation given at *Education for the Next Millennium: Environmental Workshop*, University of Sheffield, January.

Pocock, D. and Hudson, R. (1978), *Images of the Urban Environment*, Macmillan, London.

Pope, A. (1996), *Ladders*, Princeton Architectural Press, New York.

Popper, K. (1972), *Objective Knowledge*, Oxford University Press, London.

Porteous, L. (1977), *Environment and Behaviour*, Addison-Wesley, London.

Porteous, J.D. (1996), Environmental Aesthetics: Ideas, politics and planning, Routledge, London.

Porter, T. (1982), *Colour Outside*, Architectural Press, London.

Porter, T. (1997), *The Architects Eye: Visualisation and depiction of space in architecture*, E & FN Spon, London.

Porter, T. and Goodman, S. (1982), *Manual of Graphic Techniques 2*, Butterworth Architecture, Oxford.

Porter, T. and Goodman, S. (1983), *Manual of Graphic Techniques 3*, Butterworth Architecture, Oxford.

Porter, T. and Goodman, S. (1985), *Manual of Graphic Techniques 4*, Butterworth Architecture, Oxford.

Porter, T. and Greenstreet, B. (1980), *Manual of Graphic Techniques 1*, Butterworth Architecture, Oxford.

Porter, D., Phillips, P. and Lassar, T. (1988), *Flexible Zoning, How it Works*, Urban Land Institute, Washington, DC.

Portland Bureau of Planning (1992), *Central City Developers Handbook*, Portland Bureau of Planning, Portland.

Powell, K. (1999), *Architecture Reborn: The conversion and reconstruction of old buildings*, Lawrence King Publishing, London.

Project for Public Space (PPS) (2001), *How to Turn a Place Around: A Handbook for Creating Successful Public Spaces*, Project for Public Spaces, Inc., New York.

Property Council of Australia (1999), *The Design Dividend*, PCA National Office, Canberra.

Proshansky, H.M., Ittelson, W.H. and Rivlin, L.G. (1970) (eds), *Environmental Psychology: Man and His Physical Setting*, Holt Rinehart & Winston, New York.

Punter, J. (1991), Participation in the Design of Urban Space, *Landscape Design*, Issue 200, pp. 24–7.

Punter, J. (1995), Portland Cements Reputation for Design Awareness, *Planning*, No. 1114, 14th April, pp. 22–1.

Punter, J. (1998), Design, from Cullingworth, J.B. (1998), *British Planning: 50 years of Urban & Regional Policy*, The Athlone Press, London, pp. 137–55.

Punter, J. (1999), *Design Guidelines in American Cities*, Liverpool University Press, Liverpool.

Punter, J. and Carmona, M. (1997), *The Design Dimension of Planning: Theory, Content and Best Practice for Design Policies*, E & FN Spon, London.

Rabinowitz, H. (1996), The Developer's Vernacular: The owners influence on building design, *Journal of Architectural & Planning Research*, **13**, 34–42.

Rapoport, A. (1977), *Human Aspects of Urban Form: Towards a Man-Environment Approach to Urban Form and Design*, Pergamon Press, Oxford.

Read, J. (1982), Looking Backwards, *Built Environment*, **7**, 68–81.

Reade, E. (1987), *British Town and Country Planning*, Milton Keynes, Open University Press.

Reekie, R.F. (1946), *Draughtsmanship*, Edward Arnold, London.

Relph, E. (1976), *Place and Placelessness*, Pion, London.

Relph, E. (1981), *Rational Landscape and Humanistic Geography*, Croom Helm, London.

Relph, E. (1987), *The Modern Urban Landscape*, John Hopkins University Press, Baltimore.

Reps, J.W. (1965), *The Making of Urban America*, Princeton University Press, New Haven.

Richards, B. (2001), *Future Transport in Cities*, Spon Press, London.

Richards, J. (1994), *Façadism*, Routledge, London.

Robbins, K. (1991), Tradition and translation: National culture in its global context, in Corner, J. and Harvey, S. (1991) (eds), *Enterprise and Heritage: Crosscurrents of National Culture*, Routledge, London.

Robinson, N. (1992), *The Planting Design Handbook*, Gower, Aldershot.

Rogers, R. (1988), Belief in the future is rooted in memory of the past, *Royal Society of Arts Journal*, November, pp. 873–84.

Rogers, R. (1997), *Cities for a Small Planet*, Faber & Faber, London.

Rossi, A. (1982; first published in Italian, 1966), *The Architecture of the City*, MIT Press, Cambridge, Mass.

Rouse, J. (1998), The Seven Clamps of Urban Design, *Planning*, No. 1293, 6 November, pp. 18–19.

Rowe, C. and Koetter, K. (1975), Collage City, *Architectural Review*, August, pp. 203–12.

Rowe, C. and Koetter, K. (1978), *Collage City*, MIT Press, Cambridge, Mass.

Rowley, A. (1994), Definitions of Urban Design: The nature and concerns of urban design, *Planning Practice & Research*, **9**, 179–97.

Rowley, A. (1996), Mixed use development: ambiguous concept, simplistic analysis and wishful thinking? *Planning, Practice & Research*, **11**, 85–98.

Rowley, A. (1998), Private-property decision makers and the quality of urban design, *Journal of Urban Design*, **3**, 151–73.

Rowley, A., Gibson, V. and Ward, C. (1996), *Quality of Urban Design: A study of the involvement of private property decision-makers in urban design*, Royal Institution of Chartered Surveyors, London.

Rudlin, D. (2000), The Hulme and Manchester Design Guides, *Built Environment*, **25**(2).

Rudlin, D. and Falk, N. (1999), *Building the 21st Century Home: The sustainable urban neighbourhood*, Architectural Press, Oxford.

Rybczynski, W. (1994), Epilogue, in Scheer, B.C. and Preiser, W. (eds) (1994), *Design Review: Challenging Urban Aesthetic Control*, Chapman & Hall, New York, pp. 210–12.

Rybczynski, W. (1995), *City Life*, Simon & Schuster, London.

Rybczynski, W. (1997), The Pasteboard Past, *New York Times Book Review*, 6 April, p. 13.

Sandercock, L. (1997), *Towards Cosmopolis*, Academy Editions, London.

Saoud, R. (1995), *Political Influences on Urban Form*, paper presented to the New Academics in Planning Conference, Oxford Brookes University.

SceneSusTech (1998), *Car-Systems in the City: Report 1*, Department of Sociology, Trinity College, Dublin.

Schwarzer, M. (2000), The Contemporary City in Four Movements, *Journal of Urban Design*, **5**, 127–44.

Scoffham, E.R. (1984), *The Shape of British Housing*, George Godwin, London.

Scottish Office (1994), *Planning Advice Note 44: Fitting New Housing Development into the Landscape*, Scottish Office, Edinburgh.

Scruton, R. (1982), *A Dictionary of Political Thought*, Pan, London.

Sebba, R. and Churchman, A. (1983), Territories and territoriality in the home, *Environment and Behaviour*, **15**, 191–210.

Sennett, R. (1970), *The Uses of Disorder*, Faber & Faber, London.

Sennett, R. (1977), *The Fall of Public Man*, Faber & Faber, London.

Sennett, R. (1990), *The Conscience of the Eye: The design and social life of cities*, Faber & Faber, London.

Sennett, R. (1994), *Flesh and Stone: The body and the city in Western Civilisation*, Faber & Faber, London.

Sharp, T. (1953), The English Village, in Ministry of Housing and Local Government (MHLG) (1953), *Design in Town & Village*, HMSO, London.

Shearing, C.D. and Stenning, P.C. (1985), From the Panopticon to Disney World: the Development of Discipline, in *Criminological Perspectives: A Reader*, Muncie, J., McLaughlin, E. and Langan, M. (eds), London, Sage Publications, pp. 413–22.

Sheller, M. and Urry, J. (2000), The City and the Car, *International Journal of Urban & Regional Research*, **24**, 737–57.

Shelton, B. (1999), *Learning from the Japanese City: West Meets East in Urban Design*, E & FN Spon, London.

Sherman, B. (1988), *Cities fit to live in*, Channel Four Books, London.

Sherman, L., Gottfredson, D., MacKenzie, D., Eck, J., Reuter, P. and Busways, S. (2001), *Preventing Crime: What works, what doesn't, what's promising*, USA National Institute of Justice, Washington.

Shields, R. (1989), Social spatialisation and the built environment: The West Edmonton Mall, *Environment & Planning D: Society & Space*, **7**, 147–64.

Siksna, A. (1998), City centre blocks and their evolution: A comparative study of eight American and Australian CBDs, *Journal of Urban Design*, **3**, 253–83.

Sircus, J. (2001), Invented Places, *Prospect*, 81, Sept/Oct, pp. 30–5.

Sitte, C. (1889), *City Planning According to Artistic Principles* (translated by Collins, G.R. and Collins, C.C., 1965), Phaidon Press, London.

Smith, P.F. (1980), Urban Aesthetics, in Mikellides, B. (1980) (ed.), *Architecture and People*, Studio Vista, London, pp. 74–86.

Smithson, A. (ed.) (1962), Team 10 Primer, *Architectural Design*, **32**, 556–602.

Sohmer, R.R. and Lang, R.E. (2000), From Seaside to Southside: New Urbanism's Quest to Save the Inner City, *Housing Policy Debate*, **11**, 751–60.

Soja, E. (1980), The socio-spatial dialectic, *Annals, Association of American Geographers*, **70**, 207–25.

Soja, E. (1995), Postmodern Urbanisation: The six restructurings of Los Angeles, in Watson, S. and Gibson, K. (eds), *Postmodern Cities and Spaces*, Blackwell, Oxford, pp. 125–37.

Soja, E. (1996), Los Angeles, 1965–1992: The six geographies of urban restructuring, in Scott, A.J. and Soja, E. (1996) (eds), *The City: Los Angeles and Urban Theory at the End of the Twentieth Century*, University of California Press, Los Angeles, pp. 426–62.

Sorkin, M. (ed.) (1992), *Variations on a Theme Park: The New American City and the End of Public Space*, Hill & Wang, New York.

Southworth, M. (1997), Walkable Suburbs? An evaluation of neotraditional communities at the urban edge, *Journal of the American Planning Association*, **63**, 28–44.

Southworth, M. and Ben-Joseph, E. (1995), Street Standards and the Shaping of Suburbia, *Journal of the American Planning Association*, **61**, 65–81.

Southworth, M. and Ben-Joseph, E. (1997), *Streets and the Shaping of Towns and Cities*, McGraw-Hill, New York.

Southworth, M. and Owens, P.M. (1993), Studies of community, neighbourhood and street form at the urban edge, *Journal of the American Planning Association*, **59**, 271–87.

Spreiregen, P.D. (1981), *Urban Design: The Architecture of Towns and Cities*, Robert E. Krieger, Malabar, Florida.

Sternberg, E. (1996), Recuperating from market failure: Planning for bio-diversity and technological competitiveness, *Public Administration Review*, **56**, 21–9.

Sternberg, E. (2000), An Integrative Theory of Urban Design, *Journal of the American Planning Association*, **66**, 265–78.

Sudjic, D. (1992), *The 100 Mile City*, London, Harcourt Brace & Co.

Sudjic, D. (1996), Can we fix this hole at the heart of our cities? *The Guardian*, Saturday 13 January, p. 27.

Talen, E. (1999), Sense of community and neighbourhood form: An assessment of the social doctrine of New Urbanism, *Urban Studies*, **36**, 1361–79.

Talen, E. (2000), The Problem with Community in Planning, *Journal of Planning Literature*, **15**, 171–83.

Taylor, D. (2002), Highway Rules, *Urban Design Quarterly*, Issue 81, pp. 27–9.

Terence O'Rourke plc (1998), *Planning for Passive Solar Design*, BRECSU, Watford.

Thiel, P. (1961), A sequence-experience notation for architectural and urban space, *Town Planning Review*, **32**, 33–52.

Tibbalds, F. (1988a), Ten commandments of urban design, *The Planner*, **74**(12), 1.

Tibbalds, F. (1988b), Mind the Gap!, *The Planner*, March, pp. 11–15.

Tibbalds, F. (1992), *Making People Friendly Towns: Improving the public environment in towns and cities*, Longman, Harlow.

Tibbalds, F., Colbourne, Karski and Williams (1990), *City Centre Design Strategy (Birmingham Urban Design Strategy)*, City of Birmingham, Birmingham.

Tibbalds, F., Colbourne, Karski, Williams and Monro (1993), *London's Urban Environmental Quality*, London Planning Advisory Committee, Romford.

Tiesdell, S. and Oc, T. (1998), Beyond fortress and panoptic cities – Towards a safer urban public realm, *Environment & Planning B: Planning & Design*, **25**, 639–55.

Tiesdell, S., Oc, T. and Heath, T. (1996), *Revitalising Historic Urban Quarters*, Oxford: Butterworths.

Toffler, A. (1970), *Future Shock*, Random House, New York.

Tranche, H. (2001), Promoting Urban Design in Development Plans: Typo-Morphological Approaches in Montreuil, France, *Urban Design International*, Vol. 6, Issue 3/4, pp. 157–72.

Trancik, R. (1986), *Finding Lost Space: Theories of Urban Design*, Van Nostrand Reinhold, New York.

Tripp, H.A. (1938), *Road Traffic and its Control*, Arnold, London.

Tripp, H.A. (1942), *Town Planning and Road Traffic*, Arnold, London.

Tschumi, B. (1983), Sequences, *Princeton Journal*, **1**, 29–32.

Tugnutt, A. and Robertson, M. (1987), *Making Townscape: a Contextual Approach to Building in an Urban Setting*, London, Batsford, London.

University of Reading (2001), *Training for Urban Design*, DETR, London.

Unwin, R. (1909), *Town Planning in Practice: An introduction to artistic city planning*, T. Fisher Unwin, London.

Urban Design Alliance (UDAL) (1997), *The Urban Design Alliance Manifesto*, UDAL, London.

Urban Design Group (UDG) (1994), *Urban Design Sourcebook*, Urban Design Group, Oxon.

Urban Design Group (UDG) (1998a), Involving Local Communities in Urban Design, Promoting Good Practice, *Urban Design Quarterly*, Special Report, Issue 67, July, pp. 15–38.

Urban Design Group (UDG) (1998b), *Urban Design Sourcebook*, Urban Design Group, Oxon.

Urban Design Group (2002). *Urban Design Guidance, Urban Frameworks, Development Briefs and Master Plans*, London, Thomas Telford Publishing.

Urban Task Force (1999), *Towards an Urban Renaissance*, Urban Task Force, London.

Urban Villages Forum (1995), *Economics of Urban Villages*, Urban Villages Forum, London.

Urban Villages Forum/English Partnerships (1999), *Making Places: A Guide to Good Practice in Undertaking Mixed Development Schemes*, Urban Villages Forum/English Partnerships, London.pp. 2–5.

Urry, J. (1999), *Automobility, Car Culture and Weightless Travel: A Discussion Paper*, available at http://www.comp.lancs.ac.uk/sociology/soc008ju.html.

Vandell, K. and Lane, J. (1989), The economics of architecture and urban design: Some preliminary findings, *Journal of the American Real Estate and Urban Economics Association*, **17**, 235–60.

Varoufakis, Y. (1998), *Foundations of Economics: A Beginners Companion*, London, Routledge.

Venturi, R. (1966), *Complexity and Contradiction in Architecture*, MOMA, New York.

Venturi, R., Scott Brown, D. and Izenour, S. (1972), *Learning from Las Vegas: The Forgotten Symbolism of Architectural Form*, MIT Press, Cambridge, Mass.

Vischer, J.C. (1985), The adaptation and control mode of user needs: A new direction for housing research, *Journal of Environmental Psychology*, **19**, 287–98.

Von Meiss, P. (1990), *Elements of Architecture: From form to place*, E. & FN Spon, London.

Ward, G. (1997), *Postmodernism*, Hodder & Stoughton, London.

Warren, J., Worthington, J. and Taylor, S. (1998) (eds), *Context: New buildings in historic settings*, Architectural Press, Oxford.

Warren, S. (1994), Disneyfication of the metropolis: Popular resistance in Seattle, *Journal of Urban Affairs*, **16**, 89–107.

Watkin, D. (1984), *Morality and Architecture*, University of Chicago Press, Chicago.

Webber, M.M. (1963), Order, diversity: Community without propinquity, in Wingo, L. (1963) (ed.), *Cities and Space: The future use of urban land*, John Hopkins University Press, Baltimore, pp. 23–54.

Webber, M.M. (1964), The urban place and the non-place urban realm, in Webber, M.M., Dyckman, J.W., Foley, D.L. *et al.* (1964), *Explorations into Urban Structure*, University of Pennsylvania, Philadelphia pp. 79–153.

Weintraub, J. (1995), Varieties and vicissitudes of public space, in Kasinitz, P. (1995) (ed.), *Metropolis: Centre and Symbol of Our Times*, Macmillan, London, pp. 280–319.

Wells-Thorpe, J. (1998), From Bauhaus to Boiler House, in *Context: New Buildings in Historic Settings*, Warren, J., Worthington, J. and Taylor, S. (eds), Architectural Press, Oxford, pp. 102–14.

Whitehead, J.W.R. (1992), *The Making of the Urban Landscape*, Blackwell, Oxford.

Whitehead, J.W.R. and Larkham, P. (1992) (eds), *Urban Landscapes: International Perspectives*, Routledge, London.

Whyte, W.H. (1980), *The Social Life of Small Urban Spaces*, Conservation Foundation, Washington DC.

Whyte, W.H. (1988), *City: Rediscovering the Centre*, Doubleday, New York.

Wiggington, M. (1993), Architecture: the rewards of excellence, in *Better Buildings Mean Better Business*, Report of Symposium, London, Royal Society of Arts, pp. 4–7.

Wilford, M. (1984), Off to the Races or Going to the Dogs, *Architectural Design*, Vol. 54, No. 1/2, pp. 8–15.

Willmott, P. (1962), Housing density and town design in a new town: A pilot study at Stevenage, *Town Planning Review*, **33**, 115–27.

Williams, K., Burton, E. and Jenks, M. (2000a) (eds), *Achieving Sustainable Urban Form*, E & FN Spon, London.

Williams, K., Burton, E. and Jenks, M. (2000b), Achieving Sustainable Urban Form: An Introduction, in Williams, K., Burton, E. and Jenks, M. (2000) (eds), *Achieving Sustainable Urban Form*, E & FN Spon, London, pp. 1–5.

Williams, R. (1961), *The Long Revolution*, Penguin, Harmondsworth.

Williams, R. (1973), *The Country and the City*, Chatto & Windus, London.

Wilson, E. (1991), *The Sphinx in the City: The control of disorder and women*, Virago, London.

Wilson, J.Q. and Kelling, G.L. (1982), Broken Windows, *Atlantic Monthly*, March, pp. 29–36.

Wolf, C. (1994), *Markets or Government? Choosing between Imperfect Alternatives* (second edition), MIT Press, Cambridge, Mass.

Wolfe, T. (1981), *From Bauhaus to Our House*, Penguin Books, Harmondsworth.

Worskett, R. (1969), *The Character of Towns: An approach to conservation*, Architectural Press, London.

Wright, G. (1999), Urban design 12 years on: The Birmingham experience, *Built Environment*, **25**, 289–99.

Zeisel, J. (1975), *Sociology and Architectural Design*, Russell Sage Foundation, New York.

Zeisel, J. (1981), *Inquiry by Design: Tools for environment-behaviour research*, Cambridge University Press, Cambridge.

Zucker, P. (1959), *Town and Square: From the Agora to Village Green*, Columbia University Press, New York.

Zukin, S. (1989), *Loft Living: Culture and Capital in Urban Change*, Rutgers University Press, New Brunswick, NJ.

Zukin, S. (1991), *Landscapes of Power: From Detroit to Disney World*, University of California Press, Berkeley.

Zukin, S. (1995), *The Cultures of Cities*, Basil Blackwell, Oxford.

Index